Hispanic Ministry in the 21st Century: Urgent Matters

El ministerio hispano en el siglo XXI: asuntos urgentes

HOSFFMAN OSPINO
ELSIE M. MIRANDA
BRETT HOOVER
Editors

CONVIVIUMPRESS

SERIES HISPANIA

2016

Hispanic Ministry in the 21st Century: Urgent Matters

El ministerio hispano en el siglo XXI: asuntos urgentes

© Hosffman Ospino, 2016

Convivium Press 2016
All rights reserved
for the English Edition

http://www.conviviumpress.com
sales@conviviumpress.com
ventas@conviviumpress.com
convivium@conviviumpress.com

7661 NW 68th St, Suite 108
Miami, Florida 33166. USA
Phone: +1 (305) 8890489
Fax: +1 (305) 8875463

Edited by Hosffman Ospino, Elsie M. Miranda and Brett Hoover
Designed by Eduardo Chumaceiro d'E
Series: Hispania

ISBN: 978-1-934996-67-6

Printed in Colombia
Impreso en Colombia
Panamericana Formas e Impresos S.A.

Convivium Press
Miami, 2016

Hispanic Ministry in the 21st Century: Urgent Matters

El ministerio hispano en el siglo XXI: asuntos urgentes

Contents

Contenido

1

El ministerio hispano y la vida parroquial PÁGINA *181*

BRETT HOOVER *y* HOSFFMAN OSPINO

2

El ministerio hispano y el fenómeno migratorio PÁGINA *201*

DONALD KERWIN

Hispanic Ministry in the 21st Century: Urgent Matters

Acknowledgements

We are profoundly grateful to all the people who made possible that the 2014 *National Symposium on Catholic Hispanic Ministry in the United States* was the successful experience that it was, thus giving birth to this book that now serves as a resource for ministry and scholarship on the U.S. Hispanic Catholic experience.

Thanks to the army of graduate assistants and graduates from Loyola Marymount University for your tireless and meticulous work: Alejandra Angel, Raymond Camacho, Cristina Castillo, Marissa Cornejo, Marisol Gaytán Escobar, and Karen Hernández, along with undergraduate student Agueda Sofía Hernández. In particular we thank the graduate assistants who worked during the planning process: Magalí Del Bueno Riancho, Daniel Méndez, and Claudia Avila Torres. Your commitment is proof of the gift that Hispanics are and the hope that the younger generations bring to our Church.

Thanks to the scholars and administrators from the academic institutions that accepted the invitation to partner with Loyola Marymount University in the organization of the symposium: Barry University, Boston College, the Congar Institute for Ministry Development, the Graduate School of Religion and Religious Education at Fordham University, the Jesuit School of Theology of Santa Clara University (Berkeley Campus), University of Notre Dame, Santa Clara University, and Seattle University. It is gratifying to see a growing number of Catholic institutions of higher education sponsoring conversations as important as this one.

Thanks to the scholars and leaders who served as the main readers for some of these essays or offered feedback on earlier drafts: Dr. Miguel De La Torre, Dr. Luis Fraga, Dr. David Hayes-Bautista, Dra. Teodocia María Hayes-Bautista, Fr. Dempsey Rosales-Acosta, and Fr. Richard Vega. Your generosity is a true blessing to the People of God.

Thanks to all the authors of the essays in this collection. The insights shared in these essays are a precious treasure and a gift to the Church's ministerial mission in this country. We also know that there were many other thoughts born in the process of writing these essays and engaging in dialogue with colleagues during the symposium. Such thoughts rest for now in your minds and hearts, and we hope that they see the light of the day perhaps in other publications or exercises of shared reflection that continue to enrich the world of Hispanic ministry.

Thanks to all the participants in the national symposium. You shared three days of your lives discussing, in light of your passion and expertise, the urgent matters that guided the colloquium and now are at the heart of this collection. Catholic Hispanic ministry has moved a step forward because of you.

Thanks to the sponsoring publishing companies, organizations, and institutions —named and unnamed here— that made it possible that we had the appropriate resources to make the symposium a reality and publish this book: Loyola Press, Oregon Catholic Press, Our Sunday Visitor, RCL Benziger, and William H. Sadlier, Inc. The American Bible Society generously sponsored the conversation on Hispanic ministry and biblical literacy during the symposium, which led to the essay under the same title in this book. Thanks all for your generosity and support.

It was an honor to journey with all of you in this project.

Introduction

Catholicism in the United States continues to be profoundly renewed by the Hispanic presence, so much so that in many parts of the country, «Hispanic ministry is simply *ministry*»[1]. Even where this is far from the case, the diversity of Hispanic experience and identity has enriched and transformed Catholicism in the United States. Thus, the more we learn about the u.s. Hispanic experience in all of its expressions, with its contributions and challenges, the more we will be able to understand American Catholicism in the twenty-first century.

This collection is not about delineating who Hispanic Catholics are, nor is it a call to awareness about the fast-growing presence of this population, or the implications of such growth for our faith communities. Much of this was done in the work that preceded it, *Hispanic Ministry in the 21st Century: Present and Future* (Convivium, 2010), which was the result of the First National Symposium on Catholic Hispanic Ministry[2]. Immediately after that work, a number of groundbreaking texts were written providing comprehensive pictures of various levels of the Hispanic Catholic experience in this country[3]. From that starting point, this book serves as an exercise in exploration into a specific set of eight matters that are intimately related to Catholic Hispanic ministry today: parish life, immigration, u.s.-born Hispanic youth, education, social media, leadership, engagement with the Bible, and the relationship with the Church in Latin America. We call them: *Urgent Matters*.

In June of 2014, eighty-three recognized experts and consultants on Hispanic ministry were invited to Los Angeles to be part of the Second National Symposium on Catholic Hispanic Ministry, hosted by Loyola Marymount University[4]. Among those gathered for three days of reflection and study were pastoral lead-

---

1 OSPINO, H. (ed.), *Hispanic Ministry in the 21st Century: Present and Future,* Convivium Press, Miami 2010, 28.

2 The First National Symposium on Catholic Hispanic Ministry was organized and hosted by Boston College in collaboration with Barry University, Loyola Marymount University, and the Congar Institute for Ministry Development in 2009.

3 See for instance MATOVINA T., *Latino Catholicism: Transformation in America's Largest Church,* Princeton University Press, Princeton, NJ 2011; HOOVER B.C., *The Shared Parish: Latinos, Anglos, and the Future of u.s. Catholicism,* NYU Press, New York, 2014; OSPINO H., *Hispanic Ministry in Catholic Parishes: A Summary Report of Findings from the National Study of Catholic Parishes with Hispanic Ministry,* Our Sunday Visitor, Huntington, IN 2015.

4 As with the previous symposium, this effort is the result of a collaboration of several universities and pastoral institutes from around the country. The 2014 symposium was cosponsored by eight of these institutions: Barry University, Boston College, the Congar Institute for Ministry Development, the Graduate School of Religion and Religious Education at Fordham University, the Jesuit School of Theology of Santa Clara University (Berkeley Campus), Loyola Marymount University, University of Notre Dame, Santa Clara University, and Seattle University.

ers, academics, publishers, heads of advocacy organizations, and researchers. Like Jacob in the book of Genesis (32:22-31), we found ourselves wrestling with the Living God while painfully aware of the woundedness in our own communities. This was a process of reflection that aimed at engaging the complexity of the Hispanic experience in *lo cotidiano* (the everyday) with the goal of providing language and insights for pastoral leaders in Hispanic ministry to foster similar conversations in their communities. We did not propose superficial «solutions» that treat Hispanic Catholicism as an agenda item or a problem. As the essays in this collection indicate, if Hispanics are perceived as a problem to the Church in the United States, the Church will miss a critical opportunity for growth —hence the relevance and timeliness of this conversation.

The conversation at the symposium was guided by a methodological process rooted in *teología* and *pastoral de conjunto*, initially designed for the 2009 symposium in Boston. At the heart of this methodological approach is the informed conversation among participants whose lives and commitments are situated at various levels of the life of the Church and the larger society, with preferential attention to those voices coming from the grassroots. Many of the participants were pastoral leaders whose daily lives unfold in the context of Hispanic ministry. Most of the scholars at the symposium, particularly the theologians, are known for grounding their work by way of ministerial commitment and the use of research tools that demand constant engagement of Hispanic communities. Several of them authored the essays in this collection.

The selection of the urgent matters was also the result of a *conjunto* conversation, which began as a process of consultation with pastoral leaders and scholars of Hispanic Catholicism. Some of these matters were identified in 2009 during the first symposium. Others are constant referents in meetings and conversations about Hispanic ministry. Yet some matters rose to the top —such as immigration, u.s.-born Hispanic youth, and the relationship with the Church in Latin America —because of the global and national attention they have garnered as a result of the election of Pope Francis. It is important to note that symposium organizers were all aware that the selected eight matters of concern remain far from exhaustive. Many other issues in Hispanic ministry also cry out for consideration as highlighted by the recent National Study of Catholic Parishes with Hispanic Ministry[5], and our hope is that similar initiatives and future sym-

5 OSPINO, H., *Hispanic Ministry in Catholic Parishes: A Summary Report of Findings from the National Study of Catholic Parishes with Hispanic Ministry,* Our Sunday Visitor, Huntington, IN 2015, 43-44.

posia can address them in more depth. The fact remains that the 2014 symposium and the publication of this collection are providential in that they take place within the timeframe preceding the process that leads to the Fifth National Encuentro of Hispanic/Latino Ministry[6]. The symposium and the book anticipate core areas of reflection that must be addressed as part of the reflections during the Fifth Encuentro process.

The symposium also raised some other critical questions, in fact very urgent matters, that are key to strengthening the efforts of Hispanic ministry as part of the New Evangelization, even if we neglected them in part or as a whole due to the limits of the symposium process. For example, despite attempts to build into the process a critical consideration of the voices and questions raised by Hispanic women today, the symposium fell short from seriously engaging major issues such as sexuality, domestic violence, and gender inequality. Symposium participants also highlighted the under-examined tension between the social advocacy and political activism of previous generations of pastoral leaders in Hispanic ministry and the often exclusive focus on faith formation and evangelization among some younger leaders today—as if both perspectives were not two sides of the same coin, as in the best expressions of Christian praxis. The symposium experience largely did not confront the question of how and why racial biases palpably permeate the structures of our society and our Church. Though this matter was raised on a regular basis, and pastoral leaders and academics are very aware of the harmful effects of racism, we failed to speak directly about this sin of exclusion. The consequences of such silence hit home all the time. Is there an element of racial/ethnic bias, for instance, in the fact that Hispanics are over-represented in gangs and prisons and underrepresented in seminaries and ministry preparation programs? One last issue that emerged subtly at the symposium but never received appropriate treatment was the effect of secularization upon people's lives and the work of the Church, including the rising numbers of young Hispanics who choose to not affiliate with Catholicism or any other religious group (the so-called «nones»).

For the 2014 National Symposium, earlier versions of the essays in this collection were commissioned to spur dialogue in eight different groups, each corresponding to one of the urgent matters. During the gathering, the authors engaged in critical conversation with a group of experts in that particular area,

6 The Fifth National Encuentro of Hispanic/Latino Ministry will take place in 2018.

including practitioners and scholars. Eight *testigos* (witnesses), graduate students and recent pastoral theology graduates, accompanied the groups from beginning to end taking notes on the particulars of their deliberations. These notes were then reviewed by the authors and the editors. The essays that follow are a genuine attempt by the authors and editors to capture some of the best insights from the conversation in each group. However, the essays are neither summaries nor consensus statements representing those who were part of each study group, but the creative work of the authors under editorial guidance. In that sense, they are exercises of pastoral theological reflection at its best. We hope that these essays will, in turn, spur reflection and dialogue within parishes, chanceries, ecclesial organizations and apostolic movements, and universities.

In chapter one, Brett Hoover and Hosffman Ospino, also coeditors of this collection, bring their attention to parishes with Hispanic ministry. Both draw from recent groundbreaking research and publications that are helping Catholics in the United States to better appreciate the contributions as well as the challenges of parish life where Hispanic Catholics are present. They remind us of the skewed power dynamics that still characterize too many parishes that serve Hispanics, and they draw necessary attention to the role of apostolic movements in leadership development in Hispanic parishes. Hoover and Ospino raise awareness about other complex dynamics in parishes with Hispanic ministry, particularly shared parishes, and offer an analysis of emerging models of parish life that require specific types of ministerial action and models of leadership. Because the parish remains a strong referent for Hispanic Catholics as they practice and celebrate their faith, the chapter sets a strong context for the rest of the collection.

Don Kerwin, Executive Director of the Center for Migration Studies in New York, and one of the most knowledgeable experts in the country on Catholic approaches to immigration, offers a bird's eye view in chapter two of the complexity of the reality of immigration in the United States. If there is an issue that cannot be reduced to simplistic solutions or mere rhetorical positioning, it is immigration. This is an issue where Catholics definitely have much to say. Kerwin's essay calls pastoral leaders, particularly those engaged in Hispanic ministry, to draw from the best of our Catholic biblical and social teaching traditions to advocate for immigration reform that will make the lives of millions of undocumented Hispanic sisters and brothers more humane and will strengthen countless Hispanic families.

Chapter three addresses perhaps the question that is most likely to define Catholicism in the United States of America in the first half of the twenty-first century: the evangelization of u.s.-born Hispanic youth. Lynette De Jesús-Sáenz and Ken Johnson-Mondragón partner to provide a strong analysis, warning the readers that no essay or book or resource can encompass the complexity of the lives of Hispanic youth. Their essay provides an excellent set of general principles and effective practices for ministry with the new generations of Hispanic Catholics. De Jesús-Sáenz and Johnson-Mondragón speak of journeying with Hispanic youth, helping them to tell their own stories of encounter with God in light of their particular realities. To do this, parishes can be «communities of memory», places where the stories of young people, those of the larger community, and the Story of Salvation coincide all at once.

What could be more urgent for most Hispanic families and communities of faith with Hispanic ministry than the question of education? It is tempting in our Catholic circles to reduce the question of education to catechesis or to what goes on only in Catholic educational institutions. A growing number of recent resources take this focus[7]. Chapter four expands our imagination. It looks at the education of Hispanic children, of whom more than eight million are estimated to be Catholic, in the context of education in the larger society, particularly public education, since ninety seven percent (97%) of Hispanic children do not attend Catholic schools. Many attend underperforming public schools, most of these located in poor neighborhoods. We could not have thought of a more ideal person to lead this conversation than Antonia Darder, one of the foremost experts on matters related to the education of Hispanics in the United States. Her essay offers a very accurate —and we must say, sober— picture of the reality that shapes the lives of our Hispanic children. Yet, in a hopeful tone, Darder points to what she calls «principles for cultural inclusion». Success in the education of Hispanic Catholic children can only be the result of great partnerships. This chapter is a must for anyone working with Hispanic families with children.

In chapter five Patricia Jiménez and James F. Caccamo join insightfulness and a wealth of experience to set the foundations for what most likely is the first ever, research-based essay on the relationship between Catholic Hispanic min-

---

7 See for instance, OSPINO, H. and WEITZEL-O'NEILL, P., *Catholic Schools in an Increasingly Hispanic Church: A Report of Findings from the National Survey of Catholic Schools Serving Hispanic Families*, Our Sunday Visitor, Huntington, IN 2016; BRINIG, M.F. and GARNETT, N.S., *Lost Classroom, Lost Community: Catholic Schools' Importance in Urban America*, The University of Chicago Press, Chicago, IL 2014.

istry, new technology, and social media. Though the lives of u.s. Hispanics, particularly the young, are significantly driven by the use of social media and access to technological resources, and many of us use these resources in ministry, almost nothing has been written on the topic. The chapter breaks ground, raises questions, and sets the agenda for future conversations.

Chapter six resumes the conversation about pastoral leadership, a much debated matter in the context of Hispanic ministry. However, Hilda Mateo, MGSpS, does not limit herself to merely rehearsing familiar arguments about the lack of Hispanics in positions of leadership in the Church or the power dynamics that often undermine Hispanic leadership at the time of making major decisions in our communities. The chapter creatively challenges the concept of «leadership» altogether —at least as understood in many sectors of the Church influenced by business and managerial models and Western notions of the singular effectiveness of individual decision-making. Such understanding, the author argues, tends to be exclusive of many Hispanics in our Church, particularly women and minorities. Mateo invites us to reclaim the biblical and communal dimensions of ministerial service by pointing our attention to categories such as discernment, vocation, and mission. Hispanic cultures are deeply imbued in such categories, thus opening us up to a gold mine of possibilities to affirm and promote ministerial leaders in the context of Hispanic ministry.

Hispanic Catholic biblical scholar, David Sánchez, offers us one of the most interesting analyses in this collection. In chapter seven he explores the question of how Hispanic Catholics can better engage the Scriptures in the context of ministry. The encounter with the Word of God through the Scriptures happens in many instances of Hispanic ministry every day: catechesis, liturgy, Bible study groups, personal reading, *lectio divina*, and others. Sánchez highlights several of those encounters while reminding us about central guidelines from the Magisterium for reading the Bible with the Church. He also addresses the challenge of biblical illiteracy that characterizes the experience of many Hispanic Catholics. In order to respond to that challenge and promote engaged encounters with the Scriptures, Sánchez proposes four fascinating strategies for reading the Bible and promoting biblical literacy. These strategies draw profoundly from the cultural and religious experiences of Hispanic Catholics by inviting the community to read and interpret the Scriptures as «Hispanic» and «Catholic».

The planning process of the symposium leading to this collection was significantly influenced by the election of the first Pope from Latin America in the history of the Church: Pope Francis. As the reader will see in most essays of this collection, the «Francis effect» is evident as various elements of the vision and teaching of Pope Francis serve as the backbone of many core ideas proposed for the reflection on Hispanic ministry. In fact, among most U.S. Hispanic Catholics, Pope Francis is practically perceived as a Hispanic Pope. In chapter eight, Allan Figueroa Deck, SJ, and Teresa Maya Sotomayor, CCVI, turn their attention with fresh eyes to the relationship between the Latin American ecclesial experience and U.S. Hispanic Catholicism. For many decades the reflection about the pastoral care of Hispanic Catholics in the United States was influenced by the experience of pastoral leaders and spiritual categories that emerged from Latin America and the Caribbean. However, such continental conversations have lost some dynamism in recent years. Figueroa Deck and Maya Sotomayor make a very compelling case as to why the continental reflection must be strengthened, especially in light of the global perspectives that drive many contemporary conversations in our world. They set a clear agenda for conversations among pastoral leaders in Latin America, the Caribbean, and the United States, highlighting mutual influences that have unique potential for Hispanic ministry.

We hope that this collection of essays will inspire many pastoral leaders in our Church, particularly those working more directly in efforts associated with Hispanic ministry, as well as scholars of American Catholicism and the Hispanic religious experience, to embrace the call to a New Evangelization. Know that our understanding of the New Evangelization echoes Pope Francis' vision:

> The Church which «goes forth» is a community of missionary disciples who take the first step, who are involved and supportive, who bear fruit and rejoice. An evangelizing community knows that the Lord has taken the initiative, he has loved us first (cfr. 1John 4:19), and therefore we can move forward, boldly take the initiative, go out to others, seek those who have fallen away, stand at the crossroads and welcome the outcast[8].

These are the characteristics for Hispanic ministry in the twenty-first century that the essays in this collection put forward to be discussed and embraced.

HOSFFMAN OSPINO, ELSIE MIRANDA, and BRETT HOOVER
EDITORS

8 POPE FRANCIS, *Evangelii Gaudium*, n. 24.

Hispanic Ministry and Parish Life

BRETT HOOVER *and* HOSFFMAN OSPINO

According to the National Study of Catholic Parishes with Hispanic Ministry, approximately 4,300 parishes, of a total of 17,413 in 2013, offer religious services in Spanish, usually Masses and baptisms. Sixty one percent (61%) of all parishes are concentrated in the Northeast and the Midwest, where Catholic demographics are decreasing. Thirty-nine percent (39%) are in the South and the West. However, 61% of parishes with Hispanic ministry are located in the South and the West, where Catholic demographics are increasing[1]. Aware of the fact that about 60% of all u.s. Catholics under the age of eighteen are Hispanic, one can easily anticipate the future makeup of American Catholicism for the rest of the twenty-first century. People will no longer think of Hispanic ministry as a specialized ministry program, often one conducted in Spanish and directed at immigrants. The term will evoke instead the experiences of parish life of the majority of u.s. Catholics.

1

The Rise of Contemporary Hispanic Parish Life

∾

We should recall that, from the very beginning, Hispanic people have been instrumental in shaping Catholic parish life in what is now the United States of America. Long before the English colonists declared independence, Spanish speaking Catholics had founded parishes in Puerto Rico, Florida, and New Mexico. Waves of immigrants from Latin America came to the United States throughout its history, including pivotal moments like the Gold Rush (1849), the Mexican Revolution (1910-1917), and the Cristero Wars of the 1920s. During and after World War II, the *bracero* guest worker program of the United States government (1942-1964) ignited a wave of immigration from Mexico that has never really subsided. During that same postwar period, economic changes across Latin America, the rise of the Castro regime in Cuba, and a host of civil wars in Central America, characterized by frequent interventions of the United States government and military forces, brought other groups of immigrants from Latin America and diversified the Hispanic population of the country.

---

1   OSPINO, H., *Hispanic Ministry in Catholic Parishes: A Summary Report of Findings from the National Study of Catholic Parishes with Hispanic Ministry,* Our Sunday Visitor, Huntington, IN 2015, 10-14.

In the early postwar era, many Anglos involved in Hispanic ministry assumed that Hispanic ministry was a temporary phase in the larger project of assimilation into Euro-American culture. Many parishes either ignored the newcomers or accommodated them with inadequate and often paternalistic pastoral arrangements. Examples include the tiny and poor Mexican mission churches of Southern California and the church basement liturgies of New York Puerto Ricans[2]. Yet by the seventies and eighties, postwar immigration from Latin America had significantly altered the basic demographic map of u.s. Catholicism, and dioceses in immigration states like Texas and California could no longer simply ignore or «contain» the Hispanic presence. At the same time, the u.s. Catholic bishops, spurred on by ethnic and racial pride movements, distanced themselves from their former position pushing the rapid assimilation of immigrants[3]. In 1972, the bishops encouraged the fledgling Encuentro process, a collaborative dialogue which energized a generation of Hispanic pastoral leaders. Influenced by a growing embrace of Catholic Social Teaching, insights from Latin American theological thought, and socio-political movements within the United States (e.g., Civil Rights Movement), many lay leaders, priests, and religious formed during this era of Hispanic ministry spent much time and energy addressing the social needs (food, housing, neighborhood security) and the structural injustice (immigration difficulties) disproportionately affecting poor and working class Hispanics.

After 1990, a new era in Hispanic ministry began as Hispanic Catholic immigrants and their families (and internal migrants from places like California) settled in states unaccustomed to immigration such as North Carolina, Oregon, or Tennessee, and where the Hispanic presence was minimal or non-existent. It is worth noting that most parishes with Hispanic ministry nationwide typically began their outreach to Spanish-speaking Catholics, particularly celebrating Masses and baptisms, around the year 1995. Sixteen percent (16%) of parishes started doing Hispanic ministry between 1985 and 1994, 36 % between 1995 and 2004, and 15% in 2005 or later[4]. Hispanic pastoral leaders formed during this period frequently have a markedly different orientation to ministry than the gen-

---

2 See DÍAZ-STEVENS, A.M., *Oxcart Catholicism on Fifth Avenue: The Impact of the Puerto Rican Migration upon the Archdiocese of New York*, Notre Dame Studies in American Catholicism, Notre Dame University Press, Notre Dame, IN 1993.

3 GARCES-FOLEY, K., «Comparing Catholic and Evangelical Integration Efforts», in *Journal for the Scientific Study of Religion* 47, no. 1 (2008) 18-20.

4 OSPINO, H., *Hispanic Ministry in Catholic Parishes*, 14.

eration before them. Many focus their attention on the catechetical dimension of faith life under the banner of the New Evangelization. While the New Evangelization in Europe and North America has aimed to counter the effects of secularism, Latin American and u.s. Hispanic manifestations of the New Evangelization have often focused on strengthening the catechetical depth and liturgical practice of Catholics largely formed by home instruction and popular religious practice. u.s. Hispanic Catholics have engaged the New Evangelization in order to stake out a middle ground between the pastoral concerns of the Church in Latin America and in North America[5]. Regrettably, an almost exclusive focus on catechesis and spirituality in many Hispanic communities has at times replaced or sidelined the gospel-inspired commitment of earlier generations of pastoral leaders to also addressing social concerns and structural injustice. Hispanic ministry can never be a choice between a deeper knowledge of the faith or a movement toward social justice. It must be a call to a bold and integral faith that demands justice as constitutive of the content of the gospel.

2

Three Models for Hispanic Parish Life

Within parishes, different approaches to Hispanic ministry have arisen over time. While all parishes function as stable communities of the faithful (c. 515 §1) committed to celebrating the Eucharist, forming Catholics in their faith tradition, calling people to discipleship in a wounded world, and confirming the bonds of communion with our Triune God, each parish performs those functions in a slightly different way, spurred on by its own circumstances and context. While national parishes, such as those formed during the era of European immigration, are no longer an option, in some cases bishops have permitted the creation of a similar form, namely the *de jure* personal parish. However, such personal parishes rarely serve Hispanic Catholics. Most Hispanic Catholics worship in territorial parochial communities. But because the Hispanic presence in some of these communities tends to be numerous and the services offered largely focused on the pastoral, spiritual, and even social needs of Hispanic Catholics, such parishes often function as *de facto* «national» parishes, even though they are not officially

---

5 See OSPINO, H., «The u.s. Hispanic Catholic Experience and the New Evangelization: Considerations», in *Pastoral Liturgy*, 44, n. 4 (September/October 2013) 9-15.

recognized as such. These *de facto* national parishes have developed and continue to exist in heavily Hispanic areas in gateway cities like Chicago, Miami, Los Angeles, and San Antonio, and they have focused their attention on the ministerial needs of either a specific Latin American group or many groups held together either by the dominant presence of one Hispanic group (often Mexicans but in Miami Cubans) or simply by the Spanish language. Many also have English language masses attended almost entirely by Hispanics who prefer to worship in English.

In Chicago, for example, the historically Polish neighborhood of Pilsen was transformed into a largely Mexican community in the 1960s. This community included both immigrants and longtime Hispanic Chicagoans pushed out of other areas by public sector construction. In 1970, a quarter of all the Mexicans in Chicago lived there. During the late 1960s, St. Pius V parish had established several masses in Spanish, English classes for children, youth activities, a group of *guadalupanas,* a Cursillo group, and different forms of housing and economic assistance programs[6]. On a typical day in the parish office, most parish business was conducted in Spanish. Former pastor, Fr. Charles Dahm, a Euro-American priest of the Dominican Order formed in Hispanic ministry during the first Encuentros era, spent as much time helping Mexican immigrants with job, housing, and legal issues and educating his congregation on social issues as he did presiding at Mass and preaching. The parish also had multiple counseling and youth intervention programs. Some parishioners drove from far away suburbs to be able to attend worship or prepare their children for sacraments or *Quinceañera* ceremonies[7]. Today, St. Pius continues to be both a full-service community center and a longstanding cultural and spiritual home for Mexican Catholics. «The parish's development of new ways of responding culturally and pastorally to its predominantly Mexican people won their long-lasting affection», wrote Father Dahm[8].

St. Pius demonstrates the strengths of the *de facto* national parish model at the service of Hispanics, especially as it developed during the 1970s and 80s. St Pius offers «the security and clarity that comes from having one's own turf»[9],

6 DAHM, C., *Parish Ministry in a Hispanic Community,* Paulist Press, New York 2004, 15-17.
7 PUTNAM, R. and CAMPBELL D., *American Grace: How Religion Unites and Divides Us,* Simon & Schuster, New York 2010, 212-215.
8 DAHM, C., *Parish Ministry in a Hispanic Community,*18.
9 FIGUEROA DECK, A., *The Second Wave: Hispanic Ministry and the Evangelization of Cultures,* Paulist Press, New York 1989, 59.

while it provides parishioners who feel at home with the Spanish language an opportunity to express their pastoral needs with clarity and receive pastoral care. This model also helps immigrants learn to deal with the institutions of government, business, and the education system as they function in the United States. Taking seriously the Church's social teaching, St. Pius has focused necessary attention on outreach and social justice —helping people find work or housing, and advocating directly for immigrants struggling with substandard housing, employment discrimination, or lack of appropriate immigration documents.

As indicated earlier, most Hispanics in the United States do not worship at *de facto* national parishes. Instead they worship in «shared parishes» with distinct masses and ministries for two or more language or cultural groups. Forty-three percent (43%) of parishioners at parishes with Hispanic ministry are Anglos; 4% Asian, Native Hawaiian, or Pacific Islander; 3% Black, African American, or African; and 1% American Indian or Alaska Native[10]. Shared parishes generally form when, gradually or suddenly, neighborhoods change as Latin Americans or other immigrants arrive. Eventually, the number of newcomers becomes so large that the parish has to repurpose itself as a parish for multiple groups[11]. Often that repurposing is recognized and abetted by the local bishop.

For example, in one Midwestern small city during the 1990s, a group of young migrants from three different states in central Mexico led to the transformation of All Saints parish into a shared parish. In 2000, after a few years of local outreach to Hispanics, the bishop assigned a priest from Mexico, Father Ignacio (Padre Nacho)[12]. Formed in the spirit of the New Evangelization in a Mexican seminary, Padre Nacho arrived and found no faith formation programs in Spanish for a parish of recent immigrants. Everything he did thereafter, he did with an eye to teaching and forming leaders. Largely through these efforts, All Saints became not an Anglo parish with Hispanic ministry but a full-fledged shared parish with approximately equal numbers of Latino and Euro-American families. While both groups now accept the presence of the other, negotiations between groups over shared space, parking, committees, and liturgical celebrations remain complex and sometimes tense.

10 OSPINO, H., *Hispanic Ministry in Catholic Parishes*, 14.
11 See HOOVER, B.C., *The Shared Parish: Latinos, Anglos, and the Future of U.S. Catholicism*, NYU Press, New York 2014, 18-22.
12 Names of the parish and priest are pseudonyms.

Not everyone agrees that the shared parish as a model has been good for Hispanics. Some theologians and pastoral leaders worry that sharing the parish amounts to a loss of that space of «clarity and security» where immigrants can safely and gradually adapt to life in the United States. Others worry that it inexorably leads to the loss of treasured religious practices[13]. Some note that the shared parish model creates a need to keep the peace between Hispanic and other communities, and this need can create pressure for pastoral leaders to shy away from addressing the social injustices that keeps many Hispanics poor and powerless. Pastoral leaders formed in New Evangelization may already hesitate to involve themselves in these «political» struggles. Others argue that Hispanic groups bring a communitarian and sacramental ethos that naturally complements the individualism and more iconoclastic (dialectical) imagination that tends to prevail in much of Euro-American Catholicism, gently challenging its excesses. The shared parish can provide space for such complementarity to manifest itself.

Any discussion of shared parishes, however, has to take into account the inequalities of power within such parishes. True, shared parishes, like All Saints have the *potential* for symbolizing *koinonia* (communion), that ancient drawing together of Christians from different times and places together into the divine life of the Trinity. But this symbolism can be compromised by the unequal and unjust distribution of power. Hoping to stave off change, dominant cultural groups in parishes —often but not always Euro-Americans— make demands that other groups sacrifice their language, popular religion, or other distinctive customs. Treasured religious practices that coexist alongside the formal liturgical celebrations within the context of *Semana Santa* can disappear in the pressure for «unity»[14]. Minority groups are made to accept token representation in parish leadership. Anti-immigrant sentiment or grief over demographic changes exacerbates these pressures. Nevertheless, the fear that such inequalities would end in complete assimilation to «Anglo» ways has proven unfounded. As the National Study of Parishes with Hispanic Ministry notes, «Hispanic communities [within shared parishes] by and large did not become clones of their Anglo counterparts but developed alongside these. In many places Hispanic commu-

---

13 See, for example, FIGUEROA DECK, A., «Multiculturalism as Ideology», in FIGUEROA DECK, A., TARANGO, Y. and MATOVINA, T. (eds.), *Perspectivas: Hispanic Ministry,* Rowman & Littlefield, Lanham, MD 1995, 32.

14 Ibid., 32.

nities eventually became more numerous and the source of vitality for the entire parish»[15].

In *Ecclesia in America*, Pope John Paul II called for parishes in the Americas to become «communities of communities» (*Ecclesia in America*, n. 41). While the Pope was primarily addressing the alienation caused by enormous urban parishes in Latin America, the model he proposed allows for a plurality of groups and activities to co-exist and thrive in almost any context. It values dispersed experiences of community life that can only take place within smaller groups where people can truly encounter one another face-to-face. Many large shared parishes in the United States do successfully knit together distinct apostolic movements, diverse parish societies and groups, age cohorts, and different cultural groups. When their pastors and pastoral leaders call all the different communities to a strong sense of common mission that both embraces diverse experience of Catholicism and challenges all to deeper discipleship, then what we have is a true «community of communities» parish according to John Paul II's vision. Both Queen of Heaven parish in Los Angeles and St. Patrick Parish in Lawrence, Massachusetts represent such an approach[16]. Both are large and include multiple cultural groups; Queen of Heaven has some seven thousand people attending eleven weekend Masses in Spanish and English with liturgical music in Tagalog (Filipino) at one Mass. The «community of communities» model also appears in some de facto national parishes —since many include apostolic movements, groups and ministries, and distinct Hispanic cultures (Mexican, Guatemalan, Salvadoran, Puerto Rican, Cuban, etc.).

Developing the community of communities model is not easy, but there are recognizable strategies. At St. Patrick in 2001, pastor Fr. Paul O'Brien found himself leading a multicultural parish in the poorest city in New England. Fr. Paul understood that the best pastoral approach was to develop a shared sense of mission shaped by the questions and needs of the local community. For St. Patrick parish, these questions and needs involved tensions between cultures, poverty, immigration issues, violence, high geographical mobility, low educational attainment, and many other social challenges. In response, Fr. O'Brien hired a director of Hispanic ministry, ensured that every parochial vicar spoke English and at least one of the other languages common in the community, and invested in engaging and retaining bilingual and bicultural pastoral leaders at all levels. In

15 OSPINO, H., *Hispanic Ministry in Catholic Parishes,* 7.
16 Queen of Heaven is a pseudonym, as is the name of its pastor, Fr. Joe.

2006, with the help of outside donors, the communities worshipping in the parish united to build a meal center that currently feeds more than 500 people of all ethnicities daily, seven days a week, about 250,000 meals a year. In fact, the meal center became a catalyst for all parishioners to understand that, beyond linguistic and cultural differences, serving one another is where true Christian love is experienced. Parish initiatives regularly address immigration, parenting, health care, preparedness for college, and end-of-life issues.

3

The Apostolic Movements and Parish Leadership

⤳

Like Fr. Paul O'Brien at St. Patrick, Fr. Joe, pastor of Queen of Heaven parish, began his tenure with an assessment of the pastoral needs of his multiple communities and worked with his staff and parishioners to develop a common mission that would address their needs and their identity. Fr. Joe himself concentrated his energies on encouraging participation and leadership development in every corner of the parish while at the same time consciously trying to confuse anyone who wished to identify him exclusively with any group or faction. One of his strategies —as in many parishes exhibiting the community of communities model— was to build upon the already significant presence of apostolic movements within the parish. Indeed, any account of contemporary parish life for u.s. Hispanics must involve some mention of the apostolic movements. Apostolic movements (also known as ecclesial movements) consist of mission-oriented communities of the baptized called together by a common charism and spirituality, mostly lay-led, sometimes inspired by the teachings or example of charismatic founders. Two thirds of parishes with Hispanic ministry have prayer groups rooted in the spirituality of one of the movements[17].

Many of these movements —including Cursillo and the Neo-Catechumenal Way— originated in postwar Spain and then spread to Latin America and the United States. Others, like the Catholic Charismatic Renewal (ccr), emerged in the wake of the Second Vatican Council in the United States or Latin America. According to the National Study of Catholic Parishes with Hispanic Ministry, the ccr has the strongest presence in Catholic parishes with Hispanic ministry

17 OSPINO, H., *Hispanic Ministry in Catholic Parishes*, 18.

(50% of such parishes) and the largest average membership among Hispanics. While other movements also have a significant presence—for example, the Knights of Columbus, the Legion of Mary, Cursillo, Jóvenes para Cristo, and the Christian Family Movement—there are actually over a hundred different movements reported, some new and local[18]. Most people recognize that the movements have increased Hispanic people's participation in spiritual activities and disciplined reflection on their faith. All of the movements engage in structured or semi-structured spiritual practices that demand commitment from participants.

Perhaps even more important, however, the movements have provided opportunities for thousands of lay people to develop leadership skills. The National Study of Parishes with Hispanic Ministry notes, for example, that «the Catholic Charismatic Renewal…has been instrumental in fostering vocations to leadership among Hispanic Catholics. Responding parishes identified this apostolic movement as the most likely to provide formation for its leaders, have a priest and/or a permanent deacon formed in its spirituality accompanying its members, and inspire vocations to the priesthood and vowed religious life»[19]. Each of the movements has extensive regional leadership structures and networks as well as leadership formation activities that support them. In the past, those called to leadership as part of their experience in the movements have had little access to formal education or connection to official leadership roles of either the Church or in the larger society[20]. But this is changing. In some dioceses, the leadership structures and formation activities of the movements are coordinated with parish and diocesan leadership structures and formation processes. In other places, however, they still operate largely outside of parish and diocesan influence. As a result, not a few have been accused of divisive politics in the parish setting, even forming parallel parish structures. In rare cases, this has led to open schism or restrictive measures by the local bishop.

The leadership formation offered by the movements remains important since Hispanic communities often struggle to secure adequate resources and spaces to form their leaders. Today, for example, while 38-40% of adult Catholics in

18 Ibid.,17.
19 Ibid.,18.
20 See RODRÍGUEZ, R., «The Hispanic Community and Movements: Schools of Leadership», in DOLAN, J. and FIGUEROA DECK, A., (eds.), *Hispanic Catholic Culture in the U.S.: Issues and Concerns*, Notre Dame University Press, Notre Dame, IN 1994, 206-239.

the United States are Hispanic[21], only 7.5% of priests are[22]. Only 15% of permanent deacons are Hispanic[23]. A mere 9% of lay ecclesial ministers are Hispanics[24]. Of course, the model of paid, professional lay ministry is not as widespread in Latin America as it is in the United States, and it remains unfamiliar to many Hispanics. Nevertheless, a CARA study shows that only 6-10% of lay parish leaders in the United States are Hispanic[25]. We know that a growing number of Hispanic lay women and men are enrolled in ministerial leadership programs. Our hope is that these leaders are soon welcomed and promoted into key positions where they can serve the larger Church's evangelizing mission in the United States while advocating for the particular needs of Hispanic Catholics. Yet even as we push for the formation of more Hispanic pastoral leaders and for their placement in places of influence in the Church, we cannot ignore the crucial question of the clergy in Hispanic ministry. Even as the Hispanic community moves toward majority status, many seminaries are still lagging behind in preparing future priests to serve Hispanic Catholics, particularly the young. The result is that many recently ordained priests lack language skills and even a basic knowledge of Hispanic cultural customs and popular religion. Such priests find themselves greatly frustrated and confused by their lack of preparation to face this complex reality, and they may cause irreparable damage when making major pastoral decisions that have a negative impact on Hispanic Catholics. A similar concern is in place about foreign-born priests from Latin America, who sometimes lack intercultural competencies and adequate training to serve Hispanic Catholics —and others— in the particularity of the u.s. ecclesial context. A more intentional conversation at the national level about this reality is already overdue.

---

21 OSPINO, H., *Hispanic Ministry in Catholic Parishes*, 9; GRAY M., et al, *Cultural Diversity in the Catholic Church in the United States*, Center for Applied Research in the Apostolate, Georgetown University, November 2013, 4, 9.

22 OSPINO, H., *Hispanic Ministry in Catholic Parishes*, 22. Even in an era of the shrinking numbers among the ordained, the general Catholic population in the United States has about eight times as many priests as the Hispanic Catholic population. See UNITED STATES CONFERENCE OF CATHOLIC BISHOPS, *Encuentro and Mission: A Renewed Pastoral Framework for Hispanic Ministry*, USCCB, Washington, D.C. 2002, n. 67.

23 OSPINO, H., *Hispanic Ministry in Catholic Parishes*, 26.

24 GRAY, M., «Special Report: Multicultural Ministry», *Emerging Models of Pastoral Leadership Project*, Center for Applied Research in the Apostolate, Washington, D.C., July 2012, 14.

25 Ibid., 16.

4

Catholic Identity and Mission in the Hispanic Parish

Up to this point, we have looked at models of Hispanic parish life, each model an attempt, however imperfect, to respond to the social, cultural, and ecclesial context of a place and a time. All these models have raised important issues, including the marginalization of Hispanics in their own parishes, the exclusion of entire parishes when identified as mostly Hispanic, the role (and often dearth) of leadership, and the importance of apostolic movements. We have learned that the shared parish has become a dominant parish structure, and that some shared parishes become the kind of «community of communities» envisioned by John Paul II. We have also recognized that the ultimate test for any parish is how it facilitates the encounter of Christians of different cultural and ethnic backgrounds with the God of Life, through the mystery of Jesus Christ. In essence, parish life should call Hispanic (and all) Catholics to an experience of *koinonia*, that is, a drawing into the mystery of our triune God «so that God may be all in all» (1 Corinthians 15:28). What obstacles stand in the way of Hispanic parishes providing such an experience of parish life, and what can we do to clear the way?

Perhaps the greatest obstacle in the shared parishes that most Hispanics inhabit has to do with asymmetrical power relationships —both across cities and regions and within the parish itself. For example, parishes with Hispanic ministry are more likely to be located in urban settings and to struggle financially[26]. Even as the number of parishes with Hispanic ministry grows, at a much faster rate, still the vast majority of parishes are dominated by (often aging) Anglo communities[27]. Even within parishes with Hispanic ministry, most Hispanics share the parish with Anglo Catholics (about 9 out of 10)[28]. Put simply, even as the Hispanic community continues to grow, the power structure still decidedly privileges Anglo Catholics. This is true even within parishes. Many shared parishes operate under the ecclesiological assumption that the parish must have one cultural center, and that center is usually Anglo. Hispanic Catholic customs and worship are still considered temporary accommodations for immigrants who

26 Ibid., 19.
27 See GRAY, M., «Special Report: Multicultural Findings», *Emerging Models of Parish Leadership*, Center for Applied Research in the Apostolate, Washington, D.C. 2012.
28 OSPINO, H., *Hispanic Ministry in Catholic Parishes*, 15.

will eventually assimilate. The most desirable Mass times often favor Anglos. Many Anglo pastoral leaders receive a salary and status recognition as lay ecclesial ministers while many Hispanic pastoral leaders still remain unpaid volunteers. The most influential committees in parishes (finance, pastoral council, stewardship) often skew Anglo, even sometimes in parishes where Hispanics are the numerical majority.

While some of these asymmetrical power dynamics are leftovers from a church with a different demographic profile, some must be seen as the result of racial privilege, bias, and discrimination. Even with episcopal leadership prioritizing ministry to Hispanics, there remain countless unpublished stories about Hispanic Catholics being mistreated, rejected, marginalized or ignored in their parishes. Racism emerges in the constant reference to «illegals», or in stereotypical descriptions of immigrants as «invaders» or manipulators of government services[29]. The results are unambiguous —a lack of hospitality in parish life is often cited as a factor behind the high rates of desertion among Hispanic Catholics[30]. Given the long history of racial bias in Latin America and the Caribbean as well, it is not surprising that Hispanics themselves sometimes themselves display racially biased assumptions (e.g., lighter is better) that translate into self-effacing behaviors or outright discrimination against other groups, including other Hispanics[31]. Refusing to confront racism in the Church has a cost, and shared parishes run the risk of replicating the larger culture's inability to deal with issues of race[32]. As a people called to life together in Trinitarian communion, the Church must be better than that.

In response to these experiences of power inequity and racism, today's parish life demands renewed commitment to Christian *hospitality*. Christian hospitality is more than just kindness extended to strangers; it is the expectation that the stranger bears God's image and message: «The unexpected presence of God

---

29 See HOOVER, B.C., *The Shared Parish*, 210.

30 A recent study on religious identity of U.S. Latinos reveals that only 33% of Catholics who no longer self-identify as Catholic, a group that in turn constitutes about 1 in 4 of all Latinos in the country, say that the Church is very welcoming to new immigrants. 68% of Latinos who self-identify as Catholics think likewise. See FUNK, C. and HAMAR MARTÍNEZ, J., «The Shifting Religious Identity of Latinos in the United States», in *Pew Research Center Publications*, May 7, 2014, online resource, http://www.pewforum.org/files/2014/05/Latinos-and-Religion-05-06-full-report-final.pdf (accessed on May 29, 2014).

31 See POZZI, C., «Race, Ethnicity, and Color among Latinos in the United States», in PRIEST, R.J. and NIEVES, A.L., (eds.), *This Side of Heaven: Race, Ethnicity, and Christian Faith*, Oxford University Press, New York 2007, 52-54.

32 Ibid., 59.

and Christ in and through actions of hospitality is seen in Abraham and Sarah's hospitality to divine messengers at the Oaks of Mamre and the discovery of the risen Christ in the breaking of bread in Emmaus (Gen. 18:1-15; Luke 24:13-35)»[33]. If they are to be centers of true *koinonia*, Catholic parishes must be welcoming communities that excel in integrating newcomers, starting with those who are regularly initiated in the faith and those who arrive as part of national and international migratory patterns, as well as for reasons of cultural and religious mobility[34].

This process of hospitality and integration will be unique in different contexts —a majority Hispanic suburb, a historically white Southern town, and a mixed urban neighborhood will each develop a different model of integration suited to the particular circumstances. Yet one of the perennial obstacles to hospitality and integration across the nation is the use of the «assimilation» paradigm. Assimilation presumes 1) that immigrants can and ought to abandon their culture of origin in a relatively short period of time, and 2) that the normative experience into which an immigrant group is to be assimilated is Euro-American culture. This paradigm presents serious theological problems—it replaces sacramental bonds with cultural uniformity as the main principle of ecclesial unity. It refuses to recognize the cultural and existential freedom of every human person. But its practical consequences are even more damaging. It persuades many Catholics (including Hispanics) that Catholic practices or customs with Latin American roots can never be normative. Yet Catholic identity for most Hispanics is intimately associated with language and culture, just as it was for the Germans and Poles who came to this country as immigrants a century or more ago[35]. Even in the second or third generation, strict assimilation that leaves no place for the parents' or grandparents' culture creates painful generational rifts and even a loss of cultural and religious identity.

---

33 RUSSELL, L., *Just Hospitality: God's Welcome in a World of Difference,* Westminster/John Knox, Louisville, KY 2009, 19.

34 For an analysis of these different forms of mobility looking at congregations associated with different religious traditions see AMMERMAN, N.T., *Pillars of Faith: American Congregations and Their Partners,* University of California Press, Berkeley, CA 2005, 237-253.

35 For a complete analysis of this conversation, see MATOVINA, T., *Latino Catholicism: Transformation in America's Largest Church,* Princeton University Press, Princeton, NJ 2011, 42-66.

Safe space and ecclesial integration

Hispanic Ministry in the 21st Century

46

For many U.S. Catholics of all cultures, parish life remains a touchstone for religious and cultural identity. Especially for Hispanics, the act of claiming «safe space» within a shared or national parish instills self-confidence and allows for the organic adaptation of all cultural groups to demographic changes that are changing parish life in the United States. «Safe space» privileges family unity and the preservation of the best of the Catholicism of cultures of origin. At the same time, *koinonia* asks that all of us find ways for all cultural groups to recognize and experience the bonds they have with one another as fellow Catholic pilgrims on the Christian journey of faith. The United States Conference of Catholic Bishops sees this as a process of communal spiritual growth in the tension between safe space and unity across cultures: «We call this process of being changed and growing in love *ecclesial integration/inclusion*»[36]. For this to work, each group in the community must find themselves at home. This means significant time and space living Catholic faith according to the patterns of their own culture. But it also means periodic liturgies, events, meetings, and celebrations that bring all the cultural groups together for a common experience of parish life. That common experience depends on a strong sense of common Catholic identity (emphasizing common Catholic symbols, sacraments, and practices) but also a sense of mission shaped by leadership in response to the particular concerns of each parish. Whenever we gather together, we must know that God is present not only in ourselves as we were created by God but also in the other, whom we are just beginning to understand. Only then can we grow as communities of faith bound for the Reign of God where «God will be all in all».

---

[36] COMMITTEE ON CULTURAL DIVERSITY IN THE CHURCH OF THE UNITED STATES CONFERENCE OF CATHOLIC BISHOPS, *Best Practices for Shared Parishes: So That They All May Be One*, USCCB, Washington, D.C. 2013, 11.

Hispanic Ministry and Immigration

Donald Kerwin

Hispanic ministry is at the forefront of the Catholic Church's work with immigrants in the United States. To fulfill this responsibility, it must meet the spiritual and material needs of an immense, multi-cultural group comprised of persons at different points in their lives, different stages of integration into their new nation, and different socio-economic situations. It must cultivate the gifts of newcomers, their children and grand-children, and those far removed from the immigrant experience. It must advocate for the just treatment of Hispanic immigrants in the church and in society, while seeking to build unity between Catholics from all different traditions, backgrounds, and walks of life. It must model ecclesial renewal, create «inclusive and open» and «mission-oriented» ministries, and draw in «all those whom Jesus summons to friendship with him»[1].

1
The Size of the Challenge

Hispanic ministry's work with immigrants would be simplified if people migrated for the same reason, but no single theory fully accounts for this phenomenon[2]. Some theories hold that migration results from individual decisions to maximize wages or productivity. Others view migration as a family decision, meant to diversify collective resources, maximize earnings, and minimize risk. Still others see migration as an inevitable byproduct of globalization or the demands of developed nations. Other theories identify the conditions that perpetuate migration, including migrant networks between nations of origin and destination, the growth of black market and charitable institutions that serve migrants in very different ways, and the cumulative changes wrought by migration that pave the way for more migration. One theory predicts that migration should be especially likely between hegemonic states and states within their orbit, as well as between states connected by past military interventions[3].

At this writing, the large-scale migration of unaccompanied children from Honduras, Guatemala, El Salvador, and Mexico to the United States highlights how

---

1 POPE FRANCIS, *Evangelii Gaudium*, n. 27.
2 Cfr. MASSEY, D.S., ARANGO, J., GRAEME, H., KOUAOUCI, A., PELLEGRINO, A. and TAYLOR, J.D., «Theories of International Migration: A Review and Appraisal», in *Population and Development Review* 19 n. 3 (1993) 431-466.
3 Ibid., 447-448.

deep connections between nations can spur migration[4]. U.S. residents (many unauthorized) have sent for their children, so that they can escape recruitment and violence from gangs that originated in Los Angeles, whose members have been deported in substantial numbers since the 1990s and now terrorize sending communities[5].

The size of the challenge facing Hispanic ministry can be illustrated by demographic data. More than 40 million immigrants (foreign-born residents), the largest number in U.S. history, live in the United States, although the *percentage* of U.S. immigrants was slightly higher between 1860 and 1930[6]. Fifty-three percent of immigrants come from Latin America and the Caribbean, with 29 percent from Mexico[7]. U.S. immigrant populations are extraordinarily diverse: in each of the last 10 years, the United States has admitted immigrants from more than 200 nations[8]. Counting their U.S. citizen children, immigrant families from Latin American skew far younger than natives and foreign-born women have higher fertility rates[9]. Immigrants also participate in the labor force at higher rates than natives[10].

Fifty-three million Hispanics live in the United States, 35.5 percent of them foreign-born[11]. The U.S. Hispanic population is projected to grow dramatically over the next 50 years. However, the percentage of *foreign-born* Hispanics has begun to decline, falling by five percent over the last decade[12]. More than 93 percent of Hispanics under the age of 18 are U.S. citizens by birth[13].

---

4   Between 2009 and 2014, the number of unaccompanied child migrants arrested by border officials rose from 19,418 to roughly 70,000. See U.S. DEPARTMENT OF HOMELAND SECURITY, *Southwest Unaccompanied Alien Children*, Washington, D.C. 2014, available online at http://www.cbp.gov/newsroom/stats/southwest-border-unaccompanied-children (accessed September 6, 2014).

5   See JOHNSON, S., «American Born Gangs Helping to Drive Immigrant Crisis at U.S. Border», in *National Geographic*, July 23, 2014, http://news.nationalgeographic.com/news/2014/07/140723-immigration-minors-honduras-gang-violence-central-america/ (accessed September 6, 2014).

6   GRIECO, E.M., ACOSTA, Y.D., DE LA CRUZ, G.P., GAMBINO, C., GRYN, T., LARSEN, L.J., TREVELYAN, E.N. and WALTERS, N.P., *The Foreign-Born Population in the United States: 2010*, U.S. Census Bureau, Washington, DC 2012, 2, http://www.census.gov/prod/2012pubs/acs-19.pdf (accessed September 6, 2014).

7   Ibid.

8   See U.S. DEPARTMENT OF HOMELAND SECURITY, *Yearbook of Immigration Statistics*, Table 3, Washington, D.C. 2012, https://www.dhs.gov/yearbook-immigration-statistics-2012-legal-permanent-residents (accessed September 6, 2014).

9   GRIECO, E.M., ACOSTA, Y.D., DE LA CRUZ, G.P., GAMBINO, C., GRYN, T., LARSEN, L.J., TREVELYAN, E.N. and WALTERS, N.P., *The Foreign-Born Population in the United States: 2010*, 6, 9.

10 Ibid., 17.

11 See KROGSTAD, J.M., LÓPEZ, M.H. and ROHAL, M., *Hispanic Nativity Shift: U.S. births drive population growth as immigration stalls*, Pew Research Center, Washington, D.C. 2014, http://www.pewhispanic.org/files/2014/04/2014-04_hispanic-nativity-shift.pdf (accessed September 6, 2014).

12 Ibid.

13 See BROWN, A., *Statistical Portrait of Hispanics in the United States, 2012*, Table 10, Pew Research Center, Washington, D.C. 2014, http://www.pewhispanic.org/2014/04/29/statistical-portrait-of-hispanics-in-the-united-states-2012/ (accessed September 6, 2014).

Hispanics represent 35 percent of u.s. Catholics, including 58 percent of Catholics between the ages of 18 and 34 (Millennials), and 67 percent of Millennials who regularly attend mass[14]. As these numbers suggest, the vitality of the Catholic Church and nation will increasingly depend on the success and well-being of Hispanic immigrants, their u.s.-born children and their grandchildren.

2
The Biblical Roots of Hispanic Ministry and Catholic Teaching on Migrants and Newcomers

Hebrew Scripture tells of the Jewish people's exodus, exile, dispersion and return to the Promised Land[15]. Based on this experience, Israel was taught to love, extend hospitality and act justly toward the stranger (Lev 19:33). In the New Testament, God «crosses the border between divine and human worlds»[16]. Mary and Joseph cannot find a room in an inn at the end of a journey. Jesus brings light to those who walked in darkness (Isa 9:1). The wise men follow the star on their sojourn to the newborn. The Holy Family flees to Egypt in the cover of night, becoming «for all times and all places, the models and protectors of every migrant, alien and refugee»[17]. After King Herod dies, they cannot return home and must settle in Nazareth (Matt 2:22-23).

During his itinerant ministry, Jesus laments that «"foxes have dens and birds of the sky have nests, but the Son of Man has nowhere to rest his head"» (Luke 9:57-58). He identifies with the stranger and teaches that salvation depends on how truly we serve the dispossessed (Matt 25: 35). He dies to gather together God's scattered children (John 11:52).

St. Paul is converted on the road to Damascus. The disciples encounter the resurrected Lord on the road to Emmaus. The earliest Christians refer to themselves by the Greek word *paroikos*, which means sojourner or resident alien. Citing the *Epistle to Diognetus*, Pope John Paul II wrote that Christians «live in their

---

14 PUTNAM, R.D. and CAMPBELL, D.E., *American Grace: How Religion Divides and Unites Us*, Simon & Schuster, New York 2010, 299-300.

15 See HIMES, K., «The Rights of People Regarding Migration: A Perspective from Catholic Social Teaching», In U.S. CATHOLIC CONFERENCE, *Who Are My Sisters and Brothers: Reflections on Understanding and Welcoming Immigrants and Refugees*, USCC, Washington, D.C. 1996.

16 Cfr. CAMPESE, G., «The Irruption of Migrants: Theology of Migration in the 21st Century», *Theological Studies* 73, n. 1 (2012) 3-32.

17 PIUS XII, *Exsul Familia*, Introduction.

homeland, but as guests; as citizens they participate in all things, but are detached from all things as strangers. Every foreign country is a homeland to them and every homeland a foreign country»[18]. Building on its identity as a pilgrim people, the Church has developed an authoritative body of social teaching on migrants and newcomers, which is outlined in the appendix to this chapter.

3

The Need for Immigration Reform

In El Paso in 2013, a young woman with three U.S. citizen children recounted her immigrant saga. Seven years earlier, her husband had been arrested for speeding and was deported for lack of immigration status. He returned to the United States to live with his family, was arrested and sentenced to 10 months in prison. At his sentencing, the judge warned the young man that if he re-entered again, he would receive a 70-month sentence. The man re-entered, was arrested, and was sentenced to a 70-month term, leaving his wife to raise and support their three children alone. After serving his sentence, he was again deported.

The young woman had been brought to the United States by her parents as a child. She said that like every DREAMer, the first DREAMer in her family was her mother[19]. She had always dreamed that her daughter would grow up to «be somebody». The daughter seemed to have all the promise in the world, but said she was no longer confident that this dream would be fulfilled.

Her story is hardly an anomaly. It would be difficult to find a Hispanic family untouched by the failed U.S. immigration system or a Hispanic ministry program not confronted with the divided families, lost potential, and crushing pressure engendered by this system. An estimated 11.7 million U.S. residents lack immigration status[20]. More than three-quarters of the unauthorized come from

---

18 JOHN PAUL II, *Message for the 85ᵗʰ World Migration Day 1999*, n. 2. http://www.vatican.va/holy_father/john_paul_ii/messages/migration/documents/hf_jp-ii_mes_22021999_world-migration-day-1999_en.html.1999 (accessed September 6, 2014).

19 The young woman would be eligible for legal status under the Development, Relief, and Education for Alien Minors Act («the DREAM Act»), which would provide a path to permanent legal status to unauthorized persons who entered the United States prior to age 16 and could meet other requirements. It would not cover her husband.

20 Cfr. WARREN R. and WARREN J.R., «Unauthorized Immigration to the United States: Annual Estimates and Components of Change, by State, 1990 to 2010», in *International Migration Review* 47, n. 2 (2013) 296-329.

Latin America, including 52 percent from Mexico[21]. The reality of «mixed-status» families means that enforcement measures do not surgically remove the unauthorized or other removable non-citizens: they invariably impact U.S. citizen and lawful permanent resident (LPR) family members as well. Hardly «criminals» in the conventional sense, the unauthorized include:

- Long-term residents: 59 percent have resided in the United States for at least 10 years and 20 percent for 20 years or more[22].
- Parents living with 4 million U.S. citizen children[23];
- A substantial percentage of the 4.4 million persons with approved, family-based visa petitions whose visas have not yet become available[24].
- 2.1 million persons who would qualify for legal status under DREAM Act[25].
- Salvadoran and other refugee-like populations that have received temporary protected status and lived in the United States for decades[26].

In its first five years, the Obama administration removed (deported) roughly two million people, a rate of nearly 1,100 per day. The $18 billion budget of the U.S. Department of Homeland Security's (DHS's) Customs and Border Protection (CBP) and Immigration and Customs Enforcement (ICE) agencies exceeds the *combined* funding levels of the five major federal law enforcement agencies and federal and state labor standards enforcement divisions and agencies[27]. In addition, the $18 billion figure does not include the substantial immigration enforcement expenditures by other federal agencies, states and localities[28].

21 PASSEL, L., COHN, D. and GONZÁLEZ-BARRERA, A., *Population Decline of Unauthorized Immigrants Stalls, May Have Reversed*, Pew Research Center, Washington, D.C. 2013, 15, http://www.pewhispanic.org/files/2013/09/Unauthorized-Sept-2013-FINAL.pdf (accessed September 6, 2014).
22 PASSEL, J., LÓPEZ, M.H., COHN, D. and ROHAL, M., *As Growth Stalls, Unauthorized Immigrant Population Becomes More Settled*, Pew Research Center, Washington, D.C. 2014, 16, http://www.pewhispanic.org/files/2014/09/2014-09-03_Unauthorized-Final.pdf (accessed September 6, 2014)
23 Ibid., 19.
24 See BERGERON, C., «Going to the Back of the Line: A Primer on Lines, Visa Categories and Wait Times», in *MPI Issue Brief*, Migration Policy Institute, Washington, D.C. 2013, http://www.migrationpolicy.org/pubs/CIRbrief-BackofLine.pdf (accessed September 6, 2014).
25 See BATALOVA, J. and MCHUGH M., *DREAM vs. Reality: An Analysis of Potential DREAM Act Beneficiaries*, Migration Policy Institute, Washington, D.C., 2010.
26 KERWIN, D., «The Faltering U.S. Refugee Protection System: Legal and Policy Responses to Refugees, Asylum Seekers, and Others in Need of Protection», in *Refugee Survey Quarterly*, Special Edition (2012) 28-29.
27 See U.S. DEPARTMENT OF HOMELAND SECURITY, *FY 2015 Budget in Brief*, DHS, Washington, DC 2014, 49-50, 64, http://www.dhs.gov/sites/default/files/publications/FY15-BIB.pdf (accessed September 6, 2014).
28 See KERWIN, D., «"Illegal" People and the Rule of Law», in MENJÍVAR, C. and KANSTROOM, D. (eds.), *Constructing Immigrant «Illegality»: Critiques, Experiences, and Responses*, Cambridge University Press, New York 2013) 3287-352.

The growth of the Border Patrol has been accompanied by consistent and reliable reports of abuse against migrants. More than 10 percent of deportees in two studies said they had been physically abused; 20 percent in one study; and 6 percent in another, although the latter included people who had not been deported or, thus, in contact with u.s. officials[29]. In each study, the reported level of verbal abuse —racial and sexual epithets, physical threats, and assorted insults— was in the 25 percent range.

Over the last quarter century, the number of crimes leading to removal has expanded, the discretion of Immigration Judges to allow non-citizens to remain based on their ties in the United States has diminished, and the categories of non-citizens subject to mandatory detention have expanded. Many thousand long-term residents, including LPRs, have been removed based on minor crimes that they committed years in the past[30]. ICE now detains roughly 500,000 non-citizens per year[31]. In FY 2013, the United States prosecuted nearly 100,000 persons for immigration-related crimes (primarily illegal entries and re-entries), representing 40 percent of all federal criminal prosecutions[32].

In recent years, DHS has increased its immigration enforcement partnerships with states and localities. The Secure Communities program, which screens virtually everybody arrested in the United States against DHS's database for immigration violations, deters immigrants from reporting crimes and otherwise cooperating with the police out of fear that they will be deported[33].

Some states have promoted citizenship and have extended rights and benefits of state residency to unauthorized immigrants, including in-state college tuition and driver's licenses. Many jurisdictions have refused to prolong the de-

---

29 See KERWIN, D., «The Gang of Eight and Accountable Border Enforcement», in *The Huffington Post*, May 6, 2013, http://www.huffingtonpost.com/donald-kerwin/gang-of-eight-immigration-reform_b_3220803.html (accessed September 6, 2014).

30 See CATHOLIC LEGAL IMMIGRATION NETWORK, INC., *Placing Immigrants at Risk: The Impact of Our Laws and Policies on u.s. Families*, CLINIC, Washington, D.C. 2000, http://cliniclegal.org/sites/default/files/atrisk1.pdf (accessed September 6, 2014); AMERICAN BAR ASSOCIATION, COMMISSION ON IMMIGRATION, *American Justice through Immigrants' Eyes*, ABA, Chicago, IL 2004.

31 SIMANSKY, J.F. and SAPP, L.M., *Immigration Enforcement Actions 2012*, Department of Homeland Security, Washington, D.C. 2013, 5, http://www.dhs.gov/sites/default/files/publications/ois_enforcement_ar_2012_0.pdf (accessed September 6, 2014).

32 See TRANSACTIONAL RECORDS ACCES CLEARINGHOUSE, *At Nearly 100,000, Immigration Prosecutions Reach All-time High in FY 2013*, Transactional Records Access Clearinghouse, Syracuse, NY 2013, http://trac.syr.edu/immigration/reports/336/ (accessed September 6, 2014).

33 U.S. DEPARTMENT OF HOMELAND SECURITY, *Homeland Security Advisory Council: Task Force on Secure Communities Findings and Recommendations*, Department of Homeland Security, Washington, D.C. 2014, 24, http://www.dhs.gov/xlibrary/assets/hsac-task-force-on-secure-communities-findings-and-recommendations-report.pdf (accessed September 6, 2014).

tention of persons with ordinary immigration violations at the request of federal immigration officials who wish to place them in deportation proceedings. Other states, however, have pursued attrition-through-enforcement strategies that seek to compel unauthorized immigrants and their families to «self-deport» by denying them housing, work, police protection, education, public utilities, and even citizenship by birth which is constitutionally guaranteed. Several provisions in these laws have been overturned on the ground that they are pre-empted by federal law and federal prerogatives under the Supremacy Clause of the u.s. Constitution[34].

4

Catholic Principles and Strategies for Reform

The u.s. bishops lead a unified Catholic campaign, «Justice for Immigrants», in support of broad immigration reform. The campaign has several prongs. First, it supports an «earned» path to citizenship for a large percentage of the u.s. unauthorized population based on employment, good character and English language proficiency. It also strongly backs the DREAM Act and special legislation for agricultural workers. The u.s. bishops have also urged the Obama administration to use its executive authority to provide temporary relief from removal and work authorization to broad categories of unauthorized persons.

The possibility of a legalization program has mobilized many dioceses to plan for reform. Catholic Charities of Dallas Inc. has developed an ambitious plan to recruit 135 pro bono attorneys, 50 paralegals, 50 parish volunteers, 30 clerical volunteers, and a legalization coordinator at each of its 30 partner parishes. The Diocesan Pastoral Planning Department has provided parish demographic data for this initiative.

Second, the campaign supports expedited family reunification and expansion of the number of family-based immigration visas. As it stands, roughly two-thirds of the permanent visas issued each year go to persons with a close family relationship to a u.s. citizen or LPR. Yet persons from countries with high levels of immigration to the United States who seek admission in heavily subscribed «preference» categories can wait for years before a visa becomes available. During this

---

34 See *Arizona v. United States*, 567 u.s., 2012, http://www.supremecourt.gov/opinions/11pdf/11-182 b5e1.pdf (accessed September 6, 2014).

time, they must either live abroad and away from their petitioning family member, or live without status in the United States.

The campaign also supports increasing the number of visas available for necessary workers, including so-called «low-skilled» workers. In fact, these workers lack formal credentials, but are often highly skilled. Unauthorized residents constitute more than five percent of the u.s. workforce, and far higher percentages in many industries and occupations. Yet u.s. law provides only 5,000 permanent visas per year for «low-skilled» workers, a wholly insufficient number. The failure to legalize the flow of necessary workers turns self-sacrificing people into «criminals», and perversely puts them at the mercy of human smugglers, life-threatening migration conditions, harsh enforcement tactics, and unscrupulous employers.

Third, the u.s. bishops have long championed robust refugee protection policies that would allow persons fleeing danger to reach and secure protection, and would prevent the admission of persons who might threaten national security or public safety. Although the u.s. asylum system is premised on the ability of at-risk persons to reach protection, the United States blocks access to its territory through inter-locking enforcement and screening programs. It has also erected legal and procedural barriers to political asylum. For example, asylum-seekers must file their claims within one year of entry, a provision that negatively affects roughly one-third of all applicants[35].

Fourth, the campaign advocates for greater due process protections for those facing removal. It would also vest immigration judges and officials with greater discretion to allow persons to stay based on family and other ties to the United States. Because removal can have harsh, even life-and-death consequences, persons in removal proceedings can present evidence, call witnesses and apply for relief. Yet the government does not provide free legal counsel to unrepresented, indigent immigrants, which makes it far less likely that they will prevail in their claims. Moreover, three-quarters of those removed are subject to expedited, summary, and non-court processes[36].

Fifth, the campaign supports an effective, rights-respecting enforcement system. It opposes enforcement programs that erode trust between immigrant communities and public officials, and that inhibit immigrants from accessing

---

35 SCHRAG, P., SCHOENHOLTZ, A., RAMJI-NOGALES, J. and DOMBACH, J., «Rejecting Refugees: Homeland Security's Administration of the One-Year Bar to Asylum» in *William and Mary Law Review* 52, n. 3 (2010) 688.

36 See SIMANSKY, J.F. and SAPP, L.M., *Immigration Enforcement Actions 2012*.

hospitals, schools, police and other institutions that serve the common good. It also opposes treating minor immigration violations as crimes. The u.s. bishops view attrition-through-enforcement strategies as an affront to human dignity. They have also vehemently opposed legislation that would make it a crime «to assist» unauthorized immigrants and criminalize religious expression.

The Catholic Church recognizes the authority of nations to regulate migration, to ensure orderly admission procedures, and to exclude and remove persons whose presence would not serve the common good. Borders can protect a state's citizens from domination and oppression. They can also safeguard the right of distinct national and cultural groups to self-determination[37]. Yet the church also recognizes the right of human beings to migrate in order «to realize their God-given rights» and teaches that the «common good is not served when the basic human rights of the individual are violated»[38].

Sixth the u.s. bishops recognize the need to integrate the record number of u.s. immigrants and their children. Beyond legal status, immigrants need good schools, living wage jobs with an upward trajectory, safe communities, and the ability to participate in their local and national community. Integration can increase the contributions that immigrants make to the u.s. economy and to their communities of origin[39].

The Archdiocese of Chicago has developed a unique, parish-based ministry to pursue the u.s. bishops' policy priorities and to meet other needs identified by immigrant communities. Its *Pastoral Migratoria* ministry operates through «pastoral agents» in 55 Hispanic and 11 Polish parishes with substantial unauthorized immigrant populations. Since 2009, *Pastoral Migratoria* has put more than 400 lay leaders through a rigorous formation process; referred 52,000 families to housing, labor, domestic violence and other services; and accompanied roughly 500 families to detention centers during the deportation process. Its parish-based advocacy teams have led initiatives to legalize unauthorized youth, to provide driver's licenses to state residents regardless of status, and to advocate for federal immigration reform. In addition, more than 200 Archdiocesan priests

---

37 HOLLENBACH, D., «Migration as a Challenge for Theological Ethics», *Political Theology*, 12, n. 6 (2011) 809.

38 U.S. CONFERENCE OF CATHOLIC BISHOPS and CONFERENCIA DEL EPISCOPADO MEXICANO, *Strangers No Longer: Together on the Journey of Hope: A Pastoral Letter Concerning Migration from the Catholic Bishops of Mexico and the United States*, USCCB, Washington, D.C. 2003, n. 39.

39 KERWIN, D., «Migration, Development and the Right Not to Have to Migrate», in SCRIBNER, T. and APPLEBY, J.K., *On «Strangers No Longer»: Perspectives on the Historic u.s.-Mexican Catholic Bishop' Pastoral Letter on Migration*, Paulist Press, Mahwah, NJ 2013, 155-156.

in 150 parishes engage in public education and advocacy through Priests for Justice for Immigrants. A parallel group, «Sisters and Brothers of Immigrants», consists of 190 religious brothers and sisters from 59 religious orders that also advocate for reform.

5

Lessons and Recommendations from the Catholic Immigrant Integration Project
ᴄ⁄ᴐ

Over the last four years, representatives from diverse Catholic agencies and ministries have met to discuss whether Catholic institutions —which arose in response to the needs of past generations of immigrants— can increase their collective commitment to the integration and well-being of today's immigrants. Some of the themes, lessons and effective strategies surfaced by the project apply to Hispanic ministry. Indeed, some come directly from Hispanic ministry programs.

First, integration requires recognizing communion between natives and newcomers based on the universal values that find expression in diverse cultures. Communion, in turn, requires conversion. As the u.s. and Mexican bishops put it: «Faith in the presence of Christ in the migrant leads to a conversion of mind and heart, which leads to a renewed spirit of communion and to the building of structures of solidarity to accompany the migrant»[40]. Parishes can foster conversion, communion and solidarity by confronting the tensions and concerns that often accompany immigration. Yet less than one-fourth of white Catholics report that their priests often or sometimes speak about immigration[41].

Second, parishes should not dismiss popular religiosity and culturally distinct practices as archaic or superstitious. Historically, popular religious traditions and practices functioned for Hispanic parishes «like language and culture» did for European immigrant communities[42]. These traditions can serve as a building block for Hispanic ministry in a church that seeks to promote unity through diversity.

Third, the church will not be able to realize its «integrating» potential unless Catholic entities better integrate their diverse services and ministries. In addi-

---

40 U.S. CONFERENCE OF CATHOLIC BISHOPS and CONFERENCIA DEL EPISCOPADO MEXICANO, *Strangers No Longer: Together on the Journey of Hope*, 40.

41 See PUBLIC RELIGION RESEARCH INSTITUTE and BROOKINGS INSTITUTION, *Religion Values, and Immigration Reform Survey*, March 2013 (N=4,465).

42 OSPINO, H., *Hispanic Ministry in Catholic Parishes: A Summary Report of Findings from the National Study of Catholic Parishes with Hispanic Ministry*, Our Sunday Visitor, Huntington, IN 2015, 7.

tion, it cannot minister to human beings in their full dignity and promote their «integral» development[43] without partnering with non-Catholic institutions.

Fourth, integration depends on agency: people integrate, not institutions. Thus, the church should prepare immigrants, their children and grandchildren to be leaders and evangelizers. It should not treat them as mere «passive recipients of the church's mission» or «plan» for them[44]. Some of the most successful pastoral models combine leadership development, service provision and advocacy, but view their mission as evangelization. They hope to create faithful and active citizens.

Fifth, Catholic institutions must do a better job of serving Hispanics and other immigrant communities. On average, immigrants have lower levels of education, lower household income and higher poverty rates than natives[45]. They are also less likely to have health insurance[46]. Yet Hispanics, in particular, do not fully benefit from these institutions. For example, only three percent of Hispanic school-age children attend Catholic schools, despite the demonstrable educational and life «advantages» that these schools provide[47].

Sixth, the second and third generations pose the greatest challenges and offer the most potential for Hispanic ministry and other Catholic institutions. Thus, the church's investment in them should be commensurate with their needs and their importance to the church and broader society. Many scholars warn of the «downward assimilation» of the children and grandchildren of immigrants; that is, their adoption of some of the worst features of u.s. culture. Yet youth can also be a source of leadership in the Catholic community and are well-suited for this role. Not only do they have more positive views than their elders on the impact of newcomers on the nation, but they are also far more diverse[48].

43 PAUL VI, *Populorum Progressio*, n. 14.

44 GROODY, D.G., *Globalization, Spirituality and Justice*, Orbis Books, Maryknoll, NY 2007, 184; U.S. CONFERENCE OF CATHOLIC BISHOPS, *Encuentro and Mission: A Renewed Framework for Hispanic Ministry*, USCCB, Washington, D.C. 2002, n. 44.

45 GRIECO, E.M., ACOSTA, Y.D., DE LA CRUZ, G.P., GAMBINO, C., GRYN, T., LARSEN, L.J., TREVELYAN, E.N. and WALTERS, N.P., *The Foreign-Born Population in the United States: 2010*, 16-17, 21.

46 Ibid., 20.

47 See THE NOTRE DAME TASK FORCE ON THE PARTICIPATION OF LATINO CHILDREN AND FAMILIES IN CATHOLIC SCHOOLS, *To Nurture the Soul of a Nation: Latino Families, Catholic Schools, and Educational Opportunity*, University of Notre Dame, December 12, 2009, http://issuu.com/aceatnd/docs/nd_ltf_report_final_english_12.2?e=6668647/6985560 (accessed September 6, 2014).

48 See PUBLIC RELIGION RESEARCH INSTITUTE and BROOKINGS INSTITUTION, *Religion Values, and Immigration Reform Survey*.

In Nogales, Arizona, students at the Lourdes Catholic School (LCS) have initiated the «Kino Teens» club, which is devoted to serving deported migrants at the Kino Border Initiative's Center for Deported Migrants in Nogales, Sonora. Kino Teens also educate youth on migration and Catholic teaching, and advocate for immigration reform. Direct experience with migrant men, women and children allows and inspires them to evangelize their peers on this very human, but contentious phenomenon.

Seventh, the church should revisit institutions that successfully served earlier generations of immigrants. Beginning in early 1930s, for example, Catholic dioceses, religious communities, and universities began to establish labor schools for low-wage workers. The schools sought to prepare workers to participate in labor unions, instructing them on parliamentary procedure, public speaking, economics and labor law. They also provided grounding in Catholic Social Teaching and sought to instill in workers a sense of their work as a religious vocation. By the 1940s, church entities sponsored more than 150 labor schools. The church should revitalize its commitment to workplace justice in response to the needs of immigrants and others in low-paying, dangerous jobs, with high rates of labor standards violations.

6

A Reflection on Injustice and Communion

∾

On May 24, 2001, the U.S. Border Patrol found four migrants wandering east of Yuma, Arizona in the Cabeza Prieta National Wildlife Refuge. The four had splintered from a group of 26 who had come from the Mexican states of Guerrero and Veracruz. Smugglers had lied about how far the migrants needed to walk and had directed each to bring only one gallon of water. The group was trying to cross the desert in 115 degree heat. Over the next 24 hours, search and rescue teams found six clusters from the group, 14 had died and the rest were near death. Mario Castillo, a 25-year old father of a four-year old son and two-year old daughter, came from the village of Cuatro Caminos in Veracruz. He earned 35 pesos a day working on coffee and citrus plantations. He hoped to find work in the United States that would allow him to finish the construction of his family's cinder-block house.

The year before, I had researched and written a report on the border region entitled *Chaos on the U.S.-Mexico Border: A Report on Migrant Crossing Deaths,*

Immigrant Families and Subsistence-Level Laborers[49]. I later came to regret the use of the word «chaos» in the title, not because the border was not chaotic. We learned of migrants becoming separated from their children in the desert, crossing deaths (an obscenity that continues unabated), women delivering babies on ranch property, and Mexican women working in *maquilas* (assembly plants) who gave up their babies for adoption through informal channels. We learned of human rights violations by the Border Patrol, the use of deadly force against rock-throwers, and abusive treatment by officials at ports-of-entry, all conditions that persist[50].

However, there was also a predictable, well-organized quality to the predation and exploitation that was a far cry from chaos. We documented abundant criminality, but little of it from migrants. You could map, for example, where migrants were being robbed and raped and were dying in high numbers on their journey north. You still can[51]. We met farmers from Mexico who could not make a living in the wake of the North American Free Trade Agreement (NAFTA) and who had joined the U.S. migrant labor stream. One elderly farmworker spoke nostalgically of his time in the infamous Bracero Program, which he compared favorably to his subsequent work situations. We interviewed ranchers whose lands had been trashed by human smugglers. We spoke to U.S. families reeling from the deportation of husbands/fathers for drunk driving. We visited families in *colonias* (unincorporated towns) that made payment after payment without earning equity on their modest and isolated homes. We met middle-aged women whose life prospects had been irreversibly diminished when their long-time factory jobs moved abroad. We reviewed pay-stubs that combined the pay of two farmworkers in order to mask sub-minimum wages.

We met migrants who knowingly risked their lives to create a better future for their families; people who relied completely on their faith to carry them through their difficult journeys; humanitarians who drove and walked for hours to leave water and tend to the needs of the migrants in distress; Border Patrol agents on

---

49 See KERWIN, D., *Chaos on the U.S.-Mexico Border: A Report on Migrant Crossing Deaths, Immigrant Families and Subsistence-Level Laborers*, CLINIC, Washington, D.C. 2000, http://www.lexisnexis. com/practiceareas/immigration/pdfs/web305.pdf (accessed September 6, 2014).

50 KERWIN, D., «A Bipartisan Attempt to Restore Credibility to the U.S. Border Enforcement System» in *The Huffington Post*, March 28, 2014, http://www.huffingtonpost.com/donald-kerwin/a-bipartisan-attempt-to-r_b_5044761.html (accessed September 6, 2014).

51 See FOOTE, J. and SMALL, M., «Persistent Insecurity: Abuses against Central Americans in Mexico», Jesuit Refugee Service, Washington, D.C. 2013, https://www.jrsusa.org/assets/Publications/File/ Persistent_Insecurity.pdf (accessed September 6, 2014).

search and rescue missions who took a «there but for the grace of God» view of those they encountered; faith communities that ministered to detained immigrants, unaccompanied migrants, and other «near and far» neighbors; hospitals that opened their doors to the indigent and endangered from both countries; support groups of women (their children in tow) whose husbands had been deported; legal aid attorneys and countless others who had devoted their lives to service and justice. We found a community struggling in a grounded way with concepts like hospitality, justice, dignity, the human family, sovereignty, borders, the rule of law, citizenship, globalization, diversity and subsidiarity.

In the prophetic tradition, a recent statement by faith communities on the border denounced the region's manifest injustices and announced a new vision rooted in the values and strength of «families, religious communities, civic associations, neighborhoods, *colonias*, and cities»[52]. These faith leaders envisioned the border as a place of encounter, not division. They said that «God crosses borders, accompanying us —particularly the poor and marginalized— wherever we go» and they vowed to work to create a «gathering place for God's scattered children, where residents and visitors in all their diversity could work together to build the human family»[53]. So too must Hispanic ministry in its service to immigrants cross borders between diverse national and cultural groups, between natives and newcomers, between immigrants and the second and third generations, between young and old, and between new ministries and institutions created for earlier generations. So too must it create the sacred space where the church in all its wealth and diversity can build the human family.

Pope Francis has enunciated a powerful vision of migrants and refugees as a source of unity, describing them as «an occasion that Providence gives us to help build a more just society, a more perfect democracy, a more united country, a more fraternal world and a more open and evangelical Christian community»[54]. This vision animates the concept of «pastoral de conjunto» (communion in mission), which has inspired the spread of Hispanic ministry[55]. It calls us to walk to

---

52 BORDER NETWORK FOR HUMAN RIGHTS, *The New Ellis Island: Visions from the Border for the Future of America*, BNHR, El Paso, TX 2013, 17, http://www.scribd.com/doc/140208614/The-New-Ellis-Island-Visions-from-the-border-for-the-future-of-America (accessed September 6, 2014).

53 Ibid., 23.

54 See POPE FRANCIS, *Migrants and Refugees: Towards a Better World*, Message for World Day of Migrants and Refugees 2014, http://www.vatican.va/holy_father/francesco/messages/migration/documents/papa-francesco_20130805_world-migrants-day_en.html (accessed September 6, 2014).

55 U.S. CONFERENCE OF CATHOLIC BISHOPS, *Encuentro and Mission*, n. 19-20.

gether, to do what lies in our power, and to connect at the very deepest level on our spiritual journey home.

7
Appendix

7.1.   THEMES FROM CATHOLIC SOCIAL TEACHING
ON MIGRANTS AND NEWCOMERS

Politicians and the press reflexively refer to immigration «issues» and the immigration «debate». Scholars study migration through the prisms of globalization, sovereignty, national identity, demographics, economic development, labor markets, membership and integration. Policymakers and think tanks argue for effective migration «management». The church believes that these perspectives have merit, but teaches that the «human person» should always be «the focal point in the vast field of international migration»[56].

It views migration, in part, through the lens of rights and responsibilities. Pope Benedict XVI approvingly quoted Gandhi's statement that the «Ganges of rights flows from the Himalaya of duties»[57]. Catholic teaching holds that nations have a responsibility to provide the conditions that allow their members to flourish and to realize their God-given rights in their home communities. However, when states cannot fulfill this responsibility, their members have a right and responsibility to seek conditions consonant with human dignity, including by crossing borders. Nations also have a responsibility to receive migrants who, with the «local populations that welcome them … have the same right to enjoy the goods of the earth whose destination is universal»[58]. Immigrants, in turn, have a right and a responsibility to contribute to the good of their new communities.

Many view rights as a zero-sum exercise: they believe that honoring the rights of immigrants detract from the well-being of natives. The «common good»

---

56 See BENEDICT XVI, *The Migrant Family*, Message on World Day of Migrants and Refugees, http://www.justiceforimmigrants.org/documents/pope-benedict-2007-world-migrant-refugee-day-message.pdf (accessed September 6, 2014).

57 BENEDICT XVI, *World Day of Peace Message*, n. 12, http://www.vatican.va/holy_father/benedict_xvi/messages/peace/documents/hf_ben-xvi_mes_20061208_xl-world-day-peace_en.html (accessed September 6, 2014).

58 See BENEDICT XVI, *One Human Family*, Message for the 97th World Day of Migrants and Refugees, 2011, http://www.vatican.va/holy_father/benedict_xvi/messages/migration/documents/hf_ben-xvi_mes_20100927_world-migrants-day_en.html (accessed September 6, 2014).

speaks to the conditions that allow all persons in a community to flourish and to live dignified lives, including those without immigration status. As the U.S. bishops put it in 1986: «It is against the common good and unacceptable to have a double society, one visible with rights and one invisible without rights —a voiceless underground of undocumented persons»[59].

Rights contribute to the common good, but do not exhaust the conditions that allow human persons to flourish[60]. They set forth the «minimum conditions» for human dignity[61]. Catholic teaching grounds rights in Gospel values and demands a response beyond the protection of rights. It calls us to love our neighbor, to act justly, to extend hospitality.

Solidarity is the virtue that advances the common good. Pope John Paul II called solidarity a «firm and persevering commitment to commit oneself to the common good; that is to say, to the good of all and of each individual because we are all really responsible for all»[62]. The challenge is to recognize «anyone who needs me and whom I can help» as a neighbor[63].

Immigration can lead to fear of cultural displacement and loss of national identity. Yet the church views culture as the locus of people's deepest hopes and values, where faith takes root and finds expression. It teaches that migration creates an opportunity for unity based on the shared values found in diverse cultures[64], but that no culture is «permanent or perfect» and that every culture needs to be «uplifted and evangelized»[65].

Many believe that states have absolute authority to determine who enters, stays and leaves. Catholic teaching acknowledges the state's authority and responsibility to regulate immigration, but it qualifies this authority. To the church, the purpose of states —individually and collectively— is to protect human rights, promote the common good, and follow «the dictates of the natural law and the

---

59 NATIONAL CONFERENCE OF CATHOLIC BISHOPS, *Economic Justice for All: Pastoral Letter on Catholic Social Teaching and the U.S. Economy*, USCC, Washington, D.C. 1986, n. 10.

60 Cfr. BENEDICT XVI, Address to the United Nations' General Assembly, 2008, http://www.vatican.va/holy_father/benedict_xvi/speeches/2008/april/documents/hf_ben-xvi_spe_20080418_un-visit_en.html (accessed September 6, 2014).

61 NATIONAL CONFERENCE OF CATHOLIC BISHOPS, *Economic Justice for All*, 17-18, 79.

62 JOHN PAUL II, *Sollicitudo Rei Socialis*, n. 38.

63 BENEDICT XVI, *Deus Caritas Est*, n. 15.

64 KERWIN, D., «Crossing the Divide: Foundations of a Theology of Migration and Refugees», in KERWIN, D. and GERSCHUTZ, J.M. (eds.), *And You Welcomed Me: Migration and Catholic Social Teaching*, Lexington Books, Lanham, MD 2009, 99-100.

65 U.S. CATHOLIC CONFERENCE, *Welcoming the Stranger Among Us: Unity in Diversity*, USCC, Washington, D.C. 2000, n. 28.

divine law»[66]. The U.S. and Mexican bishops recognized both «the right of a sovereign state to control its borders in furtherance of the common good» and «the rights of human persons to migrate to realize their God-given rights»[67]. However, they concluded that the common good could not be «served when the basic human rights of the individual are violated»[68].

An age-old feature of anti-immigrant movements has been to scapegoat immigrants for prominent social problems or, in theological terms, for the communal sins of society. Nativists seek to brand and stigmatize immigrants, leaving them «vulnerable to control, manipulation, and exploitation»[69]. Labels like «illegal alien» or «criminal alien» controvert the God-given dignity of human beings. Beyond their deleterious political and social consequences, they can also cause immigrants to internalize a sacrilegious and scandalous view of themselves. Migrant testimonies highlight their lacerating effect[70]. To the Catholic Church, the children of God cannot be «illegal» and immigrants cannot be «alien» in a nation and church of immigrants. For the faithful, distinctions between people diminish in importance and disappear entirely (Gal 3:26-28).

The church teaches that individuals and societies have a responsibility to restore people whose rights have been violated or imperiled to full membership in the human family and to «empower them to participate in the common good»[71]. It refers to this responsibility as the «preferential option for the poor». From a pastoral perspective, the «preferential option» seeks to proclaim the Gospel in ways that reveal God's love to the poor «when much of what they experience on a daily basis is the negation of love»[72].

Some citizens argue that zero-tolerance enforcement strategies are needed to restore the rule of the law to the immigration system. They support attrition-through-enforcement laws which are designed to force immigrants to leave by denying them the means to subsist and criminalizing the exercise of rights. Ironically, such laws expose immigrants to higher levels of criminality and endanger

---

66 «Sovereignty», in *New Catholic Encyclopedia*, 2nd ed., Thomson Gale, Detroit, MI 2002, 371.

67 U.S. CONFERENCE OF CATHOLIC BISHOPS and CONFERENCIA DEL EPISCOPADO MEXICANO, *Stranger No Longer*, n. 39.

68 Ibid.

69 GROODY, D.G., «Crossing the Divide: Foundations of a Theology of Migration and Refugees», in KERWIN, D. and GERSCHUTZ, J.M. (eds.), *And You Welcomed Me: Migration and Catholic Social Teaching*, Lexington Books, Lanham, MD 2009, 3.

70 DE LA TORRE, M.A., *Trails of Hope and Terror: Testimonies on Immigration*, Orbis Books, Maryknoll, NY 2009, 46-47.

71 GROODY, D.G., *Globalization, Spirituality and Justice*, 110.

72 Ibid., 184.

the larger community. The demand for zero-tolerance enforcement of ever stricter, more punitive laws reflects a pharisaical mindset. The Pharisees and Sadducees continually sought to portray Jesus as a lawbreaker, while hardening their hearts to His message.

Many Catholics, including those that tout their fidelity to the church, evoke «prudential judgment» to signal their good-faith and loyal disagreement with the u.s. bishops' public policy positions on immigration. Catholic teaching defines prudence as the virtue that allows persons «to discern the true good in every circumstance and to choose the right means for achieving it»[73]. The bishops have rooted their immigration reform principles in Scripture, revelation, natural law and successive encyclicals. It is difficult to envision a prudent or convincing Catholic case for the criminalization of migrants, the separation of families, or making life so unbearable for non-citizens that they will be forced to leave.

73 PONTIFICAL COUNCIL FOR JUSTICE AND PEACE, *Compendium of the Social Doctrine of the Church*, 2006, n. 547, http://www.vatican.va/roman_curia/pontifical_councils/justpeace/documents/ rc_pc_justpeace_doc_20060526_compendio-dott-soc_en.html (accessed September 6, 2014).

Chapter 3

Hispanic Ministry and the Pastoral Care of the New Generations of Latino Youth

LYNETTE DE JESÚS-SÁENZ *and* KEN JOHNSON-MONDRAGÓN

When the first National Symposium for Hispanic Ministry was held at Boston College in 2009, the writing was on the wall: «Latino/a children are already about half of all Catholics under age 18 in the United States, and Latino/as are poised to become the majority of all Catholics in less than 40 years»[1]. In the last five years, the population of Latino adolescents in the u.s. has grown 16% while the number of their white counterparts has decreased by 7%[2]. Among young Catholics today, the children of Hispanic immigrants are the fastest growing segment. Given the size and continuing growth of the young Hispanic population, it is a major concern for the Catholic Church that only 6% of Hispanic Catholic teens in 2003 (the latest data) had been participating in a youth group for more than two years, and only 3% were serving as peer leaders in youth ministry—compared to 14% and 7%, respectively, for their white Catholic peers[3].

This chapter draws insights from pastoral experience and relevant social research to examine the challenge of passing a vibrant faith to the new generations of Latino youth. It will explore how their lived experience significantly impacts their engagement in faith activities and ultimately shapes their Latino Catholic identity. Six proven pastoral approaches for fostering faith among young Latinos will then be presented. All of this suggests pathways toward building a ministry with young Latinos that is sensitive to their pastoral needs and recognizes the unique gift they are to the church.

Much has already been written about the factors that inhibit the participation of young Hispanic Catholics in pastoral and faith development programs[4].

---

1   JOHNSON-MONDRAGÓN, K., «Hispanic Youth and Young Adult Ministry» in OSPINO, H. (ed.), *Hispanic Ministry in the 21ˢᵗ Century: Present and Future*, Convivium Press, Miami 2010, 104.

2   U.S. CENSUS BUREAU, *Population by Age, Sex, Race, and Hispanic Origin*, National Datasets for July 1, 2009 and December 1, 2013.

3   JOHNSON-MONDRAGÓN, K., «Youth Ministry and the Socioreligious Lives of Hispanic and White Catholic Teens in the u.s.», in INSTITUTO FE Y VIDA, *Perspectives on Hispanic Youth and Young Adult Ministry*, n. 2, Instituto Fe y Vida, Stockton, CA 2005, 7.

4   See JOHNSON-MONDRAGÓN, K., «Welcoming Hispanic Youth/Jóvenes in Catholic Parishes and Dioceses», in INSTITUTO FE Y VIDA, *Perspectives on Hispanic Youth and Young Adult Ministry*, n. 1, Instituto Fe y Vida, Stockton, CA 2003; DE JESÚS-SÁENZ, L., «Church and Youth Ministry Participation: Creating a Welcoming Environment for Latino/a Teenagers» in JOHNSON-MONDRAGÓN, K. (ed.), *Pathways of Hope and Faith Among Hispanic Teens*, Instituto Fe y Vida, Stockton, CA 2007, 81-112; JOHNSON-MONDRAGÓN, K. and CERVANTES, C.M., «The Dynamics of Culture, Faith, and Family in the Lives of Hispanic Teens, and their Implications for Youth Ministry», in INSTITUTO FE Y VIDA, *Perspectives on Hispanic Youth and Young Adult Ministry*, n. 5, Instituto Fe y Vida, Stockton, CA 2008; NATIONAL CATHOLIC NETWORK DE PASTORAL JUVENIL HISPANA — LA RED, *Conclusions, First National Encounter for Hispanic Youth and Young Adults*, USCCB, Washington, D.C. 2008, 19-24; and MATOVINA, T., *Latino Catholicism: Transformation in America's Largest Church*, Princeton University Press, Princeton, NJ 2011, 219-244.

While that is not the central focus of this chapter, a review of some common contributors to their decreasing engagement in faith-based activities sets the context for the discussion that follows. Here are brief descriptions of four of the most common reasons:

- *Language.* The connections between faith and language run deep, and the reality is that many Hispanic families today are linguistically divided, with the older generation being Spanish-dominant and the younger English-dominant. In this case, choices about language for family prayer, Mass attendance, catechesis, and youth ministry are fraught with potential conflict, differing resources, and competing agendas, with no easy answers for parents or pastoral leaders.

- *Quality of reception.* Many Hispanic communities share the parish with another ethnic community, usually the mainstream Anglo community. It is not uncommon for the Anglo youth ministry to have paid staff and abundant resources while Hispanic young people make do with volunteers and fundraisers[5]. At the individual level, Hispanic youth often feel criticized or judged by the adults and even other teens based on the way they look or dress. This type of prejudice alienates the young Latinos who stand to benefit the most from church activities.

- *Pastoral distrust.* Many young Latinos are denied meaningful participation and opportunities for leadership. The young people sense that the adults in the community do not trust them or recognize the gifts they bring. They want to participate and serve, yet the established leaders often stand in the way, or they are assigned only menial jobs like cleaning up after parish events.

- *Cultural dynamics.* Generational and cultural differences between Hispanic parents and their children can make it difficult for parents to instill the faith in their children. In some places even the parish itself may feel inhospitable or alien to immigrant parents. They often lack the frame of reference to relate to their child's experience here, while u.s.-born Latino youth feel pressured by their parents to continue family and cultural traditions they do not understand or appreciate.

---

5   OSPINO, H., *Hispanic Ministry in Catholic Parishes: A Summary Report of Findings from the National Study of Catholic Parishes with Hispanic Ministry,* Our Sunday Visitor, Huntington, IN 2015, 37. This is also discussed in HOOVER, B.C. and OSPINO, H., «Hispanic Ministry and Parish Life» in this collection.

Faith communities must «provide a safe and affirming setting in which these young people can work on their identities and life plans, for only then will the church be able to develop its corporate identity as a multigenerational institution that can serve emerging generations»[6].

1

The Parish as a Community of Memory

Pope Francis recently recommended a balanced approach for the evangelization of young people in Latin America that encompasses teaching doctrine, habits, and values together. In this process, the past (memory) and the future (utopia) come together through a process of discernment in the present (reality) that engages people across generations to work for the transformation of the world in accordance with Gospel values[7]. In Latin America, pastoral leaders and parents are supported in this effort by the Catholic religious customs and traditions that are still infused into everyday life, even though both secularism and the achievements of evangelical missionaries have significantly eroded what was once nearly a Catholic monopoly on religious affiliation.

In the United States, the broad religio-cultural ethos of Hispanic Catholicism is absent, so Latino parents look to the immigrant faith community to support the socialization and faith formation of future generations, to protect their children from the perceived harmful influences in their new social environment, and to reinforce the cultural and moral values they are trying to instill at home. In essence, the community must fill in for the grandparents —especially grandmothers, *las abuelitas*— who no longer live nearby, taking on their role in forming and sustaining the faith of the new generation.

Children and young people spending time with their grandparents is crucial for receiving the memory of their people and for discerning the present: to become teachers of discernment, spiritual advisors. And here, we see its importance with regard to trans-

6   CHA, P.T., «Ethnic Identity Formation and Participation in Immigrant Churches; Second Generation Korean Experiences», in KWON, H., KWANG, C.K. and WARNER, R.S. (eds.), *Korean Americans and Their Religions: Pilgrims and Missionaries from a Different Shore*, Pennsylvania State University, University Park, PA 2001, 141-156.

7   POPE FRANCIS, *Address to the Members of the Pontifical Commission for Latin America*, February, 28 2014.

mitting the faith to young people, a «one on one» apostolate. One cannot discern the present without… a good spiritual director who has the patience to listen to young people for hours on end. Remembrance of the past, discernment of the present, and a utopia for the future: this is the path along which a young person's faith grows[8].

Research has shown that greater assimilation into the mainstream u.s. culture —in which the popular media, public education, and most public discourse are dominated by a secular worldview— is associated with decreased religious engagement among Hispanic youth[9]. Positive relationships with the family and ethnic faith community, however, serve to mitigate these effects.

> Within the ethnic community, the church functions as a «community of memory» where the cultural values, traditions, language, and norms are reinforced and sustained through group interaction. The church becomes, in many instances, the center of cultural and social life within an often-threatening, diverse, urban environment[10].

Thus, developing youth ministry programming that is targeted specifically to Hispanic teens has great potential to strengthen a positive sense of religious and ethnic identity in young Latinos/as, especially when the leadership team is filled with Hispanic adults and peer leaders who may serve as role models.

When opportunities to participate in a parish-based ministry that responds to the needs of young Latinos are limited or unavailable, some Hispanic youth will seek out or create other avenues that allow them to minister to one another and deepen their understanding of cultural and religious traditions and how these can impact their lives. For instance, the popularity of apostolic movements has increased in part because they are peer-led and function outside of the parish structure. Parents are also doing their best to pass the faith to the next generation, but they need the support of the faith community. The reality is that many parents have limited access to their children due to language differences or lack of time with them. The parish youth ministry or apostolic movement can provide an important buffer for both parents and teens, especially when the cultural differences between generations become difficult to manage at home.

8 Ibid.
9 HERNÁNDEZ, E.I. and DUDLEY, R.L., «Persistence of Religion through Primary Group Ties Among Hispanic Seventh-Day Adventist Young People», in *Review of Religious Research* 32, n. 2 (Dec. 1990) 157-172.
10 Ibid.,158.

Immigrant congregations that generate active participation among the second-generation youth and young adults in their midst, frequently identify three factors that contribute to their success:

1) The religious and social activities within their ethnic communities provide the young people with needed support without making them feel like outsiders.

2) The immigrant congregation offers a safe space and a peer community in which they can talk about their experiences of growing up in America and the problems they are facing, knowing that they will be understood.

3) It also offers a place where they can claim their heritage on their own terms[11].

In other words, participation in the communal life of an immigrant congregation builds resilience. Not only do the young people learn about a loving, merciful God and deepen their understanding of the faith, they also grow as an individual in cultural context. The *grupo juvenil* is a place where Latino youth can ask questions and seek guidance without judgment, especially about things that they feel they cannot discuss openly with their parents. It becomes like a second family that supports them both inside and outside of church. This same sense of community can also be achieved in shared parishes by developing programs that are sensitive to the lived reality of Latino youth. A ministry with young people that acts as a «community of memory» will strengthen their identity as Catholic Latinos and promote a sense of responsibility toward the common good.

2

Journeying with Latino Youth

Given the low participation rates of young Latinos in pastoral and faith formation programs, Catholic parishes and schools have a great opportunity to increase their pastoral and missionary outreach to them. Too often, young Latinos are only offered programming options that do not touch their lives, their history, or their aspirations for the future, so they simply choose not to participate. The following six approaches offer complementary and effective ways to improve and expand the pastoral care and accompaniment of the new generations of Latino youth and young adults.

---

11 EBAUGH, H.R. and SALTMAN CHAFETZ, J., *Religion and the New Immigrants: Continuities and Adaptation in Immigrant Congregations*, AltaMira Press, Walnut Creek, CA 2000, 437.

La Familia. Hispanic families historically have communicated the Catholic faith across generations through family and community traditions that emphasize a continual awareness of God's presence in daily life. *La familia's* catechesis is an inherent part of Latino spirituality that strengthens Latino Catholic identity. It is a relational approach that involves immediate and extended family members as «traditioners» who hand on their lived faith as a set of social norms, grounded in Christian values and principles that are the foundation of *la familia's* worldview[12].

This is the primary catechetical approach used by Hispanic immigrant parents and grandparents. Latino parents who are active in the Catholic Church tend to take their kids everywhere they go: Mass, prayer groups, retreats, etc. If they are catechists, they may also take their adolescent children to help as assistants. They realize that, by their example, they are planting seeds that will help their children grow in faith. The effectiveness of this approach in the u.s., however, is influenced by many factors, especially the generational differences of culture and language and the exigencies of immigrant life in the United States. It only takes one generation to disconnect the family from regular faith practice, and the experiences of immigration, discrimination, and any number of other disruptive life experiences in adolescence —all of these can serve to separate a young person from the practice of the faith[13]. It then becomes very difficult for them to transmit the faith to their own children later in life because they have no internal resources to draw upon and they do not know how to tap into the external resources in the community, even though they may continue to identify themselves as Catholic.

Some Latino parents who are very committed in their own faith life are nevertheless cautious about spending too much time in church. They recognize that it is important to maintain a good balance, to be attentive to the needs of their children so they do not become resentful of them and/or the church. It is also important to have conversations about their experiences in the faith community. This is especially true for charismatic prayer groups and retreats, which can be confusing or unsettling for young people. The key for youth ministers and apostolic movements is to engage Latino parents, building on the faith practices they already encourage at home while equipping them with new or adapted resources suitable for their children's new linguistic and cultural context.

---

12 RAYAS, V., *La Familia's Catechesis: The Mexican American Family as a Place of Catechesis Through la Mística*, Unpublished Doctoral Dissertation, Fordham University, GSRRE, New York, 115-116.

13 See KERWIN, D., «Hispanic Ministry and Immigration» in this collection.

The National Federation for Catholic Youth Ministry has developed a process called «Strong Catholic Families» that encourages these conversations. A culturally adapted version, *Fortaleciendo Familias en la Fe*, has also been developed which follows the same outline but addresses «the unique family and cultural needs of Hispanic parents and the parishes that minister to them»[14]. Its primary purpose is to involve parents in the life and mission of the church and to support them as the primary educators of their children by strengthening the partnership between the parish/school and parents through a dynamic process that results in recommendations that can be implemented at the parish and in the home.

Popular Religious Traditions. Popular religious traditions are a central aspect of Latino spirituality and help strengthen Latino Catholic identity.

Devotions and practices of *religiosidad popular* are also moments where the faith is handed on. These include *Día de los muertos, Posadas, Fiestas, Altarcitos* (altars), *bendiciones* (blessings), *Día de San Juan, Día de los Reyes,* and holy water. The use of art, music, and drama are also significant components of *religiosidad popular*[15].

Many of these are common practices in Latino households and faith communities. These religious feasts and celebrations are not only fun for the whole family, but also reinforce its beliefs, customs, and traditions. The importance of popular religious traditions cannot be underestimated because they truly foster a devotional life across generations, and it helps to bridge the experience of faith at home with what happens at church.

The quinceañera, for example, is a religious and cultural celebration that plays a unique role in the life of young Latinas as they celebrate their fifteenth birthday. It can help the young woman develop a positive self-image, increase self-confidence, build community support networks, and heal family relationships[16]. Many parishes make the most of this period in a young Latina's life to discuss developmental concerns with the young woman while also equipping parents

14 NFCYM, «Fortaleciendo Familias en la Fe», [online]; available from http://www.nfcym.org/ programs/training/fortaleciendo.htm (accessed April 27, 2014).

15 RAYAS, V., *La Familia's Catechesis: The Mexican American Family as a Place of Catechesis Through la Mística,* 75-76.

16 See TORRES, T., «La Quinceañera: Traditioning and the Social Construction of the Mexican American Female», in ESPÍN, O. and MACY, G. (eds.), *Futuring Our Past: Explorations in the Theology of Tradition,* Orbis Books, Maryknoll, NY 2006, 277-298.

with the knowledge and skills to understand and communicate with their adolescent children.

One particular parish in Arlington, Texas offers a quinceañera program that consists of five four-hour sessions. At least one parent must be present, and separate sessions are offered for the parents and their teenage daughters. The sessions are structured in a way that empowers parents to fulfill their role and also helps the adolescent girl to better appreciate the family. A special aspect of this program is a reconciliation ritual in which the parents and child ask one another for forgiveness.

Identifying and Addressing Pastoral Needs. By focusing on the pastoral needs of young people both as individuals and in groups, pastoral workers can present the gospel message as an answer to the challenges they face in daily life[17]. When this approach is employed, even high-risk youth may begin to participate in youth ministry because they know that someone will be there to listen. They learn to manage their emotions and are encouraged to set goals. They find that church can be a welcoming and safe place where they are treated with dignity, appreciation, and respect. The recognition of the gifts they bring to the community helps to build their self-esteem.

High self-esteem and positive relationships with adults can protect young people from many behavioral problems, including gang involvement[18]. «Positive effects on the life trajectories of at-risk youth could be generated by building positive self-images in both young males and young females; building positive relationships, especially within the family; and teaching youth skills enabling them to determine how to make positive choices»[19]. Given the pervasiveness of gang activity in Latino communities, it is distressing that only 4% of the parishes in the NSCPHM study had outreach programs for Hispanic youth involved in gangs[20].

One parish in Orlando, Florida offers a community service program for youth offenders as part of their probation. In this setting, youth ministry leaders encourage gang members to make good decisions, stay off the streets, and come

---

17 BORAN, G., «Hispanic Catholic Youth in the United States» in DAVIS, K.G. and TARANGO, Y. (eds.), *Bridging Boundaries: The Pastoral Care of U.S. Hispanics,* University of Scranton Press, Scranton, PA 2000, 97.

18 JAGGERS, J. and others, «Predictors of Gang Involvement: A Longitudinal Analysis of Data from the Mobile Youth Survey», in *Journal of the Society for Social Work and Research* 4, n. 3 (2013) 277-291.

19 Ibid., 286.

20 OSPINO, H., *Hispanic Ministry in Catholic Parishes,* 37.

to church. For many of these young people, the youth minister becomes an important mother or father figure. One of their strategies is a 24-hour phone tree service called the «God Squad», for those critical moments when a young person needs special prayer support.

Apostolic movements, such as *Cursillos, Jornadas de Cristiandad, Juan XXIII,* and prayer groups for young people grounded in the Charismatic Renewal also provide ways to address the pastoral needs of young people. The profound experience of God's transforming love and the embrace of the community found in the movements have proved to be an effective pastoral response to young people whose lives have been harmed by gangs, addiction, suffering, and/or violence. These movements largely attract immigrant adults and young adults in Spanish although, in some regions, small communities in English may also be found.

The Pastoral Circle. The Pastoral Circle, sometimes referred to as a sociological approach, has been prominently used in Latin America to help «young people acquire the critical skills for analyzing structural causes of poverty and marginalization of minority groups in society»[21]. It is easy for Latino adolescents who see their families at the bottom rung of the social ladder in the United States to become discouraged and feel that the whole system is stacked against them—that they have no hope for a better life. This can also evoke a crisis of faith as they wonder why a loving God does not intervene to make things better in the face of such terrible injustice.

In the face of such challenging circumstances, the Pastoral Circle provides a reminder, first of all, that the young people are not powerless; and second, that God is at their side, with compassion and care for those who suffer or are in need. It gives them a sense of purpose in shaping the world to be a better place, even if they start in very small ways. The process itself creates leaders who can take the initiative to make a change, not only at church, but in the broader society as well.

The historical roots of the Pastoral Circle can be found in the Young Christian Workers movement —a branch of Catholic Action founded in Belgium by Cardinal Joseph Cardijn in the 1920s. His «see, judge, act» methodology offered a process for young people to become critically aware of the social forces that shape their lives, and it empowered them to become protagonists in a process of social transformation grounded in a living faith. Throughout Latin America this process has become a paradigm for continuous pastoral reflection leading to action that

---

21 BORAN, G., «Hispanic Catholic Youth in the United States», 99.

responds to the signs of the times. Likewise, Hispanic ministry in the United States has benefitted from this methodology, which has been expanded to include a total of six steps:

> The pastoral circle takes into account the uniqueness of each person and community, and encourages youth and young adults *to be*, by accepting themselves for who they are and recognizing their dignity as sons and daughters of God. It helps young people *to see* the reality of their life and *to judge* that reality in light of the Gospel and the teachings of the church. It motivates young people *to act* and develop a Christian praxis, and *to evaluate* the praxis periodically to strengthen it. The circle comes to an end and begins again with a *celebration* of life and faith[22].

Instituto Fe y Vida in particular has championed this methodology in its «Prophets of Hope» shared-leadership model for youth and young adult ministry in small communities. Its resources based on the Pastoral Circle include the *Witnesses of Hope Collection* of bilingual pastoral materials, *Diálogos Semanales con Jesús* as a weekly reflection and response in Spanish based on the Sunday lectionary readings, the bilingual *Biblical Mission for Youth and Young Adults* for empowering young leaders as missionary disciples to their peers, and Fe y Vida's *Leadership Formation System* encompassing multiple programs from the foundational level to advanced seminars, institutional leadership, and training of trainers.

When carried out properly, the Pastoral Circle methodology is much more than an exercise in social justice. It engages young people in naming and analyzing the great challenges they face in the local community. They then learn how the Good News of Jesus Christ planted in their own lives can overcome and transform all forms of human suffering. These transformative experiences, in which young people take the initiative as protagonists in building the Kingdom of God, are true reasons for communal celebration. It is in this celebration of faith that young Catholics live out the incarnation of the Church as communion and mission in a most profound way.

---

22 CERVANTES, C.M. (ed.), *Prophets of Hope, Volume 3: The Prophets of Hope Model,* Instituto Fe y Vida, Stockton, CA 1997, 46-47.

Linguistic Adaptivity. One of the great frustrations in Hispanic ministry today lies in pastoral leaders' inability to take advantage of their successes in building community among immigrant youth and young adults in Spanish in order to provide leadership for the pastoral care and accompaniment of u.s.-born Latino/a adolescents. Some parishes and apostolic movements have experimented with a bilingual approach in youth ministry settings. This works for some adolescents, but it does require at least some understanding of both languages and an openness to accommodate the needs of others. In other cases, parishes provide youth ministry and religious education opportunities for adolescents in both languages separately, allowing the young people to decide for themselves where they feel most comfortable.

Recent studies confirm that many *grupos juveniles* and apostolic movements are trying to integrate English in order to more effectively reach the u.s.-born Latinos. According to the nscphm, «Forty-five percent of parishes with pastoral programs for Hispanic youth hold their meetings mainly in Spanish, 42 percent do it bilingually, and 13 percent in English»[23]. This reflects a 15 percentage-point decrease in meetings held only in Spanish and a 13 percentage-point increase in bilingual meetings since the 2006 First National Encuentro for Hispanic Youth and Young Adult Ministry[24].

Another strategy being effectively used by parishes in liturgical settings is to provide a brief summary of the homily in English at the Spanish Masses. Young people in the congregation become more engaged because the priest expresses an interest in them as members of the community, and immigrant families do not have to sacrifice the needs of the parents in favor of their children, or vice-versa. According to the nscphm research, 84% of parishes with Hispanic ministry celebrate bilingual masses during the year, although the majority does so less than 10 times a year[25]. There are exceptions. One Hispanic national parish in Cleveland, Ohio offers a bilingual Sunday liturgy on a weekly basis in order to reach English-speaking Latinos and non-Hispanics. This Mass is celebrated primarily in English with cultural elements such as music in Spanish, and it is especially popular with Latino youth and young adults in the parish.

23 OSPINO, H., *Hispanic Ministry in Catholic Parishes*, 37.
24 NATIONAL CATHOLIC NETWORK DE PASTORAL JUVENIL HISPANA – LA RED, *Conclusions*, 97.
25 OSPINO, H., *Hispanic Ministry in Catholic Parishes*, 15.

Community of Communities. Recognizing the need for linguistic diversity in the pastoral care of young Hispanic Catholics can be the first step toward developing a broad-based «community of communities» approach to parish youth ministry. Many youth ministry leaders —especially those immersed in the dominant culture, whether or not they are of Hispanic heritage— feel that forming two or more youth groups is a step back in time toward racial segregation. In fact, this is not the case at all. When youth ministry is carried out from the mindset of «one parish, one youth group», it is not feasible to gather more than 80 or 100 teens on a regular basis because gatherings larger than that become unmanageable. It also gives pastoral leaders the mistaken impression that their programs are reaching large numbers, when in fact they may be reaching 10% or less of the young people in the community —Catholic teenagers in the largest parishes often number in the thousands.

80   Another drawback is that it limits the ability of pastoral leaders to adapt the content and methodology of a program to particular pastoral needs, such as those of high school dropouts, young immigrant workers, gang and detention ministry, teen parents, and young people of particular ethnic or linguistic groups. In most parishes with one youth group, it is the young people who are most in need of pastoral accompaniment who quickly realize that they do not «fit in» and opt not to participate, while in others it is the youth with a solid spiritual foundation at home who do not find a peer group in the parish with whom to advance in leadership and discipleship at a higher level.

In contrast, a differentiated community of communities approach to parish youth ministry does not involve segregation, but rather pastoral segmentation. It is a way to structure pastoral care and accompaniment that meets young people where they are and allows the ministry to grow without losing the human dimension of personal relationships, even if numbers surpass 50% participation rates. If the parish aspires to reach all of its teens in pastoral settings that are attuned to their particular needs, then the structural framework for the ministry should be set with that in mind from the start. Pope Francis reminds us that «the renewal of structures demanded by pastoral conversion can only be understood in this light: as part of an effort to make them more mission-oriented, to make ordinary pastoral activity on every level more inclusive and open, to inspire in pastoral workers a constant desire to go forth and in this way to elicit a positive response from all those whom Jesus summons to friendship with himself»[26].

26 POPE FRANCIS, *Evangelii Gaudium,* 27.

The community of communities approach allows for additional groups and programs to be added organically over time as the recruitment and formation of leaders permits and the perception of pastoral needs requires. One parish in Texas that has effectively implemented this approach is now reaching close to 1,000 young Catholics each year through more than 20 distinct programs that operate with more than 50 small groups or classes[27]. Such an extensive ministry does not appear overnight, but it only becomes possible when pastoral leaders embrace a vision of youth ministry that goes beyond the traditional «one youth group» mentality.

3
Conclusion

This chapter has highlighted some general principles and effective practices for ministry with the new generations of young Latino Catholics. All of these approaches can contribute independently to meeting the diverse needs of u.s.-born Latino youth and young adults. However, it is by no means a comprehensive guide to their pastoral care and accompaniment. The Pontifical Commission for Latin America recently published a set of pastoral recommendations for the transmission of the faith to the new generations of young people[28]. Many of the topics presented there are equally important for the transmission of the faith to young Latinos in the United States, such as:

- Collaboration between parishes, families, and Catholic schools to increase the enrollment of Latino youth and children (no. 10),
- Incorporating discernment of their Christian vocation more deeply into youth ministry programming (no. 14),
- Activating the protagonism of young missionary disciples (nos. 15-17),
- Social networks and evangelization on the digital «continent» (no. 19),
- Pastoral care and solidarity with young people living in poverty (no. 20),
- Social and political commitment and action of young Catholics (no. 21),
- Ecclesial movements and associations for Catholic young people (no. 22).

27 JOHNSON-MONDRAGÓN, K. and LOZANO, E., «A 'Community of Communities' Approach to Youth Ministry» in *Lifelong Faith* 7.1 (Spring 2013) 39-45.
28 See PONTIFICAL COMISSION FOR LATIN AMERICA, *La Emergencia Educativa y la* «Traditio» *de la Fe a las Nuevas Generaciones Latinoamericanas: Recomendaciones Pastorales,* Libreria Editrice Vaticana, Rome 2014.

Above all, the Church needs to develop strategies that will help young Latinos interpret their story from the perspective of what God is doing in their here and now and how their lived experience can be a real occasion of grace for themselves and the entire Church. Ideally this should be done in a linguistically-appropriate peer community of a reasonable size that allows for in-depth discussion of the particular challenges and experiences young Latinos face, accompanied by mentors and role models who have successfully navigated the treacherous waters of cultural integration. This does not mean segregating them from the broader youth community, but it may entail establishing times and settings in which Hispanic teens can congregate to address their pastoral needs, build a shared sense of ethnic and religious identity, and formulate a missionary response for their peers.

In other words, the parish must actually become a «community of memory» with all the benefits that flow from that experience for the young generations —even amid culturally diverse communities. When young Catholics are given a peer community with whom they can bond on the basis of a common history and social horizon, they become empowered to share their spiritual and cultural gifts in community-building and faith-sharing events for the entire youth community. Building a youth ministry based on these values and principles affords Latino young people the opportunity to recognize that their presence is a true gift to the entire Church. Given the size of the young Latino Catholic population in the u.s. today, this gift will become a legacy for the Church in the 21st century and beyond.

Hispanic Ministry and Education

Antonia Darder

School can and must be a catalyst, it must be a place of encounter and convergence of the entire educating community, with the sole objective of training and helping to develop mature people who are simple, competent and honest, who know how to love with fidelity, who can live life as a response to God's call, and their future profession as a service to society.

—POPE FRANCIS[1]

The words expressed by Pope Francis about education speak to salient issues that must be at the forefront of ecclesial consciousness, as the entire Christian community moves to examine the role of the Church and Hispanic ministry in supporting the education of students across diverse educational settings. To do so, however, means a careful rethinking of the Church's vision for education today beyond solely Catholic school formation, catechesis, and Church affiliation. Instead, there is a tremendous need for greater critical engagement with the lives of Latino children and their families, within the everyday communities where they struggle to make sense and meaning in these times of change and great uncertainty. This rethinking requires that the labor of the Church better engage with the particular historical, social, and material realities that define the lives of Latinos in the u.s. today. This raises serious questions as to the role that Latino ministers play in the context of education and formation of the community not just in Catholic schools and parishes, but also in the world in which they live. Is there serious urgency for proactive responses by the Church to go out into the world and meet the community where it is, as opposed to waiting for them to come knocking on the church door?

In the context of impoverished Latino communities, there is a need for a renewed Catholic vision of emancipatory education to help lead the larger society toward establishing humanizing approaches to formal and informal learning that support the development of critical consciousness, democratic voice, and community participation in the everyday culture of neighborhood churches and schools —a process that can also serve in remaking together a more just world. This speaks to a humanizing vision for democratic education and the transformation of social inequalities linked to educational priorities, ethical concerns, and teaching practices —both within Church-sponsored schools and beyond— that positively impact the social and intellectual development of Latino

1 POPE FRANCIS, *Address to the Students of the Jesuit Schools of Italy and Albania,* June 7, 2013, http://w2.vatican.va/content/francesco/en/speeches/2013/june/documents/papa-francesco_20130607_scuole-gesuiti.html (accessed August 25, 2014).

students. Moreover, this vision must be grounded on emancipatory values of community that support a universal understanding of human kinship and solidarity within and across cultural groups. This raises the need for rethinking the practices of Hispanic ministry, in order that it play a more intentional and public role in addressing the needs of the Church and world that move education from solely the promotion of human dignity and subjectivity to self-determination and a virtue and ethics of the common good.

In addressing the needs of Latinos, historical struggles for cultural and economic survival in the u.s. must encompass hard questions related to racism, class, and gender inequalities if we are to move toward a practice of social and ecclesial transformation. Since these impact the worldview of all cultural communities, understanding how people survive given disparities in opportunities and resources is key, both as a source of insight and critique. Moreover, distinct educational needs of diverse communities require an openness on the part of pastoral leaders to consider the unique situation and realities of those to whom they minister. In other words there is no «one size fits all» approach. Therefore, education with and on behalf of Latino communities must attend with the specific needs of the community and strive for greater opportunities for culturally inclusive participation and social transformation.

If the future work of Hispanic ministry in the United States is to evolve in ways that can support the diverse educational needs of Latino communities, then it will require that the societal hardships faced by Latinos become part of a larger ecumenical and political dialogue. Community organizing and the development of solidarity movements can be an essential contribution that the Church can provide to Latino communities around the country. Given the state of Latino education, the current educational crisis must be understood as a human rights issue, requiring closer interrogation of the implications it poses for Latino ministers committed to the dignity of all the people.

1

Latinos and the Grief of Poverty

> *As long as the problems of the poor are not radically resolved by rejecting the absolute autonomy of markets and financial speculation and by attacking the structural causes of inequality, no solution will be found for the world's problems or, for that matter, to any problems.*
>
> —POPE FRANCIS[2]

According to the most recent U.S. Census data, the Latino population today is nearly fifty-eight million; the largest and youngest ethnic minority population in the United States. The Mexican-origin population is estimated to comprise 67% of the total Latino population. Moreover, one-in-five schoolchildren and one-in-four newborns is Latino. Never before in the nation's history has an ethnic minority group made up so large a share of the youngest population, numbers expected to triple in the next three decades[3]. By 2036, Latino children are projected to comprise one-third of all children, ages 3 to 17[4]. Among the 30 million young people, ages 18 to 24, living in the U.S. today, six million (20%) are Latino youth. Also important are recent projections by the Pew Hispanic Center[5] that show that 82% of the future Latino population increase will be due to immigrants from Latin America and their U.S.-born descendants[6]. Hence, the trends of population shifts show a steady increase in Latino numbers, mainly due to recent Latino immigration. By the sheer force of numbers, the kind of education that Latino students receive will dramatically shape the future history of this country, as well as the Church.

Also important to this discussion, however, is the fact that Latino communities comprise one of the most economically and socially disenfranchised populations in the U.S. today. Today, over 50 million people in the U.S. are living in

2 POPE FRANCIS, *Evangelii Gaudium*, n. 202.
3 See PASSEL, J. and COHN, D. *U.S. Population Projections: 2005-2050*, Pew Hispanic Center, Washington D.C. 2008.
4 See U.S. Census Bureau.
5 Founded in 2001, the Pew Hispanic Center is a nonpartisan research organization that seeks to improve understanding of the U.S. Hispanic population and to chronicle Latinos' growing impact on the nation. See: http://www.pewhispanic.org/
6 See TAYLOR, P., GONZÁLEZ-BARRERA, A., PASSEL, J.S. and LÓPEZ, M.H., *An Awakened Giant: The Hispanic Electorate Is Likely to Double by 2030*, Hispanic Pew Center, Washington D.C. 2012.

poverty. In the Latino community, the child poverty rate is 35%, in comparison to 12% of their white peers. The total raw number of Latino children living in poverty, however, is higher than the number for any other minority ethnic group in the United States[7]. Among them, the children of Latino immigrants are most likely to face dire conditions of poverty, in comparison to other U.S. children[8]. The consequence is that Latino students have now become the new face of segregation, living in some of the poorest communities and attending some of the poorest and most segregated schools[9].

Hence, contending with poverty should be central to all facets of society, including the work of the Church. This is particularly so given that the lack of educational and labor opportunities are often associated with a variety of vulnerable life conditions. Hence, despite the important role the Church has played in providing assistance to vulnerable populations in the past, the current condition of Latino communities signal a dire need to expand education programs for youth and families through the advancement of Hispanic ministry's existing Gospel-inspired work and the expansion of ministerial outreach to the Latino community at large.

2

A Picture of Latinos and Education

> *Before all else be free persons! ... Freedom means knowing how to reflect on what we do, knowing how to evaluate ... which are the behaviors that make us grow.*
> —POPE FRANCIS[10]

7   See LÓPEZ, M.H. and VELASCO, G., *The Toll of the Great Recession: Childhood Poverty Among Hispanics Sets Record, Leads Nation,* Pew Hispanic Center, Washington, D.C. 2011, http://www.pewhispanic.org/files/2011/10/147.pdf (accessed August 25, 2014).

8   See AIZENMAN, N.C., «Left Behind: A Child's Burden», in *The Washington Post,* December 9, 2009, http://www.washingtonpost.com/wp-dyn/content/article/2009/12/08/AR2009120804446.html (accessed August 25, 2014).

9   In a report recently released by The Civil Rights Project, *E Pluribus...Separation: Deepening Double Segregation for Students,* Gary Orfield (2012) and his colleagues concludes «that segregation has increased seriously across the country for Latino students, who are attending more intensely segregated and impoverished schools than they have for generations». To access the report see: http://civilrightsproject.ucla.edu/research/k-12-education/integration-and-diversity/mlk-national/e-pluribus...separation-deepening-double-segregation-for-more-students/

10   POPE FRANCIS, Address to the Students of the Jesuit Schools of Italy and Albania, June 7, 2013, http://w2.vatican.va/content/francesco/en/speeches/2013/june/documents/papa-francesco_20130607_scuole-gesuiti.html (accessed August 25, 2014).

Educators across the country continue to grapple with the failure of mainstream education to meet the learning needs of Latino students. In the last two decades, a variety of federal and state policy initiatives have supported culturally assimilative and linguistically restrictive educational policies. As a consequence, the right to bilingual education for language minority students was abolished, while practices tied to federal mandates of *No Child Left Behind* (NCLB) and *Race to the Top* (RTTT) reinforced high-stakes testing, standardization of the curriculum, and the privatization of education. In Arizona, mean-spirited policy initiatives against Chicanos and Mexican immigrants encompass nativist efforts to restrict the use of Spanish in schools and the workplace, the elimination of Mexican American studies at the secondary level, and the banning of books considered to be subversive by ideologically-oriented proponents of curricular and textbook reforms[11]. Yet, despite the repressive intent of such policies, changing demographics across the nation point to a Latino majority population by the middle of the 21st century. How are Catholic churches in Arizona responding to these realities?

In the nation's schools, Latino students have reached a new milestone. For the first time, one-in-four (24.7%) public elementary school students are Latino, following similar milestones reached recently by Latinos among public kindergarten students (in 2007) and public nursery school students (in 2006). Among all pre-K through 12th grade public school students, a record 23.9% are Latino. And for the first time, the number of 18- to 24-year-old Latino youth enrolled in college exceeded two million, reaching a record 16.5% of all college enrollments[12]. As they progress through kindergarten to high school, Latino students are also expected to become an even larger share of all school enrollments in the coming years. This reality will also impact the numbers of children who will seek parish based catechetical instruction and other forms of education, given that access to and enrollment in Catholic schools has severely dropped.

In the last decade, graduation rates for Latino students across the country have improved. Recent data indicates that Latino students are much less likely to drop out of high school than they were a decade ago. A recent study found that 78% of Latino students graduated from high school in 2010, an increase from

11 AGUIRRE, A., «Latino Immigrants and the Framing of Anti-immigrant Policies», in *Latino Studies*, 10, n. 3 (2012) 385-394. See also DARDER, A., *Culture and Power in the Classroom*, Paradigm, Boulder, CO 2012.

12 FRY, R. and LÓPEZ, M.H., *Hispanic Student Enrollments Reach New Highs in 2011*, Hispanic Pew Center, Washington D.C. 2012, http://www.pewhispanic.org/files/2012/08/Hispanic-Student-Enrollments-Reach-New-Highs-in-2011_FINAL.pdf (accessed August 25, 2014).

64% in 2000[13]. Similarly, the rate of Latino students in the U.S. earning associate and bachelor degrees has improved dramatically. However, despite impressive gains, the Pew Research Center data indicates that of all students completing Bachelor's degrees in 2012, only 11% of degrees were conferred on Latino students, despite their increase in college enrollment[14]. In fact, only 51 percent of Latino students who enroll in college receive a degree[15].

This disturbing picture of Latino education has important implications for Hispanic ministry, with respect to the need for the Church to expand more vigorously its support toward the preparation of Latinos ministers and advocates —individuals who genuinely understand the conditions of U.S. Latino communities. This also entails broadening programs and activities within Catholic schools and beyond that support educational and social justice initiatives. Over the years, Latino communities have used both political pressure and legal remedies to struggle for equal education for their children. Often Latino parents have turned to Catholic schools, in the hopes that this would afford their children a better future. However, since only a limited number of Latino children attend Catholic schools[16], the efforts of Hispanic ministry must increase exponentially to support Latino students, wherever they attend school, by advocating for their right to a meaningful life.

Accompanying them in the struggle for educational and social justice, Latino parents also need support for claiming the inherent dignity and rights of their children, particularly when they are born to the unaccounted and undocumented in the U.S. In light of the evangelizing mission of the Church, which is rooted in both Scripture and Tradition, one of the most powerful gestures the ecclesial community can make is to stand in solidarity with the marginalized, in the simplicity of the Christ figure, to promote the emancipation of our brothers and sisters who struggle for education and for justice.

---

13 See MURNANE, R.J., «U.S. High School Graduation Rates: Patterns and Explanations», in *Journal of Economic Literature*, American Economic Association, 51, n. 2 (2013) 370-422.

14 See LÓPEZ, M.H., *Latinos and Education: Explaining the Attainment Gap*, Hispanic Pew Center, Washington D.C. 2009, http://www.pewhispanic.org/files/reports/115.pdf (accessed August 25, 2014).

15 See KELLY, A., SCHNEIDER M. and CAREY, K., *Rising to the Challenge: Hispanic College Graduation Rates as a National Priority*, American Enterprise Institute, Washington, D.C., 2010, https://www.aei.org/wp-content/uploads/2011/10/Rising-to-the-Challenge.pdf (accessed August 25, 2014).

16 OSPINO, H. and WEITZEL-O'NEILL, P., «Catholic Schools Serving Hispanic Families: Insights from the 2014 National Survey», in Journal of Catholic Education, 19, n. 2 (2016) 54-80; OSPINO, H. and WEITZEL-O'NEILL, P., Catholic Schools in an Increasingly Hispanic Church: A Summary Report of Findings from the National Survey of Catholic Schools Serving Hispanic Families, Huntington, IN: Our Sunday Visitor 2016.

More than ever, we find in the words and practice of Pope Francis a validation for standing firmly on behalf of the most vulnerable. The Pope does this reminding us about the communal dimension of Christianity. He challenges Catholics to assess the causes of the breakdown of local communities, usually worsened by the lack of access of quality educational opportunities. With him we can ask: What are the implications of a breakdown in dialogue; in unbridled consumerism that feeds markets and leaves the poor empty; in relativistic subjectivism devoid of collective consciousness and communal accountability? How has the failure of our institutions to be welcoming added to the difficulty of restoring right relationship of faith in a pluralistic landscape?[17]

3

Seven Guiding Principles for Cultural Inclusion

✑

We need… to counter the dominance of a one-dimensional vision of the human person…
—POPE FRANCIS[18]

Cultural inclusion asserts the right of all cultural communities to have a meaningful place at the table. This concept supports everyday practices for countering the one-dimensionality associated with conditions of inequality in schools and society. This understanding of community and educational practice, grounded in what Paulo Freire termed *unity-in-diversity*[19] speaks to an important recognition that all cultural traditions bring particular understandings of the world to the world. Therefore, differences between us are necessary because they shape the essence of our humanity. The intercultural inclusiveness and socially just ethos of this view counters deficit views imposed on Latino communities and other populations perceived as «other». As such, practices of cultural inclusion challenge unjust systems within Church and society that fail to respect the cultural and linguistic richness afforded by the members themselves.

17 See POPE FRANCIS, *Evangelii Gaudium*, n. 70.
18 POPE FRANCIS, Address during Audience with Representatives of the Churches and Ecclesial Communities and of the Different Religions, March 20, 2013, https://w2.vatican.va/content/francesco/en/speeches/2013/march/documents/papa-francesco_20130320_delegati-fraterni.html (accessed August 25, 2014).
19 See DARDER, A., *Freire and Education*, Routledge, New York 2014; FREIRE, P., *Pedagogy of Freedom: Ethics, Democracy and Civic Courage*, Rowman & Littlefield, Lanham: MD 1998.

Culturally inclusive practices within Latino communities challenge evangelizing structures that reproduce or remain silent before inequalities and, by so doing, create room for our many human differences. It also calls for rethinking the structures of decision-making within the Church in order to create more opportunities for Latino community participation at all levels, including financial matters. Moreover, a culturally inclusive practice opens the way for curricular innovations within both Church practices and schools to include two-way immersion programs and bilingual paradigms of instruction. In this way, an ethos of cultural inclusion supports Hispanic ministers in building rich intercultural communities of accountability, in every sector of life.

Such an approach also points to a practice of Hispanic ministry that is capable of functioning with greater ambiguity and complexity, in ways that respect both our universal humanity, as well as the particularities of the cultural knowledge that Latino communities have gained through their efforts to survive and thrive under difficult conditions. If Catholicism in the u.s. is becoming increasingly Hispanic, then an ethos of cultural inclusion calls upon Hispanic ministers to embrace more concretely the Church's long historical commitment to preferential treatment of the most vulnerable. And to do this effectively requires environments where the essence of Latino biculturalism is fueled through genuine Latino participation in establishing conditions of social justice and human dignity.

This discussion moves us to a set of seven guiding principles that inform culturally inclusive practices of ministers working within Latino communities. These guiding principles encompass a deep sensibility to issues, concerns, and Latino cultural values and beliefs, which support and enhance the intellectual, social, and spiritual ways of being of Latino communities, as both congregants and world citizens.

1 Embrace a deeply relational cultural view of the world, particularly as it relates to the multicultural needs of Latino communities and the spiritual and educational formation of *jóvenes*. This speaks to a view of education and leadership that is rooted in profoundly relational and communal processes. Herein opportunities are consistently created for Latinos to participate in the life of the Church, and to strive for justice in the world.

2 Develop an institutional memory and understanding of the dynamics of power in Church and society in order to promote strategies and relationships that can effect change for the greater good. These new ways of being and knowing point to the importance of the multilingual, multicultural pluriver-

sality that Hispanic ministers can offer the Church and world as agents of grace and wisdom.

3 Legitimate bilingual practices of dialogue within communities in order to create diverse opportunities for reflection, critique, and action, in support of democratic voices, participation, and decision-making within the Church and in the world. These practices allow for greater intergenerational relationships.

4 Promote a historical appreciation for the varied migrations and processes of integration undergone by Latino populations in the u.s. Depending on their origins, every community in our country has undergone particular struggles and many have arisen to meet the challenges that must be remembered. It is important then to build on the lessons learned and the strength of Latino communities to both survive and thrive, despite hardships.

5 Commit to the value of unity-in-diversity across the spectrum of public and private communities. Develop practices that support the cultural vitality and solidarity of Latino communities across their regional, national, linguistic, class, and gender differences.

6 Build upon principles of Catholic Social Teaching[20] as a way to challenge policies and practices of inequality in the Church and society that interfere with the spiritual and educational formation of the community. This acknowledges that bringing about societal changes requires the combined efforts of everyone working as individuals and in community. This is particularly key for those who will be most affected by the new conditions that will emerge. Ultimately, social change requires faith and personal strength to work together, as well as the courage to stand alone when necessary, in order to work toward creating a more just world.

7 Promote a covenant of well-being that expresses concern for the needs of all vulnerable populations, irrespective of culture, ethnicity, language, or faith. This again speaks to the significance of intercultural inclusiveness in the work of Hispanic ministry, which requires a deep commitment to the spiritual, social, and material health of Latino families and their communities.

These seven guiding principles of cultural inclusiveness must, of course, be intimately linked to a humanizing ethos of dignity and human rights, along with an understanding that culturally inclusive practices inspire the awakening of conscience, personal coherence, spiritual commitment, as well as cultural integrity. This entails a social consciousness that is grounded in the Freirean ideal

20 HEFT, J., «Catholic Education and Social Justice», in *Catholic Education* 10, n.1 (2013) 6-23.

that *our vocation is to be human*[21] and on a way of teaching, ministering, and living, which is anchored in a deep sense of faith, love, hope, and a vision where all cultural citizens of the world can bring the best of what we have to offer, for the evolution of our universal humanity and a growing respect for the resources of our cultural differences.

4

Building Church-Community Partnerships of Faith

⟡

We need a Church capable of walking at people's side, of doing more than simply listening to them; a Church which accompanies them on their journey; a Church able to make sense of the "night" contained in the flight of so many of our brothers and sisters from Jerusalem; a Church which realizes that the reasons why people leave also contain reasons why they can eventually return. But we need to know how to interpret, with courage, the larger picture.
—POPE FRANCIS[22]

What does the aforementioned data, propositions and reflections mean for the work of the Church within Latino communities in the United States? Latinos, as the country's largest-growing ethnic population, now make up more than 40 percent of all Catholics and this number is actually expected to grow in the coming years, as the birthrate of the Latinos exceeds all other ethnic populations in the u.s.[23]. The growing number of Hispanic youth in parish-based catechetical programs is a great opportunity to support their spiritual formation. Hence, there is no doubt that the Church continues to serve as an important hub for Latino community life. Yet the question remains: what role will the Church take in developing the hearts and minds of the future leaders of our increasingly diverse global community? How will the Church provide the prophetic witness needed to educate for what has been identified as the Freirian ideal of a common humanity, which is firmly rooted in Pauline interpretation of the organic body of Christ (1Cor 12:20-27)?

---

21 See FREIRE, P., *Pedagogy of the Oppressed,* Seabury Press, New York, 1971.

22 POPE FRANCIS, Address of Pope Francis during a Meeting with the Bishops of Brazil, Apostolic Journey to Rio de Janeiro on the Occasion of the xxviii World Youth Day, July 28, 2013 (accessed August 25, 2014).

23 See SHRANK, A. «Dwindling Catholic Schools see Future in Latino Students», in *Catholic News Service*, February 28, 2013, http://www.religionnews.com/2013/02/28/catholic-schools-seek-out-latino-students/ (accessed August 25, 2014).

Through culturally inclusive principles built upon reflection, dialogue, voice, participation, and action for the good of all, a more grounded sense of well-being and community can evolve. Such evolution will be the result of genuine relationships that the Church can foster more fully *with* Latino communities. This observation suggests that the Church's relationship with Latino populations must undergo an important transformation that extends beyond the traditional evangelizing paradigm, which oftentimes unwittingly re-inscribes deficit views of Latinos and their children. Instead, ministerial relationships within Latino communities need to be anchored in the concrete experiences and conditions of everyday life, as well as grounded in culturally inclusive practices that build empowering church-community partnerships of faith.

The Church, consequently, can work with and through its people to consider larger questions of education in ways that promote and enhance the social agency, responsibility, and consciousness of both ministers and the community. The institutional church can lead the way in the struggle for educational justice for Latino students—within and outside the traditional scope of the ecclesial structures. Just as Catholic congregants are expected to bring our faith to all secular arenas, so too should the Church be a living example of struggle for the most vulnerable in the world today. Beyond its powerful pedagogical role at the pulpit, the Church must take up Pope Francis's invitation to walk alongside Latino communities and accompany us on our journey toward making a better life for our children.

5

Hispanic Ministry as Revolutionary Commitment

> *I ask you, instead, to be revolutionaries, I ask you to swim against the tide; yes, I am asking you to rebel against this culture that sees everything as temporary and that ultimately believes you are incapable of responsibility, that believes you are incapable of true love.*
> —POPE FRANCIS[24]

24 POPE FRANCIS, *Address of Pope Francis during the Meeting with the Volunteers of xxviii World Youth Day,* July 28, 2013, https://w2.vatican.va/content/francesco/en/speeches/2013/july/documents/papa-francesco_20130728_gmg-rio-volontari.html (accessed August 25, 2014).

In many of his recent public proclamations, Pope Francis has called upon the clergy, the faithful, and the world to not only reinstate our concern for the poor, but also to be revolutionaries and rebels in this time of crisis, against the loveless forces of oppression that spiritually and materially impoverish us all. The «true love» that Pope Francis references above is reminiscent of Paulo Freire's «pedagogy of love» and Gustavo Gutierrez's notion of «theology as a love letter». This is a love for the Divine that calls into question all forms of dogmatism, disembodied theory, or ideological affiliations, to unite the love of the Church and the people in community action, inspired by the truth of the Gospel, for the betterment of the lives of our sisters and brothers and the world. This declaration of love by the Pope should fully inform the ministry of the Church and its commitment to a culturally inclusive and socially just world.

This revolutionary labor must also encompass a deep and humble commitment to communal participation and an underlying faith in the capacity of the people to evolve and reinvent together structures that can meet the essential needs of their lives. This, undoubtedly, encompasses a dramatic shift in the exercise of power and the establishment of more egalitarian relationships, which can help to promote consciousness, social responsibility, and the transformation of community life. Leadership by this definition must integrate people from the community itself, with policies and practices enacted in their primary culture and language. By so doing, a powerful praxis, founded on love and dignity, can support the dialogue required to reflect, to name, to critique, and to labor together to dismantle injustice that chokes off our existence, as Catholics and citizens of the world. Pope Francis asserts, «All the wars, all the strife, all the unsolved problems over which we clash are due to a lack of dialogue»[25]. His uncompromising faith in the power of dialogue, rooted in love, serves then as an indispensable ethical foundation for a humanizing community ministry.

Pope Francis calls for a transformation of consciousness for Catholics and non-Catholics alike, and that we take on this challenge with courage, commitment, and resolve. Hence, the Church too must continue to transform in its practice and aspire more fully to stretch beyond the boundaries of its place of sanctuary and security, as must we all. And this we must do in order to work together

---

[25] POPE FRANCIS, *Address to Students and Teachers from the Seibu Gakuen Bunri Junior High School of Saitama*, Tokyo (Japan), August 21, 2013, https://w2.vatican.va/content/francesco/en/speeches/2013/august/documents/papa-francesco_20130821_collegio-saitama-giappone.html (accessed October 23, 2015).

in the raw reality of our everyday lives —where daily and sinful forms of injustice become often normalized and persistent. It is here where Hispanic ministry can best cultivate and nurture a place for on-going public dialogue. Whether out in communities and schools or within the context of Catholic education or catechetical programs, the empowerment of youth works to transform the culture of exclusion and, instead, prepares them for participation in a world where cultural inclusion is the norm. Moreover, the revolutionary labor of Hispanic ministry is one that focuses consistently on the establishment of a humanizing world —one linked to the evolution of critical and Christian consciousness as well as social responsibility.

Culturally inclusive practices that focus on dialogue and active participation allow leaders to link effectively issues of education to the overall well-being of Latino families and their dreams of a better life for their children. The underlying assumption here is that the Church has a moral responsibility to be responsive to the integral needs of Latino populations, who constitute one of the most faithful populations in the Church. However, tending to the spiritual needs of a spiritual community, without serious regard for their culture or the larger societal forces that negatively impact their personal freedom and community development is not only shortsighted, but unconscionable in light of the historical commitment to the most vulnerable that has been central to Church's own Christian convictions. Hispanic ministry, as a formidable alliance that functions within the dual interest of Church and community seems an ideal place from which to tackle more substantively ethical and practical concerns with respect to the education of Latino students.

Through the integration of their empowered bicultural voices, moreover, pastoral leaders in Hispanic ministry can generate more effectively a deeper sense of cultural familiarity, more fluidity in communication, and communal solidarity with Latino populations, who still remain at the margins of Church and society in many places. Through encompassing an understanding of the culture, language, history, traditions, and conditions of Latinos in this hemisphere —along with a vision of faith, hope, and love— the work of Hispanic ministry can offer a genuinely participatory leadership in the transformative process of education for Latino students, whether they attend Catholic schools or not.

Hispanic ministry possesses a unique potential to accompany Latino populations on their journeys of spiritual formation and responsibility as global citizens, inviting those who have experience in the world of political participation, and empowering with the right resources those who yearn for a more just world for their children. By effectively interpreting with courage and resolve the difficult realities at work in Latino education, and grounded in the best of the Christian tradition, Hispanic ministry can serve as a viable humanizing force that leads to the affirmation of the God-given dignity of every human person. Anchored in an intimate knowledge of faith, culture, history, language, and bicultural life, the Church can enter into a renewed relationship *with* Latino communities —one in which the voices and participation of Latinos and Latinas reside squarely at the center of Church life.

Hispanic Ministry, Digital Technology, and New Media

Patricia Jiménez *and* James F. Caccamo

It is appropriate that we begin to examine digital technologies and new media, and wrestle with the way in which they are transforming our communities, while considering the questions that these transformations raise for Hispanic ministry in the 21st century. This process is essential in light of the lack of significant reflection on digital technologies within the Hispanic ministerial community.

During the *Encuentro* processes, Hispanic pastoral agents primarily reflected on the Catholic press and print publications. The First National *Encuentro in Pastoral Juvenil Hispana* expressed the desire for a website to connect with youth at a national level, and the need to develop Catholic media resources[1]. These reflections however were provisional, and while some efforts have been made to implement them, they have not been acted on in significant ways at the parish and diocesan level. Additionally, they surfaced before widespread global access to mobile communications, the development of web 2.0 technologies, and the explosion of modern social media, all of which have greatly impacted the manner in which Hispanic/Latino ministers carry out their evangelizing mission[2].

In this essay, we open a dialogue on the question of new media and digital technology in Hispanic ministry. We begin by noting some current trends in technology that demonstrate robust use within Hispanic communities. This will be followed by a theological reflection that identifies a particular resonance between digital media and the kind of contextual theology that grounds Hispanic Catholic self-understanding. In light of this resonance, the current implementation levels of new technology strategies in Hispanic ministry are of particular concern. In response, the paper will suggest four key areas of consideration that leaders could develop to diversify their media strategies and embrace technology as a new location for authentic manifestations of the Gospel: 1) «responsive flexibility», 2) being conversational rather than magisterial in speaking about media, 3) the allocation and use of resources for digital ministry, and 4) privacy in choices of technology. Through a practical theological process of seeing, judging, and considering the dynamics of action, this paper will spur reflection on the effective use of new media for ministry in the future.

---

1 NATIONAL CATHOLIC NETWORK DE PASTORAL JUVENIL HISPANA – LA RED, *Conclusiones: Primer Encuentro Nacional de Pastoral Juvenil Conclusiones*, USCCB, Washington, D.C. 2008, 50-51.
2 Definitions of «web 2.0» are varied. However, what they share is the idea that users create or affect the content that is presented. Blog posts, reader reviews, dynamic code deployment, location aware apps, and video uploading are some examples of web 2.0 technologies.

Technology and New Media Use among u.s. Hispanics[3]

The last few years has seen a wealth of coverage in secular news media highlighting the increased use of technology and new media by u.s. Hispanics. As marketing firm López Negrete notes, «with an accelerated adoption rate, and over-indexes in mobile [technology] and social media usage, Hispanics have narrowed the gap of the connected population and are set to equal, and surpass, the general market by 2015»[4]. Moving dramatically into the mobile realm, as of 2012, 94% of u.s. Hispanics ages 18-70 owned cell phones and 60% of Hispanics owned smartphones[5]. Notably, bilingual u.s. Hispanics are the most active users of mobile technologies[6]. One key area of activity is social media. Globally, Latinos

spend 56% more time on social media sites than others, and among adult internet users, Hispanics lead in social media usage[7]. Given this decisive growth trend, Zpryme Research and Consulting has gone so far as to coin the term «techno-Hispanics» to describe the emerging reality of tech savvy Hispanics/Latinos.

Tech Use in Hispanic Catholic Ministry. The rapid and decisive expansion in the use of new media technologies among Hispanics has profound implications for the way in which u.s. Hispanic Catholics live their faith, and, thus, the way that ministry leaders minister to them. As a starting point, it would be helpful to understand how technology is being utilized within Hispanic Catholic Ministry.

---

3   This essay uses «technology» to refer to the broad range of devices (i.e., cell phones, tablets, and computers) that fall under the category «information and communication technology». «New media» refers to media (i.e., email, texting, video conferencing, social media, podcasting, blogging, and microblogging) that have emerged on these technologies.

4   LÓPEZ, N., *How «Techno-Hispanics» Are Influencing Social Media,* June 2012, http://www.hispanic trending.net/2012/06/how-techno-hispanics-are-influencing-social-media.html (accessed January 22, 2014).

5   ZPRYME RESEARCH AND CONSULTING, *2012 Hispanic Mobile Consumer Trends,* June 2012, http://centerforhispanicleadership.typepad.com/files/Hispanic_Mobile_Consumer_Trends.pdf (accessed January 22, 2014); SMITH, A., «Smartphone Ownership-2013 Update», *Pew Internet & American Life Project,* Pew Research Center, Washington, D.C., June 5, 2013.

6   HEARTLAND MOBILE COUNCIL, *MobiU2013 Seminar: Mobile Hispanics –Presentation,* June 20, 2013, http://www.slideshare.net/heartlandmobile/hmc-mobi-u2013-mobile-hispanics-nielsen-final-061313 (accessed January 22, 2014).

7   VOZ DE AMÉRICA, «Los Hispanos Usan Más Las Redes Sociales», *VOANoticias.com,* December 26, 2012, available at http://www.voanoticias.com/content/eeuu-redes-sociales-facebook-latinos-hispanos-argentina-peru-/1572679.html (accessed January 22, 2014).

Unfortunately, no studies have been done which describe technological practices within Hispanic ministry. For that reason, an online survey was conducted at the beginning of 2014 to gather this information in which sixteen national Hispanic ministry/theology organizations, national apostolic movements, and non-affiliated adult Hispanic ministers participated[8].

Overall, the survey found extensive and broad usage of technology by pastoral ministers and academics. Nearly 60% of those surveyed identified themselves as confident individuals, comfortable utilizing new technologies. Nearly 70% report using a Smartphone in their ministry/profession, 54% use a Smartphone several times a day, and 62% text multiple times a day within their ministry/profession.

Social media plays a significant role among Hispanic/Latino ministers and theologians. Eighty-nine percent (89%) indicate using social media sites either for personal or professional purposes. The top three social media sites utilized by Hispanic/Latino Ministers are Facebook (71%), YouTube (51%) and Google (47%). Forty percent of social media users post only or primarily in English, 38% of respondents post both in English and Spanish, while 22% post only or primarily in Spanish. The survey points to the need for formation and training in new media as only 40% of respondents have received general computer training, 24% have received training in new media, and only 44% have received technology and new media guidelines[9].

National Organizations and New Media. Board members of national Hispanic ministry organizations were also asked to share how they utilize new media. Although national organizations have embraced new media, their use is limited and not consistent with the daily/weekly demands of Hispanic/Latino new media users. All sixteen organizations report having a website, although 10 of them update their site only several times a year, and only seven identify it as having web 2.0 features such as blogs and social media integration.

---

8 «Hispanic Ministers» are defined in this essay as anyone serving English or Spanish speaking Hispanics/Latinos.
9 See JIMÉNEZ, P., *Hispanic Ministry Technology and New Media.* For more detailed findings, see the *Summary Report* available at www.ushispanicministry.com/tr.

New Media and Technology Innovation within Hispanic Ministry. Despite new media lagging in many areas, it is being utilized in innovative ways. For example, usHispanicMinistry.com is a national website that aggregates articles, videos, resources, organizations, formation programs, and jobs in u.s. Hispanic ministry. Theologians and pastoral agents contribute articles and videos that provide unique and diverse voices. The website is presented in both English and Spanish and is integrated with social media platforms. *Instituto Fe y Vida* has also published a Facebook Page —*Biblia Católica para Jóvenes*— centered on the Bible for Hispanic young people and has an international reach of over half a million followers.

Universities and dioceses have also embraced new technologies for the purpose of delivering formation programs. Many dioceses such as San Bernardino, Stockton, and Fresno have utilized teleconferencing to deliver programs across their expansive dioceses. Some programs focus on certification of catechists who are unable to travel to training sites while others do continuing education online. Some programs are English language graduate degree programs while others are certification programs in Spanish. At the university level, the University of Dayton (*La Comunidad Cibernética Para la Formación en la Fe*) and the University of Notre Dame (*Camino*) offer online programs in Spanish that build virtual student communities. Programs may work with u.s. dioceses using a cohort model, and students receive in-person orientation at their parish or diocese to acquaint them with the technology. While these online programs are geared more towards formation and certification of pastoral ministers, there is a great need for on-line degree programs in Hispanic/Latino ministry, in Spanish and English.

2

Technology, New Media, and the Hispanic Catholic Social Reality

Beyond being simply a way of spending time, communicating, and networking, technology and new media exhibit six characteristics that may be compatible with the religious worldview of Hispanics/Latinos Catholics.

A Communal Anthropology. A local study conducted in the Diocese of Fresno, CA, surveyed Hispanic Catholics on social media usage and motivations. Ninety two percent (92%) of those surveyed use social media regularly (daily or weekly) to connect with friends; 81.7% use it regularly to connect with family and 64.4% use it regularly to build community[10]. Eighty percent (80%) affirm that social media creates community[11]; and 92% of respondents in the national survey of Hispanic organizations confirmed the findings[12].

The Material and the Spiritual. In the context of Hispanic Catholic spirituality, *mística* is often defined in terms of an organic way of experiencing reality in which the material and the spiritual are always intertwined[13]. For many Hispanics this view of *mística* also comes to life in new media where technology, chat rooms, social media site, and smartphones mediate in a quasi-sacramental way both the spiritual and material. One example is when persons unable to attend a mass become connected to a liturgy through media and experience grace and presence despite their physical absence from the event. These realities cannot be discounted despite the complexity which they bring to the question of spiritual community.

The Public Nature. One of the characteristics of the Hispanic religious worldview is its public dimension. Today, photos of home and community altars on the Day of the Dead are posted on Facebook; the Saint of the Day is tweeted; the parish *Via Crucis* is posted on YouTube; and among other events the celebration of our Lady of Guadalupe at the Archdiocese of Los Angeles is live-streamed over the internet and posted on blogs. Hispanics/Latinos continue to express and bear witness to their faith and popular practices, but now in the very public «*techno barrios*».

Life and Death. Hispanic Catholicism exhibits a particular fascination with the idea of death and the continuing relationships with those who have died as expressed in celebrations such as *Día de los Muertos* and novenas for the dead. New Media provides new spaces for blurring the separation between life and death. Profiles on Facebook and Twitter often remain after a person has died and many

10 See JIMÉNEZ, P., *Buenas Noches Facebook Familia: How Social Media is Redefining the Social Location of the Christian Community among Hispanics/Latinos in the u.s.*, Unpublished D.Min. thesis, Barry University, 2014.

11 Ibid.

12 JIMÉNEZ, P., *Hispanic Ministry Technology and New Media.*

13 See GOIZUETA, R.S., «The Symbolic World of Mexican American Religion», in MATOVINA T. and RIEBE-ESTRELLA, G., (eds.), *Horizons of the Sacred: Mexican Traditions in u.s. Catholicism*, Cornell University Press, Ithaca, NY 2002.

Hispanics —and Catholics as a whole— continue to remember those who joined the communion of saints by posting messages of remembrance on their profiles.

Lo Cotidiano. U.S. Hispanic Catholics also maneuver through this world searching for meaning in *lo cotidiano,* the everyday experience and struggle. The late Ada María Isasi-Díaz described *lo cotidiano* as situating us in our experiences[14]. New media allows Hispanic Catholics the opportunity to express *lo cotidiano* through images, quotes, and videos and to create social awareness and change through the encounter of the other.

Innovative Leadership Roles. Finally, Alicia Marill and Fr. Jorge Presmanes have stressed the importance of the ecclesiology that has underscored the National Pastoral Plan as one of *comunión y participación*[15]. Under this style of leadership, all the baptized equally share in the Christian mission through their baptismal calling. One of the foundational aspects of new media is its democratic sense and distributed power structure. Within a Christian context, the structure and functions of social media open spaces to creatively exercise our baptismal calling. Anyone can evangelize by sharing a resource, an image, a prayer or devotion. Most importantly, these events occur outside of the official liturgical celebrations and can be expressions of God's grace in our lives.

These six characteristics of new media are important to highlight, as they are compatible with the Hispanic/Latino religious worldview that rejects a dichotomous understanding of reality[16]. Considering such a reality and a prolific Hispanic new media context, we must ask, how do we prepare pastoral leaders for effective ministry in the 21st century?

3

Technology and New Media in the New Social Reality

Contemporary technology and new media have emerged as viable ways to tell and live the Gospel story, especially within the Hispanic context. However, more

14 ISASI-DÍAZ, A.M., *La Lucha Continues: Mujerista Theology,* Orbis, Maryknoll, NY 2004, 95.
15 MARILL, A. and PRESMANES, J., «Hispanic Ministry and Theology», in OSPINO, H. (ed.), *Hispanic Ministry in the 21st Century: Present and Future,* Convivium Press, Miami, FL 2010, 93.
16 GOIZUETA, R.S., «The Symbolic World of Mexican American Religion», 120-121.

than twenty years into the digital media revolution, Catholic churches —Hispanic or otherwise— are playing catch up with companies, social groups, and charities to engage users. There will be much to consider as the Church develops media strategies in ministry. The following are four key concerns that need to shape any conversation about digital ministry:

Responsive Flexibility as Fundamental. Finding a way through the many options available requires informed consideration of the avenues through which to engage the faithful technologically. The initial challenge will be selecting the adequate medium(s). Since the initial emergence of digital systems we have seen a veritable explosion of ways to communicate. Text messaging, email, websites, blogs, digital media (film, video, and images), file sharing networks, videoconferencing, and gaming provide a wealth of ways to connect with people and information. For each platform, there are different apps to choose from. Should you use Facebook, Google+, or LinkedIn? YouTube, Vevo, or Vine? Facetime, Skype, or Hangouts? The possibilities seem endless.

Effectively navigating this sea of options will require a disposition of adaptability and openness. Technology is a volatile industry that thrives on disruption. As a result, apps and platforms can fall in and out of fashion, gaining or losing millions of users in mere weeks. In this environment, ministers will succeed only when they are able to adapt and let go of outdated modalities and adapt to technologies that are more effective. Second, ministers will need to be open and nimbly respond to the particular people they serve. Knowing your audience has always been fundamental for communicators, not to mention for the see-judge-act methodology at the core of both Hispanic ministry and Catholic Social Teaching. In the twentieth century, that meant being aware of large demographic trends. Today, however, user preferences are much more specific[17]. People expect technologies to meet them in the concrete particularities of their lives. When technologies don't, people move on. As a result, ministers will need to move where church members are right in real time, not where ministers think they are, or need to be.

---

17 See MADRIGAL, A., «How Netflix Reverse Engineered Hollywood», *The Atlantic.com*, January 2, 2014, http://www.theatlantic.com/technology/archive/2014/01/how-netflix-reverse-engineered-hollywood/282679 (accessed January 9, 2014).

Admittedly, such flexible responsiveness will require leaders to critically examine our ministerial assumptions —even ones that have nothing to do with technology. For instance, one of the enduring assumptions of u. s. Catholic Hispanic ministry is that those we serve speak only Spanish, so programs should be offered in Spanish. Yet, a growing number of groups who identify as Hispanic Catholics —especially among youth— have English as their preferred language. Social media ministers who fail to reexamine their perceptions, resting instead on what was true for previous generations, are bound to leave behind members of the community.

Flexible responsiveness will, of course, also require ongoing critical examination of technological assumptions. In the wake of the sexual abuse scandal, for instance, the Archdiocese of Philadelphia issued new guidelines for those who communicate with minors. Under the heading «E-Mail, Instant Messaging, and

Text Messaging (sms —short message service)», it says:

> Teachers and administrative staff should communicate with students through the use of school based e-mail accounts and/or school-sponsored websites[18].

Such a rule makes initial sense: when communicating with youth, always use a broadcast-focused, auditable technology that is administrated by church personnel. The technologies left out —instant messaging and text messaging— are much more difficult to oversee.

Note, however, the underlying assumption about technology: web and email are effective ways to communicate with youth. Unfortunately, this assumption is only partially true. According to the Pew Center for Internet and American Life, in 2013, 78% of teens had a cell phone, almost half (47%) of which were smartphones[19]. Hispanic teens lead in smartphone ownership (43%) over Black, non-Hispanic (40%), and White, non-Hispanic (35%) teens. However, they are less likely to have mobile internet access (perhaps due to the high cost of data plans), leaving them unable to access email and websites from their phones. Instead, Hispanic teens text at a significantly higher rate. Strikingly, in 2012, Pew found

---

18 ARCHDIOCESE OF PHILADELPHIA, OFFICE FOR CHILD AND YOUTH PROTECTION, *Addendum to the Standards of Ministerial Behavior and Boundaries*, effective July 1, 2011, Philadelphia, PA, 2.

19 MADDEN, M., LENHART, A., DUGGAN, M., CORTESI, S. and GASSER, U., «Teens and Technology 2013», *Pew Internet & American Life Project*, Pew Research Center, Washington, D.C. 2013, http://www.pewinternet.org/Reports/2013/Teens-and-Tech.aspx (accessed May 12, 2013).

that Hispanic teens send a median of 100 texts per day while white, non-Hispanic teens send a median of only 50[20]. Hispanic teens send twice as many texts, despite an overall 16% lower cell ownership rate.

In their efforts to protect youth, the Archdiocese fell short of practicing flexible responsiveness regarding technology, assuming that email and the web would be equally effective for reaching all teens. Based on this faulty assumption, they created a system that favors the tech practices of some teens over others, leaving youth who don't have easy email and web access out of the loop on parish activities. Given the «on the ground» tech realities, those youth are most likely to be Hispanic.

The Trust Factor of Increased Risk in Increased Participation. A second consideration that should inform technology use in ministry is the dialogic quality of tech culture. The contemporary web is characterized by the idea that users affect the content that is presented. Readers comment on blogs, programmers share code, shutterbugs upload photos, and anyone can upload videos. As a result, online culture valorizes interaction, sharing, and contribution. While it is easy to deride the web's shrillness and vacuousness, countless communities of discourse exist where people exchange ideas, care for each other, and learn from one another. In them, one can catch glimpses of the communal anthropology and spirit of *pastoral en conjunto* fundamental to Hispanic Catholicism and leadership.

In this context, digital ministries will need to enable user contribution and participation. Youth will expect to create videos about activities and Facebook users will expect to post comments about parish events and these will need to be monitored because enabling user contribution always entails risk. However, ministry strategies that exclude these kinds of practices are bound to be short-lived. The Roman Catholic tradition has tended to favor a magisterial approach to media that avoids any risk of ambiguity or dissent. Dioceses, for example, release strong, clear, and uniform messages that express the Church's position without uncertainty or local variation. At a Priestly Formation Day in the Philadelphia Archdiocese, the assembled priests expressed grave reservations —even hostility toward— the notion that users might post criticism of Church teaching or a

---

20 LENHART, A., «Teens, Smartphones & Texting», *Pew Internet & American Life Project*, Pew Research Center, Washington, D.C. 2012, http://pewinternet.org/Reports/2013/Teens-Social-Media-And-Privacy.aspx (accessed May 12, 2013).

particular priest[21]. For some, this risk was sufficient reason to reject the web for ministry altogether.

Yet, ministers must seriously consider another factor in the equation: trust. Trust has emerged as a critical factor in technology and new media success[22]. One key part of developing successful trust relationships online is risk-taking[23]. Creating online community, it turns out, takes more than just showing up. Online communities require reciprocal acts of risk-taking involving some level of uncertainty as well as responsibility. By its nature, authentic dialogue always involves risk that facilitates community. So, while enabling participation is risky, churches that are closed off to this practice are unlikely to develop the trust necessary for successful digital ministry. Most importantly, this development must occur throughout the system, requiring church leaders to invest in well trained competent laity with whom they can have an open line of communication and whom they can trust will use technology responsibly and effectively for the greater good of the ecclesial community. Because social media moves quickly, ministers need to be empowered to speak in a timely manner without layers of oversight which will undoubtedly require correcting mistakes. However, if ministers and parishioners alike are micromanaged rather than trusted, robust use of technology will not possible.

Resources for Digital Ministry. A third consideration that should inform technology use in ministry is a realistic assessment of the resources necessary to implement digital ministry initiatives. While the Church provides priests with education and salary, many Hispanic ministry programs survive on a handful of credentialed ministers and an army of (generally female) volunteers or underpaid staff. Web and social media sites are frequently assigned to staff members and volunteers who already are over tasked. To ease the burden, some look to the growing number of Hispanic Catholic youth who are adept with digital tools who might provide a free solution to our media challenges but who will also require oversight.

Realistically, sustainable long-term ministry strategies involving technology will require adequate resources both in personnel, hardware and software. For

---

21 Witnessed by James F. Caccamo at Priestly Formation Day, Saint Helena Church, Blue Bell, PA, September 29, 2010.

22 See SOLOVE, D., *The Future of Reputation*, Yale University Press, New Haven, CT 2007.

23 FORD, H., «A Sociologist's Guide to Trust», *Phys.org*, March 29, 2012, http://phys.org/news/2012-03-sociologist.html (accessed April 10, 2012).

example, ministers need to be trained in technology; and new media needs to be an integral part of ministerial formation. To this end the Vatican has called for more extensive communications training, to only modest success[24]. However, the day when ministers could succeed without any digital skills is dwindling.

Second, if we are to invite young people who are adept with new media into ministry, a broad variety of resources will be needed for their formation. Hispanic ministers should know their tradition and understand human beings deeply and compassionately as well as exhibit a basic level of proficiency and personal boundaries when using technology. The digital world valorizes many behaviors that are disedifying when practiced by ministers. Over-sharing, strident partisan expressions, posting compromising photos, and «liking» questionable organizations for ironic value are fine for private figures, but are inappropriate for ministers who represent the Church and called to be a role model for others.

Third, in accord with the Catholic commitment to justice, resources should be allocated to compensate those who do digital ministry. Millennial Catholics who have been formed in participatory digital culture are used to spending hours creating media without compensation. Under constant fiscal pressure, it will be tempting to accept their devoted volunteerism, ignoring our responsibility to pay living wages. Additionally, ministers should be provided with the tools necessary to do their jobs (e.g., smartphones, computers, and apps). Ultimately, we are witnessing an emergence of innovative leadership roles within the Church consistent with the ecclesiological sensibilities of the Hispanic community. Creating sustainable and effective new media ministry programs will only be possible where resources are committed to these new leaders.

Privacy in Technology Choices. A final aspect that needs to inform the use of new media in ministry is the issue of privacy. As good stewards of Church resources, ministers tend to use free communication tools, information sharing systems, and media creation tools that are available. However, it is critical to maintain awareness of the implications of our choices for the privacy of those we serve. In part, this is a legal concern. Amongst the most valuable data is location information, which is collected in many apps, even ones that don't seem to have location components to them like games, social media, and video sharing sites. Location

24 CONGREGATION FOR CATHOLIC EDUCATION, *Guide to the Training of Future Priests Concerning the Instruments of Social Communication»*, Vatican, Rome 1986, http://www.vatican.va/roman_curia/pontifical_councils/pccs/documents/rc_pc_pccs_doc_19031986_guide-for-future-priests_en.html (accessed May 11, 2007).

information is particularly sensitive in the Hispanic community, where regular contact with foreign nationals or undocumented people is not unusual. We want to ensure that the Catholic commitment to freedom of movement is not undermined by the technology we use.

Beyond legal concerns, ministers must also be sensitive to what we might refer to as «existential privacy» needs. Already, ministers use digital tools for communication and reflection in their work. They might invite retreatants to use a photo app to do probing personal expression or encourage groups to use video to interpret their experiences. In these cases, technology facilitates integral human development by creating personal, private, judgment-free spaces for exploration and disclosure. However, Hayden Ramsey has made the case that privacy is a necessary precondition «for effective participation in every basic human good», including the spiritual life[25]. Without «freedom from interference and from observation» and «a measure of solitude», we lack the «freedom to grow [and] security to experiment» that is necessary for authentic self-discovery[26]. Thus, privacy is central to ministering.

Critically, while digital tools can be used to create private spaces, the robust sharing functionality built into most apps means that there is constant danger that the private will become public. In a North American culture that valorizes user contribution and creativity, sharing —even over sharing— is a constant temptation. Unfortunately, the stakes for doing so can be high, even when we exclude law enforcement issues. According to a 2012 study, 37% of u.s. companies use social media to research job candidates[27]. They do this for various reasons, yet 34% of hiring managers who look at social media chose not to hire candidates as a result. The biggest reason: Forty-nine percent (49%) found material they found provocative or inappropriate in some way. Shared imprudently, the revealing things that we invite people to create in private could easily become such an impediment.

The Hispanic Catholic emphasis on expression of religious identity in public, non-liturgical acts should be affirmed. Yet, such acts have powerful implications in a wired society. Ministers need to attend to these lest they inadvertently

25 RAMSAY, H., «Privacy, Privacies and Basic Needs», *Heythrop Journal* 60 (2010) 294.
26 Ibid., 295.
27 CAREERBUILDER, «Thirty-Seven Percent of Companies Use Social Networks to Research Potential Job Candidates, According To New Careerbuilder Survey», http://www.careerbuilder.com/share/aboutus/pressreleasesdetail.aspx?id=pr691&sd=4%2F18%2F2012&ed=4%2F18%2F2099 (accessed May 12, 2013).

compromise privacy. Ministers could do things as simple as choosing anonymous, encrypted services and teaching church members about privacy techniques, or as complex as running parish servers. In either case, developing Hispanic ministry programs that utilize technology will require making smart choices so religious practices do not lead those they serve into harm.

4
Conclusion

In this essay, we have suggested that information and communication technology represent promising new avenues for ministry that are consistent with the core insights of the Hispanic Catholic tradition. Hispanics in the United States have adopted technology and new media at rapid rates, outpacing other demographic groups in mobile and social media use. Yet, ministers have not used digital tools in as widespread a manner. Leaders in the Hispanic Catholic community would do well to develop robust programs for engaging Catholics in their new digital worlds. We have suggested that as ministers and leaders do, they adopt a stance of responsive flexibility, facilitate the contributions of those they serve, ensure that adequate resources are devoted to these efforts, and attend to the privacy of those they engage in new media spaces. Observing these dynamics will help create new connections with those they serve.

What we have not done however, has been to outline what we might consider «best practices» in using technology within Hispanic Catholic ministry. Catholics could measure success using the metrics of the business world or the evangelical Protestant community. However, doing so may very well lead the Church on a path that diverges from the kind of integral human development and social justice initiatives central to Catholic education and ministry. Thus, a key step in developing digital ministry programs for a Catholic context will be bringing together ministers and technologists to identify the goals that can be pursued authentically with technology. This collaborative engagement will need to attend to new questions related to the objectives of the Church, the needs of the people and how digital ministry can be the link that serves both. These matters must be attended to first.

Ultimately, Catholicism is not a Luddite tradition. The popes of the twentieth and twenty-first centuries have been adept media users: Pope Pius XII with radio,

St. John Paul II with television, and Pope Francis with Twitter and Instagram. Yet, many Catholic ministers are coming to understand that the instruments of social communication function best when they respond to the moral and spiritual imperatives of liberation in human communities. Thus, technology choices should always be made in light of those imperatives. We do not suggest that Hispanic media will —or even should— go completely digital. The media landscape is complex, and responsive flexibility requires that our choices respect that complexity. In the end, Hispanic Catholic ministry will greatly benefit from a wide array of social communication as it strives to serve the needs of the Church. Technology and digital media will need to play a central role in the Church's pastoral ministry in the twenty first century.

Hispanic Ministry and Leadership
Hilda Mateo, MGSpS

Where does one begin the effort to discover the path toward an authentic Latino leadership development?

—ALLAN FIGUEROA DECK, SJ[1]

Sporting his distinctive Mexican cowboy hat and boots, José, a middle-aged man of short stature, wit, humor and conviction stood before forty Catholic men and women in a rural area of his Diocese in the Southwest on a cold November morning. He repositioned the podium, ascended to the two foot ledge surrounding the stone fireplace —jokingly reminding people that he needed the extra boost to see them— and began his theological reflection on the «Exodus and the Migrant Experience». With the use of simple everyday words —*palabras cotidianas*— he contextualized the Jewish Scriptures within the framework of general Catholic Social Teaching themes and made comparisons between the mobility and plight of the ancient Israelites and that of contemporary Hispanic immigrants in the United States. Throughout his talk, José, seemingly trusting his experience more than the notes before him, did not shy away from making explicit connections between the Egyptian oppressors and the «*migra*»[2]. Summoning faith and trust in the God of the Exodus, he ended his discourse with a clear exhortation to his fellow Catholics that resulted in cheers and a standing ovation: «*Lo que hace falta hoy son nuevos Moiseses, nuevos líderes, ¿y por qué no? también nuevas Moisesas, sí, hombres y mujeres que respondan al llamado de Dios de guiar a su pueblo inmigrante*» (What is needed today are new *Moiseses* (Moseses), new leaders, and why not? Also new *Moisesas*, yes men and women to respond to God's call to lead his immigrant people».

Jose's reflection was the third talk in the curriculum for first level participants in a two day program co-sponsored by the Mexican American Cultural Center (MACC)[3] and the Catholic Migrant Farmworker Network (CMFN). Having participated three years prior in both levels of the formation program, José knew well that the objective for the weekend was to help «*develop the leadership* potential of migrant Roman Catholic farm-workers in order for them to assume

---

1 FIGUEROA DECK, A., «Latino Leaders for Church and Society: Critical Issues», in CASARELLA, P.J. and GÓMEZ RUÍZ, R. (eds.), *El Cuerpo de Cristo: The Hispanic Presence in the u.s. Catholic Church*, Academic Renewal, Lima, OH 2003,184.

2 The word «migra» is commonly used in Hispanic immigrant contexts to refer to the Immigration and Customs Enforcement (ICE) agency, which is responsible for «enforcement of federal laws governing border control, customs, trade and immigration». See http://www.ice.gov/about.

3 In 2008 MACC announced its transition into a college: Mexican American Catholic College.

their rights and responsibilities in the church and in society»[4]. Though leadership terminology was to be presumed in the context, Jose's recurrent uses of the word *líderes* and conscious inclusion of women were particularly noteworthy. However, what captivated the audience was Jose's powerful witness: he embodied the words and concepts shared and led out of his own experience.

After the talk, a woman boisterously approached me to comment on José's leadership—*liderazgo*. A civil law attorney in her native country, she was a recent émigré to the United States who had met José a few months earlier through their respective work in the *Justice for Immigrants* campaign[5]. Rather skeptical, she wondered how a man with so little schooling had acquired the power to mobilize others so effectively. Her comment made it evident to me that there are diverse interpretations of the idea of leadership. Such various interpretations generate questions not only about *who* can serve as a competent leader, but also *where* and *how* different people are called forth to exercise leadership roles. What distinguishes a «leader» from a «non-leader»? If leaders, according to classic definitions, live in a relational dynamic that requires «followers», then we need to ask: who is leading whom, to where, for what purposes, and seeking what results? Is terminology about leadership in the Church limited to name the role of bishops, clerics, religious, and lay ecclesial ministers that hold «official» positions, whether paid or volunteer, within the hierarchical ecclesial structures? Moreover, does ordination or consecration or the authorization of lay ministers who have received substantial formation, usually at the higher education level, and hold some form of official credentials make then automatically leaders? What is the relationship between leadership development and discernment, vocation, and mission? Can someone like José be strictly recognized —and seriously engaged— as «leader» according to the present standards presupposed to serve in pastoral ministry in the Catholic Church in the United States? If so, what empowers José to serve in this capacity? Formal academic education and official authorization by the hierarchy do not seem to have played a role in this case. Yet, tens of thousands of Latino Catholics like José exercise their leadership in their faith communities in very powerful ways. I suggest that it is their ability to recog

---

4   This is the objective of the program in December 2006 as it appeared in the syllabus. Emphasis and translation are mine.

5   In June 2004, the United States Conference of Catholic Bishops (USCCB) Committee on Migration and the Catholic Legal Immigration Network, INC. (CLINIC) Board of Directors resolved to make comprehensive immigration reform a major public policy priority within the Church by launching *Justice for Immigrants: A Journey of Hope campaign*. See www.justiceforimmigrants.org

nize, claim, and own their baptismal identity as missionary disciples of Jesus Christ that thrusts them into commitments that often are described as «leadership».

The role of the pastoral agent, however, echoes the operative understanding of ministry that is used in a community. If ministry is reduced to spending day and night in an office making executive decisions, raising and administering funds, and making personnel decisions, then the best model of leadership is that of a Chief Executive Officer. CEOs usually get to where they are in light of their credentials, connections in high levels, and abilities to make practical decisions. How many people have we met in the world of ministry who are excellent CEOs. Most likely very few, if any, like José. Yet, in this reflection on Latino pastoral leadership we are challenged by Pope Francis's words:

> Pastoral ministry in a missionary key seeks to abandon the complacent attitude that says: «We have always done it this way». I invite everyone to be bold and creative in this task of rethinking the goals, structures, style and methods of evangelization in their respective communities. A proposal of goals without an adequate communal search for the means of achieving them will inevitably prove illusory[6].

Statistical evidence suggests that there is a growing gap between the number of committed Hispanic ministers and the increasing Latino population[7]. According to the U.S. Census Bureau and the Pew Research Center, «The Hispanic population grew 47.5% between 2000 and 2011»[8]. This increase is paralleled in church affiliation, where figures indicate that «forty percent of all growth in registered parishioners in U.S. parishes from 2005 to 2010 was among Hispanic/ Latino(a)s»[9]. Rethinking the goals and methods for effective pastoral ministry urges us to find creative means for inspiring a vision of leadership from the His-panic perspective that provides pathways for men and women to prepare to be «missionary disciples» *latinamente*[10].

6 POPE FRANCIS, *Evangelii Gaudium*, n. 33.
7 See THE PEW FORUM ON RELIGION AND PUBLIC LIFE, *Changing Faiths: Latinos and the Transformation of American Religion*, Pew Hispanic Center, Washington, D.C. 2007; OSPINO, H., *Hispanic Ministry in Catholic Parishes: A Summary Report of Findings from the National Study of Catholic Parishes with Hispanic Ministry*, Our Sunday Visitor, Huntington, IN 2015.
8 DESILVER, D., «5 facts about Hispanics for Hispanic Heritage Month», http://www.pewresearch. org/fact-tank/2013/09/17/5-facts-about-hispanics/ (accessed October 28, 2013).
9 GRAY, M., «Special Report: Multicultural Findings», *Emerging Models of Parish Leadership*, Center for Applied Research in the Apostolate, Washington, D.C. 2012, 11. The report also underscores that «nine in ten parish leaders identify their race or ethnicity as non-Hispanic white».
10 The category «missionary disciples», closely associated with Pope Francis, is also the distinctive focus of the Fifth General Conference of the Bishops of Latin America and the Caribbean and its concluding document, commonly known as Aparecida (2007).

Undeniably, leadership is and has been, as our historical memory —*memoria histórica*—attests, a central concern for Hispanic ministries[11]. One way this is demonstrated is in the common and frequent use of «leadership» language among u.s. Hispanic Catholic ministers and theologians, especially in official documents. The *National Pastoral Plan for Hispanic Ministry* (1987) clearly prioritizes the development of Latino «leadership through integral education ... *that is a leaven for the Kingdom of God in society*[12]. In *Encuentro and Mission* (2002), the u.s. Catholic bishops state that they have «heard the voices of Hispanic *leaders* —both laity and clergy», and address the document to «all Catholics, but particularly to pastoral *leaders* involved in ministry among Hispanics»[13]. But what exactly do these documents mean when using the word leader? Are we using the term as it is used in contexts outside the Church, particularly in the business world or the political realm?

120

Recent scholarship reveals that leadership development is a fast-growing field among u.s. researchers in the political, behavioral, and social sciences, with the last two decades witnessing «an explosion of interest» in the proliferation and the implementation of «effective leadership development practices»[14]. Etymologically, the word *leadership*, as used in Anglo-American culture, extols «initiative, self-responsibility and related civic virtues»[15]. Indeed, conscious of the merits business models offer to ministry in the areas of organization, accountability, and efficacy, one must still question if *all* u.s. Catholics have a common understanding of what ecclesial «leadership» entails[16]. For instance, *Co-Workers in the Vine-*

11 For a still relevant analysis of the reality and the challenges of Hispanic Ministries, see OSPINO, H. (ed.), *Hispanic Ministry in the 21ˢᵗ Century: Present and Future,* Convivium Press, Miami 2010. I draw particular attention to the important considerations section in OSPINO, H. and MIRANDA, E.M., «Hispanic Ministry and Leadership Formation», 196-200.

12 NATIONAL CONFERENCE OF CATHOLIC BISHOPS (now the UNITED STATES CONFERENCE OF CATHOLIC BISHOPS), *National Pastoral Plan for Hispanic Ministry,* USCC, Washington, D.C. 1987. The document is found in UNITED STATES CONFERENCE OF CATHOLIC BISHOPS, *Hispanic Ministry: Three Major Documents,* USCCB, Washington, D.C. 1995, emphasis in original.

13 UNITED STATES CONFERENCE OF CATHOLIC BISHOPS, *Encuentro and Mission: A Renewed Pastoral Framework for Hispanic Ministry,* USCCB, Washington, D.C. 2002, n.1, emphasis added.

14 HERNEZ-BROOME, G. and HUGHES, R.H., «Leadership Development: Past, Present and Future», in *Human Resource Planning* 27, n.1 (2004) 25-27.

15 FIGUEROA DECK, A., «Latino Leaders for Church and Society: Critical Issues», 186. Also see MOLE, G., «Can Leadership Be Taught?», in STOREY, J. (ed.), *Leadership in Organization: Current Issues and Trends,* Routledge, New York 2011, 114-126. Mole highlights the positivistic use of the term in the context of our u.s. society and raises the need to pose challenges to such understanding.

16 A similar concern and question regarding the term «ministry» was raised by 2009 Symposium participants in the area of «Leadership Formation». Here, pointing out that «mainstream definitions of ministry in the United States... often reflect perspectives that fail to take into consideration the voices of groups that are still deemed minorities», the authors ask: «what do we mean

yard of the Lord, a major church document spelling out a vision for Lay Ecclesial Ministry in the United States, names «leadership in a particular area of ministry», as one of the four main characteristics of the lay ecclesial minister, yet it does not define the term leadership[17]. H. Richard McCord, reflecting on the development of Lay Ecclesial Ministry in the country, observes that «leadership is a term that has no particular theological or scriptural meaning»[18]. It becomes imperative, then, to explore how the omission of a basic definition of leadership affects how the evangelization, catechesis, and ministry formation of Hispanics are conceived in the intercultural milieu of the Church in the United States.

In the early 2000's Allan Figueroa Deck had pointed out that in our Latino communities the «theological underpinnings of ministry and its relationship to the secular notion of 'leadership' remain underdeveloped». He then challenged Hispanic Catholics to «develop a specifically Latino understanding of leadership» suitable for new generations[19]. Alluding to a study done among members of the National Catholic Council for Hispanic Ministry (NCCHM) in the mid-1990s, Figueroa Deck observes that when participants were asked about the words that came to mind when thinking of leadership, «service, initiative, self-responsibility, and solidarity» were mentioned alongside negative, authoritarian, and abusive notions of leadership such as «*caudillismo* (tyranny) and *caciquismo* (petty despotism)»[20]. Corroborating these findings, a 2012 study was conducted to help «understand the role of culture in transforming and adapting leadership models for the Church». The project was part of the broader *Emerging Models of Pastoral Leadership* (EMPL) initiative[21]. Father Richard Vega in his narrative of the process describes the difficulties of using leadership lexicon among so-called ethnic minorities:

when we speak of ministry?» See OSPINO, H. and MIRANDA, E.M., «Hispanic Ministry and Leadership Formation», in OSPINO, H. (ed.), *Hispanic Ministry in the 21st Century*, 196; 178-180.

17 UNITED STATES CONFERENCE OF CATHOLIC BISHOPS, *Co-Workers in the Vineyard of the Lord: A Resource for Guiding the Development of Lay Ecclesial Ministry,* USCCB, Washington, D.C. 2005, 6-10.

18 MACCORD, H.R., «Lay Ecclesial Ministry: Pastoral Leadership in a New Era», in CAHOY, W.J., (ed.), *In the Name of the Church: Vocation and Authorization of Lay Ecclesial Ministry,* Liturgical Press, Collegeville, MN 2012, 5.

19 FIGUEROA DECK, A., «Latino Leaders for Church and Society: Critical Issues», 186, 189. Related to this conversation, though in a non-ecclesial context, see DAY, D.V., «Leadership Development: A Review in Context», in *Leadership Quarterly,* 11, n. 4 (April 2001) 581-613.

20 See FIGUEROA DECK, A., «Latino Leaders for Church and Society: Critical Issues», 189.

21 VEGA, R., «Report on the Culture and Its Impact on Leadership Initiative», *Emerging Models of Pastoral Leadership* (October 2012), 3, http://emergingmodels.org/wp-content/uploads/2013/05/Final-Report-on-Culture-and-Leadership.pdf (accessed October 8, 2013). For more information on the *Emerging Models of Pastoral Leadership* initiative see www.emergingmodel.org

In framing the conversation regarding [the] *Culture and its Impact on Leadership* [initiative], the advisory group spent considerable time viewing the cultural underpinning for the concept of leadership among immigrant populations. The conversation surfaced a key concern regarding leadership among immigrant groups: leadership can be suspect because of privilege and hierarchy ... The advisory group saw the need to develop a new starting point for the conversation on leadership, which would transcend a particular cultural context[22].

One of the ten final recommendations in Vega's report was that «those involved in the various stages of formation work with lay and ordained leaders should seek to incorporate the biblical and baptismal call of leadership» in their vocabulary[23]. For the advisory group, the «call of leadership from a baptismal stance [implies] a significant shift in the paradigm through which to view the term *leadership*»[24]. The group went on to suggest language that emphasized the biblical notion of *shepherding*, which «allows for the Spirit to bestow a variety of skill sets based on relationships with varying roles within a community rather that perceiving leadership solely through a hierarchical model»[25]. Likewise, the final report for the EMPL initiative relates how participants stressed the need to frame the «conversation about pastoral leadership, not [on] academic prerequisites» but on the «common baptismal call to ministry»[26].

As I recall the cold November day when José prophetically proclaimed the liberating message of the Gospel, I am convinced that he modeled the kind of discipleship that every baptized person —laity, vowed religious, ordained— involved in Hispanic ministry should embody. And yet I wonder, would José be recognized as a ministerial «leader» in his diocese and parish? Would he be hired to lead ministry in an ecclesial context? It is not farfetched to suggest that the current shortage of committed Hispanic ministers may be symptomatic of what Franciscan theologian Kenan B. Osbourne identified as an «insufficient understanding of the common ministry that belongs to all Christians through bap-

22 Ibid., 5.
23 Ibid., 12.
24 Ibid., 5.
25 Ibid.
26 PARENT, N.A., «Final Report Executive Summary», *Emerging Models of Pastoral Leadership* (June 1, 2013), 7, http://emergingmodels.org/wp-content/uploads/2013/06/Final-Report_Executive-Summary.pdf (accessed October 8, 2013).

tism and confirmation»[27]. It is also possible that the majority of Latinos/as do not relate to the language of leadership, or its presupposed understandings in the more dominant culture. Mindful of the themes, visions, challenges and questions set forth by the 2009 *National Symposium on the Present and Future of Catholic Hispanic Ministry in the United States*, there remains an urgent need to consciously undertake Deck's challenge of developing a «contemporary [understanding of] leadership that is at once rooted in the particularity of the Latino cultures and faith traditions and rooted as well in the universality of the Catholic communion»[28].

The Church will have to initiate everyone —priests, religious and laity— into [the] «art of accompaniment» which teaches us to remove our sandals before the sacred ground of the other (cf. Ex 3:5). The pace of this accompaniment must be steady and reassuring, reflecting our closeness and our compassionate gaze which also heals, liberates and encourages growth in the Christian life ... Missionary disciples accompany missionary disciples[29].

In the May 2007 issue of the journal *Leadership*, Keith Grint writes, «Organizations that are leader-full, that is, organizations that facilitate leadership at all levels, both for formal and informal leaders, are the ones most likely to succeed

27 OSBOURNE, K.B., «Envisioning a Theology of Ordained and Lay Ministry», in WOOD, S.K., (ed.), *Ordering the Baptismal Priesthood: Theologies of Lay and Ordained Ministry,* Liturgical Press, Collegeville, MN 2003, 203.

28 See FIGUEROA DECK, A., «Latino Leaders for Church and Society: Critical Issues», 189. It is worth noting, so as not to downplay the complexity of the reality, that when speaking of Hispanic ministers we are speaking of a diverse group in terms of nationality, social class, English/Spanish language dominance, levels of formal education and even levels of religious education. For instance, Allan Figueroa Deck calls us to recognize that today «our leadership is made up of four generations, each with its own unique experience of church and levels of engagement in the processes of the past 60 years. Those generations are sometimes designated in this way: 1) Pre-Vatican II, 2) Vatican II, 3) Generation X, and 4) Millennial Generation». See FIGUEROA DECK, A., «Reflections on the Hispanic Catholic Moment», talk presented at *Raíces y Alas* 2010 (September 26, 2010). In turn, Timothy Matovina upholds that the set core of perceptions and priorities that give shape to «ministerial approaches» also reveals how diverse Hispanic ministers are. He classifies these approaches into four groups: 1) *movimiento* Hispanic Catholics (veteran leaders who helped clarify a unique identity and developed a *memoria histórica*), 2) new immigrants (which tend to equate Hispanic ministry with the Spanish language), 3) integrationists, and 4) charismatic style (who place primary emphasis on direct evangelization and tend to be involved in apostolic movements). See MATOVINA, T., *Latino Catholicism: Transformation in America's Largest Church,* Princeton University Press, Princeton, NJ 2011, 145-155; MATOVINA, T., «Hispanic Ministry in U.S. Catholicism», in OSPINO, H. (ed.), *Hispanic Ministry in the 21st Century*, 40-43.

29 POPE FRANCIS, *Evangelii Gaudium* 169-173.

in the long run»[30]. To affirm, as does *Co-Workers in the Vineyard of the Lord,* that «all of the baptized are called to work toward the transformation of the world», implies returning to a vision of Church in which all of the «faithful are continually trained to be open to others»[31]. Hoping to foster further theological reflection, I conclude by appealing for a renewed concentration on a post-Vatican II «ecclesiology of vocation», rooted in the baptismal priesthood of all the faithful and «both historically and culturally situated» in the experience of the Hispanic community[32].

The New Testament suggests that the early Church «knew no formal distinction between church leadership and the rest of the community»[33]. Christian disciples are women and men who consciously answer the call to follow Jesus the Christ as a community of disciples in order to bear the good news of God's salvation: «Go, therefore, and make disciples of all nations, baptizing them in the name of the Father, and of the Son, and of the holy Spirit, teaching them to observe all that I have commanded you» (Matthew 28:19-20a). Though some biblical terms at the time of the early Christian communities such as apostles, rulers, hosts, *episkopoi,* and *diakonoi* suggest degrees of formal ministerial responsibilities, much of how we understand them in our Church today developed many years later. Let's not forget that from a Pauline perspective, «all believers … participate in the building up of the life of the community and its mission in the world»[34].

Theologian Richard Gaillardetz observes that, from a biblical perspective, Christian initiation through baptism draws the believer into an ordered relationship with the Triune God and with the community of believers. This relationship with God and the community of believers in turn orders us to a third relationship, or better a «movement outward toward the world in mission». The essence of Christian baptism is «both being called *and* sent», a commitment to a new form of existence as disciples and a «new understanding of the human vocation» as

---

30 GRINT, K., «Learning to Lead: Can Aristotle Help Us Find the Road to Wisdom?», in *Leadership* 3 (2007) 233.

31 UNITED STATES CONFERENCE OF CATHOLIC BISHOPS, *Co-Workers in the Vineyard of the Lord,* 8; HAHNENBERG, E.P., *Awakening Vocation: A Theology of the Christian Call,* Liturgical Press, Collegeville, MN 2010, 161.

32 HAHNENBERG, E.P., *Awakening Vocation,* 161; GAILLARDETZ, R.R., *Ecclesiology for a Global Church: A People Called and Sent,* Orbis, Maryknoll, NY 2008, 162.

33 GAILLARDETZ, R.R., *Ecclesiology for a Global Church,* 174.

34 Ibid., 29-32.

primarily missionary[35]. Though this is true and inspiring, Edward Hahnenberg observes that «the category of [baptismal] vocation has been overlooked» and underplayed among Catholics[36], which calls theologians and ministers to further reflection. Where are we as Hispanic theologians and ministers in this conversation? My experience serving at parish, deanery, and diocesan levels is that most Hispanics shy away from public «*liderazgo*» (leadership) because, like most Catholics, they have difficulty appropriating their baptismal vocation, thus reducing the language of vocation and leadership to a few states of life, and reducing God's call to an institutionalized expressions[37].

For Hispanic Catholic families infant baptism is «almost a universal experience»[38]. Baptizing a child has both religious and cultural undertones. True, most Hispanic Catholics may not have much clarity about the vocational implications of baptism, and perhaps are more concerned with the impact of original sin on the individual than with the person's incorporation into the life and mission of Jesus Christ. Nonetheless, the relationality that defines the Hispanic celebration of the sacraments, including the new sets of relationships established (e.g., *padrinos, madrinas, compadres*), offers concrete possibilities for developing in our communities practical processes of initiation into a conscious Christian life that cultivate the spaces for people to discern how to live this vocation in the faith community.

One area to seriously consider in the overall conversation about leadership development among Hispanic Catholics is family catechesis in the area of sacramental preparation. Much of this happens in the parish. Hosffman Ospino reminds us that «parishes matter»[39]; parishes «continue to be privileged places where most active Catholics learn, live and celebrate their faith»[40]. The fact that millions of Latino children grow up accompanied by an average of four baptized adults provides an opportunity of developing in our parish communities a grassroots framework to discuss baptism and vocation in order to ground a theology of ministry and pastoral agency in the common call of mission and discipleship.

35 Ibid., 186-7.
36 HAHNENBERG, E.P., *Awakening Vocation*, xi-xii.
37 See Ibid., xiv, xvi.
38 EMPEREUR, J. and FERNÁNDEZ, E., *La Vida Sacra: Contemporary Hispanic Sacramental Theology*, Rowman & Littlefield, Lanham, MD 2006, 62.
39 See HOOVER, B.C. and OSPINO, H., «Hispanic Ministry and Parish Life» in this collection.
40 OSPINO, H., *Hispanic Ministry in Catholic Parishes: A Summary Report of Findings from the National Study of Catholic Parishes with Hispanic Ministry*, Our Sunday Visitor, Huntington, IN 2015, 6.

One way to proceed is to explore the possibilities of a reflection on committed Christian discipleship that builds upon what Roberto S. Goizueta has called a theology of accompaniment —*teologia de acompañamiento*. Such reflection on discipleship would intentionally take into account the historical experience as well as the anthropological and theological wisdom emerging from the world of u.s. Hispanic popular Catholicism[41]. Accompaniment for Goizueta is not only a matter of ethical action. It also incorporates an affective dimension, a spatial geographical dimension (e.g., the city, the home), a dimension of interiority (personal commitment and appropriation), and a spiritual dimension[42]. Walking with others becomes a liberating praxis that gives witness to God's Reign. If, as Goizueta suggests, community is the «birthplace of the self», how can we find ways to formally educate Catholics at all levels in the art or ministry of mutual accompaniment to promote people as agent-subjects-in-relationship to God and others for the transformation of structures of death *in* the world?[43] Before potential «leaders» are formed and commissioned, they first need to be recognized, accompanied, and promoted in their baptismal vocation.

Certainly, there are many challenges that need to be discussed. In his recent National Study of Catholic parishes with Hispanic Ministry, Hosffman Ospino highlights that one of the areas requiring most immediate pastoral attention is the development of programming and resources to consistently reach out to non-traditional Hispanic Catholic populations[44]. Ospino observes that more than two thirds of Latino/a pastoral leaders in parishes with Hispanic ministry are foreign-born. These leaders often serve according to models of ministry and leadership learned in their countries of origin that have much to offer and enrich ministerial life in our faith communities yet often clash with more dominant models of ministry and leadership in the United States. This corroborates the earlier arguments in this essay. He also observes that nine out of ten Hispanics under 18 are u.s.-born, yet this group is much less involved in ministry. Ironically —or perhaps scandalously— Hispanic Catholic youth and young adults

---

41 GOIZUETA, R.S., *Caminemos con Jesús: Toward a Hispanic/Latino Theology of Accompaniment*, Orbis Books, Maryknoll, NY 1995, ix. My desire is to center our attention on the liberating praxis of accompaniment as a possible means of referring to pastoral agency.

42 Ibid., 192.

43 See GOIZUETA, R.S., *Caminemos con Jesús*, 47-76; POPE FRANCIS, *Evangelii Gaudium*, n. 169; and MATEO, H., «*Hermeneutica Guadalupana:* Toward an Explicit Pedagogy for the Formation of Lay Associates of the *Guadalupan Missionaries of the Holy Spirit* in the United States Province», unpublished D.Min. Dissertation, Barry University 2010, 176-77.

44 OSPINO, H., *Hispanic Ministry in Catholic Parishes*, 44.

have become a de facto «non-traditional» body in the Church in the United States. The vast majority of these young Catholics are neither involved in parish cate-chetical programs, youth ministry initiatives, nor Catholic schools[45]. Most do not go to Church regularly. How will they discern their baptismal vocation if they are isolated from the rest of the community?

Another challenge is the need to study and engage the forms of «leadership» in less structured areas of Hispanic Catholic life (e.g., apostolic movements, prayer groups, confraternities), especially in cases when such roles are perceived to be abusive and controlling. Grassroots «leadership» dynamics practiced in the different *movimientos* and groups deserve to receive more attention through re-search and intentional formation programs. And perhaps one of the most urgent challenges remains the lack of acknowledgment and affirmation of the public and official dimensions of women's leadership in our faith communities —most grassroots leaders in Hispanic ministry in parishes and dioceses are Latinas.

Theologian Carmen Nanko-Fernández reminds us that «La comunidad latina is not the church's diversity» [46]. «We *are* the Church»[47], and the time for new goals and a new «communal search for the means of achieving them»[48] that include the voices of the many Josés and Josefas in our communities *¡es ya!* —is now. As the Hispanic community grows it has the opportunity to offer the u.s. Church a more integral theology of the missionary vocation of all the faithful, one that questions the «North American model of ministerial professionalism» that is deeply influenced by secular notions of leadership[49]. Only with the courage to creatively and collegially reconfigure, as Pope Francis insists, the Church's customs, language and structures, will we be able to form a new genera-tion of Hispanic ministers and leaders for Hispanic ministry that are conscious of being missionary disciples who accompany other missionary disciples[50].

---

45 See OSPINO, H. and MIRANDA, E.M., «Hispanic Ministry and Leadership Formation», 180-184.
46 NANKO-FERNÁNDEZ, C., *Theologizing en Espanglish: Context, Community, and Ministry*, Orbis Books, Maryknoll, NY 2010, 73.
47 Ibid., 20.
48 POPE FRANCIS, *Evangelii Gaudium*, n. 33.
49 GAILLARDETZ, R.R., *Ecclesiology for a Global Church*, 292.
50 CELAM, *Document of Aparecida*, v General Conference of the Bishops of Latin America and the Caribbean, USCCB Publishing, Washington, D.C. 2008, n. 276.

Hispanic Ministry and Engagement wit the Bible

David A. Sánchez

The foundation of the Catechism is Sacred Scripture[1]

«We failed them. We completely failed them». This was what I said to a woman religious one week after she had stormed out of my Bible study. The topic that evening was the 3rd chapter of the Gospel of Mark, and we had reached verses 31-34 that speak of Jesus' extended family. I challenged the class to consider what the theological implications might be if Jesus did indeed have siblings? This was, after all, a topic that led to many a lively discussion in graduate school seminars as well as heated conversations everywhere between Catholics and non-Catholics reading the Bible. That's when she got up and stormed out of the study uttering that she had never heard anything so disrespectful in all of her days. I failed that evening because I was in dialogue not only with a particular community of the contemporary faithful, but I was also in dialogue with our centuries' long tradition of interpreting the Scriptures. On the issue of Jesus' siblings, I should have acknowledged the long Catholic interpretive tradition that denied such a possibility and offered my reading as one avenue scholars had been debating more recently. On the other hand, she failed because she had no tolerance for that which existed beyond her own narrow reading of the tradition. Her readings were —at their very core— fundamentalist. We both failed because we were unable to model, for that biblically thirsty audience, what a faithful and intellectual conversation about Bible and Tradition could look like. Opportunity missed but lesson learned.

As a Latino biblical scholar, I am mindful of how difficult it is to address questions associated with biblical literacy in the context of pastoral ministry. I have for long noted the chasm between the academic «scientific» study of the Bible and the day-to-day use of the Scriptures in the Church's pastoral life. A radical disconnect between these two areas of the life of the Church can significantly hinder its mission. This observation is not new. The Pontifical Biblical Commission, in a 1993 report to Pope John Paul II, cautioned about the harmful effects of biblical exegesis that «impels some exegetes to adopt positions contrary to the faith of the Church on matters of great importance» and inadequate attitudes among the faithful that dismiss the value of biblical scholarship in favor of «simpler approaches» that lead to nothing else but fundamentalist interpretations of the sacred text[2].

---

1   UNITED STATES CONFERENCE OF CATHOLIC BISHOPS, *National Directory for Catechesis*, 24C.
2   See PONTIFICAL BIBLICAL COMMISSION, *The Interpretation of the Bible in the Church*, Rome, 1993.

With this in mind, pastoral leaders working in Hispanic ministry must ask: what does it mean for Catholics to read the Bible within Hispanic contexts? What do Hispanic Catholics contribute to the interpretation of the Scriptures as we read it in our communities and with the Church? What are some of the major obstacles that pastoral leaders involved in Hispanic ministry and their communities face in situating the Scriptures at the center of their lives? I propose to address these questions by first offering a working definition of biblical literacy that builds on the Church's magisterial guidance and key insights from the field of u.s. Hispanic biblical scholarship. I then describe several reading strategies that have hindered attempts towards biblical literacy among Hispanics. Pastoral leaders must be aware of these limitations in order to envision effective models of engagement with the Scriptures in their ministries. The core contribution of this essay is the proposal of four alternative reading strategies that aim at bridging the chasm between academic and pastoral readings of Scripture in the context of Hispanic ministry. I conclude with a number of recommendations for pastoral practice.

1

What Is Biblical Literacy?

The question of what is meant by biblical literacy is fascinating. I have been teaching Bible for the last decade and a half, and this is a question that never ceases to cause me to pause and reflect. It is also a question Latino/a Catholics should not take lightly in response to the Second Vatican Council directive in its Constitution *Sacrosanctum Concilium* for «the treasures of the Bible ... to be opened up more lavishly so that a richer share of God's word may be provided for the faithful»[3]. Within the Catholic faith tradition we should pay great attention to what can be called a *reformational* invitation (i.e. echoing Martin Luther's invitation to the laity to read the Bible) by the Church to claim that which is foundational for the catechetical development of the community.

From the perspective of the Catholic tradition, the commitment to strengthening biblical literacy cannot be overstated, as the Dogmatic Constitution on Divine Revelation of Vatican II, *Dei Verbum,* clearly notes:

---

[3] Second Vatican Council, *Sacrosanctum Concilium,* n. 51.

This present council wishes to set forth authentic doctrine on divine revelation and how it is handed on. So that by hearing the message of salvation the whole world may believe, by believing it may hope, and by hoping it may love[4].

Thus, it is clear that from the point of view of the Church's teaching, divine revelation is in part embodied in Sacred Scripture, containing the Christian message of salvation and the Church's access to that salvific message as embodied in the Word. A closer investigation of *Dei Verbum* demonstrates how the interpreter is to go about coming to that richer understanding of Sacred Scripture, which is at least part of what we mean by biblical literacy:

> For the correct understanding of what the sacred author wanted to assert, due attention must be paid to the customary and characteristic styles of feeling, speaking, and narrating which prevailed at the time of the sacred writer ... The interpreter must investigate what meaning the sacred writer intended to express and actually expressed in particular circumstances by using contemporary literary forms in accordance with the situation of his [sic] own time and culture[5].

In addition, the Pontifical Biblical Commission's report, «The Interpretation of the Bible in the Church», clearly specifies that this understanding is enhanced, from the perspective of both individual and communal engagements of the Scriptures, through the practice of *lectio divina*, a familiar strategy to read and interpret the Scriptures among Catholics[6].

In terms of the process of interpretation of the Scriptures, *Dei Verbum* reminds us that the Church, rooted in the richness of the Tradition, is the ultimate home where this takes place: «Through the same tradition the Church's full canon of the sacred books is known, and the sacred writings themselves are more profoundly understood and unceasingly made active in her»[7]. For Catholics, the Magisterium is the final arbiter of the validity and utility of all biblical interpretation for the faithful: «But the task of authentically interpreting the word of God, whether written or handed on, has been entrusted exclusively to the living teach-

---

4   Second Vatican Council, *Dei Verbum*, n.1.
5   *Dei Verbum*, n. 12.
6   For example see PONTIFICAL BIBLICAL COMMISSION, *The Interpretation of the Bible in the Church*, n.181-86.
7   *Dei Verbum*, n. 8.

ing office of the Church»[8]. Nonetheless, the teaching office of the Church, especially exercised by those whose ministry involves preaching the Word of God, is called to do so with an *ear to the people,* as noted recently by Pope Francis in his *Evangelii Gaudium,* that recognizes «their language [i.e., that of the faithful], their signs and symbols, to answer the questions they ask». These are essential elements of the interpretive process[9]. Thus, the living teaching office of the Church is called into direct and active dialogue with those whom they serve (i.e. the faithful), and the laity is called into the service of the ministry of the Word by sharing their lived experiences in light of the Gospel. The result is a fully *embodied* interpretation of the Word that recognizes the lived realities of the faithful in dialogue with those called to serve them.

A Catholic approach to engagement with the Bible therefore presumes:

① Exegesis —engagement of the actual text and its world in a scholarly way,
② Historical interpretation—reading the text in dialogue with the larger Tradition,
③ Contemporary interpretation —understanding the community's present reality or situation.

This is precisely the approach to the Bible that must be present in any form of pastoral activity associated with Hispanic ministry. As scholars and pastoral leaders we know that context and cultural identity profoundly shape people's relationship with God and others. Therefore, we must ask: Can we speak of Hispanic reading(s) and interpretation(s) of the Bible? We can and we do, and such readings and interpretations add something important to the Catholic approach just described.

The words of Protestant theologian Justo González might in fact help us address this question:

In the Hispanic community, the biblical interpretation that is most appreciated is not the one that helps us understand the difficult passages in the text but rather the one that helps us understand our own difficult passages in the pilgrimage of obedience[10].

---

8 *Dei Verbum,* n. 10.
9 POPE FRANCIS, *Evangelii Gaudium,* n. 154.
10 GONZÁLEZ, J.L., *Mañana: Christian Theology from a Hispanic Perspective,* Abingdon Press, Nashville, TN 1990, 87.

This observation correctly recognizes that biblical interpretation occurs on multiple levels. The first, González notes, occurs at the level of interpretation of the text and the textual world. He goes on, however, to emphasize the most germane level of interpretation in the context of Hispanic ministry: the applicability of the biblical text for Hispanics here and now in the negotiation of *our own* contemporary pilgrimages. Understood in this manner, we encounter once again the multi-layered schema for biblical interpretation identified earlier: the world before and of the text (biblical exegesis); the life of the text in the Christian/Catholic tradition (history of interpretation); and the modern understanding and applicability of the text (contemporary interpretation). This is the type of sophisticated reading of the Scriptures that ideally pastoral leaders should foster in our Hispanic communities today. Pastoral leaders must read the Bible with Hispanic communities taking into careful consideration the communal and pastoral life situations in which they exist, the teachings of the Church, *and* the insight derived from the findings of biblical scholarship in conjunction. Grounding pastoral leaders in informed and faithful biblical literacy allows for the community's encounter with the God of history in the here and now. In turn, Latino/a biblical scholars must not limit themselves to only critically engage the world before and of the text, but also the long history of interpretation of the text and the current contemporary situations from which we interpret as both Latinos/as and Catholics in our pilgrimages. Thus, a dynamic hermeneutic circle is established: ancient, historical, and modern; each informing each other, each incomplete without the other in the interpretive process.

When Justo González speaks of «obedience», I suggest instead a focus on *liberation*[11]. This change of focus is especially important for Latino/a Catholics in light of the colonial encounter(s) that brought Catholicism to the Americas and the multiple conditions of marginality that presently shape the lives of millions of Latinos/as in the United States[12]. Therefore, the message of the Gospel

11 In sharp contrast to obedience as passive submission, the Scriptures call us to hear and to go towards the path set forth by God (via Moses, the Prophets, Jesus), which yields liberation. In the Old Testament the Hebrew word *shama* was used to mean to «to hear, listen, obey». In the New Testament the word *hupakou* refered «to listen under, to obey». Indeed, the etymology of obedience suggests listening—*ob*, «towards» and *oedire*, «to hear or listen». All of these words have a profoundly relational and personal context.

12 Let us remember that many Latinos/as never crossed the border but the border crossed them in 1848 when the United States annexed a large section of Mexico to its territory. In 1898 Puerto Rico became a u.s. colony. Millions of Latin American and Caribbean people arrived in the United States fleeing conditions of poverty, violence, and even persecution, and presently face a new set of struggles in a society that often refuses to fully embrace them.

embedded in the Scripture is one that leads to liberation and emancipation of our peoples rather than a call to mere obedience —a rich term yet whose meaning is frequently distorted. Therefore, biblical literacy presupposes both worldly and otherworldly concerns. Reading the Bible with an eye only to otherworldly pursuits is to reduce the inherent value of the sacred text for our historical lives, here and now, making it almost irrelevant, thus degrading our human existence to a life (*especially* from a Latino/a perspective) of obedient, silent servitude to powers that dehumanize us. I want to affirm the insights of African-American biblical scholar Vincent Wimbush who has for long emphasized the *this worldly* relevance of the Bible as a resource for both social and political hope, *worldly* critique and challenge[13].

Biblical literacy requires knowledge of the texts and stories embedded in the canon, the insights that Catholics and other Christian communities have gained interpreting those texts across the centuries, and the exegesis of those passages deemed most difficult. But biblical literacy does not stop there. It cannot. The ultimate goal of biblical literacy in the context of Hispanic ministry is to empower Hispanic women and men to engage those passages that help us make meaning in the pilgrimage of our own lives, here in the United States, now in our shared present.

2

Challenges to Biblical Literacy

Before moving on to consider alternative reading strategies that have historically been employed in Latino pastoral settings, a series of observations on contemporary challenges to biblical literacy are in order. The first challenge to an enhanced Latino biblical literacy is the lack of resources in our community that would allow for a deeper and more sophisticated engagement of the Bible. Allan Figueroa Deck sets the context:

---

13 WIMBUSH, V.L., «Reading Darkness, Reading Scriptures», in WIMBUSH, V.L., (ed.), *African Americans and the Bible: Sacred Texts and Social Textures*, Continuum, New York 2001, 12.

Despite the relentless growth of the Hispanic presence [in the United States] over the past 50 years there has not been anywhere near the appropriate development of what I would call a Hispanic ministry infrastructure[14].

This lack of infrastructure directly affects the engagement of the Scriptures among Hispanics and can be attributed to multiple causes. Let us be clear. It is more than mere access to the Bible. What Deck here refers to is the lack of a well-resourced and permanent organizational structure that can effectively address Hispanic Catholic concerns. As Hispanics quickly become the majority of Catholics in many parts of the country, it is imperative that Church leaders be proactive in preparing clergy and ministers to adequately serve this constituency[15]. This means preparing biblically literate clergy and pastoral ministers. Most Latinos/as called to pastoral ministry lack the financial means and resources (e.g. undergraduate degrees) to enter into either specialized graduate schools of theology or seminaries. Thus, the majority of the training they are exposed to comes from *institutos pastorales*, parish Bible studies, or self-training. This limited exposure to in-depth biblical training corroborates Hosffman Ospino's observation:

> [E]mpirical observation among scholars and church leaders [is] that many, perhaps most, leaders and catechists in these groups are poorly prepared in the study of Sacred Scripture. The immediate consequences of such lack of preparation are erroneous readings and interpretations of the Bible, as well as a tendency to read the sacred text in fundamentalistic [literal] ways[16].

Secondly, those of us who are trained and hold advanced degrees in Biblical Studies are appallingly few to meet the needs of the vast masses of Hispanic Catholics who wish to be trained in Bible in order to enhance their ministries. There are just not enough Latino/a biblical scholars to do that training. This matter is complicated by the fact that the majority of Latino/a biblical scholars are

14 FIGUEROA DECK, A., *Hispanic Ministry: New Realities and Choices*, lecture delivered during the Symposium on Hispanic/Latino/a Catholics in the United States, Center for Applied Research in the Apostolate, Georgetown University, Washington, D.C. October 5-6, 2008, 6.

15 See MATEO, H., «Hispanic Ministry and Leadership», and HOOVER, B. and OSPINO, H., «Hispanic Ministry and Parish Life» in this collection.

16 OSPINO, H., «The Bible and Catechesis», in RUÍZ, J.P. and PAREDES, M.J., (eds.), *The Word of God and Latino Catholics: The Teachings of the Road to Emmaus*, American Bible Society, New York 2011, 64.

full-time employees at universities and seminaries where we are already over-committed.

Another challenge to biblical literacy from a Latino/a perspective is that in many Catholic venues, biblical literacy is understood via the evangelical lens of literacy that is common in many Latino Protestant Churches, including but not limited to fundamentalist movements. Raúl Gómez-Ruíz offers the following vignette that will sound quite familiar to pastoral leaders doing Hispanic ministry:

> I was approached by a group of Hispanic women who asked me to start a Bible study for them. They wanted to know more about the Bible for several reasons: one was they noticed it being read more at Eucharist, and second, they were being challenged by Evangelicals who claimed that Catholics did not use or know the Bible[17].

Now, the goal here is not to demean fundamentalist or Evangelical readings of Scripture. We should not forget that biblical fundamentalism brings millions of Christians into relationship with the Word of God. Yet, this is not the Catholic way of reading the Scriptures since it largely circumvents the critical engagement with Tradition. This makes perfect sense, however, from a Protestant perspective. What we should glean from our Protestant brothers and sisters of a fundamentalist persuasion is their comprehensive engagement and somewhat «rabbinical» knowledge of the Bible. I am constantly amazed and pleasantly surprised when I teach in fundamental and Evangelical settings by their vast knowledge of the content of the Bible. We as Roman Catholics could gain much from this level of textual literacy albeit in conversation with the hermeneutic circle articulated above.

The last challenge I would like to highlight is related to the use of the Lectionary. It has to do with the problem of pastoral leaders, ordained and non-ordained, who view the Lectionary as a comprehensive reading strategy of Scriptural engagement. Gómez-Ruíz observes:

> The Lectionary becomes another «Bible», a «liturgical Bible» that is selective of which texts are used/read/reflected upon so as to communicate what the Church believes about what is essential in the revelation of God's salvific work in creation and to foster its application into daily life by the faithful[18].

---

17 GÓMEZ-RUÍZ, R., «In the Breaking of Bread: The Bible and Liturgy», in RUÍZ, J.P. and PAREDES, M.J. (eds.), *The Word of God and Latino Catholics*, 33.
18 Ibid., 34.

What I gather from Gómez-Ruiz's observation is not so much that the Lectionary is a hindrance to a comprehensive approach to the Bible, but rather, that we as hearers of the Lectionary must take our study deeper with an in-depth examination of the Lectionary reading for a particular day. It is particularly the responsibility of clergy and other pastoral ministers to use the Lectionary readings as an invitation to further study of the passage in its historical context, in the history of interpretation, and in its present application.

3
Alternative Reading Strategies as Alternative Literacies:
Latino/a Readings of the Bible

In recent decades, new avenues of biblical research have emerged that address the lived realities of the reader, thus challenging Latino/a biblical scholars to consider their own life situations as influences on their interpretation of the biblical text(s). These personal readings —or subjectivities— are not necessarily impositions upon biblical interpretation[19]. They are actually vital factors that enrich the exercise of contemporary biblical interpretation. It is widely accepted in our day that so-called «objective» approaches to the study of Bible are far from being objective and, by extension, biblical truth. Human beings are involved in the process. We need to acknowledge that the once perceived «objective» scholarship of traditional biblical studies was in fact, «a class specific cultural practice» of the historically dominant North Atlantic culture of biblical scholars[20]. Therefore, «objective» biblical scholarship —as has been traditionally practiced over the last two centuries— is in fact an unacknowledged culturally specific and political reading of Bible, and one that has very little to do with our lived realities as Latino/a Catholics. Because the stories of the people of faith are important, as well as their socio-cultural location, I propose the following four reading strategies as models for our collective consideration.

19 Scholars call this *eisegesis*: interpreting a text largely through the lens of one's presuppositions and ideological convictions.
20 WIMBUSH, V.L., «Reading Darkness, Reading Scriptures», 10.

Reading Strategy 1: Reading in Community: Pastors, Scholars and Communities of Faith. To challenge dominant readings of Scripture and their unacknowledged, subjective agendas, Jean-Pierre Ruíz argues:

> Latino biblical scholarship insists that not only is it impossible to check one's assumptions and presuppositions at the door prior to engaging in biblical interpretation, but that such assumptions and presuppositions (theological, sociocultural, and otherwise) are no less important for biblical interpretation than the grammatical, linguistic, and historical tools that are the standard equipment of academic biblical interpretation[21].

This observation is nothing short of an invitation for Latino clergy and pastoral ministers to take seriously their social locations and ministerial concerns in the engagement of Bible. Thus, the traditional one-directional approach of biblical scholars educating clergy, pastoral ministers, and the laity becomes a true *dialogue* in which the aforementioned enter into critical dialogue with biblical scholars foregrounding their lived realities in their faith pilgrimages seeking liberation and salvation (*teología de conjunto*). Ruíz summarizes this collective interpretive approach: «The work of theology takes place not in the first person singular, but in the first person plural, for the primary subject of the theological endeavor is the community—the Church»[22].

Reading Strategy 2: The Flesh-and-Blood Reader. Cuban-American Scripture scholar Fernando Segovia has promoted a second approach to biblical interpretation. Like Jean-Pierre Ruiz, he «calls into question the construct of a *neutral* and *disinterested* reader presupposed by historical criticism»[23]. In its place, Segovia promotes the value of the contemporary flesh-and blood reader as one consideration in the interpretation of Bible. He acknowledges from the onset that this flesh-and-blood reader is, «always positioned and interested, socially and historically conditioned and unable to transcend such conditions»[24].

21 RUÍZ, J.P., «Beginning with Moses and All of the Prophets: Latino Biblical Interpretation and the Word of God in the Church», in RUÍZ, J.P. and PAREDES, M.J., (eds.), *The Word of God and Latino Catholics*, 99.

22 Ibid., 100.

23 SEGOVIA, F.F., «And They Began to Speak in Other Tongues: Competing Modes of Discourse in Contemporary Biblical Criticism», in SEGOVIA, F.F. and TOLBERT, M.A. (eds.), *Reading From this Place: Social Location and Biblical Interpretation in the United States*, vol. 1, Augsburg Fortress Press, Minneapolis, MN 1995, 28. Emphasis added.

24 Ibid., 28-29.

Segovia's approach brings together biblical studies and the field of cultural studies: «a joint critical studies of texts and readers, perspectives and ideologies»[25]. Segovia's approach to biblical scholarship is an invitation to pastoral leaders to openly bring their social and cultural identities and realities into the interpretation of the Bible —and empower others to do likewise.

Reading Strategy 3: Reading the Bible «in Spanish». Justo González, not a Catholic scholar yet one who has been highly influential among u.s. Hispanic Catholic theologians because of the depth and familiarity of his insights, argues:

> If it is true that we bring a particular perspective to history and to theology, then we must bring a particular perspective to the interpretation of Scripture. And, once again, it may be that this perspective will prove useful not only to us but also to the church at large[26].

González proposes that a specific Latino/a subjectivity may in fact provide an advantage when interpreting the Scriptures —a hermeneutical advantage— that challenges more dominant reading strategies. González calls for a non-innocent reading of the Bible «in Spanish»:

> In short, biblical history is a history beyond innocence ... Since this is also the nature of Hispanic history, it may well be that on this score we have a hermeneutical advantage over those whose history is still at the level of guilty innocence, and who therefore must read Scripture in the same way in which they read their own history[27].

González further adds: «The parallel between the 'Bible stories' read in our Sunday schools and the 'American stories' that pass for history in our daily schools is striking»[28]. As an alternative to these «innocent» —and often complicit— readings of the Bible, González promotes a non-innocent reading that embraces both positive and negative examples from Scripture. Rather than just highlighting triumphant story lines and successful or righteous biblical actors, González invites to a thicker, more honest reading of Scripture. He challenges us to engage

25 Ibid., 29.
26 GONZÁLEZ, J.L., *Mañana,* 75.
27 Ibid., 77.
28 Ibid., 79.

stories such as Abraham's misrepresentation of Sarah to save his own life, Moses' hesitation in accepting his call, the comprehensive apostasy detailed in the Book of Judges, the transgression of King David who had one of his generals killed to take his wife, and the multiple transgressions of Jesus' own disciples in the Christian Testament. What then are the results when we engage these stories into our interpretive biblical landscape? How does the disruption of innocent readings of Scripture challenge our relationship to Scripture and the innocent (and triumphant) worldviews that are subsequently derived? And more importantly, how does this proposed non-innocent reading of Scripture facilitate a more critical evaluation of our pilgrimage(s) as Latino/a scriptural scholars, clergy and pastoral ministers with the very people we attempt to serve in our parishes?

Reading Strategy 4: Through the Lens of Popular Catholicism. The last alternative reading strategy I propose is one to which I have devoted the majority of my scholarly life, namely through the lens of *popular* Latino Catholicism. The theological category of popular Catholicism, according to theologian Orlando Espín, is vital to any notions of Latino spirituality —biblical or otherwise— because the majority of Latino/a Catholics are «usually so in a 'popular' way»[29]. According to Espín,

> By «popular» I do not mean «widespread», although popular Catholicism certainly is. «Popular», rather, is the adjective to the noun «people». Thus, popular Catholicism is «popular» because it is the people's own. Although it is evident that not every single Latino Catholic person shares in this tradition within Catholicism, most Latinos do, and all of our cultures are clearly grounded in it[30].

It should not come as any surprise to the reader that popular religion has a strong history in our faith communities. It is so central to some of our Latino theological expressions that Espín has categorized it as a «true *locus theologicus* and not solely or mainly as a pastoral, catechetical problem»[31]. It is the faith of the people, the *faith of our people* and merits serious theological reflection. According to Hosffman Ospino, «[p]opular Catholicism is simultaneously a way

---

29 ESPÍN, O.O., *The Faith of the People: Theological Reflections on Popular Catholicism*, Orbis Books, New York 1997, 3.
30 Ibid.
31 Ibid., 2.

of knowing and the most available language for the majority of u.s. Latino/a Catholics, many of whom live in the margins of our society, to express our faith in a way that is accessible and familiar»[32]. It is both pervasive and life giving in the communities in which we exist and serve.

What I have discovered in my own research on the Guadalupan mural tradition of East Los Angeles is that some forms of popular Latino Catholicism are quite literate in their biblical appropriations and exegetical savvy[33]. When I first started collecting photographs of murals of Guadalupe in East Los Angeles, it quickly became clear that her modern depictions, as well as her original icon, were visual representations of the Book of Revelation, chapter 12: «And a great sign appeared in heaven, a woman clothed with the sun, with the moon under her feet, and on her head a crown of twelve stars»[34]. These representations demonstrate a complex knowledge of the ancient world and of the biblical stories that allow sophisticated modern appropriations. Such knowledge also reveals an impressive biblical appreciation for the text embedded in contemporary popular Catholicism.

Biblical scholars, theologians, and pastoral ministers can gain much by paying close attention to the deep-rooted connections between the Scriptures and expressions of popular Catholicism. For too long we have looked at expressions of popular Catholicism as being somewhat contrary or less than official doctrine and practices. At second glance, this may not be the entire story. It is an interpretive tradition that is indeed worthy of serious and sustained theological reflection.

4
Epilogue
⧸⧹

As the Church in the United States becomes increasingly Hispanic and creative models of ministry and evangelization become necessary, a passive reception of the Bible is no longer an option. It is the responsibility especially of those actively engaged in pastoral ministry to heed the directive of *Sacrosanctum Concilium*

---

32 OSPINO, H., «The Bible and Catechesis», 60.
33 See SÁNCHEZ, D.A., *From Patmos to the Barrio: Subverting Imperial Myths*, Fortress Press, Minneapolis, MN 2008.
34 Author's translation of Rev 12:1.

noted above: «The treasures of the Bible... [must] be opened up more lavishly so that a richer share of God's word may be provided for the faithful». The alternative reading strategies described above, born out of the dialogue with Latino/a biblical scholars and theologians, all deeply rooted in ministerial life, validate the role of lived experience in the biblical interpretive process. The work and lived ministerial experiences of these scholars, the world of biblical scholarship, and the rich tradition of the Church constitute the hermeneutical circle at the heart of Latino biblical interpretation.

All pastoral leaders involved in Hispanic ministry can further enhance biblical literacy. This is already happening week after week through catechesis, preaching, prayer groups, and Bible study sessions in thousands of communities across the country serving Hispanic Catholics. Their ministries are often supported by efforts such as the *Biblia Católica para Jóvenes* (sponsored by Instituto Fe y Vida), the *Biblia Católica de la Familia* (sponsored by the Center for Ministry Development and Editorial Verbo Divino), Renew International, the Little Rock Scripture Study in Spanish, among others. Much more needs to be done to foster a deeper love for the Scriptures. It is time for Latino/a pastoral leaders to take their rightful place in this faithful circle so that we may all become whole.

Chapter 8

Hispanic Ministry and the Church in Latin America and the Caribbean

ALLAN FIGUEROA DECK, SJ *and* TERESA MAYA SOTOMAYÒR, CCVI

The Catholic Church in the United States has become the most globalized church in the world[1]. No other church on the planet has experienced the multi-cultural and inter-cultural reality as have the parishes and dioceses of the United States[2]. The challenges for ministry are evident, while the potential this hyper-diversity holds for the future of the Catholic Church is promising. A new wine is pouring into our life as a Church. Are new wineskins ready?[3] This diversity constitutes the «theological place» for reimagining the Church in a globalized, rapidly changing world; and ministry with the Latino/Hispanic population has been for decades the space *par excellence* where this re-imagination has been gradually taking place in creative and dynamic ways.

The possibilities imagined in the «Pan American» dream of early fighters for independence from New England to Buenos Aires, or the fulfillment of Karl Rahner's «World Church» prophesy[4], or simply the continental church Pope John Paul II proclaimed in *Ecclesia in America* are taking shape in many U.S. parishes! The crossroads of cultures and traditions that Hispanic ministry represents is creating a new model of Church unique to the Third Millennium and its new evangelization. The ever present tension between the charismatic and the institutional has begun to reintegrate in hopeful ways in Hispanic ministry where the Global South and the West meet[5]. The Church of «the Americas» thus becomes a theological paradigm for the future: ministering in diversity, creating a new form of *mestizaje* that integrates contributions of the Latin American Church with those of the North American one and birthing something new.

The Church in the United States has been linked with the Church in Latin America for centuries, but linkages have become stronger and systematic since the early 1960s. This essay explores the melding of ecclesial cultures and contributions of the Latin American Church to Hispanic ministry today, and outlines

---

1 See CENTER FOR APPLIED RESEARCH IN THE APOSTOLATE, *Cultural Diversity in the Catholic Church of the United States,* CARA, Washington, D.C. 2014, http://www.usccb.org/issues-and-action/cultural-diversity/upload/cultural-diversity-cara-report-phase-1.pdf (accessed on August 26, 2014).

2 See HOOVER, B.C. and OSPINO, H., «Hispanic Ministry and Parish Life» in this collection.

3 PARKS, S., «A Reflection on Religious Vocation: The Wine Is Ready, but the Wineskin Is Not», National Catholic Reporter, *Global Sisters Report,* May 14, 2014, http://globalsistersreport.org/column/speaking-god/trends/reflection-religious-vocation-wine-ready-wineskin-not-371 (accessed August 26, 2014).

4 SAMMON, S.D., «The Birth of a World Church», in *America Magazine,* October 15, 2012, http://americamagazine.org/issue/100/birth-world-church (accessed August 23, 2014).

5 ALLEN, J.L., *The Future Church: How Ten Trends Are Revolutionizing the Catholic Church,* Doubleday, New York 2009, 17-20.

how Hispanic ministry has something to offer Latin America in return. It seeks to identify several sources for a pastoral vision which gains new vigor under the aegis of the reform-minded Pope Francis, the first Latin American pope. Hispanic ministry thus becomes the place of exchange between the Global South and Western culture offering the Church at large new expressions and methods.

1

What Latin America? A Context

∾

U.S. Hispanic ministry has roots in the creative pastoral productivity of the Latin American Church since the Second Vatican Council. This influence began in the exchanges that took place through the bishops' conferences. The recommendations of the general conferences of the Latin American bishops (CELAM) were also felt in the United States. Efforts at collaboration had begun earlier, but after the 1960s, gatherings brought North and South American bishops together. These initiatives supported by the U.S. Catholic Bishops' Latin American Bureau in Washington, DC created a conduit for the dissemination in the United States of the exciting ecclesial vision of Medellín, Puebla, and other pastoral initiatives of CELAM. These contacts led to the founding of the Northeast Regional Office for the Spanish-speaking. Father Edgar Beltrán, a Colombian priest who had worked for CELAM in Bogotá, was employed by the Division of the Spanish-Speaking of the National Conference of Catholic Bishops. The charismatic Father Beltrán traveled extensively and communicated the extraordinary message of pastoral conversion explicit in pastoral initiatives of the Latin American Church[6]. An

6   The idea of «pastoral conversion» has been familiar to Latin American pastoral leaders for several decades. Most recently, Aparecida (2007) reclaimed it. For instance: «No community should excuse itself from entering decidedly with all its might into the ongoing processes of missionary renewal and from giving up outdated structures that are no longer helpful for handing on the faith» (n. 365); «Hence the need, in fidelity to the Holy Spirit who leads it, for an ecclesial renewal that entails spiritual, pastoral, and also institutional reforms» (n. 367); «Pastoral conversion requires that ecclesial communities be communities of missionary disciples around Jesus Christ, Master and Shepherd» (n. 368); «The pastoral conversion of our communities requires moving from a pastoral ministry of mere conservation to a decidedly missionary pastoral ministry» (n. 370). See CELAM, *Document of Aparecida, v General Conference of the Bishops of Latin America and the Caribbean*, USCCB Publishing, Washington, D.C. 2008. Pope Francis has also made it a central category of his pontificate: «The renewal of structures demanded by pastoral conversion can only be understood in this light: as part of an effort to make them more mission-oriented, to make ordinary pastoral activity on every level more inclusive and open, to inspire in pastoral workers a constant desire to go forth and in this way to elicit a positive response from all those whom Jesus summons to friendship with himself», *Evangelii Gaudium*, n. 27.

entire generation of u.s. Hispanic leaders was set on fire and a new period of u.s. church renewal began within the emerging context of Hispanic ministries.

The influence of Latin America was also felt through encounters taking place within religious institutes of men and women. The Inter-American Conference of Religious met in 1971, and ever since there have been conversations between all the conferences of religious in the region. New currents of thought and action arrived from Latin America through the agency of thousands of u.s. missionaries—priests, religious and laity. They had founded missions throughout the continent in response to St. John xxiii's call for missionary volunteers. Outstanding missionaries returned with first-hand experience of the theory and practice of Latin America's emerging pastoral vision. They immediately went about applying what they had seen and learned in their mission experience to pastoral contexts throughout the United States. Hence the seeds were planted for the distinctive pastoral orientation that the u.s. Conference of Catholic Bishops Office of the Spanish-Speaking (later named the Secretariat of Hispanic Affairs and currently the Secretariat of Cultural Diversity in the Church) was to endorse and enshrine in what came to be called the *Encuentro* process, which has shaped Hispanic ministry ever since.

Another equally important influence that the u.s. Church has experienced comes from Latin American immigrants themselves who have made their home in our communities. The sheer numbers of this presence have transformed the demographic reality of the Church in the United States. This is not one more historical migration that the United States is once more merely assimilating. The ceaseless movement of people, ideas and resources in every direction throughout the continent creates a dynamic effect throughout the region that has required an equally dynamic pastoral approach. Hispanic ministry has been learning for decades to live with newcomers and second and third generations, with departures, and with the diversity. This reality requires ministry in the United States to stay engaged with the evolution also taking place in Latin America since the Second Vatican Council.

Latin America has experienced dramatic political, social and economic shifts over the last 50 years. Economic progress is evident in some sectors but entire regions are still suffering dehumanizing poverty. Grave human rights violations are still rampant and the plague of violence surrounding the drug trade is epidemic. Social change has been keeping pace as the population of the continent rapidly made its way into the cities. Today, despite some regional differences, the people of Latin American live mostly in urban settings. Massive migrations have come to represent an important characteristic of Latin American life. Movement from rural areas to cities, and then between cities and countries has grown exponentially to the point that this is one of the regions with the most people on the move in the world[7]. Families increasingly straddle different cities and countries. This ongoing Latin American diaspora has both cultural and religious repercussions.

Latin American cultures and cities mirror all of these changes. Cities resemble one another both in their unplanned, chaotic growth, and in the rings of poverty that surround them. Youth cultures and secularization are beginning to characterize urban life. The growing erosion of popular religiosity in younger Latin Americans has become evident in recent years. The growing distance these youth keep from their family traditions results in an increasingly spiritual yet secular (non-religious) population in the span of just one generation. The net result does not present an optimistic outlook as percentages of church affiliation continue to drop in every country of Latin America. The fact is that Latin America may boast the largest concentration of Catholics in the world, but it may not be far behind the churches of Europe and North America in terms of declining numbers[8].

Religious pluralism has been steadily on the rise in Latin America. Pentecostalism has grown exponentially in the Americas over the last 50 years. Surveys, though limited, show tendencies that are dramatically transforming the religious profiles of countries like Guatemala, El Salvador, Uruguay or Nicaragua where Catholics may no longer be in the majority[9]. Cities everywhere harbor an increasing religious diversity. Tension accompanies this pluralism and the continent slowly shifts away from majority Catholicism. The Latin American Church has not fully acknowledged that Christians of other confessions are no longer

---

7   See HOOVER, B.C., *The Shared Parish: Latinos, Anglos, and the Future of U.S. Catholicism,* NYU Press, New York, 2014,165. Also: INTERNATIONAL ORGANIZATION FOR MIGRATION, *Facts and Figures,* http://www.iom.int/cms/en/sites/iom/home/about-migration/facts—figures-1.html (accessed September 19, 2014).

8   Cfr. CHESTNUT, A.R., as quoted by GOODWIN, L., «First Latin American Pope Could Counter Declining Catholicism», March 13, 2013, http://www.news.yahoo.com/blog/the-lookout/first-latin-american-pope (accessed September 19, 2014).

9   LATIN AMERICAN PUBLIC OPINIONPROJECT, Vanderbilt University «Nota metodológica: midiendo religión en encuestas de Latinoamérica», available online at http://www.vanderbilt.edu/lapop/insights/I0829es.pdf (accessed September 19, 2014).

necessarily recent converts; indeed, some are third or fifth generation non-Catholics[10].

The erosion of cultural Catholicism and the Constantinian paradigm of Christendom has given way to a new moment. The Church's stance has been reactive as a majority religion, often protected by law from Protestant proselytism. In this paradigm, parishes functioned as sacramental way stations, not necessarily for other purposes. Customs and traditions rooted in the concessions made under colonial arrangements (*Patronato Real)* have persisted. For most of Latin America, Catholics find the church where they feel connected. The idea of registering at a local parish or having sufficient administrative personnel to keep track of those registered is probably unthinkable for the vast majority of parishes around the continent. The parish still lacks the administrative organization common in the United States. Moreover, financial agreements whereby parishes regularly support the diocese by means of a parish tax are fewer and less significant for dioceses throughout Latin America and the Caribbean than in the United States. Parishes throughout Latin America are not very structured, far from the U.S. institutional model.

Lay organization is a significant characteristic of Latin American Catholic culture. Parishes are often run by lay volunteers or lay organizations who often take up the slack due to the priest shortage. The historical and sociological reasons for this core identity of the Church in Spanish and Portuguese America are rooted in the early evangelization of the continent. The chronic lack of ordained clergy to care for the pastoral needs of the local churches, the vibrant culture of medieval confraternities that crossed the Atlantic, and the racial separation that became prevalent as an evangelization strategy conspired to create self-organized groups that cared for the spiritual needs of the community. Popular religiosity is one of the consequences of this self-organization, not its cause. Lay organizations flourish in both urban and rural contexts. Depending on the region, an astounding percentage of Catholics do not engage in the regular sacramental life of the Church, yet do identify as Catholic[11]. Remote regions have long had

---

10 MARTÍNEZ, J.F., *Los Protestantes: An Introduction to Latino Protestantism in the United States,* Praeger, Santa Barbara, CA 2011, 55.

11 The Catholic Church in Mexico reports only between 6-9% of Catholics attend Mass on Sundays out of the 84% that identified as Catholic in the 2010 census. See Oficina de Planificación y Estadística de la Arquidiócesis de México, «Disminuye la asistencia a misa», Línea Directa http://www.linearecta.com.mx/?p=1356. Sistema Informativo de la Arquidiócesis de México, http://www.siame.mx/ (accessed on December 16, 2013).

the standard practice of «circuit-riding priests» who visit periodically. Smaller and midsize cites may have a higher concentration of priests, yet the number of Masses they offer in a few locations on Sundays and the sheer volume of the population under their care makes them remote and largely unknown to most Catholics.

The Church in Latin America is challenged in the area of formation/catechesis. New generations of Catholic parents are not necessarily enrolling their children in local catechetical programs and Catholic schools account for less than 7 percent of total schools in countries like Mexico. The Latin American bishops in the Aparecida document identify formation as a significant challenge and call the continent to religious formation centered on a personal encounter with Jesus Christ[12]. The conferences of bishops have declared an «educational emergency» in Latin America because the commitment to be disciples and missionaries «requires a clear and firm option for the formation of our communities»[13]. Pope Francis is endorsing this focus with renewed vigor, calling for the reform of seminaries and houses of religious formation as well as catechetical programs[14]. Seminary and religious formation programs are challenged in Latin America perhaps as a result of the use of poor pedagogy: rote memorization, text book compilations or summaries, and little emphasis on critical thinking. In some countries or cities, the lack of professors with the appropriate credentials often leads to substandard teaching. However, priests and religious that accompany migrant communities in the United States often have to undergo more rigorous formation since they are confronted with disparity of working in one of the most educated Catholic communities in the world, where parish ministry has reached a level of professionalization unimaginable in their countries. As a result, ministers migrating to the u.s. experience tensions due to the more sophisticated levels of theological formation among Euro American and Hispanic lay ministers, especially women, upon whom parishes greatly depend.

These are just a few of the lights and shadows in which the Latin American Church came of age after the Vatican Council. Exemplifying the words of Pope Francis in *Evangelii Gaudium*, «Realities are more important than ideas», the Conference of Latin American Bishops (celam) has been struggling to under-

12 celam, *Document of Aparecida*, n. 246-247.

13 Ibid., 276, 328.

14 spadaro, a., «Wake up the world! Conversation with Pope Francis about Religious Life», in *La Civilitá Cattólica*, 1 (2014) 3, 17. Available at http://www.laciviltacattolica.it/articoli_download/extra/Wake_up_the_world.pdf.

152

stand the right place for the Church in Modern Latin America in view of these significant challenges[15]. This context is the backdrop where the Church in Latin America has flourished. The pastoral responses to these realities are the core of the many positive developments that have made an impact on the Church in the United States.

2

Latin American Contributions to Pastoral Life in the United States

Timothy Matovina has identified several contributions of Hispanic Catholicism to the life of the Church in the United States[16]. These contributions are explained in great measure by the distinctive ecclesial renewal already noted that began in Latin America immediately after the Second Vatican Council. This reform was carried out under the leadership of the Conference of Latin American Bishops (CELAM) with the incisive reflection of a new generation of Latin American thinkers, among them liberation theologians such as Gustavo Gutiérrez[17]. Some core features of this renewal which resonated throughout the United States were: 1) the vision of the Church's mission as an expansive outward movement of evangelization rather than an inward, defensive one, 2) the option for the poor which includes a commitment to socioeconomic change, 3) a theology of the Church as pilgrim People of God in history not as a static «perfect society», 4) an emphasis on church as community as well as hierarchy, and hence the parish as a «community of communities»[18].

Over the last fifty years these elements have taken root in the pastoral life of the U.S. Catholic Church in connection with the Hispanic presence and manifest themselves in at least four ways. First, in regard to liturgy, Latin American popular religion has brought color, movement, passion and beauty not only to

---

15 POPE FRANCIS, *Evangelii Gaudium*, n. 231-233.

16 MATOVINA, T., *Latino Catholicism: Transformation in America's Largest Church*, Princeton University Press, Princeton, NJ 2011, 98-131.

17 For Cardinal Muller on Pope Francis' attitude toward Liberation Theology, see PONGRATZ-LIPPITT, C., «CDF Head: Pope Francis has close ties with Liberation Theology», *The Tablet* (May 2, 2014).

18 NATIONAL CONFERENCE OF CATHOLIC BISHOPS (now the UNITED STATES CONFERENCE OF CATHOLIC BISHOPS), *National Pastoral Plan for Hispanic Ministry*, USCC, Washington, D.C. 1987, n. 2-21. The document is found in UNITED STATES CONFERENCE OF CATHOLIC BISHOPS, *Hispanic Ministry: Three Major Documents*, USCCB, Washington, D.C. 1995.

burgeoning Latino congregations throughout the country but also to mainstream U.S. Catholicism. The natural tendencies of Latino cultures to hold ritual, narrative and symbol in high regard has contributed to renewing the sacramental character of Catholic tradition, which is challenged by the modern world's tendency to silence symbols, eliminate rituals and dismiss the experience of mystery and transcendence. Hispanic Catholicism, however, does not promote the restoration of liturgical practices of other centuries or the championing of the old Latin liturgy. Rather, it advances the integration of the people's vital symbols, rituals, and narratives into official forms of worship.

Latinos bring popular religious practices to parishes, movements, schools and other institutions in which they participate. By integrating piety and official worship, Latinos follow the lead of Vatican II's Constitution on the Sacred Liturgy, *Sacrosanctum Concilium,* in promoting full, conscious participation in the liturgy. The feast of Our Lady of Guadalupe has *de facto* become the most popular Marian feast in the United States even though the Immaculate Conception is the Marian holy day of obligation[19]. Moreover, the strong devotional thrust of Latino Catholicism with its rich musical repertoire moderates tendencies toward formalism in worship sometimes found in more mono-cultural, middle class contexts. The Latino presence serves to restrain a tendency to impose dry doctrinal norms on liturgical practice at the expense of stifling expressivity, spontaneity and life in worship. In addition, an orientation to fiesta among Hispanics enhances the inherent celebratory nature of the sacraments[20].

The second contribution of Latino Catholicism is in the area of spiritual renewal. What would U.S. Catholicism be if there were no Cursillos, Marriage Encounters, Catholic Charismatic Renewal groups, Teen Search retreats, or Christian Base Communities? All these developments which have prospered in the United States over the last fifty years were either brought from Spain and Latin America or primarily put into action by U.S. Latino Catholics. At the heart of these practical approaches to renewing Christian life is a spiritual regard for human affectivity and for the interior life. Consequently, many aspects of parish life and spirituality have benefitted by adopting features of movements which make the riches of faith accessible and appealing to ordinary people.

---

19 PALMO, R., «A Morenita Mass and Procession», 2011, http://whispersintheloggio.blogspot.com/2011/12/big-week-begins-in-la-mass-and.html (accessed on February 24, 2014).

20 See BURGALETA, C., *La fe de los hispanos: diversidad religiosa de los pueblos latinoamericanos,* Libros Liguori, Liguori, MO 2013.

The third contribution of Latinos to the u.s. Church is in the area of linking faith with justice. In the mid-twentieth century, u.s. Catholicism moved upward from being the faith of working class, immigrant peoples of European descent to a decidedly middle class church. John F. Kennedy's election as president was a watershed moment in this process. While the presence of Latinos actually antedates that of European Americans in this country, it was in the twentieth century that a new northward migration of Latin Americans began. This migration, of course, has brought challenges but most certainly blessings. Most notably, the Latino presence has helped maintain and expand the deep-seated Catholic tradition of advocacy for migrants, workers and human dignity in general in the United States. Church-based community organizations such as the Pacific Institute for Community Organizations (PICO) and the Industrial Areas Foundation (IAF), often under Catholic auspices or ecumenical in nature, have arisen with seed monies from the Catholic Campaign for Human Development (CCHD). Scores of organizations have arisen made up of poor Latinos, African Americans and other marginal groups for the purpose of tackling serious social justice issues such as access to education, medical care and security. Today there exists a new multicultural generation of Catholic laity formed in social action and inspired by Catholic Social Doctrine, the option for the poor and Liberation Theology.

A fourth outstanding contribution of Latino Catholicism to the u.s. Catholic Church is found in the application of pastoral methodologies from Medellín to Aparecida in pastoral contexts of parish, diocese, and nation. These have been embraced especially by the u.s. bishops in the process of *Encuentros* that have taken place from 1972 to 2006. Of particular importance is the pastoral circle method for pastoral planning and methodologies which proceed inductively rather than deductively[21]. Pastoral care and planning must first assess reality and discern using insights from human sciences before applying theological and doctrinal considerations to decision making. The *Encuentro* approach insists on a dynamic understanding of church life whereby the mission to evangelize requires ongoing attention to sociocultural realities together with serious pastoral planning. This has taken place in many diocese and parishes. The vision of such a Church is found in the remarkable documents of the *Encuentros* published by the USCCB and especially in the work of the Bishops Conference over the past sixty years together with dioceses, pastoral institutes, ministry organizations and

---

21 WIFSEN, F., HENRIOT, P. and MEJÍA, R. (eds.), *The Pastoral Circle Revisited,* Orbis Books, Maryknoll, NY 2005.

movements throughout the United States[22]. Several dioceses have developed quite sophisticated pastoral plans along these lines.

3
U.S. *Contributions to Latin America and to Hispanic Ministry*

⁀

The relationship between pastoral practice in Latin America and the United States, however, has been reciprocal and symbiotic. This is seen in the emergence of a new generation of Hispanic ministry leaders who themselves are immigrants but have either arrived with considerable pastoral/theological formation or, over the years, gained a solid formation through experience and study in U.S. Catholic colleges and universities and in U.S. pastoral institutes. Hispanic ministry has prospered in the U.S. environment as a result of the stress placed upon education in the United States and the middle class drive toward professionalization from which many Hispanic ministers and pastoral programs have benefitted. Institutes like the Mexican American Cultural Center[23] or the Southwest Pastoral Institute initiated what has become an ongoing relationship between Latin America and the United States. They brought Latin America pastoralists to give workshops and engage Hispanic ministers in dialogue on how to translate Latin American initiatives such as the basic ecclesial communities or pastoral planning into U.S. parish and diocesan contexts.

These initiatives, nevertheless, were inculturated and took on a U.S. expression. For instance, Renew International took the base ecclesial community and translated them quite successfully into a U.S. small group, parish-based faith-sharing dynamic. Movements like the Catholic Charismatic Renewal or the Christian Family Movement—all with foundations in Latin America—took root in the more organizationally structured U.S. Church. The case of the Catholic Charismatic Renewal is of particular interest. The movement actually began in the United States as is well known, but it prospered more in Latin America than in the United States. Eventually U.S. Hispanic charismatics were to receive ongoing support from animators from Latin America who facilitated charismatic communities throughout the United States. The communities that developed,

---

22 See SECRETARIAT OF CULTURAL DIVERSITY IN THE CHURCH, SUBCOMMITTE ON HISPANIC AFFAIRS, *A New Beginning: Hispanic Ministry-Past, Present, Future,* USCCB, Washington, D.C. 2012.

23 In 2008 MACC announced its transition into a college: Mexican American Catholic College.

however, despite occasional tensions with local authorities, generally exhibit an ability to remain in communion with their pastors, and conform to a more structured U.S. approach to church[24].

These interactions are only the tip of the iceberg. Over the past four decades inter-American cooperation has increased through organizations such as Catholic Relief Services, Jesuit Refugee Services, the U.S. Bishops' Collection for Latin America, and participation of U.S. bishops at both the Synod of the Americas in 1997 and with voice and vote at the Aparecida Conference in 2007. The movement of priests, religious men and women, and laity between the U.S. and Latin America occurs more than ever. It takes place at Catholic universities, colleges, seminaries, and theological centers as the percentage of Latino priests, seminarians, religious and laity —native and non-native— rises in the United States, and significant numbers of Latin Americans study in the United States and return to Latin America. This means that Latin American ecclesial leaders are regularly being exposed to U.S. culture and pastoral trends and vice-versa through language and graduate studies, immersions and formation programs. Indeed, a dramatic transformation of presbyterates in the United States is now under way. Significant numbers of the clergy are now immigrants from Latin America and many other world regions. United States religious congregations are being transformed by the inclusion of Latin Americans in critical numbers[25]. For instance, the Trinitarian Fathers and Brothers with headquarters in Silver Spring, Maryland, a U.S. foundation, have reached out to Latin America in recent decades. In time they may become a primarily Latin American congregation. Congregations of women such as the Company of Mary or the Sisters of Charity of the Incarnate Word are combining with their Latin American provinces to create international ones. In places like the Archdiocese of Denver, creative formation programs in Hispanic ministry like those of the San Juan Diego Center bring together the vision of Latin America with the challenges of immigrant and first generation Latinos. Access to excellent internet resources and distance learning opportunities are provided by the Latin American bishops on their excellent

24 See MATOVINA T., *Latino Catholicism*, 118-19; also THE PEW FORUM ON RELIGION AND PUBLIC LIFE, *Changing Faiths: Latinos and the Transformation of American Religion*, Pew Hispanic Center, Washington, D.C. 2007, 23-30.

25 Mary Gautier and others at the Center for Applied Research in the Apostolate at Georgetown University document the cultural transformation underway in the U.S. Catholic Church including seminaries, universities and presbyterates. See GAUTIER, M., *Catholic Ministry Formation Enrollment: Statistical Overview for 2013-2014*, CARA, Washington, D.C. 2014, http://cara.georgetown. edu/Overview201314.pdf (accessed August 28, 2014).

CELAM webpage and by the U.S. bishops on theirs. Hence, throughout the hemisphere, unprecedented conditions are created for a truly symbiotic relationship —a cross-cultural, bilingual formation for church ministers across borders.

One of the areas where mutual influences between Latin America and the United States are clearly seen is in the field of youth ministry. Recent guidelines for certification of ministers have adopted the Spanish term *Pastoral Juvenil Hispana* to refer to the approach taken in the development of effective outreach and formation of youth and young adults, an approach grounded in several characteristics of pastoral ministry in Latin America[26]. This approach integrates the pastoral circle methodology, the focus on active leadership by the youth and young adults themselves, the raising of social consciousness, emphasis on small community development and many other qualities of a contemporary Latin American pastoral vision. At the same time Instituto Fe y Vida has engaged in ongoing dialogue with U.S. youth ministry leaders and adopted approaches from fund development and professional training that are typical of U.S. Catholicism. Thus *Pastoral Juvenil Hispana* has taken a place at the table of contemporary U.S. Catholic outreach to youth and is gaining recognition as a creative alternative to more Euro-American youth ministry approaches[27].

4

New Pope: Times Are Changing

෴

The crowd was impressive by any standard. Millions of young people gathered on Copacabana Beach for the closing liturgy of World Youth Day. Bishops dancing! Yes, dancing. The Argentine Pope fired up in Spanish, «¡Hagan lío!» which means, «Shake things up!» Startled pastoral ministers of every stripe must have been wondering whether their programs were any match for this challenge[28].

---

26 See NATIONAL CATHOLIC NETWORK DE PASTORAL JUVENIL HISPANA – LA RED, *Conclusions, First National Encounter for Hispanic Youth and Young Adults,* USCCB, Washington, D.C. 2008. Also, Instituto Fe y Vida at www.feyvida.org

27 See CERVANTES, C.M., FIGUEROA DECK, A., and JOHNSON-MONDRAGÓN, K., «Pastoral Ministry and Vision: Latino/a Contributions to the Transformation of Practical Theology in the United States», in WOLFTEICH, C. (ed.), *Invitation to Practical Theology,* Paulist Press, Mahwah, NJ 2014.

28 See POPE FRANCIS, *Address during Meeting with Young People from Argentina, Apostolic Journey to Rio de Janeiro on the Occasion of the XXVIII World Youth Day,* July 25, 2013, http://w2. vatican.va/content/francesco/en/speeches/2013/july/documents/papa-francesco_20130725_gmg-argentini-rio.html (accessed August 28, 2014).

A new chapter opens up for the Church under Pope Francis extraordinary leadership. He is moving the global Church beyond a stale and wintry period characterized by drawing lines in the sand and by obsessions with certain teachings to a period of freshness, dialogue, and inclusivity.

It is not easy for pastoral leaders, from bishops to parish catechists, to grasp the implications of Pope Francis' reforms. There is still plenty of disorientation and even grieving the fact that a defensive Tridentine Church is finally being laid to rest. He represents a surprising and unusually energetic leader that literally came from «the ends of the earth» and has a way of proceeding that does not neatly fall into the ideological silos of conservatives or progressives. Nevertheless, this brief analysis of pastoral developments shows that Hispanic/Latino ministry constitutes a meeting point and bridge between the emerging, new vision of Pope Francis' *Iglesia siempre en salida* (Church always reaching out) and the vision and practices of the u.s. Catholic Church. Hispanics have thus been catalysts of a process for creating and «putting new wine into new wineskins». This can be seen in the widespread acceptance of popular devotions like that to the Virgin Mary, the reinvigorated celebrations of All Souls' Day through practices inspired by the Latin American Day of the Dead and by the more graphic aesthetics of Hispanic representations of death and the dying. The persistent effort to make parishes communities of communities is boosted by the Latino presence where small faith-sharing communities are deeply valued. Moreover, the strong social justice orientation of Latin American Catholicism, its grounding in Catholic Social Teaching and in contextual theology and pastoral planning as advanced by CELAM, represents a growing current among pastoral leaders in the u.s.

In the content and methodologies of the *Encuentro* processes of the past four decades, the pastoral vision that nurtured the thought and practice of Jorge Mario Bergoglio and many other pastoral leaders throughout Latin America and the Caribbean has found a home in the United States. The underlying ecclesiology of the People of God, the option for the poor, justice flowing from faith, the inductive pastoral circle methodology, the deep respect for the peoples' popular religion, and the missionary mindset that inspired the basic documents of u.s. Hispanic ministry are now enshrined in *Evangelii Gaudium*, the foundational document of Pope Francis' Petrine ministry[29]. Both u.s. Hispanic ministry and

29 See *The National Pastoral Plan for Hispanic Ministry (1987)* and *Encuentro and Mission (2002)* in
SECRETARIAT OF CULTURAL DIVERSITY IN THE CHURCH, SUBCOMMITTE ON HISPANIC AFFAIRS, *A New Beginning*, 3-24, 61-88.

Pope Francis' reforms for the universal Church have their deepest sources in Latin America's creative post-Vatican II initiatives.

Hence the United States has become the place of gestation for a truly inter-American pastoral vision, struggling for recognition and sometimes the victim of benign neglect. Hispanic ministry in the age of Pope Francis emerges as a source of knowledge, experiences and vision for the U.S. Church striving to grasp where this papacy is leading. The U.S. Catholic Church in turn is making a significant contribution to this encounter with its emphasis on education and professionalism. Catholic universities and pastoral centers have been at the forefront of this endeavor. But what they offer is still not enough. This encounter offers a singular opportunity to bridge the gap. Latin American approaches rooted in intense cultural dialogue, inculturation, and liberation must continue to engage U.S. educational and formational initiatives[30]. Something new and better may derive from this encounter. The Latin American emphasis on missionary discipleship and inclusion of all the baptized, for example, empowers laity more broadly than the more professionalized —and potentially more elitist— approach to lay ecclesial ministry that prevails in the United States[31].

Hispanic ministry is the privileged place for finding ways to engage all the faithful in discipleship, no matter their educational backgrounds, while advancing knowledge and skills[32]. As a result, Hispanic ministry offers alternative models suitable for a globalized world while benefitting from the educational and technical achievements of U.S. know-how. Finally, U.S. Hispanic ministry as a child of both Latin America and the United States offers the wider world examples and models of pastoral engagement firmly grounded in the insights of *Evangelii Gaudium*. It thus becomes a creative resource for advancing the process of *conversión pastoral* (pastoral conversion) proposed by Pope Francis as the goal of a worldwide Church that is forever reaching out and seeking to remain on a permanent missionary footing.

---

30 IRARRÁZABAL, D., *Inculturación: Amanecer Eclesial en América Latina*, Ediciones Abya-Yala, Quito, Ecuador 2000, 169-75.

31 CELAM, *Document of Aparecida*, n. 201-205.

32 See MATEO, H., «Hispanic Ministry and Leadership» in this collection.

Contributors

James F. Caccamo, Ph.D., is Associate Professor of Theology and Chair of Theology and Religious Studies at Saint Joseph's University in Philadelphia, PA.

Antonia Darder, Ph.D., is Leavey Presidential Chair of Ethics and Moral Leadership in the School of Education at Loyola Marymount University, Los Angeles, CA.

Lynette De Jesús-Sáenz, is Director of the Office for Cultural Diversity and the Hispanic Pastoral Institute in the Diocese of Rochester, NY.

Allan Figueroa Deck, SJ, Ph.D., is a Distinguished Scholar in Pastoral Theology and Latino Studies and holds a dual appointment as Lecturer in the Departments of Theological Studies and Chicano/Latino/a Studies at Loyola Marymount University, Los Angeles, CA.

Brett Hoover, Ph.D., is Assistant Professor of Theological Studies, Department of Theological Studies, Loyola Marymount University, Los Angeles, CA; Book Coeditor.

Donald Kerwin, Jr., is the Executive Director of the Center for Migration Studies (CMS) in New York.

Patricia Jiménez, D.Min., is founder of ushispanicministry.com and works as an independent scholar in California.

Ken Johnson-Mondragón, D.Min candidate, is Director of Latino Research and Development at RCL Benziger.

Hilda Mateo, MGSpS, D.Min., is Director of Theological Research —Carisma Sacerdotal— Guadalupano, Our Lady of Guadalupe Province, Missionaries Guadalupanas of the Holy Spirit.

Teresa Maya Sotomayor, CCVI, Ph.D., currently serves on the leadership team for the Congregation of the Sisters of Charity of the Incarnate Word, San Antonio, TX.

Elsie M. Miranda, D.Min., is Associate Professor of Practical Theology, and Director of Ministerial Formation at Barry University, Miami, FL; Book Coeditor.

Hosffman Ospino, Ph.D., is Assistant Professor of Hispanic Ministry and Religious Education, and Director of Graduate Programs in Hispanic Ministry at Boston College's School of Theology and Ministry, Boston, MA; Book Coeditor.

David Sánchez, Ph.D., is Associate Professor of Theological Studies and Director of American Cultures at Loyola Marymount University, Los Angeles, CA.

El ministerio hispano en el siglo XXI: asuntos urgentes

Agradecimientos

Estamos agradecidos profundamente con todas las personas que hicieron posible que el *simposio nacional sobre el ministerio católico hispano en los Estados Unidos*, el cual tuvo lugar en el año 2014, tuviera el éxito que tuvo, dando así vida a este libro que ahora sirve como recurso para el ministerio y la investigación sobre la experiencia católica hispana en los Estados Unidos.

Damos gracias al equipo de asistentes de postgrado y exalumnos de Loyola Marymount University por su trabajo incansable y esmerado: Alejandra Ángel, Raymond Camacho, Cristina Castillo, Marissa Cornejo, Marisol Gaytán Escobar, y Karen Hernández, junto con la estudiante de pregrado Águeda Sofía Hernández. De manera particular agradecemos a los asistentes de postgrado que trabajaron durante el proceso de planeación: Magalí Del Bueno Riancho, Daniel Méndez y Claudia Ávila Torres. Su compromiso es prueba del don que los hispanos son y de la esperanza que las nuevas generaciones traen a la Iglesia.

Muchas gracias a los profesores y administradores de las instituciones académicas que aceptaron trabajar en conjunto con Loyola Marymount University en la organización del simposio: Barry University, Boston College, Congar Institute for Ministry Development, Graduate School of Religion and Religious Education at Fordham University, Jesuit School of Theology of Santa Clara University (Campus de Berkeley), University of Notre Dame, Santa Clara University y Seattle University. Es alentador ver un número cada vez más grande de instituciones católicas de educación superior patrocinando conversaciones tan importantes como ésta.

Damos gracias a los académicos y líderes pastorales que leyeron distintas versiones de estos ensayos y ofrecieron sus reacciones a los primeros borradores: Dr. Miguel De La Torre, Dr. Luis Fraga, Dr. David Hayes-Bautista, Dra. Teodocia María Hayes-Bautista, Rev. Dempsey Rosales-Acosta y Rev. Richard Vega. Su generosidad realmente es una bendición para el Pueblo de Dios.

Agradecemos a todos los autores de los ensayos en este volumen. Las ideas que se comparten en estos ensayos son un tesoro precioso y un regalo para la misión evangelizadora de la Iglesia en este país. Sabemos también que muchas más ideas nacieron en el proceso de escribir estos ensayos y el diálogo con otros colegas durante el simposio. Dichas ideas quedan por ahora en sus mentes y corazones, y esperamos que vean la luz del día quizás en otras publicaciones o ejercicios de reflexión compartida que sigan enriqueciendo el mundo del ministerio hispano.

Muchas gracias a todos los participantes en el simposio nacional. Ustedes compartieron tres días de sus vidas discutiendo, a la luz de su pasión y conocimiento, los asuntos urgentes que guiaron el coloquio y ahora están al centro de este volumen. El ministerio católico hispano ha avanzado un gran paso gracias a ustedes.

Gracias a las editoriales, organizaciones e instituciones —nombradas y anónimas— que hicieron posible que tuviéramos los recursos apropiados para hacer realidad el simposio y publicar este libro: Loyola Press, Oregon Catholic Press, Our Sunday Visitor, RCL Benziger, y William H. Sadlier, Inc. La Sociedad Bíblica Americana (*American Bible Society*) patrocinó generosamente la conversación sobre el ministerio hispano y el estudio de la Biblia durante el simposio, el cual condujo al ensayo bajo el mismo título en este libro. Gracias a todos por su generosidad y su apoyo.

Fue un honor caminar con todos ustedes en este proyecto.

Introducción

El catolicismo en los Estados Unidos continúa siendo renovado profundamente por la presencia hispana. Tanto es así que en muchos sitios del país, «el ministerio hispano es simplemente *el ministerio*»[1]. Aun en aquellos lugares en los que esto dista de ser realidad, la diversidad e identidad de la experiencia hispana ha transformado y enriquecido el catolicismo en los Estados Unidos. Por lo tanto, cuanto más aprendamos acerca de la experiencia hispana en este país, con todas sus manifestaciones, contribuciones y desafíos, más podremos entender el catolicismo estadounidense en el siglo XXI.

Esta colección de ensayos no busca describir quiénes son los católicos hispanos. Tampoco es un llamado a crear conciencia sobre la presencia de esta creciente población, ni sobre las implicaciones de tal crecimiento para nuestras comunidades de fe. Mucho de esto fue objeto de un trabajo previo, *El ministerio hispano en el siglo XXI: presente y futuro* (Convivium, 2010), que fue el resultado del primer simposio nacional sobre el ministerio católico hispano[2]. Después de aquel trabajo se escribieron varias obras innovadoras que ofrecieron panoramas completos de distintos niveles de la experiencia católica hispana en este país[3]. Usando ese libro como base, el presente trabajo es una exploración de ocho asuntos particulares que están íntimamente relacionados con el ministerio católico hispano en nuestros días: la vida parroquial, la inmigración, los jóvenes hispanos nacidos en los Estados Unidos, la educación, los medios de comunicación social, el liderazgo, el estudio de la Biblia, y la relación con la Iglesia en Latinoamérica. Estos han sido identificados como *asuntos urgentes*.

En junio del año 2014, ochenta y tres expertos y consultores reconocidos en el mundo del ministerio hispano fueron invitados a Los Ángeles, California para participar del segundo simposio nacional sobre el ministerio católico hispano, bajo el auspicio de Loyola Marymount University[4]. Entre las voces reunidas

---

1 OSPINO, H. (ed.), *El ministerio hispano en el siglo XXI: Presente y futuro,* Convivium Press, Miami 2010, 234.

2 El primer simposio nacional sobre el ministerio católico hispano fue organizado y auspiciado por Boston College, en colaboración con Barry University, Loyola Marymount University y el Congar Institute for Ministry Development en el año 2009.

3 Véase MATOVINA, T., *Latino Catholicism: Transformation in America's Largest Church,* Princeton University Press, Princeton, NJ 2011; HOOVER, B.C., *The Shared Parish: Latinos, Anglos, and the Future of U.S. Catholicism,* NYU Press, New York 2014; OSPINO, H., *El ministerio hispano en parroquias católicas: Reporte inicial de los resultados del studio nacional de parroquias católicas con ministerio hispano,* Our Sunday Visitor, Huntington, IN 2015.

4 Al igual que con el simposio anterior, este esfuerzo es el resultado de una colaboración de varias universidades e institutos pastorales de todo el país. El simposio del año 2014 fue copatrocinado por ocho de estas instituciones: Barry University, Boston College, Congar Institute for Ministry Development, Graduate School of Religion and Religious Education en Fordham University,

durante tres días de reflexión y estudio se encontraban líderes pastorales, académicos, editoriales, organizaciones que apoyan el ministerio hispano, e investigadores. Como Jacob en el libro del Génesis (32,22-31), nos encontramos allí en una lucha con el Dios vivo mientras dolorosamente nos hacíamos conscientes de las heridas que aquejan a nuestras propias comunidades. Fue un proceso de reflexión que intentó adentrarse en la complejidad de la experiencia hispana en *lo cotidiano* con el deseo de proporcionar un lenguaje y unas ideas adecuadas para que los agentes pastorales en el ministerio hispano puedan fomentar intercambios similares en sus comunidades. No se propusieron «soluciones» superficiales que trataran al catolicismo hispano como un tema más de diálogo o como un problema. Tal como lo demuestran los ensayos en esta colección, si se percibe a los hispanos como un problema para la Iglesia en los Estados Unidos, la Iglesia perderá una oportunidad crucial para crecer. De ahí la pertinencia y la conveniencia de estos diálogos.

La conversación durante el simposio fue guiada por un proceso metodológico fundamentado en una teología y una pastoral de conjunto, el cual fue diseñado inicialmente para el simposio que tuvo lugar en Boston en el año 2009. Al centro de este enfoque metodológico está un diálogo informado entre los participantes cuyas vidas y compromisos se sitúan en diferentes niveles de la realidad de la Iglesia y de la sociedad, poniendo atención en particular a aquellas voces que vienen de las bases. Muchos de los participantes son agentes pastorales trabajando día a día en el contexto del ministerio hispano. La mayoría de los académicos en el simposio, especialmente los teólogos, son conocidos por avanzar su trabajo manteniendo un compromiso firme con el ministerio y usar herramientas de investigación que exigen un diálogo constante con las comunidades hispanas. Varios de ellos son autores en esta colección.

La selección de los asuntos urgentes también fue el resultado de un diálogo de conjunto, el cual comenzó como un proceso de consulta con líderes pastorales y académicos familiarizados con la experiencia católica hispana. Algunos de estos temas fueron identificados en el año 2009, durante el primer simposio. Otros son referentes constantes en las reuniones y conversaciones sobre el ministerio hispano. La urgencia de algunos de estos asuntos tales como la inmigración, los jóvenes hispanos nacidos en los Estados Unidos y la relación con la Iglesia en Latinoamérica incrementó gracias a la atención que han recibido, tanto mundial

Jesuit School of Theology de Santa Clara University (Berkeley Campus), Loyola Marymount University, University of Notre Dame, Santa Clara University y Seattle University.

como nacionalmente, como resultado de la elección del Papa Francisco. Es importante señalar que los organizadores del simposio fuimos conscientes de que la selección de los ocho asuntos urgentes está lejos de ser exhaustiva. Muchos otros asuntos en el ministerio hispano piden a gritos ser considerados también, como lo destacó el reciente *Estudio nacional de parroquias católicas con ministerio hispano*[5]. Nuestra esperanza es que iniciativas similares y futuros simposios puedan referirse a ellos con mayor profundidad. El simposio del año 2014 y la publicación de esta colección son providenciales, pues ocurren dentro del período que antecede el proceso del Quinto Encuentro Nacional del Pastoral Hispana/Latina[6]. El simposio y el libro anticipan áreas centrales de reflexión que deben ser abordadas en el marco de las reflexiones durante el proceso del Quinto Encuentro.

El simposio también planteó varios interrogantes claves, de hecho asuntos muy urgentes, que son clave para el fortalecimiento de los esfuerzos en el ministerio hispano como parte de la Nueva Evangelización, pero que lamentablemente no fueron abordados en parte o en su totalidad debido a los límites del proceso del simposio. Por ejemplo, a pesar del deseo de integrar en el proceso una conversación crítica sobre las voces e interrogantes planteados por las mujeres hispanas en nuestro momento actual, el simposio no hizo lo suficiente para explorar conscientemente temas tan importantes como la sexualidad, la violencia doméstica y la desigualdad de género. Los participantes en el simposio también resaltaron la tensión poco examinada entre el compromiso social y el activismo político que caracterizó a generaciones de agentes pastorales en el ministerio hispano en el pasado, y el enfoque casi exclusivo sobre temas de formación en la fe y evangelización que caracteriza a algunos agentes pastorales más jóvenes hoy en día. Es como si ambas perspectivas no fuesen dos caras de la misma moneda tal como lo demuestran las mejores expresiones de vida cristiana. La experiencia del simposio no enfrentó en gran medida el tema de cómo y por qué los prejuicios raciales permean palpablemente las estructuras de nuestra sociedad y nuestra Iglesia. Aunque este asunto surgió frecuentemente y los agentes pastorales y académicos somos muy conscientes de los efectos nocivos del racismo, no hicimos lo suficiente para hablar con más claridad sobre este pecado de exclusión. Las consecuencias de tal silencio nos afectan directamente todo el tiempo. ¿Hay, por ejemplo, un elemento de sesgo racial / étnico en el

5 OSPINO, H., *El ministerio hispano en parroquias católicas*, 91-92.
6 El evento central del Quinto Encuentro Nacional de Pastoral Hispana/Latina tendrá lugar en el año 2018.

hecho de que los hispanos estén excesivamente representados en las pandillas y las prisiones e insuficientemente representados en los seminarios y los programas de preparación para el ministerio? Una última cuestión que surgió de manera sutil en el simposio, pero que nunca recibió el tratamiento adecuado, fue el impacto de la secularización en la vida del Pueblo de Dios y en el trabajo de la Iglesia, incluyendo el número creciente de jóvenes hispanos que deciden no afiliarse al catolicismo ni a ningún otro grupo religioso (los llamados «*nones*» o *non-religiously affiliated*, en inglés).

Versiones preliminares de los ensayos en este volumen fueron comisionados para estimular el diálogo durante el simposio nacional en el año 2014 en ocho grupos diferentes, cada uno correspondiente a uno de los asuntos urgentes. Durante la convocación, los autores entablaron un intercambio crítico con un grupo de expertos en cada área, incluyendo agentes pastorales y académicos. Ocho testigos, estudiantes de postgrado y algunos recién graduados de un programa de teología pastoral, acompañaron a los grupos de principio a fin tomando notas sobre los detalles de sus deliberaciones. Estas notas fueron revisadas por los autores y los editores. Los ensayos que siguen son un esfuerzo genuino de los autores y los editores de articular las mejores ideas que sobresalieron en cada grupo. Sin embargo, los ensayos no son resúmenes ni declaraciones que representen el consenso de quienes fueron parte de cada grupo de estudio. Los ensayos son el ejercicio del trabajo creativo de los autores en diálogo con los editores, proveyendo la mejor reflexión teológico-pastoral posible. Esperamos que estos ensayos a su vez estimulen la reflexión y el diálogo en parroquias, cancillerías, organizaciones eclesiales, movimientos apostólicos y universidades.

En el primer capítulo, Brett Hoover y Hosffman Ospino, coeditores de esta colección, centran su atención en las parroquias con ministerio hispano. Ambos fundamentan su análisis en investigaciones recientes y publicaciones innovadoras que están ayudando a los católicos en los Estados Unidos a apreciar mejor las contribuciones de los católicos hispanos así como los desafíos de la vida parroquial donde están presentes. Los autores hacen referencia a las dinámicas sesgadas de poder que aún caracterizan a demasiadas parroquias que sirven a los hispanos e invitan a poner atención al papel de los movimientos apostólicos en el proceso de cultivar agentes pastorales en las parroquias hispanas. Hoover y Ospino crean conciencia sobre otras dinámicas complejas en las parroquias con ministerio hispano, especialmente en parroquias compartidas, y ofrecen un análisis de modelos emergentes de vida parroquial que exigen tipos específicos de acción ministerial y modelos de liderazgo. Dado que la parroquia sigue siendo un referente firme para los católicos hispanos en la práctica y la celebración de su fe, el capítulo provee un contexto sólido de reflexión para el resto del volumen.

Don Kerwin, director ejecutivo del Centro de Estudios Migratorios (*Center for Migration Studies*) en Nueva York, y uno de los expertos más reconocidos el país sobre temas de inmigración desde una perspectiva católica, ofrece en el capítulo dos una visión panorámica de esta compleja realidad en los Estados Unidos. Si hay un tema que no se puede reducir a soluciones simplistas o a un mero posicionamiento retórico, es la inmigración. Éste es un tema donde los católicos sin duda alguna tenemos mucho que decir. El ensayo de Kerwin invita a los agentes pastorales, sobre todo a los que trabajan en el ministerio hispano, a entrar en diálogo con lo mejor de nuestra tradición bíblica y la Doctrina Social de la Iglesia para abogar por una reforma migratoria que haga más humanas las vidas de millones de hermanas y hermanos hispanos indocumentados y fortalezca innumerables familias hispanas.

El capítulo tres aborda el tema que seguramente definirá al catolicismo en los Estados Unidos de América en la primera mitad del siglo XXI: la evangelización de los jóvenes hispanos nacidos en los Estados Unidos. Lynette De Jesús-Sáenz y Ken Johnson-Mondragón se unen para ofrecer un análisis sólido, advirtiendo a los lectores que ningún ensayo o libro u otro recurso puede abarcar la complejidad de la vida de los jóvenes hispanos. Su ensayo ofrece un conjunto excelente de principios generales y prácticas eficaces para el ministerio con las nuevas generaciones de católicos hispanos. De Jesús-Sáenz y Johnson-Mondragón proponen caminar con los jóvenes hispanos, ayudándolos a contar sus propias historias de encuentro con Dios a la luz de sus realidades particulares. Para esto, las parroquias pueden ser «comunidades de memoria», lugares en los que las historias de los jóvenes y las del resto de la comunidad coincidan al mismo tiempo con la Historia de la Salvación.

¿Qué pudiera ser más urgente para la mayoría de las familias hispanas y las comunidades de fe con ministerio hispano que el tema de la educación? Es tentador en nuestros círculos católicos reducir el tema de la educación a la catequesis o a lo que sucede sólo en las instituciones educativas católicas. Un número creciente de recursos escritos recientemente se enfocan en estas realidades7. El ca-

---

7 Véanse por ejemplo, OSPINO, H. y WEITZEL-O'NEILL, P., *Escuelas católicas en una Iglesia cada vez más hispana: Reporte general de los resultados del Estudio nacional de escuelas católicas al servicio de familias hispanas,* Our Sunday Visitor, Huntington, IN 2016; BRINIG, M.F. y GARNETT, N.S.,

pítulo cuatro expande nuestra imaginación analizando la educación de los niños hispanos, de los cuales se estima que más de ocho millones son católicos, en el contexto de los procesos educativos de nuestra sociedad, en particular procesos de educación pública, pues el 97% de los niños hispanos en los Estados Unidos no están matriculados en escuelas católicas. Muchos van a escuelas públicas de bajo rendimiento, la mayoría de éstas situadas en barrios pobres. No podíamos haber pensado en una persona más ideal para guiar este intercambio que Antonia Darder, una de las mayores expertas en asuntos relacionados con la educación de los hispanos en los Estados Unidos. Su ensayo ofrece un análisis preciso —y muy sobrio, hay que decirlo— de las realidades que determinan la vida de nuestros niños hispanos. Sin embargo, en un tono esperanzador, Darder apunta a lo que ella llama «principios para la inclusión cultural». El éxito de la educación de los niños católicos hispanos sólo puede ser el resultado de grandes alianzas. Este capítulo es imprescindible para cualquier persona que trabaje con familias hispanas que tengan niños en edad escolar.

En el capítulo cinco Patricia Jiménez y James F. Caccamo unen la habilidad de hacer un análisis conciso junto con una amplia experiencia para establecer las bases de lo que probablemente es el primer ensayo investigativo sobre la relación entre el ministerio católico hispano, las nuevas tecnologías y los nuevos medios de comunicación social. Aunque las vidas de los hispanos en los Estados Unidos, particularmente las de los jóvenes, son significativamente influenciadas por el uso de medios de comunicación social y el acceso a recursos tecnológicos, y muchos de nosotros utilizamos estos recursos en el ministerio, casi nada se ha escrito sobre el tema. El capítulo abre brechas, plantea interrogantes y establece un derrotero para futuras conversaciones.

El capítulo seis reanuda la conversación sobre el liderazgo pastoral, un asunto muy debatido en el contexto del ministerio hispano. Sin embargo, Hilda Mateo, MGSpS, no se limita a repetir los conocidos argumentos sobre la falta de hispanos en posiciones de liderazgo en la Iglesia o las dinámicas de poder que a menudo socavan el liderazgo hispano a la hora de tomar decisiones en nuestras comunidades. El capítulo desafía creativamente el concepto de «liderazgo» en general —al menos tal como se entiende en muchos sectores de la Iglesia influenciados por modelos empresariales y administrativos, y por las nociones que predominan en las sociedades occidentales sobre la eficacia única del poder de deci-

Lost Classroom, Lost Community: Catholic Schools' Importance in Urban America, The University of Chicago Press, Chicago, IL 2014.

sión individual. Tal perspectiva, afirma la autora, tiende a excluir a muchos hispanos en nuestra Iglesia, particularmente a las mujeres y a las minorías. Mateo nos invita a recuperar las dimensiones bíblicas y comunitarias del servicio ministerial, guiando nuestra atención hacia categorías como el discernimiento, la vocación y la misión. Las culturas hispanas están profundamente marcadas por dichas categorías, abriéndonos a una mina de oro de posibilidades para afirmar y promover agentes pastorales en el contexto del ministerio hispano.

David Sánchez, católico hispano experto en estudios bíblicos, nos ofrece uno de los análisis más interesantes en esta colección. En el capítulo siete explora cómo los católicos hispanos podemos explorar mejor las Escrituras en el contexto del ministerio. El encuentro con la Palabra de Dios a través de las Escrituras ocurre todos los días y de manera constante en el ministerio hispano: la catequesis, la liturgia, los grupos de estudio bíblico, la lectura personal, la *lectio divina*, etc. Sánchez destaca varios de esos encuentros mientras nos recuerda las directrices centrales del Magisterio sobre la lectura de la Biblia con la Iglesia. También aborda el desafío de la falta de formación bíblica que caracteriza la experiencia de muchos católicos hispanos. Con el fin de responder a ese desafío y promover encuentros participativos con las Escrituras, Sánchez propone cuatro estrategias fascinantes para la lectura de la Biblia y fomentar el conocimiento de las Escrituras. Estas estrategias afirman decididamente las experiencias culturales y religiosas de los católicos hispanos, invitando a la comunidad a leer e interpretar las Escrituras como «hispanos» y «católicos».

El proceso de planeación del simposio que dio origen a este volumen fue influenciado profundamente por la elección del primer Papa latinoamericano en la historia de la Iglesia: el Papa Francisco. Como se puede observar en la mayoría de los ensayos de esta colección, el «efecto Francisco» es evidente, pues varios elementos de la visión y las enseñanzas del Papa Francisco sirven como eje central de muchas ideas fundamentales propuestas para la reflexión sobre el ministerio hispano. De hecho, para la mayoría de los católicos hispanos, el Papa Francisco es prácticamente un Papa hispano. En el capítulo ocho, Allan Figueroa Deck, SJ, y Teresa Maya Sotomayor, CCVI releen con visión renovada la relación entre la experiencia eclesial latinoamericana y el catolicismo hispano estadounidense. Por muchas décadas la reflexión sobre la atención pastoral a los católicos hispanos en los Estados Unidos fue influenciada por la experiencia de agentes pastorales y categorías espirituales que emergían desde Latinoamérica y el Caribe. Sin embargo, este tipo de diálogos continentales ha perdido algo de dinamismo en los últimos años. Figueroa Deck y Maya Sotomayor argumentan convincentemente que la reflexión continental debe fortalecerse, especialmente a la luz de las perspectivas globales que impulsan muchos diálogos contemporáneos en nuestro mundo. Los autores proponen una agenda clara de diálogo entre agentes pastorales en Latinoamérica, el Caribe y los Estados Unidos, destacando las influencias mutuas que tienen un potencial singular para el ministerio hispano.

Esperamos que esta colección de ensayos inspire a muchos agentes pastorales en nuestra Iglesia, en particular a quienes trabajamos más directamente en esfuerzos asociados con el ministerio hispano, así como a académicos estudiando el catolicismo estadounidense y la experiencia religiosa hispana, a hacer nuestra la llamada a la Nueva Evangelización. Entendemos la Nueva Evangelización según la visión del Papa Francisco:

> La Iglesia en salida es la comunidad de discípulos misioneros que primerean, que se involucran, que acompañan, que fructifican y festejan. «Primerear»: sepan disculpar este neologismo. La comunidad evangelizadora experimenta que el Señor tomó la iniciativa, la ha primereado en el amor (cf. 1 Jn 4,10); y, por eso, ella sabe adelantarse, tomar la iniciativa sin miedo, salir al encuentro, buscar a los lejanos y llegar a los cruces de los caminos para invitar a los excluidos[8].

Estas son precisamente las características para el ministerio hispano en el siglo XXI que los ensayos en este volumen proponen para ser acogidas por medio del diálogo.

HOSFFMAN OSPINO, ELSIE MIRANDA y BRETT HOOVER
EDITORES

---

8 PAPA FRANCISCO, *Evangelii Gaudium*, n. 24.

El ministerio hispano y la vida parroquial

Brett Hoover *y* Hosffman Ospino

Según el Estudio nacional de parroquias católicas con ministerio hispano, aproximadamente 4.300 parroquias, de un total de 17.413 en el año 2013, ofrecen servicios religiosos en español, por lo general Misas y bautizos. El 61% de todas las parroquias católicas se concentran en el Noreste y el Medio Oeste, donde la población de católicos está disminuyendo. El 39% se encuentran en el Sur y el Oeste. Sin embargo, el 61% de las parroquias con ministerio hispano se encuentran en el Sur y el Oeste, donde la población de católicos está aumentando. Consciente del hecho de que alrededor del 60% de todos los católicos estadounidenses menores de dieciocho años son hispanos, podemos anticipar fácilmente el rostro del catolicismo estadounidense durante el resto del siglo XXI. Ya no se pensará en el ministerio hispano como un programa pastoral especializado, que a menudo se lleva a cabo en español y está dirigido a los inmigrantes. Más bien, el término evocará las experiencias de la vida parroquial de la mayoría de los católicos estadounidenses.

1

El crecimiento actual de la vida parroquial hispana

Recordemos que desde un comienzo los hispanos han jugado un papel decisivo en la definición de la vida parroquial católica en lo que hoy es los Estados Unidos de América. Mucho antes de que los colonos ingleses declararan la independencia, los católicos de habla hispana habían fundado parroquias en Puerto Rico, Florida y Nuevo México. Olas de inmigrantes de Latinoamérica han llegado a los Estados Unidos a lo largo de su historia, incluyendo momentos claves como la Fiebre del Oro (1849), la Revolución Mexicana (1910-1917) y las guerras de los Cristeros de los años veinte. Durante la Segunda Guerra Mundial y los años que le siguieron, el programa de trabajadores braceros del gobierno de los Estados Unidos (1942-1964) incitó una ola migratoria procedente de México que en realidad nunca ha culminado. Durante ese mismo periodo de la posguerra, los cambios económicos en toda Latinoamérica, el ascenso del régimen de Fidel Castro en Cuba, y una serie de guerras civiles en América Central, caracterizadas por frecuentes intervenciones del gobierno y las fuerzas militares de los Estados Unidos, impulsaron a otros grupos de inmigrantes latinoamericanos a llegar al país y así diversificar la población hispana aún más.

En la era de la posguerra, muchos de los líderes anglos involucrados en el ministerio hispano asumieron que éste era una fase temporal en el gran proceso de asimilación de los hispanos a la cultura euroamericana. Muchas parroquias ignoraron a los recién llegados o los acomodaron con propuestas pastorales inadecuadas y a menudo paternalistas. Entre los ejemplos que se pueden citar están los pequeños centros mexicanos de misión en el sur de California, los cuales eran muy pobres, y las liturgias que los puertorriqueños celebraban en las iglesias de abajo, los sótanos, en Nueva York[1]. Sin embargo, hacia los años setenta y ochenta, la inmigración desde Latinoamérica que siguió a los años de posguerra ya había alterado significativamente el mapa demográfico del catolicismo estadounidense, y las diócesis en los estados con alto nivel de inmigración, como Texas y California, ya no podían simplemente ignorar o «contener la presencia hispana». Al mismo tiempo, los obispos católicos de los Estados Unidos,

motivados por los movimientos de orgullo étnico y racial, se distanciaron de su antigua posición de promover una asimilación rápida de los inmigrantes[2]. En 1972, los obispos animaron el proceso de Encuentro que acababa de nacer, el cual generó un diálogo de colaboración que avivó a toda una generación de líderes pastorales hispanos. Influenciados por la cada vez más estudiada Doctrina Social de la Iglesia, ideas provenientes del pensamiento teológico latinoamericano y movimientos sociopolíticos en los Estados Unidos (por ejemplo, el Movimiento de los Derechos Civiles), muchos líderes laicos, sacerdotes y religiosos formados durante esta época del ministerio hispano dedicaron bastante tiempo y energía a responder a las necesidades sociales (alimentación, vivienda, seguridad local) y a la injusticia estructural (dificultades relacionadas con el proceso migratorio) que afectaban de manera desproporcionada a los hispanos pobres y de clase obrera.

Después del año 1990 comenzó una nueva era en el ministerio hispano a medida que los inmigrantes católicos hispanos (e hispanos que migraban internamente desde lugares como California) se establecían con sus familias en estados con poco historial migratorio tales como Carolina del Norte, Oregón o Tennessee, donde la presencia hispana era pequeña o inexistente. Vale la pena señalar que

---

1 Véase DÍAZ-STEVENS, A.M., *Oxcart Catholicism on Fifth Avenue: The Impact of the Puerto Rican Migration upon the Archdiocese of New York*, Notre Dame Studies in American Catholicism, Notre Dame University Press, Notre Dame, IN 1993.

2 GARCES-FOLEY, K., «Comparing Catholic and Evangelical Integration Efforts», en *Journal for the Scientific Study of Religion* 47, no. 1 (2008) 18-20.

en general la mayoría de las parroquias con ministerio hispano en el país comenzaron a servir a los católicos de habla hispana, especialmente celebrando Misas y bautizos, alrededor del año 1995. El 16% de las parroquias comenzaron a implementar el ministerio hispano entre 1985 y 1994, el 36 % entre 1995 y 2004, y el 15% desde el año 2005 en adelante[3]. Los agentes pastorales hispanos formados durante este período con frecuencia exhiben una orientación hacia el ministerio bastante diferente en comparación a la de la generación anterior. Muchos centran su atención en la dimensión catequética de la experiencia de fe con el espíritu de la Nueva Evangelización. Mientras que los esfuerzos de la Nueva Evangelización en Europa y América del Norte han tratado de contrarrestar los efectos del secularismo, las manifestaciones latinoamericanas e hispanas de la Nueva Evangelización en los Estados Unidos con frecuencia se centran en el fortalecimiento de la actividad catequética y la vida litúrgica de aquellos católicos formados en su fe primordialmente en el contexto del hogar y por medio de la religiosidad popular. Los católicos hispanos han hecho suya la Nueva Evangelización estableciendo un punto medio entre las preocupaciones pastorales de la Iglesia en Latinoamérica y en Norteamérica[4]. Lamentablemente, en muchas comunidades hispanas la preocupación casi exclusiva por asuntos de catequesis y espiritualidad en ocasiones ha reemplazado o dejado de lado el celo evangélico que llevó a las primeras generaciones de agentes pastorales a confrontar también los problemas sociales y la injusticia estructural del momento. El ministerio hispano no puede caer en la trampa de tener que escoger entre invitar a un conocimiento más profundo de la fe o ser un movimiento que promueva la justicia social. Debe ser una llamada a una fe audaz e integral que exija la justicia como parte fundamental del contenido del Evangelio.

3 OSPINO, H., *El ministerio hispano en parroquias católicas: Reporte inicial de los resultados del Estudio Nacional de parroquias católicas con ministerio hispano*, Our Sunday Visitor, Huntington, IN 2015, 62.
4 Véase OSPINO, H., «The U.S. Hispanic Catholic Experience and the New Evangelization: Considerations», en *Pastoral Liturgy*, 44, n. 4 (septiembre/octubre 2013) 9-15.

Tres modelos de vida parroquial hispana

Con el paso del tiempo las parroquias han dado vida a distintas maneras de hacer ministerio hispano. Mientras que todas las parroquias funcionan con cierto nivel de estabilidad como comunidades de fieles (*Código de Derecho Canónico*, canon 515 § 1) comprometidas con la celebración de la Eucaristía y la formación de los católicos en su tradición de fe, invitando a los creyentes al discipulado en un mundo herido y confirmando los vínculos de comunión con nuestro Dios Uno y Trino, cada parroquia lleva a cabo estas funciones de una manera ligeramente diferente, respondiendo a sus propias circunstancias y a su contexto. Aunque las parroquias nacionales de la época de la inmigración europea ya no son una opción, los obispos han permitido en algunos casos la creación de una estructura similar llamada la parroquia personal *de jure*. Sin embargo, estas parroquias personales raramente sirven a los católicos hispanos. La mayoría de los hispanos católicos celebran su fe en comunidades parroquiales territoriales. Pero debido a que la presencia hispana en algunas de estas comunidades tiende a ser numerosa y los servicios ofrecidos en gran medida se centran en las necesidades pastorales, espirituales e incluso sociales de los católicos hispanos, tales parroquias suelen funcionar como parroquias «nacionales» *de facto*, a pesar de que no son oficialmente reconocidas como tal. Estas parroquias nacionales *de facto* se han formado y continúan existiendo en zonas con grandes poblaciones hispanas en centros urbanos como Chicago, Miami, Los Ángeles y San Antonio. Estas comunidades usualmente centran su atención en las necesidades ministeriales ya sea de un grupo latinoamericano en particular o de muchos grupos que se mantienen unidos por la presencia dominante de un grupo hispano (a menudo los mexicanos, pero en Miami son los cubanos) o simplemente por el idioma español. Muchas también tienen Misas en inglés a las que asisten primordialmente hispanos que prefieren la celebración en inglés.

En Chicago, por ejemplo, Pilsen, un histórico barrio polaco, se transformó en una comunidad mayoritariamente mexicana en la década de los sesenta. Esta comunidad incluye tanto a inmigrantes como a hispanos que han vivido por mucho tiempo en Chicago que han llegado a este sector de otras áreas debido al impacto de proyectos de construcción en el sector público. En 1970 una cuarta parte de todos los mexicanos de Chicago vivía allí. A finales de la década de los sesenta, la parroquia St. Pius V había instituido varias Misas en español, clases de inglés para niños, actividades para los jóvenes, un grupo de guadalupanas, un grupo de Cursillos de Cristiandad y diferentes iniciativas de vivienda y programas de asistencia económica[5]. En un día típico en la oficina de la parroquia, la mayor parte de los asuntos parroquiales se tramitaban en español. El P. Charles Dahm, párroco en aquel entonces, un sacerdote euroamericano de la orden de los dominicos quien a su vez fue formado en el ministerio hispano durante la primera época de los Encuentros, pasaba tanto tiempo ayudando a los inmigrantes mexicanos con asuntos de empleo, vivienda y cuestiones legales, al igual que educando a su congregación sobre temas sociales, como celebrando Misa y predicando. La parroquia también tenía varios programas de consejería e intervención para los jóvenes. Algunos feligreses viajaban largas distancias desde barrios lejanos para participar en la Misa o preparar a sus hijos para recibir los sacramentos o las ceremonias de quinceañera[6]. Hoy St. Pius sigue siendo un centro comunitario que ofrece muchos servicios y funciona como un hogar cultural y espiritual para los católicos mexicanos. «El que la parroquia haya establecido maneras nuevas de responder cultural y pastoralmente a su pueblo predominantemente mexicano le valió para ganarse el afecto perdurable de ellos», escribió el Padre Dahm[7].

St. Pius confirma las fortalezas del modelo de parroquia nacional *de facto* al servicio de los hispanos, especialmente como se forjó durante los años setenta y ochenta. St. Pius ofrece «la seguridad y la claridad que crecen en la comunidad al tener su propio territorio»[8], mientras que provee a los feligreses, que se sienten como en casa hablando español, la oportunidad de expresar sus necesidades pastorales con claridad y de recibir atención pastoral. Este modelo también ayuda a los inmigrantes a aprender detalles sobre cómo las instituciones gubernamentales, los negocios y el sistema educativo funcionan en los Estados Unidos. Haciendo suya seriamente la Doctrina Social de la Iglesia, St. Pius ha puesto atención suficiente a asuntos de servicio y justicia social: ayudando a la gente a encontrar trabajo o vivienda y abogando directamente por los inmigrantes que

5   DAHM, C., *Parish Ministry in a Hispanic Community,* Paulist Press, New York 2004, 15-17.
6   PUTNAM, R. y CAMPBELL, D., *American Grace: How Religion Unites and Divides Us,* Simon & Schuster, New York 2010, 212-215.
7   DAHM, C., *Parish Ministry in a Hispanic Community,*18.
8   FIGUEROA DECK, A., *The Second Wave: Hispanic Ministry and the Evangelization of Cultures,* Paulist Press, New York 1989, 59.

viven en condiciones precarias o son discriminados en sus lugares de trabajo o carecen de documentos migratorios adecuados.

Como indicamos anteriormente, la mayoría de los hispanos en los Estados Unidos no van a parroquias nacionales *de facto*. La mayoría de hecho van a «parroquias compartidas», las cuales ofrecen Misas distintas y servicios pastorales para dos o más grupos culturales o grupos que hablan distintos idiomas. El 43% de los feligreses en las parroquias con ministerio hispano son anglos; el 4% asiáticos, nacidos en Hawái, y provenientes de las islas del Pacífico; el 3% son de raza negra, afroamericanos o africanos; y el 1% indígenas estadounidenses o indígenas de Alaska[9]. Las parroquias compartidas se forman por lo general cuando, poco a poco o de repente, los barrios cambian a medida que llegan los latinoamericanos u otros inmigrantes. Con el tiempo, el número de recién llegados es tan grande que la parroquia tiene que reorientarse como una parroquia sirviendo a múltiples grupos[10]. A menudo, esa reorientación es reconocida y afirmada por el obispo local.

Por ejemplo, en una pequeña ciudad del Medio Oeste durante la década de los noventa, un grupo de jóvenes migrantes de tres estados diferentes en el centro de México comenzó un proceso de transformación de All Saints convirtiéndola en una parroquia compartida. En el año 2000, después de algunos años ofreciendo servicios a los hispanos del área, el obispo asignó a un sacerdote mexicano, el Padre Ignacio (Padre Nacho)[11]. Formado en el espíritu de la Nueva Evangelización en un seminario de México, el Padre Nacho llegó y no encontró programas de formación en la fe en español en una parroquia de inmigrantes recién llegados. Todo lo que hizo de ahí en adelante tenía como objetivo educar y formar agentes pastorales. Gracias a estos esfuerzos en particular, All Saints no se convirtió en una parroquia anglo con un ministerio hispano, sino en una parroquia compartida en todo sentido, aproximadamente con el mismo número de familias latinas y euroamericanas. Aunque cada grupo hoy en día acepta la presencia del otro, la negociación de los espacios compartidos, el estacionamiento, los comités y las celebraciones litúrgicas entre los dos grupos sigue siendo una tarea compleja y a veces tensa.

---

9   OSPINO, H., *El ministerio hispano en parroquias católicas*, 62.
10 Véase HOOVER, B.C., *The Shared Parish: Latinos, Anglos, and the Future of U.S. Catholicism*, NYU Press, New York 2014, 18-22.
11 Los nombres de la parroquia y del sacerdote son seudónimos.

No todo el mundo está de acuerdo con la idea que la parroquia compartida es un buen modelo para los hispanos. Algunos teólogos y agentes pastorales se preocupan de que el compartir la parroquia equivalga a una pérdida de ese espacio de «claridad y seguridad» donde los inmigrantes pueden adaptarse de forma segura y paulatina a la vida en los Estados Unidos. A otros les preocupa que el modelo conduzca inexorablemente a la pérdida de prácticas religiosas que son muy apreciadas[12]. Algunos señalan que el modelo de parroquia compartida crea una necesidad de mantener la paz entre las comunidades hispanas y las demás comunidades, y esta necesidad puede crear cierta presión para que los agentes pastorales se abstengan de confrontar aquellas injusticias sociales que mantienen a muchos hispanos pobres y sin poder de decisión. Los agentes pastorales formados en el espíritu de la Nueva Evangelización posiblemente ya evitan involucrarse en estas disputas «políticas». Otros argumentan que los grupos hispanos comparten un espíritu comunitario y sacramental que complementa naturalmente el individualismo y la imaginación más iconoclasta (dialéctica) que tiende a prevalecer en gran parte de la experiencia católica estadounidense, desafiando así sus excesos de manera gentil. La parroquia compartida puede proporcionar un espacio para que esa complementariedad se haga evidente.

Sin embargo, cualquier conversación sobre las parroquias compartidas ha de tener en cuenta las desigualdades en cuanto al poder de decisión dentro de esas comunidades. Es cierto que las parroquias compartidas como All Saints tienen el *potencial* de simbolizar el ideal de *koinonía* (comunión), es decir la visión de aquellos primeros cristianos que venían de distintas épocas y lugares para formar comunidad y participar juntos en la vida divina de la Trinidad. Pero este simbolismo puede ser sólo un sueño ante la distribución desigual e injusta del poder de decisión. Con el deseo de evitar cualquier cambio, los grupos culturales predominantes en las parroquias —muchas veces euroamericanos aunque no siempre— exigen que otros grupos sacrifiquen su idioma, su religiosidad popular u otras costumbres distintivas. La riqueza de las prácticas religiosas que coexisten junto a las celebraciones litúrgicas formales en el contexto de la Semana Santa puede desaparecer ante la presión de procurar la «unidad»[13]. Los grupos considerados minoría son obligados a aceptar una representación sim-

---

12 Véase, por ejemplo, FIGUEROA DECK, A., «Multiculturalism as Ideology», en FIGUEROA DECK, A., TARANGO, Y. y MATOVINA, T. (eds.), *Perspectivas: Hispanic Ministry,* Rowman & Littlefield, Lanham, MD 1995, 32.

13 Ibid.

bólica en el liderazgo de la parroquia. El sentimiento anti-inmigrante o la desazón que surge por los cambios demográficos exacerban estas presiones. Sin embargo, el temor de que tales desigualdades conduzcan a los hispanos a asimilarse de lleno según modelos de vida «anglo» no tienen mucho fundamento. Como señala el Estudio nacional de parroquias católicas con ministerio hispano, «las comunidades hispanas [dentro de las parroquias compartidas] no se transformaron de sus contrapartidas angloparlantes, sino que crecieron junto a ellas. En muchos lugares, después de un tiempo, las comunidades hispanas se hicieron más numerosas y se convirtieron en la fuente de vitalidad para parroquias enteras»[14].

En *Ecclesia in America* el Papa Juan Pablo II invitó a las parroquias en las Américas a convertirse en «comunidades de comunidades» (*Ecclesia in America*, n. 41). Aunque el Papa se refería principalmente a la alienación causada por el fenómeno de enormes parroquias urbanas en Latinoamérica, el modelo que propuso permitía que una pluralidad de grupos y actividades coexistieran y prosperaran en casi cualquier contexto. El modelo valora aquellas experiencias dispersas de vida comunitaria que sólo pueden existir dentro de grupos más pequeños, donde realmente la gente puede encontrarse unos con otros cara a cara. Muchas de las parroquias compartidas en los Estados Unidos con grandes poblaciones hacen un buen trabajo entretejiendo la experiencia de distintos movimientos apostólicos, sociedades y grupos parroquiales diversos, grupos organizados según la edad de los participantes, y diferentes grupos culturales. Cuando los párrocos y los líderes pastorales de estas parroquias convocan a todas las comunidades a hacer suyo un fuerte sentido de misión común que incorpore las diversas experiencias ser católico y desafíe a todos a vivir un discipulado más profundo, tenemos entonces es una verdadera parroquia que es «comunidad de comunidades» según la visión de Juan Pablo II. Tanto la parroquia Queen of Heaven en Los Ángeles como la Parroquia St. Patrick en Lawrence, Massachusetts ilustran este modelo[15]. Ambas son grandes e incluyen múltiples grupos culturales. Queen of Heaven tiene unas siete mil personas que van a once Misas en inglés y en español durante el fin de semana. Una de las Misas se celebra con música litúrgica en tagalo (filipino). El modelo de «comunidad de comunidades» aparece también en algunas parroquias nacionales *de facto* —puesto que mu-

14 OSPINO, H., *El ministerio hispano en parroquias católicas*, 55.
15 Queen of Heaven es un seudónimo, así como el nombre de su sacerdote, Padre Joe.

chas incluyen movimientos apostólicos, grupos y ministerios, y culturas hispanas distintas (mexicanos, guatemaltecos, salvadoreños, puertorriqueños, cubanos, etc.).

Implementar el modelo de comunidad de comunidades no es fácil, pero hay estrategias reconocibles. En la parroquia de St. Patrick en el año 2001, el Padre Paul O'Brien se encontró como líder de una parroquia multicultural en la ciudad más pobre de Nueva Inglaterra. Él entendió que el mejor modelo pastoral era crear un sentido compartido de misión determinado por las preguntas y necesidades de la comunidad local. Para la parroquia St. Patrick estas preguntas y necesidades nacen en medio de tensiones culturales, pobreza, realidades migratorias, violencia, alta movilidad poblacional, bajos niveles educativos y muchos otros desafíos sociales. Para responder a esta realidad, el Padre O'Brien contrató a un director del ministerio hispano, se aseguró de que cada vicario parroquial hablara inglés y al menos uno de los otros idiomas comunes en la comunidad (español y vietnamita), e invirtió en la identificación y retención de líderes pastorales bilingües y biculturales en todos los niveles de la vida parroquial. En el año 2006, con la ayuda de fondos provenientes de fuera de St. Patrick, las comunidades de la parroquia se unieron para construir un comedor público que actualmente sirve alimentos diariamente a más de 500 personas de todas razas y etnicidades durante los siete días de la semana, alrededor de 250.000 comidas al año. De hecho, el comedor público se convirtió en un espacio propicio para que todos los feligreses entendieran que, más allá de las diferencias lingüísticas y culturales, el verdadero amor cristiano se experimenta en el servicio mutuo. Las distintas iniciativas parroquiales abordan con frecuencia temas claves como la inmigración, la crianza de los hijos, el cuidado de la salud, la preparación para la universidad e interrogantes sobre qué hacer cuando una persona se acerca al final de su vida.

3
Los movimientos apostólicos y el liderazgo parroquial

Al igual que el Padre Paul O'Brien en St. Patrick, el Padre Joe, sacerdote de la parroquia Queen of Heaven, comenzó su servicio ministerial evaluando las necesidades pastorales de las varias comunidades parroquiales y trabajó con su equipo pastoral y los feligreses para delinear una misión común que respondiera a sus necesidades al igual que a su identidad. El mismo Padre Joe dedicó su energía a fomentar la participación y la formación de agentes pastorales en todos los rincones de la parroquia, mientras que conscientemente trataba de despistar a cualquier persona que quisiera identificarlo exclusivamente con algún grupo o facción. Una de sus estrategias —como en muchas parroquias que exhiben el modelo de comunidad de comunidades— fue afirmar la presencia significativa presencia de los movimientos apostólicos que ya existían en la parroquia. De hecho, cualquier análisis de la vida parroquial contemporánea de los hispanos en los Estados Unidos debe hacer referencia a los movimientos apostólicos. Los movimientos apostólicos (también conocidos como movimientos eclesiales) son comunidades de bautizados con un sentido profundo de misión, convocadas por un carisma y una espiritualidad compartidas, en su mayoría dirigidas por laicos, a veces inspiradas en las enseñanzas o el ejemplo de sus fundadores conocidos por su personalidad carismática. Dos terceras partes de las parroquias con ministerio hispano tienen grupos de oración arraigados en la espiritualidad de uno de los movimientos[16].

Muchos de estos movimientos, incluyendo los Cursillos de Cristiandad y el Camino Neocatecumenal, se originaron en España después de la guerra y luego se expandieron a Latinoamérica y a los Estados Unidos. Otros como la Renovación Carismática Católica (RCC) surgieron poco después del Concilio Vaticano II en los Estados Unidos o en Latinoamérica. Según el Estudio nacional de parroquias católicas con ministerio hispano, la RCC es el movimiento eclesial con más presencia en las parroquias católicas con ministerio hispano (el 50% de dichas parroquias) y tiene el promedio más grande de simpatizantes entre los hispanos. Mientras que otros movimientos también están presentes en las parroquias hispanas de manera significativa —por ejemplo, los Caballeros de Colón, la Legión de María, los Cursillos de Cristiandad, los Jóvenes para Cristo y el Movimiento Familiar Cristiano— es bueno saber que se han identificado más de un centenar de movimientos distintos, algunos nuevos y locales[17]. Muchos agentes pastorales reconocen que los movimientos tienen una influencia positiva en la participación de los hispanos en actividades espirituales y experiencias organizadas de reflexión sobre la fe. Todos los movimientos promueven prácticas espirituales estructuradas o semiestructuradas que exigen el compromiso de los participantes.

16 OSPINO, H., *El ministerio hispano en parroquias católicas,* 66.
17 Ibid., 65.

Quizás más importante es el hecho que los movimientos han proporcionado oportunidades para que miles de laicos se preparen para ejercer el liderazgo pastoral. El Estudio nacional de parroquias católicas con ministerio hispano señala, por ejemplo, que «la Renovación Carismática Católica… ha jugado un papel fundamental al momento de fomentar vocaciones al liderazgo entre los católicos hispanos. Las parroquias que respondieron identificaron este movimiento apostólico como el más proclive a brindar formación para sus líderes, tiene un sacerdote o un diácono permanente instruido en su espiritualidad que acompaña a sus miembros, e inspira vocaciones al sacerdocio ministerial y a la vida consagrada»[18]. Cada uno de los movimientos tiene amplias estructuras y redes regionales de liderazgo, apoyadas por actividades de formación para el liderazgo. En el pasado, quienes fueron llamados a ejercer liderazgo pastoral como parte de su experiencia en los movimientos tenían poco acceso a educación formal y pocos asumían puestos oficiales de liderazgo en la Iglesia o en la sociedad en general[19]. Pero esto está cambiando. En algunas diócesis, las estructuras de liderazgo y las actividades de formación de los movimientos se coordinan con las estructuras de liderazgo y los procesos de formación parroquiales y diocesanos. En otros lugares, sin embargo, estos todavía operan en gran parte en las márgenes de la influencia parroquial y diocesana. Como resultado, un buen número ha sido acusado de prácticas divisorias en las dinámicas diarias de la vida parroquial, formando incluso estructuras parroquiales paralelas. En ciertos casos esto ha llevado a cismas o a que el obispo local tome medidas restrictivas.

La formación de agentes pastorales en el contexto de los movimientos apostólicos sigue siendo importante ya que las comunidades hispanas a menudo tienen dificultades para asegurar recursos y espacios adecuados que les permitan preparar a sus líderes. Hoy en día, por ejemplo, mientras que entre un 38% y un 40% de los católicos adultos en los Estados Unidos son hispanos[20], sólo el 7.5% de los sacerdotes lo son[21]. Solamente el 15% de los diáconos permanentes son

18 Ibid., 66.
19 Véase RODRÍGUEZ, R., «The Hispanic Community and Movements: Schools of Leadership», en DOLAN, J. y FIGUEROA DECK, A. (eds.), *Hispanic Catholic Culture in the u.s.: Issues and Concerns*, Notre Dame University Press, Notre Dame, IN 1994, 206-239.
20 OSPINO, H., *El ministerio hispano en parroquias católicas*, 57; GRAY, M., et al, *Cultural Diversity in the Catholic Church in the United States*, Center for Applied Research in the Apostolate, Georgetown University, noviembre del 2013, 4, 9.
21 OSPINO, H., *El ministerio hispano en parroquias católicas*, 70. Incluso en una época en la que el número de sacerdotes disminuye, la población católica en general en los Estados Unidos tiene ocho veces más sacerdotes que la población católica hispana. Véase UNITED STATES CONFERENCE OF CATHOLIC BISHOPS, *Encuentro and Mission: A Renewed Pastoral Framework for Hispanic Ministry*, USCCB, Washington, D.C. 2002, n. 67.

hispanos[22]. Y apenas el 9% de los ministros eclesiales laicos son hispanos[23]. Por supuesto, el modelo de ministros laicos profesionales contratados con salarios y beneficios no es tan generalizado en Latinoamérica como lo es en los Estados Unidos, y todavía sigue siendo poco común entre muchos hispanos. Sin embargo, un estudio del Center for Applied Research in the Apostolate (CARA, por su siglas en inglés) indica que sólo el 10.6% de los agentes pastorales parroquiales laicos en los Estados Unidos son hispanos[24]. Sabemos que un número cada vez más grande de laicos hispanos se matriculan en programas de liderazgo ministerial. Nuestra esperanza es que estos agentes pastorales pronto sean bienvenidos y promovidos a posiciones de toma de decisión en las que puedan avanzar la misión evangelizadora de la Iglesia en los Estados Unidos mientras que abogan por las necesidades particulares de los católicos hispanos. Sin embargo, al fomentar la formación de más agentes pastorales laicos hispanos y su promoción en puestos de influencia dentro de la Iglesia, no podemos ignorar el asunto urgente del clero en el ministerio hispano. A pesar de que la comunidad hispana se mueve hacia un estatus de mayoría, muchos seminarios siguen rezagados en la preparación de futuros sacerdotes que puedan servir adecuadamente a los católicos hispanos, especialmente los jóvenes. El resultado es que muchos sacerdotes recién ordenados carecen de habilidades lingüísticas e incluso de un conocimiento básico de las costumbres culturales y de la religiosidad popular hispanas. Estos sacerdotes se encuentran enormemente frustrados y confundidos por su falta de preparación para hacerle frente a esta realidad compleja, y pueden causar daños irreparables al tomar decisiones pastorales de gran trascendencia con un impacto negativo para los católicos hispanos. La misma preocupación aplica a la realidad de los sacerdotes nacidos en Latinoamérica, quienes muchas veces carecen de las competencias interculturales y la formación necesaria para servir a los católicos hispanos —y a otros católicos en el país— en la singularidad del contexto eclesial estadounidense. Necesitamos tener una conversación más definida a nivel nacional sobre esta realidad.

---

22 OSPINO, H., *El ministerio hispano en parroquias católicas*, 74.
23 GRAY, M., «Special Report: Multicultural Ministry», *Emerging Models of Pastoral Leadership Project*, Center for Applied Research in the Apostolate, Washington, D.C., julio del 2012, 14.
24 Ibid., 16.

Hasta ahora hemos analizado varios modelos de vida parroquial hispana. Cada modelo es un esfuerzo, aunque imperfecto, para responder aquí y ahora a un contexto social, cultural y eclesial. Todos estos modelos apuntan a realidades importantes tales como la marginación de los hispanos en sus propias parroquias, la exclusión de parroquias enteras cuando son identificadas como primordialmente hispanas, el papel (y a menudo escasez) del liderazgo, y la importancia de los movimientos apostólicos. Hemos aprendido que la parroquia compartida se ha convertido en una estructura parroquial típica, y que algunas parroquias compartidas exhiben el modelo de «comunidad de comunidades» concebido por Juan Pablo II. También hemos descubierto que la prueba de fuego para cualquier parroquia es la manera en la que facilita el encuentro de los creyentes cristianos de diferentes orígenes culturales y étnicos con el Dios de la Vida a través del misterio de Jesucristo. En esencia, la vida parroquial debe invitar a los católicos hispanos (y a todo otro católico) a una experiencia de *koinonia,* es decir, a entrar en el misterio de nuestro Dios que es Trinidad «a fin de que Dios sea todo en todos» (1Cor 15,28). ¿Qué obstáculos se interponen en el camino de las parroquias hispanas que proporcionan dicha experiencia de vida parroquial, y qué podemos hacer para despejar el camino?

Tal vez el mayor obstáculo que muchos hispanos confrontan en las parroquias compartidas que frecuentan tiene que ver con las relaciones asimétricas de poder de decisión, las cuales varían de ciudad a ciudad, región a región, e incluso están presentes dentro de la misma parroquia. Por ejemplo, es más probable que las parroquias con ministerio hispano se encuentren en sectores urbanos y experimenten dificultades económicas[25]. A pesar de que las parroquias con ministerio hispano crecen a un ritmo mucho más acelerado que el resto de parroquias en el país, la gran mayoría de ellas siguen dominadas por comunidades anglo, con frecuencia con un promedio de edad bastante alto. Incluso en las mismas parroquias con ministerio hispano, la mayoría de los hispanos comparten la parroquia con católicos anglos (aproximadamente 9 de cada 10 parroquias)[26]. En pocas palabras, aunque la comunidad hispana sigue creciendo a un gran rit-

25 Ibid.,19.
26 OSPINO, H., *El ministerio hispano en parroquias católicas,* 62.

mo, las estructuras de poder de decisión aún privilegian decididamente a los católicos anglos. Esto es cierto incluso en las parroquias. Muchas parroquias compartidas operan bajo el supuesto eclesiológico de que la parroquia debe tener un centro cultural y ese centro por lo general es anglo. Las costumbres católicas hispanas y la Eucaristía en español todavía se consideran servicios temporales para los inmigrantes, quienes algún día se asimilarán. Los horarios de Misas más cómodos a menudo favorecen a los anglos. Muchos líderes pastorales anglos reciben un salario y el reconocimiento de su status como ministros eclesiales laicos, mientras que muchos líderes pastorales hispanos siguen siendo voluntarios sin remuneración. Los comités más influyentes en las parroquias (consejo financiero, consejo pastoral, comité de corresponsabilidad) suelen servir los intereses de los feligreses anglos, incluso cuando en muchos casos los hispanos son una mayoría numérica en las parroquias.

196

Es cierto que algunas de estas dinámicas asimétricas de poder son residuos de comunidades eclesiales con un perfil demográfico diferente. Sin embargo, algunas deben ser vistas también como el resultado de privilegios, prejuicios y discriminación raciales. Aun cuando los obispos hacen del ministerio hispano una prioridad, son muchas las historias desconocidas de católicos hispanos que son maltratados, rechazados, marginados o ignorados en sus parroquias. El racismo es evidente en las referencias constantes a personas como «ilegales» o en los estereotipos asociados con la población migrante como «invasores» o manipuladores de los servicios del gobierno[27]. Los resultados son inequívocos: la falta de hospitalidad en la vida parroquial es a menudo citada como un factor central en las altas tasas de deserción entre los católicos hispanos[28]. Dada la larga historia de prejuicios raciales en Latinoamérica y también en el Caribe, no es de extrañar que los mismos hispanos a veces exhiban actitudes fundadas en prejuicios raciales (por ejemplo, es mejor tener un color de piel claro) que se traducen en comportamientos humillantes o en actitudes abiertamente discrimina-

27 Véase HOOVER, B.C., *The Shared Parish,* 210.
28 Un estudio reciente sobre la identidad religiosa de los hispanos en los Estados Unidos reveló que tan solo el 33% de los católicos que ya no se identifican como tal, grupo que a su vez representa aproximadamente un cuarto de todos los latinos en el país, dicen que la Iglesia tiene una actitud bastante acogedora hacia los inmigrantes que acaban de llegar. El 68% de los latinos que se identifican como católicos piensan de manera similar. Véase FUNK, C. y HAMAR MARTÍNEZ, J., «The Shifting Religious Identity of Latinos in the United States», en *Pew Research Center Publications,* 7 de mayo del 2014, recurso *en línea,* http://www.pewforum.org/files/2014/05/Latinos-and-Religion-05-06-full-report-final.pdf (documento visitado el 29 de mayo del 2014).

torias contra otros grupos, incluso contra otros hispanos[29]. Negarse a confrontar el racismo en la Iglesia tiene un costo, y las parroquias compartidas corren el riesgo de reproducir la incapacidad de la cultura en la que vivimos de hacerle frente a realidades de discriminación racial[30]. Como un pueblo llamado a vivir unido en la comunión Trinitaria, la Iglesia tiene que ser mejor.

Para responder a estas experiencias de racismo e inequidad en cuanto al poder de decisión, la vida parroquial hoy en día exige un compromiso renovado de la idea de *hospitalidad* cristiana. La hospitalidad cristiana es más que la simple bondad extendida hacia los extranjeros; es la convicción de que el extranjero es en sí mismo la imagen de Dios y su mensaje: «La presencia inesperada de Dios y de Cristo en acciones hospitalarias y a través de éstas se ve en la hospitalidad de Abraham y Sara ante los mensajeros divinos en el encinar de Mamré y el descubrimiento de Cristo resucitado en la fracción del pan en Emaús (Gn 18,1-15; Lc 24,13-35)»[31]. Si han de ser centros de verdadera *koinonía,* las parroquias católicas deben ser comunidades acogedoras que se destaquen por la integración de los que acaban de llegar, comenzando con aquellos que se inician con regularidad en la fe y los que llegan como parte de los patrones migratorios nacionales e internacionales, al igual que por razones de movilidad cultural y religiosa[32].

Este proceso de hospitalidad e integración será único en diferentes contextos. Un barrio periférico de mayoría hispana, una ciudad históricamente de población blanca en el Sur, o un barrio urbano mixto, cada uno desarrollará un modelo distinto de integración, adecuado a las circunstancias particulares. Sin embargo, uno de los obstáculos perennes para la hospitalidad y la integración en el país es el uso del paradigma de «asimilación». La asimilación presume 1) que los inmigrantes pueden y deben abandonar su cultura original en un período de tiempo relativamente corto, y 2) que la experiencia normativa a la cual un grupo de inmigrantes debe ser asimilado es la cultura euro-americana. Este paradigma presenta serios problemas teológicos: reemplaza los vínculos sacramentales imponiendo la uniformidad cultural como el principio fundamental de uni-

---

29 Véase POZZI, C., «Race, Ethnicity, and Color among Latinos in the United States», en PRIEST, R.J. y NIEVES, A.L. (eds.), *This Side of Heaven: Race, Ethnicity, and Christian Faith,* Oxford University Press, New York 2007, 52-54.

30 Ibid., 59.

31 RUSSELL, L., *Just Hospitality: God's Welcome in a World of Difference,* Westminster/John Knox, Louisville, KY 2009, 19.

32 Para un análisis de las diferentes formas de movilidad que se observan en las congregaciones asociadas a distintas tradiciones religiosas, véase AMMERMAN, N.T., *Pillars of Faith: American Congregations and Their Partners,* University of California Press, Berkeley, CA 2005, 237-253.

dad eclesial. Se niega a reconocer la libertad cultural y existencial de toda persona humana. Pero sus consecuencias prácticas son aún más perjudiciales. Se convence a muchos católicos, incluyendo a muchos hispanos, de que las prácticas católicas o costumbres con raíces latinoamericanas nunca pueden ser normativas. Sin embargo, la identidad católica de la mayoría de los hispanos está íntimamente relacionada con el idioma y la cultura, tal como lo fue para los alemanes y los polacos que llegaron a este país como inmigrantes hace más de un siglo[33]. Incluso en la segunda o tercera generación, la asimilación estricta que no deja espacio para la cultura de los abuelos o de los padres crea divisiones generacionales dolorosas e incluso una pérdida de identidad cultural y religiosa.

5
Espacio seguro e integración eclesial

Para muchos católicos de distintas culturas en los Estados Unidos, la vida parroquial sigue siendo un punto de referencia central para su identidad religiosa y cultural. Especialmente para los hispanos, el acto de buscar un «espacio seguro» dentro de una parroquia compartida o una parroquia nacional infunde confianza y permite la adaptación orgánica de todos los grupos culturales a los cambios demográficos que están transformando la vida parroquial en los Estados Unidos. El «espacio seguro» privilegia la unidad familiar y la preservación de lo mejor del catolicismo tal como lo vivieron en sus culturas de origen. Al mismo tiempo, *la koinonia* exige que encontremos maneras para que todos los grupos culturales reconozcan y experimenten vínculos mutuos como compañeros y peregrinos católicos en el camino cristiano de la fe. La Conferencia de Obispos Católicos de los Estados Unidos ve esto como un proceso de crecimiento espiritual comunitario en medio de la tensión que existe entre la idea de un espacio seguro y la unidad entre las culturas: «Llamamos a este proceso de transformación y crecimiento en el amor *integración/inclusión eclesial*»[34]. Para que esto funcione, cada grupo en la comunidad debe encontrarse como en casa. Esto im-

---

33 Para un análisis completo de esta conversación, véase MATOVINA, T., *Latino Catholicism: Transformation in America's Largest Church,* Princeton University Press, Princeton, NJ 2011, 42-66.

34 COMITÉ SOBRE DIVERSIDAD CULTURAL EN LA IGLESIA, CONFERENCIA DE OBISPOS CATÓLICOS DE LOS ESTADOS UNIDOS, *Mejores prácticas en parroquias compartidas: Para que todos sean uno,* USCCB, Washington, D.C. 2013, 67.

plica que cada grupo tenga el tiempo y el espacio apropiado para vivir la fe católica de acuerdo con los patrones de su propia cultura. Pero también exige planear liturgias periódicas, eventos, reuniones y celebraciones que reúnan a todos los grupos culturales en una experiencia comunitaria de vida parroquial. Esta experiencia comunitaria depende de un fuerte sentido de identidad católica común, haciendo énfasis en símbolos católicos comunes, sacramentos y prácticas de fe, aunque también de un sentido de misión guiado por agentes pastorales que respondan a las preocupaciones específicas de cada parroquia. Siempre que nos reunimos, sabemos que Dios está presente no sólo en nosotros por ser sus creaturas, sino también en el otro, a quien estamos justamente comenzando a entender. Sólo entonces podremos crecer como comunidades de fe unidos por el Reino de Dios, donde «Dios sea todo en todos».

El ministerio hispano y el fenómeno migratorio

Donald Kerwin

El ministerio hispano está a la vanguardia del compromiso de la Iglesia Católica hacia los inmigrantes en los Estados Unidos. Para cumplir con esta responsabilidad, este ministerio debe responder a las necesidades espirituales y materiales de un grupo inmenso y multicultural conformado por personas que se encuentran en distintos momentos de sus vidas, distintas etapas de integración en la nueva nación y distintas situaciones socioeconómicas. Es importante que el ministerio hispano cultive lo que los recién llegados, sus hijos y nietos contribuyen al país, lo mismo que lo que contribuyen aquellos para quienes la experiencia migrante es parte de un pasado distante. Este ministerio debe luchar por el trato justo a los inmigrantes hispanos en la Iglesia y en la sociedad, buscando así fomentar la unidad entre los católicos de todas las tradiciones, orígenes y condiciones sociales. El ministerio hispano debe modelar una renovación eclesial, crear ministerios «incluyentes y abiertos» al igual que «orientados a la misión», y atraer a «todos aquellos a quienes Jesús convoca a su amistad»[1].

1

La magnitud del desafío

La labor del ministerio hispano con los inmigrantes se simplificaría si la gente migrara por la misma razón, pero este fenómeno no se puede explicar en su totalidad con una sola teoría[2]. Algunas teorías sugieren que la migración es el resultado de decisiones individuales que buscan maximizar los salarios o la productividad. Otros ven la migración como una decisión familiar cuya intención es diversificar los recursos colectivos, maximizar las ganancias y minimizar los riesgos. Otros ven la migración como un subproducto inevitable de la globalización o de las necesidades de las naciones ricas. Otras teorías identifican las condiciones que perpetúan la migración, incluidas las redes de migrantes entre los países de origen y destino, el crecimiento del mercado negro y las instituciones benéficas que sirven a los migrantes aunque de muy diversas maneras, y los cambios acumulativos provocados por un historial migratorio que incentiva más migración. Una teoría predice que la migración ha de esperarse naturalmente entre

---

1 PAPA FRANCISCO, *Evangelii Gaudium*, n. 27.
2 Cfr. MASSEY, D.S., ARANGO, J., GRAEME, H., KOUAOUCI, A., PELLEGRINO, A. y TAYLOR, J.D., «Theories of International Migration: A Review and Appraisal», en *Population and Development Review* 19 n. 3 (1993) 431-466.

naciones similares y las naciones vecinas, así como entre aquellas que comparten una historia de intervenciones militares[3].

Recientemente, las migraciones a gran escala hacia los Estados Unidos por parte de niños viajando solos procedentes de Honduras, Guatemala, El Salvador y México ilustran cómo las conexiones profundas entre naciones pueden estimular este fenómeno[4]. Las personas residentes en los Estados Unidos, muchas sin la debida autorización, han mandado a buscar a sus hijos para que puedan escapar del reclutamiento y la violencia de las pandillas que se formaron en Los Ángeles, cuyos miembros han sido deportados en gran número desde la década de los noventas y ahora crean pánico en los países de donde vienen los inmigrantes[5].

La magnitud del desafío que enfrenta el ministerio hispano puede ser ilustrada con datos demográficos. Más de 40 millones de inmigrantes, residentes nacidos en el extranjero, viven en los Estados Unidos. Es el número más grande en la historia de este país, aunque el *porcentaje* de inmigrantes con respecto al resto de la población fue mayor entre los años 1860 y 1930[6]. Cincuenta y tres por ciento de los inmigrantes provienen de Latinoamérica y el Caribe, el 29% de México[7]. Las poblaciones migrantes en los Estados Unidos son extraordinariamente diversas: en cada uno de los últimos 10 años los Estados Unidos ha admitido inmigrantes provenientes de más de 200 naciones[8]. Contando a sus hijos que ya son ciudadanos estadounidenses, las familias inmigrantes latinoamericanas son mucho más jóvenes que aquellas nacidas en el país y la tasa de fertili-

---

3   Ibid., 447-448.

4   Entre el 2009 y el 2014 el número de niños migrantes viajando sin la compañía de sus padres o un adulto que fueron detenidos por funcionarios de la frontera pasó de 19.418 a cerca de 70.000. Véase U.S. DEPARTMENT OF HOMELAND SECURITY, *Southwest Unaccompanied Alien Children*, Washington, D.C. 2014, http://www.cbp.gov/newsroom/stats/southwest-border-unaccompanied-children (documento visitado el 6 de septiembre del 2014).

5   Véase JOHNSON, S., «American Born Gangs Helping to Drive Immigrant Crisis at U.S. Border», en *National Geographic*, 23 de julio del 2014, http://news.nationalgeographic.com/news/2014/07/140723-immigration-minors-honduras-gang-violence-central-america/ (documento visitado el 6 de septiembre del 2014).

6   GRIECO, E.M., ACOSTA, Y.D., DE LA CRUZ, G.P., GAMBINO, C., GRYN, T., LARSEN, L.J., TREVELYAN, E.N. y WALTERS, N.P., *The Foreign-Born Population in the United States: 2010*, U.S. Census Bureau, Washington, DC 2012, 2, http://www.census.gov/prod/2012pubs/acs-19.pdf (documento visitado el 6 de septiembre del 2014).

7   Ibid.

8   Véase U.S. DEPARTMENT OF HOMELAND SECURITY, *Yearbook of Immigration Statistics*, Table 3, Washington, D.C. 2012, https://www.dhs.gov/yearbook-immigration-statistics-2012-legal-permanent-residents (documento visitado el 6 de septiembre del 2014).

dad entre las mujeres nacidas en el extranjero es más alta[9]. Los inmigrantes también se integran en la fuerza laboral en mayor proporción que quienes nacieron en el país[10].

Cincuenta y tres millones de hispanos viven en los Estados Unidos, un 35.5% de ellos nacidos en el extranjero[11]. Se estima que la población hispana de los Estados Unidos crecerá de un modo impresionante en los próximos 50 años. Sin embargo, el porcentaje de hispanos *nacidos en el extranjero* es cada vez menor, disminuyendo un 5% durante la última década[12]. Más del 93% de los hispanos menores de 18 años son ciudadanos estadounidenses de nacimiento[13].

Los hispanos representan el 35% de los católicos en los Estados Unidos, incluyendo un 58% de los católicos entre las edades de 18 y 34 años (los llamados «Generación del milenio»). De todos los católicos en la Generación del milenio que van a Misa, el 67% son hispanos[14]. Como sugieren estas cifras, la vitalidad de la Iglesia Católica y de la nación entera dependerá cada vez más del éxito y el progreso de los inmigrantes hispanos al igual que el de sus hijos y nietos nacidos en los Estados Unidos.

2

*Raíces bíblicas del ministerio hispano y de la enseñanza católica
sobre de los migrantes*

El Antiguo Testamento habla del éxodo del pueblo judío, su exilio, su dispersión y el regreso a la Tierra Prometida[15]. Partiendo de esta experiencia, a Israel se le enseñó a amar al extranjero, a ofrecerle hospitalidad y a practicar la justicia con

9   GRIECO, E.M., ACOSTA, Y.D., DE LA CRUZ, G.P., GAMBINO, C., GRYN, T., LARSEN, L.J., TREVELYAN, E.N. Y WALTERS, N.P., «The Foreign-Born Population in the United States: 2010», 6, 9.

10 Ibid., 17.

11 Véase KROGSTAD, J.M., LÓPEZ, M.H. Y ROHAL, M., «Hispanic Nativity Shift: U.S. births drive population growth as immigration stalls», *Pew Research Center*, Washington, D.C. 2014, http://www.pewhispanic.org/files/2014/04/2014-04_hispanic-nativity-shift.pdf (documento visitado el 6 de septiembre del 2014).

12 Ibid.

13 Véase BROWN, A., «Statistical Portrait of Hispanics in the United States, 2012», Table 10, *Pew Research Center*, Washington, D.C. 2014, http://www.pewhispanic.org/2014/04/29/statistical-portrait-of-hispanics-in-the-united-states-2012/ (documento visitado el 6 de septiembre del 2014).

14 PUTNAM, R.D. Y CAMPBELL, D.E., *American Grace: How Religion Divides and Unites Us*, Simon & Schuster, New York 2010, 299-300.

15 Véase HIMES, K., «The Rights of People Regarding Migration: A Perspective from Catholic Social Teaching», en U.S. CATHOLIC CONFERENCE, *Who Are My Sisters and Brothers: Reflections on Understanding and Welcoming Immigrants and Refugees*, USCC, Washington, D.C. 1996.

esta persona (Lv 19,33). En el Nuevo Testamento Dios «cruza la frontera entre los mundos divino y humano»[16]. María y José no pueden encontrar un espacio en una posada al final de su viaje. Jesús trae luz a los que caminaban en tinieblas (Is 9,1). Los reyes magos siguen la estrella hasta la morada del recién nacido. La Sagrada Familia huye a Egipto bajo el manto de la noche y se convierten en «los modelos y protectores de todos los migrantes, extranjeros y refugiados de todos los tiempos y lugares»[17]. Después de que el rey Herodes muere, no pueden regresar a su hogar y se instalan en Nazaret (Mt 2,22-23).

Durante su ministerio itinerante, Jesús se lamenta de que «los zorros tienen sus cuevas y las aves del cielo sus nidos, pero el Hijo del hombre no tiene dónde reclinar la cabeza» (Lc 9,57-58). Se identifica con el desconocido y enseña que la salvación depende de cómo servimos verdaderamente a los desamparados (Mt 25,35). Él muere para reunir a todos los hijos de Dios que estaban dispersos (Jn 11,52).

San Pablo tiene una experiencia de conversión en el camino a Damasco. Los discípulos se encuentran con el Señor resucitado en el camino a Emaús. Los primeros cristianos se refieren a sí mismos usando la palabra griega *paroikos*, que significa forastero o extranjero residente. Citando la Carta a Diogneto, el Papa Juan Pablo II escribió que los cristianos «viven en su patria, pero como forasteros; participan en todo como ciudadanos y todo lo soportan como extranjeros. Toda tierra extraña es para ellos patria, y toda patria, tierra extraña»[18]. Afirmando su identidad como pueblo peregrino, la Iglesia ha concebido un conjunto importante de enseñanzas sociales sobre la migración, el cual se describe en detalle al final de este capítulo.

3
La necesidad de una reforma migratoria

En El Paso, Texas en el año 2013, una mujer joven con tres hijos ciudadanos estadounidenses relató su saga migratoria. Siete años atrás, su marido fue detenido por exceso de velocidad y deportado por falta de estatus migratorio. Regresó a los Estados Unidos para vivir con su familia, fue detenido y condenado a 10 meses

---

16 Cfr. CAMPESE, G., «The Irruption of Migrants: Theology of Migration in the 21st Century», *Theological Studies* 73, n. 1 (2012) 3-32.

17 PIO XII, *Exsul familia nazarethana*, prólogo.

18 JUAN PABLO II, *Mensaje del Santo Padre para la Jornada Mundial del emigrante*, 1999, n. 2.

de prisión. En su sentencia, el juez advirtió al joven que si volvía a entrar al país, recibiría una sentencia de 70 meses. El hombre regresó, fue arrestado y condenado a una pena de 70 meses, dejando sola a su esposa para criar y mantener a sus tres hijos. Después de cumplir su condena, fue deportado de nuevo.

La joven llegó a los Estados Unidos con sus padres cuando era una niña. Relató que como todo «*dreamer*» («soñador(a)», término que se usa para referirse a inmigrantes que llegaron cuando eran niños pero que carecían de status migratorio legal), la primera de su familia en ser una «soñadora» (en el sentido amplio de soñar) fue su madre[19]. Siempre había soñado que su hija creciera y llegara a «ser alguien». Su hija parecía tener el futuro más prometedor, pero dijo que había perdido la confianza en que este sueño se hiciera realidad.

Su historia no es una excepción. Es difícil encontrar una familia hispana que no haya sido afectada por las fallas del sistema migratorio de los Estados Unidos o un programa de ministerio hispano que no haya tenido que trabajar con familias divididas, la pérdida de potencial, y la presión agobiante que genera esta realidad. Se estima que 11.7 millones de habitantes en los Estados Unidos carecen de estatus migratorio legal[20]. Más de tres cuartas partes de este sector de la población estadounidense provienen de Latinoamérica. El 52% son mexicanos[21]. La realidad de las familias «con estatus migratorio mixto» deja claro que las medidas que buscan aplicar rigurosamente las leyes migratorias de hecho no deportan con exactitud a quienes carecen de estatus legal y a otras personas que no son ciudadanas que también pueden ser deportadas. Dichas medidas afectan invariablemente a familiares ciudadanos que son tanto estadounidenses como residentes permanentes legales. Las personas sin autorización migratoria, a quienes es muy difícil considerarlas como «criminales» en el sentido convencional, incluyen:

---

19 La joven sería elegible para regularizar su estatus legal bajo un proyecto de ley llamado *Development, Relief, and Education for Alien Minors Act* («DREAM Act, en inglés»), es decir «Acta del Sueño», que ofrecería un camino hacia el estatus legal permanente a personas no autorizadas si entraron a los Estados Unidos antes de la edad de 16 años y cumplen con otros requisitos. La ley no cubriría a los esposos de estos beneficiarios.

20 Cfr. WARREN, R. Y WARREN, J.R., «Unauthorized Immigration to the United States: Annual Estimates and Components of Change, by State, 1990 to 2010», en *International Migration Review* 47, n. 2 (2013) 296-329.

21 PASSEL, J., COHN, D. Y GONZÁLEZ-BARRERA, A., «Population Decline of Unauthorized Immigrants Stalls, May Have Reversed», en *Pew Research Center*, Washington, D.C. 2013, 15, http://www.pewhispanic.org/files/2013/09/Unauthorized-Sept-2013-FINAL.pdf (documento visitado el 6 de septiembre del 2014).

- Residentes a largo plazo: un 59% han residido en los Estados Unidos al menos por 10 años y un 20% por 20 años o más[22].
- Padres de familia que viven con 4 millones de niños que son ciudadanos estadounidenses[23].
- Un porcentaje significativo de los 4.4 millones de personas que no han recibido todavía sus visas aprobadas gracias a peticiones familiares[24].
- 2.1 millones de personas que calificarían para estabilizar su estatus legal bajo el «*Dream Act*» (conocida en español como el «Acta del Sueño»)[25].
- La población salvadoreña y otros inmigrantes en la categoría de refugiados que han recibido estatus de protección temporal y han vivido en los Estados Unidos por décadas[26].

En sus primeros cinco años, el gobierno del Presidente Barack Obama deportó aproximadamente a dos millones de personas, casi 1.100 por día. El presupuesto de 18.000 millones de dólares de las agencias del Departamento de Seguridad Nacional de los Estados Unidos (DHS, por sus siglas en inglés), la Oficina de Aduanas y Protección Fronteriza (CBP, por sus siglas en inglés) y el Servicio de Inmigración y Control de Aduanas (ICE, por sus siglas en inglés) supera los niveles de financiación combinados de los cinco principales organismos de seguridad y orden público federales al igual que de las divisiones y organismos laborales federales y estatales[27]. Además, la cifra de 18.000 millones de dólares no incluye los gastos considerables de control migratorio de otros organismos federales, estatales y locales[28].

22 PASSEL, J., LÓPEZ, M.H., COHN, D. y ROHAL, M., «As Growth Stalls, Unauthorized Immigrant Population Becomes More Settled», en *Pew Research Center*, Washington, D.C. 2014, 16, http://www.pewhispanic.org/files/2014/09/2014-09-03_Unauthorized-Final.pdf (documento visitado el 6 de septiembre del 2014).

23 Ibid., 19.

24 Véase BERGERON, C., «Going to the Back of the Line: A Primer on Lines, Visa Categories and Wait Times», en *MPI Issue Brief*, Migration Policy Institute, Washington, D.C. 2013, http://www.migrationpolicy.org/pubs/CIRbrief-BackofLine.pdf (documento visitado el 6 de septiembre del 2014).

25 Véase BATALOVA, J. y MCHUGH, M., «DREAM vs. Reality: An Analysis of Potential DREAM Act Beneficiaries», *Migration Policy Institute*, Washington, D.C., 2010.

26 KERWIN, D., «The Faltering U.S. Refugee Protection System: Legal and Policy Responses to Refugees, Asylum Seekers, and Others in Need of Protection», en *Refugee Survey Quarterly*, Special Edition (2012) 28-29.

27 Cfr. U.S. DEPARTMENT OF HOMELAND SECURITY, FY 2015 *Budget in Brief*, DHS, Washington, D.C. 2014, 49-50, 64, http://www.dhs.gov/sites/default/files/publications/FY15-BIB.pdf (documento visitado el 6 de septiembre del 2014).

28 Véase KERWIN, D., «"Illegal" People and the Rule of Law», en MENJÍVAR, C. y KANSTROOM, D. (eds.), *Constructing Immigrant «Illegality»: Critiques, Experiences, and Responses*, Cambridge University Press, New York 2013).

La expansión de la Patrulla Fronteriza (*Border Patrol*) ha estado acompañada de informes coherentes y fidedignos de abusos contra los migrantes. Más del 10% de los deportados en dos estudios dijeron que habían sido abusados físicamente: un 20% en un estudio y un 6% en otro, aunque este último incluyó a personas que no habían sido deportadas y, por consiguiente no habían estado en contacto con funcionarios oficiales de los Estados Unidos[29]. En cada estudio, el nivel de abuso verbal reportado —calificativos raciales y sexuales, amenazas físicas e insultos variados— estaba en el rango del 25%.

Durante los últimos 25 años ha incrementado el número de delitos que ahora conducen a la deportación mientras que ha disminuido el poder de discreción los jueces de inmigración para permitir que quienes no son ciudadanos permanezcan en los Estados Unidos en función de sus vínculos. Las categorías de personas que no son ciudadanas sujetas a detención obligatoria se han ampliado. Miles de residentes que han vivido en el país por un largo tiempo, incluyendo residentes permanentes legales, han perdido su estatus por delitos menores cometidos en el pasado[30]. Actualmente el Servicio de Inmigración y Control de Aduanas detiene cada año a aproximadamente 500.000 personas que no son ciudadanas[31]. En el año fiscal 2013, los Estados Unidos procesó a cerca de 100.000 personas por delitos relacionados con asuntos migratorios, principalmente por entradas ilegales y reingresos, lo que representa un 40% de todos los procesos criminales a nivel federal[32].

En los últimos años, el Departamento de Seguridad Nacional (DHS, por siglas en inglés) de los Estados Unidos ha incrementado sus alianzas de control migratorio con los gobiernos estatales y locales. El programa de Comunidades Seguras, que monitorea prácticamente a todas las personas arrestadas en los Estados Unidos, compartiendo información con la base de datos del Departamento de Seguridad Nacional que registra violaciones del sistema migratorio,

29 Véase KERWIN, D., «The Gang of Eight and Accountable Border Enforcement», en *The Huffington Post*, 6 de mayo, 2013, http://www.huffingtonpost.com/donald-kerwin/gang-of-eight-immigration-reform_b_3220803.html (documento visitado el 6 de septiembre del 2014).

30 Véase CATHOLIC LEGAL IMMIGRATION NETWORK, INC., *Placing Immigrants at Risk: The Impact of Our Laws and Policies on U.S. Families*, CLINIC, Washington, D.C. 2000, http://cliniclegal.org/sites/default/files/atrisk1.pdf (documento visitado el 6 de septiembre del 2014); AMERICAN BAR ASSOCIATION, COMMISSION ON IMMIGRATION, *American Justice through Immigrants' Eyes*, ABA, Chicago, IL 2004.

31 SIMANSKY, J.F. Y SAPP, L.M., *Immigration Enforcement Actions 2012*, Department of Homeland Security, Washington, D.C. 2013, 5, http://www.dhs.gov/sites/default/files/publications/ois_enforcement_ar_2012_0.pdf (documento visitado el 6 de septiembre del 2014).

32 Véase TRANSACTIONAL RECORDS ACCESS CLEARINGHOUSE, *At Nearly 100,000, Immigration Prosecutions Reach All-time High in FY 2013*, Transactional Records Access Clearinghouse, Syracuse, NY 2013, http://trac.syr.edu/immigration/reports/336/ (documento visitado el 6 de septiembre del 2014).

desanima a que los inmigrantes denuncien delitos o cooperen de otra forma con la policía por temor de ser deportados[33].

Algunos estados han promovido la ciudadanía y han ampliado los derechos y beneficios a los inmigrantes no autorizados para vivir en ellos, incluyendo el pago del costo de matrícula para residentes en las universidades estatales y la obtención de licencias de conducir. Muchas jurisdicciones se han negado a prolongar la detención de personas con violaciones migratorias ordinarias, a pesar de las peticiones de las autoridades federales de inmigración que desean iniciar procesos de deportación. Otros estados, sin embargo, han seguido estrategias que buscan disuadir y desmotivar aplicando las leyes de manera rigurosa, obligando a los inmigrantes no autorizados y a sus familias a «auto-deportarse» al negarles vivienda, trabajo, protección policial, educación, servicios públicos, e incluso la ciudadanía por nacimiento, la cual está garantizada por la Constitución. Varias provisiones que son parte de estas leyes han sido revocadas al afirmar la primacía de las leyes y prerrogativas federales conforme a la Cláusula de Supremacía de la Constitución de los Estados Unidos[34].

4

Principios católicos y estrategias para una reforma

Los obispos católicos de los Estados Unidos dirigen una campaña católica unificada llamada «Justicia para los Inmigrantes», la cual apoya una reforma migratoria integral. La campaña tiene varias dimensiones. Primero, apoya un camino hacia la ciudadanía para un gran porcentaje de la población no autorizada de los Estados Unidos por razón de «mérito» basándose en un historial de empleo, buen carácter y dominio del idioma inglés. También respalda firmemente el *Dream Act* y legislación especial para los trabajadores del campo. Los obispos estadounidenses han instado al gobierno del Presidente Obama a usar su autoridad ejecutiva para proporcionar una excepción provisional a la deportación y a la autorización de trabajo para varias categorías de personas no autorizadas.

33 U.S. DEPARTMENT OF HOMELAND SECURITY, *Homeland Security Advisory Council: Task Force on Secure Communities Findings and Recommendations*, Department of Homeland Security, Washington, D.C. 2014, 24, http://www.dhs.gov/xlibrary/assets/hsac-task-force-on-secure-communities-findings-and-recommendations-report.pdf (documento visitado el 6 de septiembre del 2014).

34 *Arizona v. United States*, 567 U.S., 2012, http://www.supremecourt.gov/opinions/11pdf/11-182b5e1.pdf (documento visitado el 6 de septiembre del 2014).

La posibilidad de un programa de legalización ha movilizado a muchas diócesis a establecer planes para una reforma. Caridades Católicas (*Catholic Charities*) de Dallas Inc. ha diseñado un plan ambicioso para reclutar a 135 abogados *pro bono*, 50 paralegales, 50 voluntarios parroquiales, 30 voluntarios para ayudar con asuntos administrativos y un coordinador de procesos de legalización en cada una de las 30 parroquias que son parte del proyecto. El Departamento de Planeación Pastoral de la diócesis ha proporcionado datos demográficos de las parroquias para esta iniciativa.

Segundo, la campaña de los obispos apoya la reunificación familiar acelerada y la ampliación del número de visas de inmigración por razones familiares. En este momento más o menos dos tercios de las visas permanentes emitidas cada año se conceden a personas que tienen una relación familiar cercana con un ciudadano estadounidense o un residente permanente. Sin embargo, las personas procedentes de países con altos niveles de migración hacia los Estados Unidos que buscan ser admitidos en las categorías migratorias consideradas como de mucha «preferencia» pueden esperar durante varios años antes de que una visa esté disponible para ellos. Durante este tiempo deben vivir ya sea en el extranjero y lejos del familiar que ha hecho la petición o vivir sin estatus legal en los Estados Unidos.

La campaña también apoya el aumento del número de visas disponibles para los trabajadores esenciales, incluyendo aquellos trabajadores «con pocas cualificaciones». De hecho, estos trabajadores pueden carecer de credenciales oficiales pero a menudo son altamente cualificados para trabajar en su área. Los residentes no autorizados constituyen más del 5% de la fuerza laboral de los Estados Unidos y los porcentajes son mucho más altos en ciertas industrias y ocupaciones. Sin embargo, la ley estadounidense ofrece sólo 5.000 visas permanentes por año para los trabajadores «con pocas cualificaciones», un número realmente insuficiente. El fiasco de no poder legalizar el flujo de trabajadores esenciales convierte en «criminales» a personas que están haciendo muchos sacrificios y las pone perversamente a merced de traficantes de personas y empleadores sin escrúpulos, de condiciones migratorias que amenazan sus vidas, y de procedimientos legales severos.

Tercero, los obispos estadounidenses han defendido siempre las políticas firmes de protección de refugiados que permitan a las personas que huyen de situaciones peligrosas alcanzar y asegurar cierto nivel de protección. También afirman políticas que eviten el ingreso de personas que puedan amenazar la seguridad nacional o la seguridad pública. Aunque el sistema de asilo de los Estados Unidos se basa en la habilidad de las personas que viven en situaciones de riesgo de buscar protección, el país bloquea el acceso a su territorio a través de una combinación de medidas de aplicación rigurosa de leyes migratorias y de identificación. También ha creado barreras legales y de procedimiento que afectan los procesos de aplicación al asilo político. Por ejemplo, quienes solicitan asilo deben presentar sus peticiones en el transcurso de un año después de su entrada, una disposición que afecta negativamente a aproximadamente un tercio de todos los solicitantes[35].

Cuarto, la campaña busca que haya mayores garantías en los procesos que afectan a quienes enfrentan procedimientos de deportación. También otorgaría a jueces y funcionarios de inmigración mayor discreción para permitir que las personas se queden en los Estados Unidos por razones familiares u otros vínculos. Como la deportación puede tener consecuencias severas, incluso de vida o muerte, las personas en dicho proceso pueden presentar pruebas, llamar testigos y solicitar exenciones. Sin embargo, el gobierno no proporciona asistencia jurídica gratuita a los inmigrantes que no tienen representación ni tienen los recursos para pagar dicho servicio, lo que reduce significativamente la posibilidad de que sus solicitudes tengan éxito. Por otra parte, tres cuartas partes de quienes son deportados están sujetos a procesos expeditos y sumarios fuera de las cortes[36].

Quinto, la campaña apoya un sistema de aplicación de leyes migratorias que sea eficaz y respete los derechos de las personas involucradas. Se opone a los programas de aplicación de la ley que erosionan la confianza entre las comunidades de inmigrantes y los funcionarios públicos, y que limitan el acceso de los inmigrantes a los hospitales, las escuelas, la policía y otras instituciones al servicio del bien común. También se opone a que se traten las violaciones migratorias menores como delitos. Los obispos católicos de los Estados Unidos consideran las estrategias que buscan disuadir y desmotivar aplicando las leyes de manera rigurosa como una afrenta a la dignidad humana. También se han opuesto vehementemente a propuestas legislativas que convertirían en delito «ayudar»

---

35 SCHRAG, P., SCHOENHOLTZ, A., RAMJI-NOGALES, J. y DOMBACH, J., «Rejecting Refugees: Homeland Security's Administration of the One-Year Bar to Asylum», en *William and Mary Law Review* 52, n. 3 (2010), 688.

36 Véase SIMANSKY, J.F. y SAPP, L.M., *Immigration Enforcement Actions 2012*.

a los inmigrantes no autorizados y por consiguiente criminalizarían ciertas prácticas y expresiones religiosas.

La Iglesia Católica reconoce la autoridad de las naciones para regular políticas migratorias, garantizar procedimientos de admisión ordenada y excluir y deportar a personas cuya presencia amenace el bien común. Las fronteras pueden proteger a los ciudadanos de una nación de la dominación y la opresión. También pueden salvaguardar el derecho a la libre determinación de distintos grupos nacionales y culturales[37]. Sin embargo, la Iglesia también reconoce el derecho de los seres humanos a migrar con el fin de «hacer realidad sus derechos dados por Dios», y enseña que «no se sirve al bien común cuando se va contra los derechos humanos básicos del individuo»[38].

Sexto, los obispos estadounidenses reconocen la necesidad de integrar al número récord de inmigrantes y sus hijos en los Estados Unidos. Más allá de su estatus legal, los inmigrantes necesitan buenas escuelas, trabajos que remuneren dignamente con posibilidades de ascenso, comunidades seguras, y la capacidad de participar en sus comunidades local y nacional. La integración puede aumentar los aportes de los inmigrantes a la economía de los Estados Unidos y a sus comunidades de origen[39].

La Arquidiócesis de Chicago ha delineado un ministerio único a nivel parroquial para hacer realidad las prioridades de las políticas de los obispos católicos de los Estados Unidos y para satisfacer otras necesidades identificadas por las comunidades inmigrantes. Su ministerio de Pastoral Migratoria opera a través de «agentes pastorales» en 55 parroquias hispanas y 11 polacas, las cuales sirven poblaciones numerosas de inmigrantes no autorizados. Desde el año 2009, la *Pastoral Migratoria* ha capacitado a más de 400 líderes laicos siguiendo un proceso riguroso de formación. El ministerio ha referido a 52.000 familias a los servicios relacionados con vivienda, trabajo y violencia doméstica, entre otros. También ha acompañado a aproximadamente 500 familias en centros de deten-

---

37 HOLLENBACH, D., «Migration as a Challenge for Theological Ethics», en *Political Theology*, 12, n. 6 (2011) 809.

38 CONFERENCIA DE OBISPOS CATÓLICOS DE LOS ESTADOS UNIDOS Y CONFERENCIA DEL ESPICOPADO MEXICANO, *Juntos en el camino de la esperanza, ya no somos extranjeros: carta pastoral de los obispos católicos de los Estados Unidos y México sobre la migración*, USCCB, Washington, D.C. 2003, n. 39, http://www.usccb.org/issues-and-action/human-life-and-dignity/immigration/juntos-en-el-camino-de-la-esperanjuntos-en-el-camino.cfm (documento visitado el 6 de septiembre del 2014).

39 KERWIN, D., «Migration, Development and the Right Not to Have to Migrate», en SCRIBNER, T. y APPLEBY, J.K., *On «Strangers No Longer»: Perspectives on the Historic U.S.-Mexican Catholic Bishop' Pastoral Letter on Migration*, Paulist Press, Mahwah, NJ 2013, 155-156.

ción durante procesos de deportación. Sus equipos parroquiales de asistencia legal han liderado iniciativas para legalizar a jóvenes no autorizados, procurar licencias de conducir para residentes del estado sin importar su estatus migratorio, y abogar por una reforma migratoria a nivel federal. Además, más de 200 sacerdotes arquidiocesanos en 150 parroquias participan en iniciativas para educar al público y abogar por causas relacionadas con la realidad inmigrante a través de la organización *Priests for Justice for Immigrants* (Sacerdotes por la Justicia para Inmigrantes). Un grupo paralelo, *Sisters and Brothers of Immigrants* (Hermanas y Hermanos de Inmigrantes) está constituido por 190 religiosas y religiosos de 59 congregaciones religiosas, quienes abogan también por una reforma migratoria.

5

214 *Lecciones y recomendaciones del Proyecto Católico para la Integración de Inmigrantes*

En los últimos cuatro años, representantes de diversos organismos y ministerios católicos se han reunido para considerar si las instituciones católicas, las cuales se formaron para responder a las necesidades de las anteriores generaciones de inmigrantes, pueden intensificar su compromiso colectivo para facilitar la integración y el bienestar de los inmigrantes hoy en día. Algunos de los temas, lecciones y estrategias eficaces que han surgido del proyecto se aplican al ministerio hispano. De hecho, algunos de estos provienen directamente de los programas del ministerio hispano.

Primero, la integración exige cultivar un sentido de comunión entre quienes ya viven aquí y los recién llegados partiendo de los valores universales que ya se encuentran expresados en diversas culturas. La comunión a su vez exige la conversión. Como expresaron los obispos mexicanos y estadounidenses: «La fe en la presencia de Cristo en el migrante, conlleva así a la conversión de corazón y mente, a un espíritu renovado de comunión, y a la construcción de estructuras de solidaridad para acompañar al migrante»[40]. Las parroquias pueden fomentar la conversión, la comunión y la solidaridad haciéndole frente a las tensiones

---

40 CONFERENCIA DE OBISPOS CATÓLICOS DE LOS ESTADOS UNIDOS Y CONFERENCIA DEL ESPICOPA-DO MEXICANO, *Juntos en el camino de la esperanza ya no somos extranjeros*, n. 40.

y preocupaciones que con frecuencia acompañan a la realidad migratoria. Sin embargo, menos de una cuarta parte de los católicos euroamericanos reporta que sus sacerdotes hablan, a menudo o de vez en cuando, sobre temas migratorios[41].

Segundo, las parroquias no deben menospreciar la religiosidad popular y las prácticas culturalmente diferentes como si fueran arcaicas o supersticiosas. Históricamente, las tradiciones y las prácticas religiosas populares han funcionado en las parroquias hispanas «del mismo modo que el lenguaje y la cultura» lo hicieron en las comunidades de inmigrantes europeos[42]. Estas tradiciones pueden servir como puntos de partida para el ministerio hispano en una Iglesia que busca promover la unidad en la diversidad.

Tercero, la Iglesia no será capaz de afirmar su potencial «integrador» a menos que las entidades católicas de hecho integren mejor sus diversos servicios y ministerios. Además, no podrá abogar en favor de la plena dignidad de las personas y promover su desarrollo «integral» sin asociarse con instituciones no católicas[43].

Cuarto, la integración depende del tipo de compromiso que se adquiere: las personas se integran, no las instituciones. Por lo tanto, la Iglesia debe preparar a los inmigrantes, a sus hijos y nietos para ser líderes y evangelizadores. No debe tratarlos como meros «receptores pasivos de la misión de la Iglesia» o «planear» por ellos[44]. Algunos de los modelos pastorales con más éxito combinan la formación de agentes pastorales, la prestación de servicios y la mediación, aunque considerando su misión como evangelización. Estos modelos buscan formar ciudadanos fieles y activos.

Quinto, las instituciones católicas deben hacer un mejor trabajo al servicio de los hispanos y otras comunidades con altos números de inmigrantes. En promedio, los inmigrantes tienen niveles más bajos de educación, menores ingresos familiares e índices de pobreza más elevados que quienes nacieron en el país[45].

---

41 Véase PUBLIC RELIGION RESEARCH INSTITUTE Y BROOKINGS INSTITUTION, *Religion Values, and Immigration Reform Survey*, marzo del 2013 (N=4,465).

42 OSPINO, H., *El ministerio hispano en parroquias católicas: Reporte inicial de los resultados del Estudio Nacional de parroquias católicas con ministerio hispano*, Our Sunday Visitor, Huntington, IN 2015, 55.

43 PABLO VI, *Populorum Progressio*, n. 14.

44 GROODY, D.G., *Globalization, Spirituality and Justice*, Orbis Books, Maryknoll, NY 2007, 184; CONFERENCIA DE OBISPOS CATÓLICOS DE LOS ESTADOS UNIDOS, *Encuentro y misión: Un Marco Pastoral Renovado para el Ministerio Hispano*, USCCB, Washington, D.C. 2002, n. 44.

45 GRIECO, E.M., ACOSTA, Y.D., DE LA CRUZ, G.P., GAMBINO, C., GRYN, T., LARSEN, L.J., TREVELYAN, E.N. Y WALTERS, N.P., «The Foreign-Born Population in the United States: 2010», 16-17, 21.

Al mismo tiempo, tienen menos posibilidades de tener un seguro de salud[46]. Sin embargo, de manera particular los hispanos no se benefician de lleno de las instituciones católicas. Por ejemplo, sólo el 3% de los niños hispanos en edad escolar están matriculados en escuelas católicas a pesar de las «ventajas» educativas y de vida demostrables que estas escuelas ofrecen[47].

Sexto, la segunda y tercera generación de latinos plantean los mayores desafíos y ofrecen el mayor potencial para el ministerio hispano y otras instituciones católicas. Por lo tanto, la inversión de la Iglesia en ellas debe estar de acuerdo con sus necesidades y su importancia para la Iglesia y la sociedad en general. Muchos académicos advierten sobre la «asimilación descendente» de los hijos y nietos de los inmigrantes, refiriéndose a la adopción de algunos de los peores rasgos de la cultura estadounidense. Sin embargo, los jóvenes también pueden ser una fuente de liderazgo en la comunidad católica y están en mejor posición para desempeñar este papel. No sólo sus perspectivas hacia quienes han migrado recientemente a la nación son más positivas, sino que también son mucho más diversos[48].

En Nogales, Arizona, los estudiantes de la escuela católica de Nuestra Señora de Lourdes han puesto en marcha el club *Kino Teens*, el cual se dedica a servir a los migrantes deportados que se quedan en el Centro para Migrantes Deportados, parte de la Iniciativa Fronteriza Kino (*Kino Border Initiative*), en Nogales, Sonora. *Kino Teens* también educa a otros jóvenes sobre lo que la Doctrina Social de la Iglesia enseña en cuanto al tema de la migración y aboga por una reforma migratoria. La experiencia directa con los hombres, mujeres y niños migrantes los inspira a evangelizar a otros jóvenes sobre este fenómeno tan humano, aunque polémico.

Séptimo, la Iglesia debe releer la historia de las instituciones que sirvieron con éxito a las generaciones anteriores de inmigrantes. En la primera parte de los años 1930s, por ejemplo, algunas diócesis católicas, comunidades religiosas y universidades comenzaron a establecer escuelas laborales para trabajadores con

---

46 Ibid., 20.

47 Véase THE NOTRE DAME TASK FORCE ON THE PARTICIPATION OF LATINO CHILDREN AND FAMILIES IN CATHOLIC SCHOOLS, *To Nurture the Soul of a Nation: Latino Families, Catholic Schools, and Educational Opportunity*, University of Notre Dame, 12 de diciembre del 2009, http://issuu. com/aceatnd/docs/nd_ltf_report_final_english_12.2?e=6668647/6985560 (documento visitado el 6 de septiembre del 2014).

48 Véase PUBLIC RELIGION RESEARCH INSTITUTE y BROOKINGS INSTITUTION, *Religion Values, and Immigration Reform Survey*.

bajos salarios. Estas escuelas buscaban preparar a los trabajadores para participar en sindicatos, enseñándoles procedimientos parlamentarios, oratoria, economía y derecho laboral. También enseñaban conceptos fundamentales de la Doctrina Social de la Iglesia y trataron de inculcar en los trabajadores un sentido del trabajo como vocación religiosa. Hacia los años 1940s, distintas entidades eclesiales patrocinaban más de 150 escuelas laborales. La Iglesia debe revitalizar su compromiso con la justicia laboral en respuesta a las necesidades de los inmigrantes y de otras personas en trabajos peligrosos, mal remunerados y con altas tasas de violaciones de las normas laborales.

6

Una reflexión sobre la injusticia y la comunión

El 24 de mayo del 2001, la Patrulla Fronteriza encontró cuatro migrantes errantes al este de Yuma, Arizona, en el Refugio Nacional de Vida Salvaje de Cabeza Prieta. Los cuatro se habían separado de un grupo de 26 que habían venido de los estados mexicanos de Guerrero y Veracruz. Los coyotes (contrabandistas de personas) les habían mentido sobre cuán lejos era necesario caminar y les habían indicado que llevaran sólo un galón de agua por persona. El grupo estaba tratando de cruzar el desierto bajo una temperatura de 115 grados Fahrenheit (46 grados centígrados). Durante las siguientes 24 horas los equipos de búsqueda y rescate encontraron el resto en seis grupos pequeños, 14 habían muerto y el resto estaban a punto de morir. Mario Castillo, de 25 años de edad, padre de un niño de cuatro años y de una niña de dos años, salió del pueblo de Cuatro Caminos en Veracruz. Ganaba 35 pesos al día trabajando en las plantaciones de café y cítricos. Tenía la esperanza de encontrar un trabajo en los Estados Unidos que le permitiera terminar la construcción de la casa de bloque para su familia.

El año anterior yo había investigado y escrito un informe sobre la región fronteriza titulado: *El caos en la frontera entre los Estados Unidos y México: Un informe sobre las muertes entre migrantes, las familias inmigrantes y los trabajadores remunerados injustamente*[49]. Más tarde lamenté el uso de la palabra «caos» en el títu-

49 Véase KERWIN, D., *Chaos on the U.S.-Mexico Border: A Report on Migrant Crossing Deaths, Immigrant Families and Subsistence-Level Laborers*, CLINIC, Washington, D.C., 2000, http://www.lexisnexis.com/practiceareas/immigration/pdfs/web305.pdf (documento visitado el 6 de septiembre del 2014).

lo del reporte, no porque la frontera no fuera caótica. Supimos de migrantes que quedan separados de sus hijos en el desierto, que mueren al tratar de cruzar la frontera (una atrocidad que no ha disminuido), mujeres que dan a luz en los ranchos, y mujeres mexicanas que trabajan en las maquilas (plantas de ensamblaje) que entregan a sus bebés en adopción a través de canales informales. Nos enteramos de violaciones de los derechos humanos por parte de la Patrulla Fronteriza, el uso de fuerza letal contra personas que tiran piedras, y el trato abusivo por parte de funcionarios en los puertos de entrada —condiciones que todavía persisten[50].

Sin embargo, también descubrimos redes bien organizadas de abuso y explotación que estaban lejos de ser caóticas. Documentamos índices alarmantes de criminalidad, los cuales por lo general no eran causados por los migrantes. Uno podía dibujar un mapa e identificar, por ejemplo, dónde estaban robando y violando a los migrantes y dónde morían grandes números de ellos en su viaje hacia el norte. Todavía se puede dibujar ese mapa[51]. Conocimos a campesinos de Méjico que no podían ganarse la vida como consecuencia del Tratado de Libre Comercio de América del Norte (TLCAN en español, NAFTA en inglés) y decidieron unirse al grupo de trabajadores de camino hacia los Estados Unidos. Un campesino anciano habló con nostalgia de su época en el criticado Programa Bracero, el cual veía favorablemente al compararlo con su realidad laboral durante los siguientes años. Entrevistamos a dueños de ranchos cuyas tierras habían sido destrozadas por los traficantes de personas. Hablamos con familias estadounidenses que no se habían recuperado de la deportación de esposos y padres de familia después de ser sorprendidos conduciendo bajo el influjo del alcohol. Visitamos familias en las colonias (barrios sin personalidad jurídica) que pagaban cuotas una y otra vez sin amortizar capital sobre sus casas modestas y aisladas. Conocimos a mujeres de mediana edad cuyas posibilidades de progreso en su vida se habían reducido de manera irreversible desde el momento en que sus antiguos trabajos en fábricas se trasladaron al extranjero. Revisamos talones de pago que combinaban el sueldo de dos trabajadores campesinos con el fin de enmascarar prácticas de remuneración laboral que no llegaban siquiera a un salario mínimo.

50 KERWIN, D., «A Bipartisan Attempt to Restore Credibility to the U.S. Border Enforcement System» en *The Huffington Post*, 28 de marzo del 2014, http://www.huffingtonpost.com/donald-kerwin/a-bipartisan-attempt-to-r_b_5044761.html (documento visitado el 6 de septiembre del 2014).
51 Véase FOOTE, J. y SMALL, M., *Persistent Insecurity: Abuses against Central Americans in Mexico*, Jesuit Refugee Service, Washington, D.C. 2013, https://www.jrsusa.org/assets/Publications/File/Persistent_Insecurity.pdf (documento visitado el 6 de septiembre del 2014).

Conocimos a migrantes que sabiendo los riegos para sus vidas, los aceptaron deliberadamente para procurar un futuro mejor para sus familias; personas que dependían totalmente de su fe como apoyo durante sus viajes difíciles; voluntarios con espíritu humanitario que conducían y caminaban durante horas para llevar agua y ocuparse de las necesidades de los migrantes en peligro; agentes de la Patrulla Fronteriza en misiones de búsqueda y rescate con la convicción de que estaban allí «por la gracia de Dios»; comunidades de fe que servían a inmigrantes detenidos, a migrantes no acompañados, y a otros que consideraban hermanas y hermanos; hospitales que abrieron sus puertas a indigentes y a personas en peligro de ambos países; grupos de apoyo de mujeres (con sus hijos a cuestas) cuyos maridos habían sido deportados; abogados defensores y un sinnúmero de personas que habían dedicado su vida al servicio y a la justicia. Encontramos una comunidad luchando de una manera profunda con conceptos como hospitalidad, justicia, dignidad, familia humana, soberanía, fronteras, estado de derecho, ciudadanía, globalización, diversidad y subsidiariedad.

Haciéndole eco a la tradición profética, una declaración reciente de las comunidades de fe en la frontera denunció las injusticias evidentes en la región y anunció una nueva visión enraizada en los valores y la fuerza de «familias, comunidades religiosas, asociaciones cívicas, barrios, colonias y ciudades»[52]. Estos líderes religiosos conciben la frontera como un lugar de encuentro, no de división. Afirmaron que «Dios cruza las fronteras, acompañándonos —especialmente a los pobres y marginados— dondequiera que vayamos» y se comprometieron a trabajar para crear un «lugar de reunión para los hijos dispersos de Dios, donde los residentes y visitantes en toda su diversidad pudieran trabajar juntos en la construcción de la familia humana»[53]. Así también el ministerio hispano debe, en su servicio a los inmigrantes, cruzar las fronteras entre los que nacieron en diversos grupos nacionales y culturales, entre los que nacieron en el país y los recién llegados, entre los inmigrantes y las segundas y terceras generaciones, entre jóvenes y viejos, y entre los nuevos ministerios y las instituciones creadas para las generaciones anteriores. El ministerio hispano debe crear el espacio sagrado donde la Iglesia en toda su riqueza y diversidad pueda construir la familia humana.

---

52 BORDER NETWORK FOR HUMAN RIGHTS, «The New Ellis Island: Visions from the Border for the Future of America», BNHR, El Paso, TX, 2013, 17, http://www.scribd.com/doc/140208614/The-New-Ellis-Island-Visions-from-the-border-for-the-future-of-America (documento visitado el 6 de septiembre del 2014).
53 Ibid., 23.

El Papa Francisco ha propuesto la poderosa idea de ver a los migrantes y refugiados como fuente de unidad, describiéndolos como «una ocasión que la Providencia nos ofrece para contribuir a la construcción de una sociedad más justa, una democracia más plena, un país más solidario, un mundo más fraterno y una comunidad cristiana más abierta, de acuerdo con el Evangelio»[54]. Esta visión anima el concepto de «pastoral de conjunto» que ha inspirado el crecimiento del ministerio hispano[55]. Se nos llama a caminar juntos para hacer lo que está a nuestro alcance y para unirnos profundamente en nuestro viaje espiritual de camino a nuestro destino final con Dios.

7

Apéndice

7.1. TEMAS DE LA DOCTRINA SOCIAL DE LA IGLESIA SOBRE LOS MIGRANTES Y LOS RECIÉN LLEGADOS

Los políticos y la prensa hacen referencia constante a los «asuntos» y al «debate» sobre la inmigración. Los académicos estudian la migración a través de los prismas de la globalización, la soberanía, la identidad nacional, la demografía, el desarrollo económico, los mercados de trabajo, el sentido de pertenencia y la integración. Los políticos y los grupos de expertos exploran una manera eficaz de «manejar» la migración. La Iglesia cree que estas perspectivas tienen mérito, pero enseña que «en el vasto campo de las migraciones internacionales es preciso poner siempre en el centro a la persona humana»[56].

En gran parte, la Iglesia ve el tema de la migración desde la perspectiva de derechos y responsabilidades. El Papa Benedicto XVI citó con aprobación a Gandhi cuando señaló que «el Ganges de los derechos desciende del Himalaya de los

---

54 Véase PAPA FRANCISCO, *Emigrantes y refugiados: Hacia un mundo mejor*, Mensaje del Santo Padre para la Jornada Mundial del Emigrante y del Refugiado 2015, http://w2.vatican.va/content/francesco/es/messages/migration/documents/papa-francesco_20130805_world-migrants-day.html (documento visitado el 10 de enero del 2016).

55 CONFERENCIA DE OBISPOS CATÓLICOS DE LOS ESTADOS UNIDOS, *Encuentro y misión*, n. 19-20.

56 Véase BENEDICTO XVI, *Angelus*, Mensaje del Santo Padre para la Jornada Mundial del Emigrante y del Refugiado 2007, http://w2.vatican.va/content/benedict-xvi/es/messages/migration/documents/hf_ben-xvi_mes_20061018_world-migrants-day.html (documento visitado el 6 de septiembre del 2014).

deberes»[57]. La enseñanza católica sostiene que las naciones tienen la responsabilidad de crear las condiciones que permitan a sus miembros prosperar y hacer realidad los derechos que Dios les ha dado en el contexto de sus comunidades de origen. Sin embargo, cuando las naciones no pueden cumplir con esta responsabilidad, sus miembros tienen el derecho y la responsabilidad de buscar condiciones conformes a la dignidad humana, en particular cruzando fronteras. Las naciones también tienen la responsabilidad de recibir a los migrantes quienes, junto con las «poblaciones locales que los acogen… tienen el mismo derecho a gozar de los bienes de la tierra, cuya destinación es universal»[58]. Los inmigrantes, a su vez, tienen el derecho y la responsabilidad de contribuir al bien de sus nuevas comunidades.

Muchos consideran el tema de los derechos como una realidad en la que no hay ganadores ni perdedores: creen que afirmar los derechos de los inmigrantes causa detrimento al bienestar de las poblaciones locales. El «bien común» se refiere a las condiciones que permiten prosperar y vivir una vida digna a todas las personas de una comunidad, incluidos los que no tienen estatus migratorio. Tal como los obispos católicos de los Estados Unidos declararon en 1986: «Contradice el bien común y es inaceptable tener dos sociedades paralelas, una visible con derechos y otra invisible sin derechos —clandestina y sin voz, de personas indocumentadas»[59].

Los derechos contribuyen al bien común, pero no agotan las condiciones que permiten prosperar a las personas[60]. Estos establecen las «condiciones mínimas» para la dignidad humana[61]. La enseñanza católica fundamenta los derechos en los valores del Evangelio y exige una respuesta más allá de la protección de los derechos. Nos llama a amar a nuestro prójimo, a actuar con justicia y a practicar la hospitalidad.

57 BENEDICTO XVI, *Mensaje del Santo Padre para la celebración de la XL Jornada Mundial de la Paz*, http://w2.vatican.va/content/benedict-xvi/es/messages/peace/documents/hf_ben-xvi_mes_20061208_xl-world-day-peace.html (documento visitado el 6 de septiembre del 2014).

58 Véase BENEDICTO XVI, *Una sola familia humana*, Mensaje del Santo Padre para la Jornada Mundial del Emigrante y del Refugiado 2011, http://w2.vatican.va/content/benedict-xvi/es/messages/migration/documents/hf_ben-xvi_mes_20100927_world-migrants-day.html (documento visitado el 6 de septiembre del 2014).

59 CONFERENCIA DE OBISPOS CATÓLICOS DE LOS ESTADOS UNIDOS, *Justicia económica para todos* USCCB, Washington, D.C. 1986, n. 10.

60 BENEDICTO XVI, *Encuentro con los miembros de la Asamblea General de las Naciones Unidas*, 2008, http://w2.vatican.va/content/benedict-xvi/es/speeches/2008/april/documents/hf_ben-xvi_spe_20080418_un-visit.html (documento visitado el 6 de septiembre del 2014).

61 CONFERENCIA DE OBISPOS CATÓLICOS DE LOS ESTADOS UNIDOS, *Justicia económica para todos*, n. 17-18, 79.

La solidaridad es la virtud que hace posible que el bien común se haga realidad. El Papa Juan Pablo II definió la solidaridad como «la *determinación firme y perseverante* de empeñarse por el *bien común*; es decir, por el bien de todos y cada uno, para que todos seamos verdaderamente responsables de todos»[62]. El desafío es reconocer a «cualquiera que tenga necesidad de mí y a quien yo pueda ayudar» como prójimo[63].

La inmigración puede generar un temor al desplazamiento cultural y a la pérdida de la identidad nacional. Sin embargo, la Iglesia considera la cultura como el lugar de las esperanzas y los valores más profundos de las personas, el espacio donde la fe se arraiga y se expresa. La Iglesia está convencida de que la migración crea una oportunidad para procurar una unidad basada en los valores compartidos que se encuentran en las diversas culturas[64], pero ninguna cultura es «permanente o perfecta» y por consiguiente cada cultura necesita ser «mejorada y evangelizada»[65].

Muchos creen que las naciones tienen autoridad absoluta para determinar quién entra, quién se queda y quién se va. La enseñanza católica reconoce la autoridad y la responsabilidad del Estado para regular la inmigración, pero matiza esta autoridad. Para la Iglesia, el propósito de las naciones —individual y colectivamente— es proteger los derechos humanos, promover el bien común y seguir «los dictámenes de la ley natural y de la ley divina»[66]. Los obispos estadounidenses y mexicanos reconocieron tanto «el derecho de un Estado soberano a controlar sus fronteras para promover el bien común» como «el derecho que tienen las personas de migrar para gozar de los derechos que poseen como hijos de Dios»[67]. Sin embargo, concluyeron que no se sirve al bien común «cuando se va contra los derechos humanos básicos del individuo»[68].

Una antigua característica de los movimientos anti-inmigrantes ha sido tratar a los migrantes como chivos expiatorios y culparlos de los grandes problemas sociales o, en términos teológicos, de los pecados comunitarios de la socie-

---

62 JUAN PABLO II, *Sollicitudo rei socialis*, n. 38.

63 BENEDICTO XVI, *Deus caritas est*, n. 15.

64 KERWIN, D., «Crossing the Divide: Foundations of a Theology of Migration and Refugees», en KERWIN, D. y GERSCHUTZ, J.M. (eds.), *And You Welcomed Me: Migration and Catholic Social Teaching*, Lexington Books, Lanham, MD 2009, 99-100.

65 CONFERENCIA DE OBISPOS CATÓLICOS DE LOS ESTADOS UNIDOS, *Acogiendo al forastero entre nosotros: Unidad en la diversidad*, USCCB, Washington, D.C. 2000, n. 28.

66 «Sovereignty», en *New Catholic Encylopedia*, 2ⁿᵈ ed., Thomson Gale, Detroit, MI 2002, 371.

67 CONFERENCIA DE OBISPOS CATÓLICOS DE LOS ESTADOS UNIDOS y CONFERENCIA DEL EPISCOPADO MEXICANO, *Juntos en el camino de la esperanza ya no somos extranjeros*, n. 39.

68 Ibid.

dad. Quienes enfatizan radicalmente la primacía de las poblaciones locales tratan de marcar y estigmatizar a los inmigrantes, haciéndolos «vulnerables al control, la manipulación y la explotación»[69]. Estereotipos negativos como «inmigrante ilegal» o «extranjero criminal» (*«criminal alien»* en inglés) desdicen de la dignidad de hijos de Dios que poseemos todos los seres humanos. Más allá de sus consecuencias perjudiciales a nivel político y social, también pueden causar que los inmigrantes internalicen una visión sacrílega y escandalosa de sí mismos. Los testimonios de migrantes resaltan dicho efecto lacerante[70]. Para la Iglesia Católica, los hijos de Dios no pueden ser «ilegales» y los inmigrantes no pueden ser «extranjeros» en una nación y en una comunidad eclesial de inmigrantes. Para los creyentes las distinciones entre las personas disminuyen en importancia y desaparecen por completo (Ga 3,26-28).

La Iglesia enseña que las personas y las sociedades tienen la responsabilidad de restaurar la membresía plena en la familia humana a quienes sus derechos han sido violados o puestos en entredicho y «darles la posibilidad de participar en el bien común»[71]. Esta responsabilidad se conoce como la «opción preferencial por los pobres». Desde una perspectiva pastoral, la «opción preferencial» busca proclamar el Evangelio de maneras que revelen el amor de Dios a los pobres, «cuando gran parte de lo que experimentan a diario es la negación del amor»[72].

Algunos ciudadanos argumentan que se necesitan estrategias que apliquen la ley sin tolerancia alguna para restablecer el estado de derecho en el sistema de inmigración. Estas personas apoyan leyes que buscan disuadir y desmotivar, diseñadas para obligar a los inmigrantes a marcharse al negarles los medios básicos para subsistir mientras se criminaliza el ejercicio de sus derechos. Irónicamente, esas leyes exponen a los inmigrantes a niveles más altos de criminalidad que también ponen en peligro al resto de la comunidad. Exigir la aplicación intolerante de leyes cada vez más estrictas y más punitivas refleja una mentalidad «farisaica». Los fariseos y los saduceos trataron continuamente de presentar a Jesús como un transgresor de la ley, mientras endurecían sus corazones ante su mensaje.

69 GROODY, D.G., «Crossing the Divide: Foundations of a Theology of Migration and Refugees», en KERWIN, D. y GERSCHUTZ, J.M. (eds.), *And You Welcomed Me*, 3.

70 DE LA TORRE, M.A., *Trails of Hope and Terror: Testimonies on Immigration*, Orbis Books, Maryknoll, NY 2009, 46-47.

71 GROODY, D.G., *Globalization, Spirituality and Justice*, 110.

72 Ibid., 184.

Muchos católicos, incluidos aquellos que pregonan su fidelidad a la Iglesia, evocan el uso del «juicio prudente» para señalar su buena fe y al mismo tiempo su desacuerdo leal con las políticas públicas de los obispos católicos de los Estados Unidos sobre el tema de la inmigración. La doctrina católica define la prudencia como la virtud que permite a las personas «discernir en cada circunstancia el verdadero bien y elegir los medios adecuados para llevarlo a cabo»[73]. Los obispos han fundamentado sus principios sobre la reforma migratoria en las Escrituras, la Revelación, el derecho natural y varias cartas encíclicas. Es difícil concebir un argumento católico prudente o convincente en favor de la criminalización de los migrantes, la separación de las familias, o hacerle la vida tan imposible a quienes no son ciudadanos para obligarles a marcharse.

73 PONTIFICIO CONSEJO «JUSTICIA Y PAZ», *Compendio de la doctrina social de la Iglesia*, 2006, n. 547, http://www.vatican.va/roman_curia/pontifical_councils/justpeace/documents/rc_pc_just peace_doc_20060526_compendio-dott-soc_sp.html (documento visitado el 6 de septiembre del 2014).

El ministerio hispano y el acompañamiento pastoral de las nuevas generaciones de adolescentes latinos

LYNETTE DE JESÚS-SÁENZ Y KEN JOHNSON-MONDRAGÓN

Cuando se celebró el Primer simposio nacional de ministerio católico hispano en Boston College en el año 2009, la presente realidad era más que evidente: «los jóvenes latinos ya constituyen la mitad de los católicos menores de 18 años en los Estados Unidos, y el pueblo latino constituirá la mayoría de la población católica en menos de 40 años»[1]. Durante los últimos cinco años la población adolescente latina estadounidense ha incrementado un 16% mientras que el número de sus compañeros blancos ha disminuido un 7%[2]. Entre los católicos adolescentes hoy en día, los hijos de los inmigrantes hispanos son el segmento poblacional que crece más rápido. Debido al tamaño y crecimiento continuo de la población hispana joven, es motivo de gran preocupación para la Iglesia Católica que solo el 6% de los adolescentes católicos hispanos en el año 2003 (los últimos datos disponibles) participaban en un grupo juvenil durante más de dos años y solo el 3% ejercían su liderazgo con otros adolescentes en programas de pastoral con adolescentes —comparados con el 14% y el 7%, respectivamente, de los adolescentes católicos blancos[3].

Este capítulo incorpora observaciones e ideas que vienen de la experiencia pastoral y de investigaciones sociológicas pertinentes para examinar el desafío de comunicar una fe viva a las nuevas generaciones de adolescentes latinos. Explorará cómo su experiencia de vida afecta significativamente su participación en actividades de fe y en última instancia forma su identidad católica latina. Luego presentará seis enfoques pastorales que han sido probados para fomentar la fe entre los adolescentes latinos. Todo esto sugiere caminos hacia el desarrollo de un ministerio con adolescentes latinos que es sensible a sus necesidades pastorales y reconoce el don que son para la Iglesia.

Mucho ya se ha escrito sobre los factores que impiden la participación de los jóvenes católicos hispanos en la pastoral y los programas de formación en la fe[4].

---

1   JOHNSON-MONDRAGÓN, K., «El ministerio hispano y la pastoral juvenil hispana» en OSPINO, H. (ed.), *El ministerio hispano en el siglo XXI: presente y futuro,* Convivium Press, Miami 2010, 320.

2   U.S. CENSUS BUREAU, *Population by Age, Sex, Race, and Hispanic Origin,* bases de datos nacionales entre el 1 de julio del 2009 y el 1 de diciembre del 2013.

3   JOHNSON-MONDRAGÓN, K., «Youth Ministry and the Socioreligious Lives of Hispanic and White Catholic Teens in the U.S.», en INSTITUTO FE Y VIDA, *Perspectives on Hispanic Youth and Young Adult Ministry,* n. 2, Instituto Fe y Vida, Stockton, CA 2005, 7.

4   Véase JOHNSON-MONDRAGÓN, K., «Welcoming Hispanic Youth/Jóvenes in Catholic Parishes and Dioceses», en INSTITUTO FE Y VIDA, *Perspectives on Hispanic Youth and Young Adult Ministry,* n. 1, Instituto Fe y Vida, Stockton, CA 2003; DE JESÚS-SÁENZ, L., «Church and Youth Ministry Participation: Creating a Welcoming Environment for Latino/a Teenagers» en JOHNSON-MONDRAGÓN, K. (ed.), *Pathways of Hope and Faith Among Hispanic Teens,* Instituto Fe y Vida, Stockton, CA 2007, 81-112; JOHNSON-MONDRAGÓN, K. Y CERVANTES, C.M., «Las dinámicas de cultura, fe y familia en la vida de los adolescentes hispanos, y sus implicaciones para la pastoral con adoles-

Mientras que éste no es el enfoque de este capítulo, una sinopsis de algunos de los factores que contribuyen a disminuir su compromiso en actividades religiosas nos permite delinear el contexto para la reflexión más adelante. He aquí descripciones breves de cuatro de las razones más comunes:

- *Idioma.* Las conexiones entre la fe y el idioma son profundas y la verdad es que muchas familias hispanas hoy en día están divididas a nivel lingüístico: la generación mayor habla más español y la generación más joven habla más inglés. En este caso, las opciones para orar en familia, ir a Misa, recibir catequesis y participar en programas de pastoral con adolescentes están acompañadas de posibles conflictos, variedad de recursos y agendas que generalmente compiten, sin respuestas fáciles para los padres o los líderes pastorales.

- *Calidad de acogida.* Muchas comunidades hispanas comparten la parroquia con otra comunidad étnica, usualmente la comunidad angloparlante que todavía predomina en muchas partes. No es infrecuente que el ministerio con adolescentes anglos tenga personal contratado y recursos abundantes mientras que los hispanos tienen que contentarse con voluntarios y actividades para recaudar fondos[5]. A nivel individual, los adolescentes hispanos con frecuencia se sienten criticados o juzgados por parte de los adultos e incluso otros adolescentes por la manera como se ven o se visten. Esta clase de prejuicio aleja sobre todo a los adolescentes latinos que más necesitan el apoyo de las actividades eclesiales.

- *Desconfianza pastoral.* Muchos adolescentes latinos están privados de la posibilidad de participar y ocupar posiciones de liderazgo. Perciben que los adultos en la comunidad no confían en ellos o no reconocen los talentos que traen. Quieren participar y servir, sin embargo los líderes con frecuencia son un obstáculo o solo les permiten hacer tareas mínimas como limpiar después de los eventos parroquiales.

- *Dinámicas culturales.* Las diferencias generacionales y culturales entre los padres de familia hispanos y sus hijos pueden dificultar la transmisión de la fe

centes», en INSTITUTO FE Y VIDA, *Perspectivas sobre la Pastoral Juvenil Hispana*, n. 5, Instituto Fe y Vida, Stockton, CA 2008; NATIONAL CATHOLIC NETWORK DE PASTORAL JUVENIL HISPANA - LA RED, *Conclusiones: Primer Encuentro Nacional de Pastoral Juvenil Hispana*, PENPJH, USCCB, Washington, D.C. 2008, 19-24; y MATOVINA, T., *Latino Catholicism: Transformation in America's Largest Church*, Princeton University Press, Princeton, NJ 2011, 219-244.

5 OSPINO, H., *El ministerio hispano en parroquias católicas: Reporte inicial de los resultados del Estudio Nacional de parroquias católicas con ministerio hispano*, Our Sunday Visitor, Huntington, IN 2015, 85. Esto se menciona también en HOOVER, B.C. y OSPINO, H., «El ministerio hispano y la vida parroquial» en este volumen.

a los hijos. En algunos lugares la misma parroquia es poco acogedora o se siente extraña para los padres de familia inmigrantes. Estos padres de familia con frecuencia carecen del marco de referencia para relacionarse con la experiencia de su hijo/a aquí, mientras que el adolescente latino nacido en los Estados Unidos se siente presionado por sus padres a continuar practicando tradiciones familiares y culturales que ni entiende ni aprecia.

Las comunidades de fe tienen que «proveer un espacio seguro y favorable en el que estas personas jóvenes puedan discernir sus identidades y su proyecto de vida, pues solo allí la Iglesia será capaz de desarrollar su identidad corporativa como una institución multi-generacional que pueda servir a las generaciones que irrumpen»[6].

1

La parroquia como comunidad de memoria

El Papa Francisco recientemente recomendó una perspectiva balanceada para la evangelización de la juventud en Latinoamérica, la cual abarca enseñar doctrina, hábitos y valores al mismo tiempo. En este proceso, el pasado (memoria) y el futuro (utopía) se unen por medio de un proceso de discernimiento en el presente (realidad) que involucre a las personas de todas las generaciones a comprometerse en la transformación del mundo según los valores del Evangelio[7]. En Latinoamérica, los líderes pastorales y los padres de familia cuentan con las costumbres y tradiciones religiosas católicas que les apoyan en este esfuerzo, las cuales están todavía infusas en la vida cotidiana, aunque el secularismo y el éxito de los misioneros evangélicos han disminuido el monopolio católico en términos de afiliación religiosa.

En los Estados Unidos, el ambiente religioso y cultural del catolicismo hispano no está presente, así que los padres de familia latinos esperan que la comunidad de fe inmigrante les ayude en la socialización y la formación en la fe de las generaciones futuras, a proteger a sus hijos de lo que se percibe como influencias

---

6   CHA, P.T., «Ethnic Identity Formation and Participation in Immigrant Churches; Second Generation Korean Experiences», en KWON, H., KWANG, C.K. y WARNER, R.S. (eds.), *Korean Americans and Their Religions: Pilgrims and Missionaries from a Different Shore*, Pennsylvania State University, University Park, PA 2001, 141-156.

negativas en su nuevo ambiente social, y a reafirmar los valores culturales y morales que intentan transmitir en sus hogares. En el fondo, la comunidad tiene que tomar el lugar de los abuelos —especialmente de las abuelitas— quienes no viven cerca, asumiendo el papel de formar y sostener la fe de la nueva generación.

Este encuentro de los chicos y los jóvenes con los abuelos es clave para recibir la memoria de un pueblo y el discernimiento en el presente. Ser maestros de discernimiento, consejeros espirituales. Y aquí es importante para la transmisión de la fe de los jóvenes el apostolado cuerpo a cuerpo. El discernimiento en el presente no se puede hacer sin…un buen director espiritual que se anime a aburrirse horas y horas escuchando a los jóvenes. Memoria del pasado, discernimiento del presente, utopía del futuro, en ese esquema va creciendo la fe de un joven[8].

230

Investigaciones recientes han demostrado que a la medida que los adolescentes hispanos se asimilen a la cultura estadounidense predominante —en la cual los medios populares de comunicación, la educación pública y la mayor parte del discurso público son dominados por perspectivas seculares— va bajando su compromiso a nivel religioso[9]. Sin embargo, las relaciones positivas con la familia y la comunidad de fe étnica sirven para disminuir estos efectos.

Dentro de la comunidad étnica, la iglesia funciona como una «comunidad de memoria» en donde los valores culturales, tradiciones, idioma y normas se refuerzan y se mantienen por medio de la interacción con el grupo. La iglesia se convierte, en muchas instancias, en el centro de la vida cultural y social dentro de un ambiente que es con frecuencia amenazador, diverso y urbano[10].

Por consiguiente, el desarrollar programas de pastoral con adolescentes que sirvan específicamente a los adolescentes hispanos tiene el gran potencial de fortalecer un sentido positivo de identidad religiosa y étnica en los adolescentes

7   PAPA FRANCISCO, *Discurso del Santo Padre Francisco a los miembros de la Pontificia Comisión para América Latina*, 28 de febrero del 2014.
8   Ibid.
9   HERNÁNDEZ, E.I. y DUDLEY, R.L., «Persistence of Religion through Primary Group Ties Among Hispanic Seventh-Day Adventist Young People», en *Review of Religious Research* 32, n. 2 (Diciembre 1990) 157-172.
10 Ibid., 158.

latinos, especialmente cuando el equipo de liderazgo cuenta con un buen número de adultos y adolescentes hispanos, quienes sirven de modelo para los demás.

Cuando las oportunidades de participar en un ministerio parroquial que responda a las necesidades de los adolescentes latinos son limitadas o no existen, algunos de ellos buscarán o crearán otros caminos que les permitan acompañarse pastoralmente y compartir la manera como entienden sus tradiciones culturales y religiosas y cómo éstas influencian sus vidas. Por ejemplo, los movimientos apostólicos han incrementado en parte porque son guiados por personas de la misma edad y funcionan fuera de la estructura parroquial. Los padres de familia también están haciendo lo mejor que puedan para transmitir la fe a la siguiente generación, pero necesitan del apoyo de la comunidad de fe. La realidad es que muchos padres de familia tienen acceso limitado a sus hijos debido a las diferencias lingüísticas o la falta de tiempo para estar con ellos. El ministerio parroquial de pastoral con adolescentes o el movimiento apostólico pueden convertirse en un recurso inestimable tanto para los padres de familia como para los adolescentes, especialmente cuando las diferencias culturales estorban la relación entre las generaciones en el hogar.

Las congregaciones inmigrantes que generan una participación activa de adolescentes y jóvenes de segunda generación con frecuencia señalan tres factores que posibilitan sus logros:

1 Las actividades religiosas y sociales en las comunidades étnicas ofrecen el apoyo que los adolescentes necesitan sin hacerlos sentir como si no pertenecieran.

2 La congregación inmigrante abre un espacio seguro y una comunidad de compañeros en la cual pueden hablar de lo que significa la experiencia de crecer en los Estados Unidos y los problemas que enfrentan, sabiendo que alguien les entenderá.

3 La congregación inmigrante también ofrece un espacio en el cual pueden reencontrarse con su herencia cultural y hacerla suya a su manera[11].

En otras palabras, participar en la vida comunitaria de una congregación inmigrante permite desarrollar habilidades de adaptación. Los adolescentes no solo aprenden sobre un Dios amoroso y misericordioso y profundizan en el conocimiento de su fe, sino que también crecen como individuos en su contexto cultural. El grupo juvenil es un lugar en donde los adolescentes latinos pueden hacer preguntas y buscar consejo sin ser juzgados, especialmente cuando se trata

11 EBAUGH, H.R. Y SALTZMAN CHAFETZ, J., *Religion and the New Immigrants: Continuities and Adaptation in Immigrant Congregations*, AltaMira Press, Walnut Creek, CA 2000, 437.

de asuntos que ellos creen que no pueden dialogar abiertamente con sus padres. El grupo se convierte en una segunda familia que les apoya dentro y fuera de la Iglesia. Ese mismo sentido de comunidad se puede lograr en las parroquias compartidas al desarrollar programas sensibles a la realidad de los adolescentes latinos. Un ministerio juvenil que se lleva a cabo como una «comunidad de memoria» fortalecerá su identidad como latinos católicos y promoverá un sentido de corresponsabilidad hacia el bien común.

2

Caminando con adolescentes latinos

Teniendo en cuenta los niveles bajos de participación de los adolescentes latinos en los programas pastorales y de formación en la fe, las parroquias y las escuelas católicas tienen una gran oportunidad de incrementar sus esfuerzos pastorales y misioneros para servir a esta población. Con demasiada frecuencia se les ofrece a los adolescentes latinos programas que no conectan con sus vidas, su historia o sus aspiraciones para el futuro, y por consiguiente deciden no participar. Los siguientes seis enfoques ofrecen alternativas complementarias y eficaces para mejorar y expandir el acompañamiento pastoral de las nuevas generaciones de adolescentes y jóvenes latinos.

La Familia. Las familias hispanas han transmitido la fe católica de generación a generación por medio de tradiciones familiares y comunitarias que enfatizan la presencia de Dios en lo cotidiano. Esa catequesis familiar es un aspecto integral de la espiritualidad latina que fortalece la identidad católica latina. Es una manera relacional de compartir la fe que involucra a los miembros inmediatos de la familia y a la familia extensa, quienes juegan el papel de «comunicadores de la tradición» compartiendo una fe viva a través de normas sociales inspiradas en los valores y principios cristianos que son la base de la manera como la familia ve la realidad[12].

Éste es el enfoque catequético primordial que usan los padres de familia y abuelos inmigrantes. Los padres de familia latinos que están activos en la Iglesia Católica tienden a llevar a sus hijos personalmente a todas partes, donde sea que

---

12 RAYAS, V., *La Familia's Catechesis: The Mexican American Family as a Place of Catechesis Through la Mística*, disertación doctoral sin publicar, Fordham University, GSRRE, New York, 115-116.

vayan: la Misa, grupos de oración, retiros, etc. Si son catequistas, es posible que lleven a sus hijos adolescentes para que les ayuden como asistentes. Ellos saben que por su ejemplo están plantando las semillas que ayudarán a sus hijos a crecer en la fe. Qué tan eficaces pueden ser estas prácticas en los Estados Unidos depende de muchos factores, especialmente de las diferencias culturales y de idioma entre las generaciones y de las exigencias de la vida del inmigrante en el país. Solo requiere una generación para desconectar a la familia del hábito de practicar la fe regularmente. Experiencias tales como la inmigración, la discriminación y muchas otras clases de experiencias disruptivas pueden servir para separar a un adolescente de la práctica de la fe[13]. Será muy difícil para ellos transmitir la fe a sus propios hijos más adelante en la vida puesto que no tienen los recursos internos para hacerlo y no saben cómo valerse de recursos externos en la comunidad, aún si siguen identificándose como católicos.

Algunos padres de familia latinos que son bien comprometidos con su vida de fe, sin embargo, son precavidos en cuanto a pasar demasiado tiempo en la iglesia. Ellos reconocen que es importante mantener un buen balance y estar atentos a las necesidades de sus hijos para que no tengan ningún resentimiento hacia ellos o hacia la Iglesia. Es importante también tener conversaciones sobre las experiencias en la comunidad de fe. Esto tiene sentido sobre todo para los grupos de oración y retiros carismáticos, los cuales pueden ser confusos o desconcertantes para los adolescentes. La clave para quienes coordinan la pastoral con adolescentes y los movimientos apostólicos es entrar en diálogo con los padres de familia latinos, usar como punto de partida las prácticas de fe que ya son parte de la vida del hogar mientras se les ofrecen recursos adaptados al nuevo contexto lingüístico y cultural de sus hijos.

La *National Federation for Catholic Youth Ministry* (Federación Nacional para el Ministerio Católico con Adolescentes) ha diseñado un proceso llamado «*Strong Catholic Families*» (Familias Católicas Fuertes) que promueve estas conversaciones en el hogar. Ha sido adaptado culturalmente bajo el título «Fortaleciendo Familias en la Fe», siguiendo el mismo esquema pero tomando en cuenta «la particularidad de las necesidades familiares y culturales de los padres de familia hispanos y las parroquias que les sirven»[14]. El objetivo principal es involucrar a los padres de familia en la vida y misión de la Iglesia, y apoyarlos como los

---

13 Véase KERWIN, D., «El ministerio hispano y el fenómeno migratorio» en este volumen.
14 NFCYM, «Fortaleciendo Familias en la Fe», disponible en línea http://www.nfcym.org/programs/training/fortaleciendo.htm (documento visitado el 27 de abril del 2014).

primeros educadores de sus hijos al fortalecer su colaboración con la parroquia, la escuela y otros padres de familia por medio de un proceso dinámico que conduzca a recomendaciones que puedan ser implementadas en la parroquia y el hogar.

Tradiciones religiosas populares. Las tradiciones religiosas populares son un aspecto central de la espiritualidad latina y ayudan a fortalecer la identidad católica latina.

> Las devociones y prácticas de religiosidad popular son también momentos en los cuales se transmite la fe. Éstas incluyen el día de los muertos, las posadas, fiestas, altarcitos, bendiciones, el día de San Juan, el día de los reyes y agua bendita. El uso de artesanías, música y dramatizaciones también son componentes importantes de la religiosidad popular[15].

Muchas de estas prácticas son comunes en los hogares y comunidades de fe latinos. Estas fiestas y celebraciones religiosas no solo son agradables para toda la familia, sino que también refuerzan sus creencias, costumbres y tradiciones. La importancia de las tradiciones religiosas populares no se puede subestimar porque éstas verdaderamente promueven una vida devocional entre las generaciones y ayudan a crear puentes entre la experiencia de fe que se vive en el hogar con lo que ocurre en la iglesia.

La quinceañera, por ejemplo, es una celebración religiosa y cultural que juega un papel único en la vida de las adolescentes latinas al celebrar sus quince años. Esta celebración puede ayudarlas a desarrollar una autoimagen positiva, incrementar la confianza en sí misma, establecer redes de apoyo comunitario y sanar relaciones familiares[16]. Muchas parroquias aprovechan al máximo este momento en la vida de una muchacha latina para dialogar sobre su desarrollo mientras que se ofrece a los padres de familia el conocimiento y las habilidades para entender y comunicarse con sus hijas adolescentes.

---

15 RAYAS, V., *La Familia's Catechesis: The Mexican American Family as a Place of Catechesis Through la Mística*, 75-76.
16 Cfr. TORRES, T., «La Quinceañera: Traditioning and the Social Construction of the Mexican American Female», en ESPÍN, O. y MACY, G. (eds.), *Futuring Our Past: Explorations in the Theology of Tradition*, Orbis Books, Maryknoll, NY 2006, 277-298.

Una parroquia en particular ubicada en Arlington, Texas ofrece un programa de quinceañera que consiste en cinco sesiones de cuatro horas. Al menos uno de los padres de familia debe estar presente y se ofrecen sesiones separadas para los padres y sus hijas adolescentes. Estas sesiones están estructuradas de tal manera que preparen a los padres de familia para que cumplan su papel y ayuden a su hija adolescente a apreciar mejor a su familia. Un aspecto especial de este programa es un rito de reconciliación en el cual los padres y la quinceañera se piden perdón mutuamente.

Identificar y responder a las necesidades pastorales. Al concentrarse en las necesidades pastorales de los adolescentes tanto a nivel individual como colectivamente, los agentes pastorales pueden presentar el mensaje del Evangelio como una respuesta a los desafíos que enfrentan en su vida diaria[17]. Cuando este enfoque se emplea, incluso los adolescentes que viven en situaciones de alto riesgo pueden comenzar a participar en la pastoral con adolescentes porque saben que alguien estará allí para escucharles. Los adolescentes aprenden a controlar sus emociones y se les motiva a establecer metas. Descubren que la iglesia puede ser un lugar seguro que les da la bienvenida en el cual son tratados con dignidad, aprecio y respeto. El reconocimiento de los dones que traen a la comunidad les ayuda a fortalecer su autoestima.

Una autoestima alta y relaciones positivas con adultos pueden proteger a los adolescentes de muchos problemas de conducta, incluyendo participación en pandillas[18]. «Efectos positivos en la trayectoria de las vidas de adolescentes en situaciones de alto riesgo se pueden generar al crear autoimágenes positivas tanto entre los muchachos como las muchachas; al establecer relaciones positivas, especialmente dentro de la familia, y al enseñar hábitos a los adolescentes que les permitan elegir opciones positivas»[19]. Sabiendo qué tan común es la presencia de pandillas en las comunidades latinas, es de gran preocupación que solo el 4% de las parroquias en el Estudio nacional de parroquias católicas con ministerio hispano tenían programas para llegar y atender a los adolescentes hispanos involucrados en pandillas[20].

---

17 BORAN, G., «Hispanic Catholic Youth in the United States» en DAVIS, K.G. y TARANGO, Y. (eds.), *Bridging Boundaries: The Pastoral Care of U.S. Hispanics,* University of Scranton Press, Scranton, PA 2000, 97.
18 JAGGERS, J. et al, «Predictors of Gang Involvement: A Longitudinal Analysis of Data from the Mobile Youth Survey», en *Journal of the Society for Social Work and Research* 4, n. 3 (2013) 277-291.
19 Ibid., 286.
20 OSPINO, H., *El ministerio hispano en parroquias católicas,* 85.

Una parroquia en Orlando, Florida ofrece un programa de servicio comunitario supervisado para adolescentes que han cometido un delito. En este ambiente los líderes de la pastoral con adolescentes motivan a los pandilleros a tomar buenas decisiones, a estar lejos de las calles y venir a la iglesia. Para muchos de ellos, el líder de la pastoral con adolescentes se convierte en una figura maternal o paternal importante. Una de sus estrategias es un servicio telefónico disponible las 24 horas del día llamado «*God Squad*» (Escuadrón de Dios), disponible para ayudar en aquellos momentos críticos cuando el adolescente necesita el apoyo especial de la oración.

Los movimientos apostólicos tales como los Cursillos, las Jornadas de Cristiandad, Juan XXIII y los grupos de oración juveniles sostenidos por la espiritualidad de la Renovación Carismática también ofrecen maneras de responder a las necesidades pastorales de los adolescentes. Se ha demostrado que la experiencia profunda del amor transformador de Dios y la acogida de la comunidad que se siente en los movimientos son respuestas pastorales eficaces para los adolescentes cuyas vidas han sido impactadas negativamente por las pandillas, la adicción, el sufrimiento y/o la violencia. Estos movimientos en gran parte atraen a adultos y jóvenes inmigrantes en español, aunque en algunas regiones se pueden encontrar pequeñas comunidades en inglés también.

El círculo pastoral. El círculo pastoral, conocido también como un enfoque sociológico, se ha usado prominentemente en Latinoamérica para ayudar a los «jóvenes a adquirir habilidades necesarias para analizar causas estructurales de la pobreza y la marginación de grupos minoritarios en la sociedad»[21]. Es fácil que los adolescentes latinos se desanimen al ver a sus familias al fondo de las estructuras sociales en los Estados Unidos y sientan que el sistema social está en su contra, que no tienen esperanza de una vida mejor. Dicha realidad también puede generar una crisis de fe cuando estos adolescentes se preguntan por qué un Dios amoroso no interviene para mejorar su situación frente a injusticias tan terribles.

Ante estas circunstancias desafiantes, el círculo pastoral nos recuerda en primer lugar que los adolescentes no son sujetos pasivos. En segundo lugar, Dios está con ellos a su lado, con compasión cuidando a aquellos que sufren o padecen una necesidad. El círculo pastoral les ofrece el propósito de transformar el mundo para que sea un lugar mejor, aun cuando tengan que comenzar con

21 BORAN, G., «Hispanic Catholic Youth in the United States», 99.

pasos pequeños. El proceso mismo crea líderes que pueden tomar la iniciativa de buscar el cambio no solo en la Iglesia, sino también en el resto de la sociedad.

Las raíces históricas del círculo pastoral se pueden trazar al movimiento de la Juventud Obrera Cristiana en Bélgica —una rama de la Acción Católica fundada por el Cardenal Joseph Cardijn en los años 1920. Su metodología «ver, juzgar, actuar» ofreció un proceso para que los jóvenes se hicieran críticamente conscientes de las fuerzas sociales que afectan sus vidas y les inspiró a ser protagonistas en un proceso de transformación social fundamentado en una fe viva. Este proceso ha sido un paradigma para la reflexión pastoral continua en toda Latinoamérica, generando acciones que responden a los signos de los tiempos. De la misma manera, el ministerio hispano en los Estados Unidos se ha beneficiado de esta metodología, la cual se ha expandido incluyendo un total de seis pasos:

> El círculo pastoral toma en cuenta lo original de cada ser humano y comunidad, y motiva a los jóvenes a *ser* personas, a aceptarse a sí mismos, a reconocer su dignidad como hijos e hijas de Dios; los ayuda a *ver* la realidad de su vida y a *juzgarla* a la luz del Evangelio y de las enseñanzas de la iglesia; motiva a los jóvenes a *actuar* para desarrollar una praxis cristiana y a *evaluar* esta praxis periódicamente para reforzarla. El círculo se cierra y vuelve a empezar al *celebrar* la vida y la fe[22].

El Instituto Fe y Vida de manera particular ha promovido esta metodología en su modelo de liderazgo compartido «Profetas de Esperanza» para la pastoral juvenil en pequeñas comunidades. Sus recursos basados en el círculo pastoral incluyen la colección de materiales bilingües *Testigos de Esperanza; Diálogos Semanales con Jesús* que ofrecen una reflexión y respuestas basadas en las lecturas del leccionario dominical; la *Misión Bíblica Juvenil* bilingüe para potenciar líderes jóvenes como discípulos misioneros con sus compañeros; y el *Sistema de Formación de Líderes* que integra varios programas desde un nivel intermedio hasta seminarios avanzados, liderazgo institucional y capacitación de formadores.

Cuando se lleva a cabo de manera apropiada, la metodología del círculo pastoral es mucho más que un ejercicio de justicia social. Invita a los adolescentes a nombrar y a analizar los grandes desafíos que enfrentan en la comunidad local. Luego aprenden cómo la Buena Nueva de Jesucristo sembrada en sus propias

---

22 CERVANTES, C.M. (ed.), *Profetas de Esperanza, Volumen 3: El Modelo Profetas de Esperanza*, Instituto Fe y Vida, Stockton, CA 1997, 46-47.

vidas puede vencer y transformar toda forma de sufrimiento humano. Estas experiencias transformadoras en las que los adolescentes toman la iniciativa como protagonistas en la construcción del Reino de Dios son verdaderas razones para celebrar en comunidad. Es en esta celebración de fe que los adolescentes católicos viven la encarnación de la Iglesia como comunión y misión de manera más profunda.

Adaptabilidad lingüística. Una de las grandes frustraciones en el ministerio hispano hoy en día radica en la inhabilidad de los líderes pastorales de aprovechar el buen trabajo hecho en la formación de comunidades entre los jóvenes inmigrantes en español para proveer liderazgo en el acompañamiento pastoral de los adolescentes nacidos en los Estados Unidos. Algunas parroquias y movimientos apostólicos han experimentado con modelos bilingües en la pastoral con adolescentes. Esto funciona para algunos adolescentes, pero exige al menos un conocimiento básico de los dos idiomas y apertura a acomodarse a las necesidades de los demás. En otros casos, las parroquias ofrecen iniciativas de pastoral con adolescentes y educación religiosa por separado para los adolescentes en ambos idiomas, permitiendo que decidan por sí mismos en cuál idioma se sienten más cómodos.

Estudios recientes confirman que muchos grupos juveniles y movimientos apostólicos están tratando de integrar inglés para involucrar de manera más eficaz a los latinos nacidos en los Estados Unidos. De acuerdo con el Estudio nacional de parroquias católicas con ministerio hispano, «El 45% de parroquias con programas pastorales para los jóvenes hispanos realizan sus reuniones primordialmente en español; el 42% de manera bilingüe; y el 13% en inglés»[23]. Esto refleja una disminución de 15 puntos porcentuales en cuanto a reuniones llevadas a cabo solo en español y un incremento de 13 puntos porcentuales en las reuniones bilingües desde el Primer Encuentro Nacional de Pastoral Juvenil Hispana en el año 2006[24].

Otra estrategia que se usa con éxito en el contexto litúrgico de algunas parroquias es ofrecer un resumen breve de la homilía en inglés durante las Misas en español. Los adolescentes en la congregación se sienten más acogidos porque el sacerdote expresa interés en ellos como miembros de la comunidad, y las familias inmigrantes no tienen que sacrificar las necesidades de los padres con rela-

---

23 OSPINO, H., *El ministerio hispano en parroquias católicas,* 85.
24 NATIONAL CATHOLIC NETWORK DE PASTORAL JUVENIL HISPANA - LA RED, *Conclusiones,* 97.

ción a las de sus hijos, o viceversa. Según la investigación del estudio nacional de parroquias católicas con ministerio hispano, el 84% de las parroquias con ministerio hispano celebra Misas bilingües durante el año, aunque la mayoría lo hace menos de diez veces en un determinado año[25]. Hay excepciones. Una parroquia nacional hispana en Cleveland, Ohio ofrece una liturgia bilingüe todos los domingos para servir a católicos latinos de habla inglesa y no latinos. Esta Misa se celebra primordialmente en inglés con elementos culturales en español tales como la música. Esa Misa es popular especialmente entre los jóvenes latinos de la parroquia.

Comunidad de comunidades. Reconocer la necesidad de una diversidad lingüística en el cuidado pastoral de los adolescentes católicos hispanos puede ser el primer paso para desarrollar un enfoque amplio de «comunidad de comunidades» para la pastoral con adolescentes. Muchos líderes de la pastoral con adolescentes —especialmente aquellos más influenciados por la cultura predominante, hispanos o no— sienten que formar dos o más grupos juveniles es un paso de retroceso hacia una segregación racial. De hecho, esto no es correcto. Cuando la pastoral con adolescentes se lleva a cabo con una mentalidad que asume «una parroquia, un grupo de adolescentes», no es posible reunir más de 80 o 100 adolescentes de manera regular porque sería difícil conducir reuniones más grandes. Esto también daría a los líderes pastorales la impresión falsa de que sus programas están sirviendo grandes números cuando, de hecho, solo están involucrando un 10% o menos de los adolescentes de la comunidad. En realidad, hay miles de adolescentes católicos en las parroquias más grandes.

Otra limitación es que dicha perspectiva limita la habilidad de los líderes pastorales de adaptar el contenido y la metodología de un programa a las necesidades pastorales particulares de grupos tales como adolescentes que dejaron de estudiar, jóvenes inmigrantes trabajadores, adolescentes asociados con pandillas o detenidos por algún delito, los que tienen hijos y adolescentes de grupos étnicos o lingüísticos específicos. En la mayoría de parroquias con un solo grupo de adolescentes, son los que tienen mayor necesidad de acompañamiento pastoral los que rápido descubren que no «encajan» y deciden no participar, mientras que en otras son los adolescentes que vienen con una base espiritual sólida desde sus hogares quienes no encuentran un grupo en la parroquia que les permita crecer en su liderazgo y discipulado.

25 OSPINO, H., *El ministerio hispano en parroquias católicas,* 63.

Por el contrario, un enfoque diferenciado de comunidad de comunidades para la pastoral parroquial con adolescentes no implica segregación sino más bien una estrategia de segmentación pastoral. Es una manera de estructurar el acompañamiento pastoral para servir a los adolescentes desde su realidad permitiéndole a dicho ministerio expandirse sin perder la dimensión humana de las relaciones personales, aún si los números sobrepasan el 50% de los posibles participantes. Si la parroquia aspira a servirles a todos sus adolescentes en ambientes pastorales que realmente toman en cuenta sus necesidades particulares, el marco estructural de este ministerio debe definirse de esta manera desde un principio. El Papa Francisco nos recuerda que «La reforma de estructuras que exige la conversión pastoral sólo puede entenderse en este sentido: procurar que todas ellas se vuelvan más misioneras, que la pastoral ordinaria en todas sus instancias sea más expansiva y abierta, que coloque a los agentes pastorales en constante actitud de salida y favorezca así la respuesta positiva de todos aquellos a quienes Jesús convoca a su amistad»[26].

El enfoque de comunidad de comunidades permite que se añadan orgánicamente nuevos grupos y programas con el paso del tiempo a medida que se identifiquen y formen líderes, y según las necesidades pastorales que se perciban. Una parroquia en Texas que ha implementado con éxito este enfoque ya sirve a cerca de mil adolescentes y jóvenes católicos cada año por medio de más de 20 programas distintos que operan con más de 50 clases o grupos pequeños[27]. Un ministerio de esta magnitud no aparece de la noche a la mañana, sino que solo es posible cuando los líderes pastorales asumen una visión de pastoral con adolescentes que va más allá de la mentalidad tradicional de «un solo grupo de adolescentes».

3

Conclusión

Este capítulo ha resaltado algunos principios generales y prácticas eficaces para el ministerio con las nuevas generaciones de católicos latinos. Todos estos enfoques pueden contribuir independientemente a responder a las distintas necesi-

---

26 PAPA FRANCISCO, *Evangelii Gaudium*, 27.
27 JOHNSON-MONDRAGÓN, K. Y LOZANO, E., «A "Community of Communities" Approach to Youth Ministry» en *Lifelong Faith* 7.1 (Spring 2013) 39-45.

dades de los adolescentes y jóvenes latinos nacidos en los Estados Unidos. Sin embargo, la presente no es una guía definitiva para su acompañamiento pastoral. La Pontificia Comisión para Latinoamérica publicó recientemente un conjunto de recomendaciones pastorales para la transmisión de la fe a las nuevas generaciones de jóvenes[28]. Muchos de los temas que aparecen allí tienen la misma importancia para el esfuerzo de transmitir la fe a los adolescentes latinos en los Estados Unidos. Por ejemplo:

- Colaboración entre parroquias, familias y escuelas católicas para incrementar la participación de adolescentes y niños latinos (n. 10),
- Incorporar más profundamente el discernimiento de su vocación cristiana en los programas de pastoral juvenil (n. 14),
- Activar el protagonismo de los discípulos misioneros jóvenes (n. 15-17),
- Redes sociales y evangelización en el «continente» digital (n. 19),
- Compañía y solidaridad con la juventud que vive en la pobreza (n. 20),
- Compromiso social y político y la acción de los católicos jóvenes (n. 21),
- Movimientos y asociaciones eclesiales para jóvenes católicos (n. 22).

Lo más importante es que la Iglesia plantee estrategias que ayuden a los adolescentes latinos a interpretar su historia desde la perspectiva de lo que Dios hace en el aquí y el ahora, y cómo su experiencia diaria puede ser realmente una ocasión de gracia para ellos y para toda la Iglesia. Idealmente esto debería hacerse en una comunidad no muy grande de adolescentes, según el idioma con el que se sientan más cómodos, que les permita dialogar en profundidad los desafíos y experiencias particulares que los adolescentes latinos enfrentan, acompañados por asesores y modelos a seguir que han navegado con cierto éxito las aguas traicioneras de la integración cultural. Esto no implica segregarlos del resto de la comunidad juvenil, aunque sí puede exigir establecer momentos y espacios en que los adolescentes hispanos se puedan reunir para hablar de sus necesidades pastorales, articular un sentido de identidad étnica y religiosa, y formular una respuesta misionera para otros adolescentes como ellos.

En otras palabras, la parroquia tiene que convertirse en «comunidad de memoria» con todos los beneficios que se derivan de dicha experiencia para las nuevas generaciones —aun en medio de comunidades culturalmente diversas. Cuando los adolescentes católicos encuentran una comunidad de compañeros

---

28 Véase PONTIFICIA COMISIÓN PARA AMÉRICA LATINA, *La Emergencia Educativa y la «Traditio» de la Fe a las Nuevas Generaciones Latinoamericanas: Recomendaciones Pastorales*, Libreria Editrice Vaticana, Roma 2014.

con quienes se pueden relacionar a la luz de una historia y un horizonte social en común, se descubren potenciados para compartir sus dones espirituales y culturales en eventos diseñados para construir comunidad y compartir la fe con la comunidad entera de adolescentes en la parroquia. La organización de una pastoral con adolescentes basada en estos valores y principios ofrece a los adolescentes latinos la oportunidad de reconocer que su presencia es un verdadero don para toda la Iglesia. Considerando el tamaño de la población católica latina en los Estados Unidos en nuestro día, ese don será un legado para la Iglesia en el siglo XXI y más allá.

El ministerio hispano y la educación

Antonia Darder

La escuela puede y tiene que ser espacio de fermento, un lugar en el que se encuentra y converge la comunidad educadora entera con el sólo objetivo de capacitar y ayudar a madurar a las personas que son simples, competentes y honestas, que conocen cómo amar con fidelidad, que pueden vivir sus vidas como una respuesta al llamado de Dios, y en su futura profesión servir a la sociedad.

—Papa Francisco[1]

Las palabras expresadas por el Papa Francisco sobre la educación hacen referencia a los asuntos urgentes que tienen que ser prioridad en la conciencia eclesial, a medida que la comunidad cristiana entera se mueve a examinar el papel de la Iglesia y del ministerio hispano en cuanto al apoyo de la educación de los estudiantes en ambientes educativos diversos. Hacer esto significa repensar con atención la visión de la Iglesia para la educación más allá del simple identificarse como católicos y de los procesos educativos que ocurren en las escuelas católicas y la catequesis. En estos tiempos de cambio e incertidumbre, existe una necesidad urgente de involucrarse críticamente en las vidas de los niños latinos y sus familias, en la realidad diaria de las comunidades donde se esfuerzan por realizarse. Este repensar exige que la Iglesia se esfuerce por entrar en diálogo con las realidades históricas, sociales y materiales específicas que definen las vidas de los latinos en los Estados Unidos hoy en día. Este compromiso nos cuestiona con relación al papel que los agentes pastorales latinos deben jugar en el contexto de la educación y la formación de la comunidad, no sólo en las escuelas católicas y las parroquias, sino también en los ambientes en donde viven. ¿Existe un sentido de urgencia por parte de la Iglesia para responder proactivamente saliendo al mundo y encontrando a la comunidad latina en donde vive, en lugar de esperar a que ésta venga a tocar las puertas de nuestros templos y oficinas?

En el contexto de las comunidades latinas empobrecidas, se necesita una visión católica renovada de educación emancipadora que ayude al resto de la sociedad a establecer estrategias humanizadoras de aprendizaje formal e informal que fomenten el desarrollo de una conciencia crítica, una voz democrática y una participación comunitaria en la cultura diaria de las iglesias y escuelas en los barrios. Este proceso también puede servir para reconstruir juntos un mundo más justo. Esta propuesta apunta a una visión humanizadora para una educación

---

1 PAPA FRANCISCO, *Discurso a los estudiantes de las escuelas de los jesuitas de Italia y Albania,* 7 de junio del 2013, http://w2.vatican.va/content/francesco/en/speeches/2013/june/documents/papa-francesco_20130607_scuole-gesuiti.html (documento visitado el 25 de agosto del 2014).

democrática y a la transformación de inequidades sociales asociadas con prioridades educacionales, preocupaciones éticas y prácticas de enseñanza, tanto en escuelas patrocinadas por la Iglesia como más allá de ellas, que impacten positivamente el crecimiento social e intelectual de los estudiantes latinos. Es más, esta visión tiene que estar fundamentada en los valores emancipadores de una comunidad que afirma la convicción universal de una humanidad fraterna y solidaria en las dinámicas de los grupos culturales. Esto exige que repensemos nuestras prácticas de ministerio hispano para que puedan jugar un papel más intencional en el proceso de responder a las necesidades de la Iglesia y del mundo, haciendo que la tarea educativa no se reduzca sólo a promover la dignidad humana y la subjetividad, sino que también cultiven la autodeterminación y la virtud al igual que una ética del bien común.

Al hacer nuestras las necesidades de los latinos, las luchas históricas para sobrevivir cultural y económicamente en los Estados Unidos exigen incorporar las preguntas fundamentales relacionadas con inequidades raciales, de clase y de género si la meta es adoptar prácticas de transformación social y eclesial. Como dichas dinámicas impactan la realidad de todas las comunidades culturales, entender cómo las personas sobreviven disparidades relacionadas con oportunidades y recursos es importante tanto como fuente de reflexión como crítica. Es más, las necesidades educacionales distintas de las comunidades diversas requieren una apertura por parte de los agentes pastorales a considerar la situación única y las realidades de aquellos a quienes sirven. En otras palabras, no existe un enfoque que sea igual para todos. Por consiguiente, la educación con las comunidades latinas y en favor de estas comunidades tiene que tener en cuenta las necesidades específicas de cada una, promoviendo más oportunidades para una participación culturalmente inclusiva y la transformación social.

Si la tarea futura del ministerio hispano en los Estados Unidos es fomentar nuevos espacios e iniciativas para apoyar las diversas necesidades educacionales de las comunidades latinas, este ministerio entonces necesita asegurarse de que los desafíos sociales que los latinos enfrentan sean parte del diálogo ecuménico y político. La organización comunitaria y el impulso de movimientos de solidaridad pueden ser contribuciones que la Iglesia haga a las comunidades latinas en todo el país. Considerando el estado de la educación de los latinos, la crisis educacional actual tiene que entenderse como un asunto de derechos humanos, lo cual exige preguntarnos de qué manera interpela a los agentes pastorales latinos que están comprometidos a afirmar la dignidad de todas las personas.

1

Los latinos y la aflicción de la pobreza

Mientras no se resuelvan radicalmente los problemas de los pobres, renunciando a la autonomía absoluta de los mercados y de la especulación financiera y atacando las causas estructurales de la inequidad, no se resolverán los problemas del mundo y en definitiva ningún problema.

—PAPA FRANCISCO[2]

Según datos recientes de la Oficina del Censo de los Estados Unidos, la población Latina es de casi 58 millones de personas, la minoría étnica más grande y joven dentro de la población estadounidense. La población de origen mexicano constituye aproximadamente el 67% del total de la población latina. Uno de cada cinco niños en edad escolar y uno de cada cuatro niños que nacen es latino. Nunca antes en la historia de este país un número tan grande de niños pertenecía a una minoría étnica; se espera que los números se tripliquen en las próximas tres décadas[3]. Se proyecta que para el año 2036 los niños latinos constituirán un tercio de todos los niños entre las edades de 3 y 17 años[4]. De los 30 millones de jóvenes entre los 18 y los 24 años en los Estados Unidos hoy en día, seis millones (20%) son latinos. También es importante tener en cuenta que las proyecciones del Pew Hispanic Center[5] estiman que el 82% del crecimiento de la población latina estará impulsado por la presencia de inmigrantes latinoamericanos y sus hijos[6]. Estas tendencias de cambios poblacionales nos muestran que la población latina seguirá creciendo como resultado de la reciente ola migratoria. Si sólo tenemos en cuenta la presencia numérica, es fácil afirmar que el tipo de educación que reciban los estudiantes latinos determinará de manera dramática la historia futura de este país —y de la Iglesia.

2 PAPA FRANCISCO, *Evangelii Gaudium*, n. 202.
3 Véase PASSEL, J. y COHN, D., *U.S. Population Projections: 2005-2050*, Pew Hispanic Center, Washington D.C. 2008.
4 Véase U.S. CENSUS BUREAU.
5 Fundado en el año 2001, el Pew Hispanic Center es una organización investigativa independiente que busca mejorar la manera como se entiende la realidad de la población hispana estadounidense y ofrecer una crónica del creciente impacto de los latinos en la nación. Véase http://www.pewhispanic.org/
6 Véase TAYLOR, P., GONZÁLEZ-BARRERA, A., PASSEL, J.S. y LÓPEZ, M.H., *An Awakened Giant: The Hispanic Electorate Is Likely to Double by 2030*, Hispanic Pew Center, Washington D.C. 2012.

También es importante tener en cuenta en esta conversación el hecho de que las comunidades latinas se encuentran entre las poblaciones que más dificultades tienen en los Estados Unidos hoy en día a nivel económico y social. Más de 50 millones de personas en los Estados Unidos viven en la pobreza. En la comunidad latina, la tasa de pobreza infantil es del 35%, comparada con el 12% entre los niños de raza blanca. El número total de niños latinos viviendo en la pobreza es más alto que el de cualquier grupo étnico en los Estados Unidos[7]. Entre ellos, los hijos de familias inmigrantes son los que más cerca están de vivir en condiciones de pobreza, comparados con otros niños en los Estados Unidos[8]. La consecuencia más notable de esta realidad es que los estudiantes latinos hoy en día se han convertido en el nuevo rostro de la segregación, viviendo en las comunidades más pobres y estudiando en las escuelas más pobres y segregadas[9].

Es por ello que hacerle frente a la pobreza debe ser una prioridad en todas las dinámicas sociales, incluyendo el trabajo de la Iglesia. Esto se hace más urgente antes la falta de oportunidades educativas y laborales que con frecuencia están asociadas con condiciones de vida en un contexto de vulnerabilidad. A pesar del papel tan importante que la Iglesia ha jugado en el pasado ayudando a las poblaciones más vulnerables, la situación actual de las comunidades latinas exige ampliar programas educativos para los jóvenes y las familias en el contexto de un ministerio hispano inspirado en el Evangelio y la multiplicación de los esfuerzos para servirle al resto de la comunidad hispana.

248

7   Véase LÓPEZ, M.H. y VELASCO, G., *The Toll of the Great Recession: Childhood Poverty Among Hispanics Sets Record, Leads Nation*, Pew Hispanic Center, Washington, D.C. 2011, http://www.pewhispanic.org/files/2011/10/147.pdf (documento visitado el 25 de Agosto del 2014).

8   Véase AIZENMAN, N.C., «Left Behind: A Child's Burden», en *The Washington Post*, 9 de diciembre del 2009, http://www.washingtonpost.com/wp-dyn/content/article/2009/12/08/AR2009120804446.html (documento visitado el 25 de agosto del 2014).

9   En un reporte reciente producido por The Civil Rights Project, *E Pluribus...Separation: Deepening Double Segregation for Students*, Gary Orfield (2012) y sus colegas concluyeron «que la segregación de estudiantes latinos hoy en día ha incrementado seriamente en el país, yendo a escuelas más intensamente segregadas y más pobres que en varias generaciones». El reporte está disponible en: http://civilrightsproject.ucla.edu/research/k-12-education/integration-and-diversity/mlk-national/e-pluribus...separation-deepening-double-segregation-for-more-students/

Un retrato de la realidad educacional de los latinos

cℐo

¡Antes que nada, sean personas libres!… Ser libres significa saber reflexionar sobre lo que
hacemos, saber cómo evaluar… cuáles son las conductas que nos ayudan a crecer.
—PAPA FRANCISCO[10]

Los educadores en todo el país siguen tratando de entender las razones por las
cuales el sistema educativo estadounidense sigue siendo incapaz de responder
a las necesidades de los estudiantes latinos. En las últimas dos décadas, una serie
de iniciativas federales y estatales han promovido la asimilación cultural junto
con políticas educacionales restrictivas. Una de las consecuencias es que el derecho a la educación bilingüe de los estudiantes que son parte de una minoría
lingüística ha sido abolido mientras que prácticas asociadas con programas como Que Ningún Niño Se Quede Atrás (*No Child Left Behind*) y Carrera a la Cima
(*Race to the Top*) enfatizaron pruebas de alta exigencia, la estandarización del
currículo y la privatización de la educación. En Arizona, iniciativas fundamen-
tadas en políticas parcializadas ideológicamente en contra de los chicanos y los
inmigrantes mexicanos llevaron a esfuerzos nativistas de restringir el uso del
español en las escuelas y el lugar de trabajo, la eliminación de los estudios mexi-
coamericanos en los niveles de secundaria, y la prohibición de libros considerados subversivos por parte de líderes sociales que proponen reformas curriculares y de libros de texto[11]. A pesar de la intención represiva de estas políticas, los
cambios demográficos a nivel nacional anticipan que la población latina en el
estado será la mayoría a mediados del siglo XXI. ¿Cómo responden las comunidades católicas a estas realidades en Arizona?

En las escuelas del país, los estudiantes latinos siguen haciendo historia. Por
primera vez, uno de cada cuatro estudiantes (24.7%) en escuelas primarias son
latinos. Dicha presencia histórica le hace eco a lo que ocurrió con estudiantes
en kindergarten (en el 2007) y niños en niveles preescolares (en el 2016). De entre todos los estudiantes entre kindergarten y grado 12 en las escuelas públicas,
el 23.9% son latinos —un número récord. Y por primera vez el número de lati-

---

10 PAPA FRANCISCO, *Discurso a los estudiantes de las escuelas de los jesuitas de Italia y Albania.*
11 AGUIRRE, A., «Latino Immigrants and the Framing of Anti-immigrant Policies», en *Latino Studies*,
    10, n. 3 (2012) 385-394. Véase también DARDER, A., *Culture and Power in the Classroom*, Paradigm,
    Boulder, CO 2012.

nos entre las edades de 18 y 24 años matriculados en universidades es más de dos millones, constituyendo el 16.5% de todos los estudiantes universitarios[12]. A medida que avanzan desde kindergarten hasta terminar la escuela secundaria, el número de estudiantes latinos será aún más grande en todos los niveles educativos durante los próximos años. Esta realidad también impactará el número de niños que buscarán instrucción catequética en las parroquias y otras formas de educación en la fe, teniendo en cuenta que el acceso y las matrículas en las escuelas católicas han disminuido notablemente.

En la última década, los niveles de graduación de los estudiantes latinos en el país han mejorado. Datos recientes indican que los estudiantes latinos tienen más posibilidades de graduarse de la secundaria que hace diez años. Un estudio reciente notó que el 78% de los estudiantes latinos se graduaron de escuela secundaria en el 2010, comparado con el 64% en el año 2000[13]. Igualmente, la tasa de estudiantes latinos en los Estados Unidos graduándose de programas universitarios de dos y cuatro años ha incrementado positivamente. Pero a pesar de los avances, datos del Centro de Investigación Pew indican que de todos los estudiantes que recibieron un título universitario equivalente a cuatro años de estudio (*bachelor's degree*, en inglés), sólo el 11% eran latinos[14]. De hecho, sólo el 51% de los estudiantes latinos que se matriculan en una universidad reciben un título[15].

Este retrato preocupante de la educación latina tiene mucho que ver con el ministerio hispano en cuanto que afirma la necesidad de que la Iglesia amplíe con más entusiasmo su apoyo a la preparación de agentes pastorales y líderes latinos, personas que entiendan genuinamente las condiciones de las comunidades latinas en los Estados Unidos. Esto también exige que se expandan programas y actividades dentro de las escuelas católicas y en otros espacios para fomentar iniciativas de apoyo educativo y de justicia social. A través de los años, las comunidades latinas han usado estrategias de cabildeo político y alternativas

12 FRY, R. Y LÓPEZ, M.H., *Hispanic Student Enrollments Reach New Highs in 2011*, Hispanic Pew Center, Washington D.C. 2012, http://www.pewhispanic.org/files/2012/08/Hispanic-Student-Enrollments-Reach-New-Highs-in-2011_FINAL.pdf (documento visitado el 25 de agosto del 2014).

13 Véase MURNANE, R.J., «U.S. High School Graduation Rates: Patterns and Explanations», en *Journal of Economic Literature*, American Economic Association, 51, n. 2 (2013) 370-422.

14 Véase LÓPEZ, M.H., *Latinos and Education: Explaining the Attainment Gap*, Hispanic Pew Center, Washington D.C. 2009, http://www.pewhispanic.org/files/reports/115.pdf (documento visitado el 25 de agosto del 2014).

15 Véase KELLY, A., SCHNEIDER, M. Y CAREY, K., *Rising to the Challenge: Hispanic College Graduation Rates as a National Priority*, American Enterprise Institute, Washington, D.C. 2010, https://www.aei.org/wp-content/uploads/2011/10/Rising-to-the-Challenge.pdf (documento visitado el 25 de agosto del 2014).

legales para abogar por equidad en cuanto a la educación de sus hijos. Con frecuencia los padres de familia latinos han recurrido a las escuelas católicas con la esperanza de forjar un futuro mejor para sus hijos. Sin embargo, como sólo un número muy pequeño de niños latinos van a escuelas católicas[16], más esfuerzos en el ministerio hispano tienen que orientarse a apoyar a los estudiantes latinos sin importar a dónde van a estudiar, abogando por su derecho a una vida plena.

Al acompañarles en la lucha por condiciones justas a nivel educacional y social, los padres de familia latinos también necesitan apoyo para abogar por la dignidad inalienable y los derechos de sus hijos, especialmente cuando estos nacen en familias en donde hay alguien indocumentado. A la luz de la misión evangelizadora de la Iglesia, arraigada en las Escrituras y la Tradición, uno de los gestos más significativos que la comunidad eclesial puede hacer es estar en solidaridad con los marginalizados, con la simplicidad de Jesucristo, para promover la emancipación de nuestras hermanas y hermanos que buscan mejores condiciones educativas y de justicia.

Más que nunca encontramos en las palabras y las acciones del Papa Francisco una afirmación para caminar firmemente con los más vulnerables. El Papa hace esto recordándonos sobre la dimensión comunitaria del cristianismo. Él reta a los católicos a evaluar las causas por las cuales las comunidades sufren, lo cual es agravado por la falta de acceso a oportunidades educacionales de calidad. Con él podemos preguntarnos: ¿cuáles son las implicaciones de la falta de diálogo, de un consumismo que beneficia al sistema de mercado pero deja a los pobres vacíos, de un subjetivismo relativista que carece de conciencia colectiva y responsabilidad hacia la comunidad? ¿De qué manera nuestras instituciones han dejado de darle la bienvenida a todos y cómo dicha actitud hace difícil que se restaure una relación de justicia a la luz de la fe en un ambiente pluralista?[17]

---

16 Ver OSPINO, H. y WEITZEL-O'NEILL, P., «Catholic Schools Serving Hispanic Families: Insights from the 2014 National Survey», en *Journal of Catholic Education*, 19, n. 2 (2016) 54-80; OSPINO, H. y WEITZEL-O'NEILL, P., *Escuelas católicas en una Iglesia cada vez más hispana: Reporte general de los resultados del Estudio nacional de escuelas católicas al servicio de familias hispanas*, Our Sunday Visitor, Huntington, IN 2016.

17 Véase PAPA FRANCISCO, *Evangelii Gaudium*, n. 70.

3
Siete principios claves para la inclusión cultural

[No podemos] permitir que prevalezca una visión de la persona humana unidimensional...
—PAPA FRANCISCO[18]

Una cultura de inclusión afirma el derecho de las comunidades culturales a tener un lugar apropiado en la mesa de diálogo social. Este concepto afirma aquellas prácticas cotidianas que confrontan perspectivas unidimensionales asociadas con condiciones de inequidad en las escuelas y la sociedad. Esta idea de práctica comunitaria y educacional, fundamentada en lo que Paulo Freire llamó *unidad-en-la-diversidad*[19], apunta a la importancia de reconocer que todas las tradiciones culturales ofrecen una interpretación del mundo para el mundo. Por lo tanto, nuestras diferencias son necesarias porque forman la esencia de nuestra humanidad común. La inclusividad intercultural y las presuposiciones socialmente justas de esta visión desafían las perspectivas de déficit que se imponen a las comunidades latinas y a otras poblaciones percibidas como «otros». Dichas prácticas de inclusión cultural confrontan sistemas injustos dentro de la Iglesia y la sociedad que no respetan la riqueza cultural y lingüística que los miembros de las comunidades particulares saben que poseen.

Las prácticas culturalmente inclusivas en las comunidades latinas desafían las estructuras evangelizadoras que reproducen o se mantienen en silencio ante las inequidades y, al hacer esto, crean espacio para las muchas diferencias humanas. Todo esto nos llama a repensar las maneras como se toman las decisiones dentro de la Iglesia para crear más posibilidades de que la comunidad latina participe en todos los niveles de vida social, incluyendo en asuntos económicos. Una práctica culturalmente inclusiva abre derroteros para innovaciones curriculares dentro de las prácticas eclesiales y escolares para fomentar programas de inmersión lingüísticas (ej., español e inglés) y paradigmas bilingües de instrucción. De esta manera, un ambiente de inclusión cultural apoya el trabajo de

---

18 PAPA FRANCISCO, *Discurso durante el encuentro con los representantes de las iglesias y comunidades eclesiales, y de las diversas religiones,* 20 de marzo del 2013, https://w2.vatican.va/content/francesco/es/speeches/2013/march/documents/papa-francesco_20130320_delegati-fraterni.html (documento visitado el 25 de agosto del 2014).

19 Véase DARDER, A., *Freire and Education,* Routledge, New York 2014; FREIRE, P., *Pedagogy of Freedom: Ethics, Democracy and Civic Courage,* Rowman & Littlefield, Lanham, MD 1998.

El ministerio hispano en el siglo XXI

252

los agentes pastorales hispanos en la construcción de comunidades interculturales responsables en todo sector de la vida de las personas.

Esta manera de proceder también invita a expresiones del ministerio hispano que son capaces de funcionar mejor en ambientes ambiguos y complejos, respetando la universalidad de nuestra humanidad y las particularidades del saber cultural que las comunidades latinas han acumulado gracias a sus esfuerzos de sobrevivencia y florecimiento en medio de circunstancias difíciles. Si el catolicismo en los Estados Unidos asume cada vez más características hispanas, entonces un ambiente de inclusión cultural exige que los agentes pastorales hispanos hagan suyo el compromiso que la Iglesia ha asumido por siglos de tratar a los más vulnerables con cierta preferencia. Para hacer esto eficazmente se necesitan ambientes en donde la esencia de la realidad bicultural sea animada por una participación genuina de los latinos en el proceso de establecer condiciones que favorezcan la justicia social y la dignidad humana.

Esta conversación nos lleva entonces a los siente principios claves que informan las prácticas de inclusividad cultural para los agentes pastorales trabajando en las comunidades latinas. Al fondo de estos principios claves se halla una sensibilidad profunda a asuntos, preocupaciones, convicciones y valores latinos, los cuales apoyan y optimizan la vida intelectual, social y espiritual de las comunidades latinas, tanto como feligreses y ciudadanos del mundo.

1 Asumir una perspectiva del mundo profundamente relacional, especialmente en cuanto a las necesidades multiculturales de las comunidades latinas y la formación educativa y espiritual de los jóvenes. Dicha perspectiva exige modelos de educación y liderazgo enraizados en procesos intensamente relacionales y comunitarios. Desde esta perspectiva se crean consistentemente oportunidades para que los latinos participen en la vida de la Iglesia y luchen por condiciones de justicia en el mundo.

2 Articular una memoria y una comprensión institucional de las dinámicas de poder en la Iglesia y la sociedad para promover estrategias y relaciones que puedan conducir a un cambio para mejorar la realidad. Estas nuevas maneras de ser y conocer afirman la importancia de la pluriversalidad multilingüe y multicultural que los agentes pastorales hispanos pueden ofrecer a la Iglesia y al mundo como agentes de gracia y sabiduría.

3 Prácticas de diálogo legítimamente bilingües que permitan crear oportunidades diversas dentro de las comunidades para la reflexión, la crítica y la acción, apoyando voces democráticas, la participación y la capacidad de tomar

decisiones en la Iglesia y en el mundo. Estas prácticas facilitan una mejor dinámica en las relaciones intergeneracionales.

4 Promover una apreciación de la historia de las distintas migraciones y los procesos de integración en los que las poblaciones latinas en los Estados Unidos han participado. Dependiendo de sus orígenes, cada comunidad en nuestro país ha tenido su propio caminar y ha salido adelante a pesar de los desafíos, lo cual debe ser recordado. Es importante construir a partir de las lecciones aprendidas y de la fortaleza de las comunidades latinas para sobrevivir y florecer en medio de las dificultades.

5 Comprometerse a valorar la unidad-en-la-diversidad tanto en las comunidades públicas y privadas. Se necesita promover prácticas que apoyen la vitalidad cultural y la solidaridad de las comunidades latinas en medio de las diferencias regionales, nacionales, lingüísticas, sociales y de género.

6 Afirmar los principios de la Doctrina Social de la Iglesia[20] como una manera de confrontar políticas y prácticas de inequidad en la Iglesia y en la sociedad que interfieren con la formación espiritual y educativa de la comunidad. Esto requiere reconocer que para hacer cambios sociales se necesitan los esfuerzos combinados de cada persona tanto individual como comunitariamente. Esto es particularmente clave para aquellos que serán más afectados por las nuevas condiciones que han de surgir. En última instancia, el cambio social exige la fe y la fortaleza personal de trabajar juntos, al igual que el valor para moverse solos cuando sea necesario, para crear un mundo más justo.

7 Promover una colaboración que busque el bienestar y responda a las necesidades de todas las poblaciones vulnerables, sin importar la cultura, la etnicidad, el lenguaje o la fe. Este principio nos recuerda una vez más la importancia de la inclusividad intercultural en el ministerio hispano, la cual requiere un compromiso de promover el bienestar espiritual, social y material de las familias latinas y sus comunidades.

Estos siete principios claves de inclusividad cultural tienen que estar vinculados, por supuesto, a un ambiente de afirmación de la dignidad de la persona humana y de los derechos humanos, junto con un conocimiento de prácticas culturalmente inclusivas que inspiren el despertar de la conciencia, coherencia personal, compromiso espiritual e integridad cultural. Todo esto supone una conciencia social fundamentada en el ideal Freireano: *nuestra vocación es a ser*

---

20 HEFT, J., «Catholic Education and Social Justice», en *Catholic Education* 10, n.1 (2013) 6-23.

humanos[21]. También una conciencia social fundamentada en una manera de enseñar, acompañar pastoralmente y vivir que estén fundamentados en un sentido profundo de fe, esperanza y visión desde el cual todos los ciudadanos culturales del mundo puedan compartir lo mejor que tienen para ofrecer, para que nuestra humanidad universal madure y crezca en el respeto por los recursos de nuestras diferencias culturales.

4
Estableciendo colaboraciones de fe entre la Iglesia y la comunidad

> *Hace falta… una Iglesia que acompañe en el camino poniéndose en marcha con la gente; una Iglesia que pueda descifrar esa noche que entraña la fuga de Jerusalén de tantos hermanos y hermanas; una Iglesia que se dé cuenta de que las razones por las que hay gente que se aleja, contienen ya en sí mismas también los motivos para un posible retorno, pero es necesario saber leer el todo con valentía.*
> —PAPA FRANCISCO[22]

¿Qué significan todos los datos, proposiciones y reflexiones anteriores para la tarea evangelizadora de la Iglesia en las comunidades latinas en los Estados Unidos? Los Latinos, el sector étnico de la población en el país que más crece, hoy en día constituye más del 40% de todos los católicos y este número seguramente crecerá en los próximos años a medida que la tasa de nacimiento de los latinos excede la del resto de las poblaciones étnicas en los Estados Unidos[23]. Este número cada vez mayor de jóvenes hispanos en los programas catequéticos parroquiales es una gran oportunidad para apoyar su formación espiritual. No cabe duda alguna de que la Iglesia sigue siendo un hogar para la vida de la comunidad latina. Pero aun así hemos de preguntarnos: ¿qué papel jugará la Iglesia en la formación de los corazones y las mentes de los futuros líderes de nuestra comunidad global que es cada vez más diversa? ¿De qué manera proveerá la

21 Véase FREIRE, P., *Pedagogy of the Oppressed*, Seabury Press, New York 1971.
22 PAPA FRANCISCO, *Discurso durante el encuentro con el episcopado brasileño, viaje apostólico a Río de Janeiro con ocasión de la xxviii jornada mundial de la juventud,* 28 de julio del 2013, https://w2.vatican.va/content/francesco/es/speeches/2013/july/documents/papa-francesco_20130727_gmg-episcopato-brasile.html (documento visitado el 25 de Agosto del 2014).
23 Véase SHRANK, A., «Dwindling Catholic Schools see Future in Latino Students», en *Catholic News Service,* 28 de febrero del 2013, http://www.religionnews.com/2013/02/28/catholic-schools-seek-out-latino-students/ (documento visitado el 25 de Agosto del 2014).

Iglesia el testimonio profético para educar hacia lo que identificamos como el ideal Freireano de una humanidad común, el cual está firmemente sostenido en la interpretación paulina del Cuerpo de Cristo como una realidad orgánica (1Cor 12,20- 27)?

Por medio de los principios de inclusividad cultural, los cuales son basados en reflexión diálogo, potenciamiento y acción para el bien de todos, puede surgir un sentido más firme de bienestar y vida en comunidad. Dicho surgir será el resultado de las relaciones auténticas que la Iglesia pueda fomentar más de lleno *con* las comunidades latinas. Esta observación sugiere que la relación de la Iglesia con las poblaciones latinas necesita ir más allá del paradigma tradicional de sólo evangelización, el cual de vez en cuando y sin intención reafirma perspectivas de déficit hacia los latinos y sus hijos. Así que las relaciones ministeriales en las comunidades latinas tienen que estar sostenidas por experiencias concretas de la vida diaria, al igual que por prácticas culturalmente inclusivas que permitan el surgir de colaboraciones de fe potenciadoras entre las comunidades eclesiales y la comunidad.

La Iglesia puede trabajar con y por medio de su gente para hacer suyos los interrogantes del campo de la educación, de manera que promueva el actuar, la responsabilidad y la conciencia social tanto de agentes pastorales como de la comunidad. La iglesia institucional puede liderar el camino de lucha para obtener justicia educacional para los estudiantes latinos, dentro y fuera de los campos tradicionales de acción en que se mueven las estructuras eclesiales. Así como se espera que los feligreses lleven su fe a los ambientes seculares, también la iglesia institucional debe ser un ejemplo vivo de lucha por los más pobres en nuestro día. Más allá del papel pedagógico ejercido desde el púlpito, la Iglesia tiene que aceptar la invitación del Papa Francisco a caminar junto con las comunidades latinas y acompañarnos en nuestro caminar en búsqueda de una mejor vida para nuestros hijos.

El ministerio hispano como compromiso revolucionario

Yo, en cambio, les pido que sean revolucionarios, les pido que vayan contracorriente; sí, en esto les pido que se rebelen contra esta cultura de lo provisional, que, en el fondo, cree que ustedes no son capaces de asumir responsabilidades, cree que ustedes no son capaces de amar verdaderamente.

—PAPA FRANCISCO[24]

En muchas de sus declaraciones públicas recientes, el Papa Francisco ha llamado al clero, los fieles y a todos el mundo no sólo a renovar nuestra preocupación por los pobres, sino a ser revolucionarios y rebeldes en este tiempo de crisis, en contra de las fuerzas opresoras y sin amor que nos empobrecen a todos espiritual y materialmente. El «amor verdadero» del que habla el Papa Francisco le hace eco a la «pedagogía del amor» de la que habló Paulo Freire y la noción de Gustavo Gutiérrez de que «la teología es una carta de amor». Se trata de un amor por lo divino que cuestiona toda forma de dogmatismo, teoría desencarnada y afiliación ideológica para unir el amor de la Iglesia y el pueblo en acción comunitaria, inspirados por la verdad del Evangelio, para mejorar la vida de nuestras hermanas y hermanos en el mundo. Esta declaración de amor del Papa debe informar de lleno el ministerio de la Iglesia y su compromiso con un mundo culturalmente inclusivo y socialmente justo.

Esta tarea revolucionaria tiene que incorporar un compromiso profundo y humilde a fomentar la participación comunitaria y una fe en la capacidad de las personas a crecer y juntos reinventar estructuras que ayuden a responder a las necesidades esenciales de sus vidas. Sin lugar a duda, esto exige un cambio en el ejercicio del poder y la adopción de relaciones más equitativas que ayuden a promover la conciencia, la responsabilidad social y la transformación de la vida comunitaria. Al hablar de «liderazgo» tenemos que integrar a las personas que son parte de la comunidad, asegurándonos de que las políticas y las prácticas que nos guían están disponibles en su propio idioma y cultura. Al hacer esto, una praxis profunda, fundamentada en el amor y la dignidad, puede apoyar el diálogo re-

---

24 PAPA FRANCISCO, *Discurso durante el encuentro con los voluntarios de la xxviii jornada mundial de la juventud,* 28 de julio del 2013, https://w2.vatican.va/content/francesco/es/speeches/2013/july/documents/papa-francesco_20130728_gmg-rio-volontari.html (documento visitado el 25 de Agosto del 2014).

querido para nombrar, criticar y trabajar juntos para desmantelar la injusticia que asfixia nuestra existencia como católicos y ciudadanos del mundo. El Papa Francisco afirma: «Todas las guerras, todas las luchas, todos los problemas que no se resuelven, con los cuales nos encontramos, se dan por falta de diálogo »[25]. Su fe inamovible en el poder del diálogo, sostenido en el amor, sirve como una base ética indispensable para un ministerio que humanice a la comunidad.

El Papa Francisco nos llama tanto a católicos como a quienes no son católicos a la transformación de la conciencia y a que lo hagamos con valor, compromiso y audacia. La Iglesia tiene que seguir transformándose en su práctica y aspirar a extender sus límites como santuario y lugar seguro. Todos tenemos que hacer esto también para trabajar juntos en medio de la realidad como se nos presenta en lo cotidiano de nuestras vidas, en donde expresiones de injusticia que son pecaminosas con frecuencia se han normalizado y se mantienen. Es aquí en donde el ministerio hispano verdaderamente puede cultivar y ser un lugar de diálogo público continuo. Ya sea en fuera de nuestras comunidades y escuelas o dentro del contexto de la educación católica y los programas catequéticos, potenciar a los más jóvenes sirve para transformar una cultura de exclusión y les prepara para participar en un mundo en donde la inclusión cultural sea la norma. La labor revolucionaria del ministerio hispano es una que se enfoca consistentemente en establecer un mundo que nos haga más humanos, un mundo que facilite una conciencia crítica y cristiana al igual que la responsabilidad social.

Prácticas culturalmente inclusivas que se enfoquen en el diálogo y la participación activa permiten a los agentes pastorales relacionar los asuntos educativos como el bienestar general de las familias latinas y sus sueños de procurar una mejor vida para sus hijos. Esta observación presupone que la Iglesia tiene una responsabilidad moral de responder a las necesidades integrales de las poblaciones latinas, las cuales constituyen uno de los grupos más fieles dentro de la Iglesia. Sin embargo, acompañar espiritualmente a la comunidad sin tener en cuenta su cultura o las realidades sociales que afectan negativamente su libertad personal y crecimiento comunitario no sólo es contraproducente, sino contradictorio teniendo en cuenta la larga historia de compromiso con los más vulnerables al centro de las convicciones cristianas de la Iglesia. El ministerio hispano,

25 PAPA FRANCISCO, *Discurso a un grupo de estudiantes y profesores del colegio Japonés Seibu Gakuen Bunri Junior High School de Saitama, Tokio (Japón)*, 21 de agosto del 2013, https://w2.vatican.va /content/francesco/es/speeches/2013/august/documents/papa-francesco_20130821_collegio-saitama-giappone.html (documento visitado el 23 de octubre del 2014).

como colaboración formidable que responde a los intereses de la Iglesia y de la comunidad, parece ser el contexto ideal para responder a las preocupaciones éticas y prácticas más urgentes con relación a la educación de los estudiantes latinos.

Por medio de la integración de sus voces biculturales, los agentes pastorales en el ministerio hispano pueden generar de manera eficaz un sentido más profundo de familiaridad cultural, mayor fluidez en la comunicación y solidaridad hacia las comunidades latinas, las cuales en muchos lugares siguen habitando en las márgenes de la Iglesia y de la sociedad. Con un conocimiento sólido de la cultura, idioma, historia, tradiciones y condiciones de los latinos en este hemisferio —junto con una visión de fe, esperanza y amor— la labor del ministerio hispano puede facilitar un tipo de liderazgo que realmente promueva procesos educativos transformadores entre los estudiantes latinos, tanto en escuelas católicas como en otras instituciones.

El ministerio hispano posee un potencial único para acompañar a las poblaciones latinas en su caminar de formación espiritual y su responsabilidad como ciudadanos globales, invitando a quienes tienen experiencia en el mundo de la participación política y capacitando con los recursos apropiados a quienes anhelan un mundo más justo para sus hijos. Al interpretar eficazmente con valor y ánimo las realidades difíciles que acompañan a la educación de los latinos, sostenidos por lo mejor de la tradición cristiana, el ministerio hispano puede servir como un fuerza humanizadora que conduzca a la afirmación del don de Dios que es la dignidad de cada persona. Con un conocimiento íntimo de la fe, la cultura, la historia, el idioma y las realidades biculturales, la Iglesia puede entrar en una relación renovada *con* las comunidades latinas, una relación en la que las voces y la participación de los latinos es parte fundamental de la vida eclesial.

El ministerio hispano, la tecnología digital y los nuevos medios de comunicación social

Patricia Jiménez *y* James F. Caccamo

Éste es el momento apropiado para que quienes estamos involucrados en el ministerio hispano comencemos a examinar las tecnologías digitales y los nuevos medios de comunicación social, investiguemos cómo estas realidades están transformando nuestras comunidades y reflexionemos sobre los interrogantes que dichas transformaciones nos proponen en el siglo XXI. Este proceso es esencial puesto que ha sido muy poco lo que se ha dicho y escrito sobre tecnologías digitales en el mundo del ministerio hispano.

Durante los procesos de *Encuentro*, los agentes pastorales hispanos reflexionaron primordialmente sobre la prensa y las publicaciones católicas impresas. El Primer Encuentro Nacional de Pastoral Juvenil Hispana expresó el deseo de un portal electrónico que conectara a los jóvenes a nivel nacional al igual que la necesidad de crear recursos mediáticos desde una perspectiva católica[1]. Estas reflexiones fueron sin embargo provisionales, y mientras se han hecho algunos esfuerzos para implementarlas, no se han tomado llevado suficientemente a la práctica a nivel parroquial y diocesano. Además, dichas reflexiones fueron formuladas antes de que el acceso a las comunicaciones móviles se hiciera global, el desarrollo de tecnologías web 2.0 y el crecimiento explosivo de los medios de comunicación social, lo cual ha impactado profundamente la manera como los agentes pastorales hispanos adelantan su misión evangelizadora[2].

En este ensayo queremos abrir un diálogo sobre el tema de los nuevos medios de comunicación social y la tecnología digital en el ministerio hispano. Comenzamos observando tendencias actuales que demuestran el amplio uso de tecnología en las comunidades hispanas. Hacemos luego una reflexión teológica que identifica una resonancia particular entre los medios de comunicación y la clase de teología contextual que caracteriza la experiencia católica hispana. A la luz de esta resonancia, es pertinente pensar en los niveles actuales de implementación de estrategias que involucren el uso de nuevas tecnologías en el ministerio hispano. Para responder a ello, este ensayo sugiere cuatro áreas de atención que líderes pastorales pueden apropiar para diversificar sus estrategias mediáticas y adoptar la tecnología como un nuevo espacio en donde el Evangelio

---

1 NATIONAL CATHOLIC NETWORK DE PASTORAL JUVENIL HISPANA - LA RED, *Conclusiones: Primer Encuentro Nacional de Pastoral Juvenil Conclusiones*, USCCB, Washington, D.C. 2008, 50-51.
2 Las definiciones de lo que es «web 2.0» varían. Sin embargo, estas definiciones comparten en común la idea de que los usuarios pueden crear o alterar el contenido de lo que se presenta. Contribuciones a blogs, reseñas por partes de los lectores, compartir dinámico de códigos de programación, aplicaciones que revelan la ubicación del usuario, y la capacidad de publicar video son algunos ejemplos de tecnologías web 2.0.

se manifiesta auténticamente: 1) «flexibilidad de respuesta», 2) una actitud dialógica en lugar de una autoritaria al hablar de los medios de comunicación social, 3) la asignación y uso de recursos para un ministerio digital, y 4) privacidad al tomar decisiones relacionadas con la tecnología. Por medio de un proceso teológico práctico que involucra ver, juzgar y considerar dinámicas de acción, este ensayo busca fomentar una reflexión sobre el uso futuro de los nuevos medios de comunicación social en el ministerio.

1

El uso de tecnología y medios de comunicación social
entre los hispanos estadounidenses[3]

264   En los últimos años, los medios de comunicación seculares han hablado abundantemente sobre la manera como los hispanos en los Estados Unidos usan cada vez más la tecnología y los nuevos medios de comunicación social. La firma de mercadeo López Negrete observa: «con una tasa de adopción acelerada y con índices más amplios en el uso de [tecnología] móvil y medios de comunicación social, los hispanos han reducido la brecha de la población que está conectada y están en camino de igualar, incluso sobrepasar, el mercado general para el año 2015»[4]. Adoptando rápidamente la tecnología móvil, para el año 2012 el 92% de los hispanos en los Estados Unidos entre las edades de 18 y 70 años tenían teléfonos celulares y el 60% tenían teléfonos inteligentes[5]. Es de notar que los hispanos bilingües son los que más usan las tecnologías móviles[6]. Un área clave de

3   Este ensayo usa el término «tecnología» para referirse a una serie amplia de accesorios electrónicos (ej., teléfonos celulares, tabletas y computadores) que son parte de la categoría «tecnología de información y comunicación». «Los nuevos medios de comunicación social» se refieren a medios masivos de comunicación (ej., correo electrónico, mensajes de texto, videoconferencias, medios de comunicación social, podcasts, blogs y micro-blogs) que han surgido con estas tecnologías.

4   LÓPEZ, N., *How «Techno-Hispanics» Are Influencing Social Media,* junio del 2012, http://www.hispanictrending.net/2012/06/how-techno-hispanics-are-influencing-social-media.html (documento visitado el 22 de enero del 2014).

5   ZPRYME RESEARCH AND CONSULTING, *2012 Hispanic Mobile Consumer Trends,* junio 2012, http://centerforhispanicleadership.typepad.com/files/Hispanic_Mobile_Consumer_Trends.pdf (documento visitado el 22 de enero del 2014); SMITH, A., «Smartphone Ownership-2013 Update», *Pew Internet & American Life Project,* Pew Research Center, Washington, D.C., 5 de junio del 2013.

6   HEARTLAND MOBILE COUNCIL, *MobiU2013 Seminar: Mobile Hispanics - Presentation,* 20 de junio del 2013, http://www.slideshare.net/heartlandmobile/hmc-mobi-u2013-mobile-hispanics-nielsen-final-061313 (documento visitado el 22 de enero del 2014).

actividad son los medios de comunicación social. A nivel general, los latinos invierten un 56% más tiempo en espacios de comunicación social que el resto de la población. Entre los adultos que usan el internet, los hispanos son los que más usan medios de comunicación social[7]. Teniendo en cuenta esta tendencia contundente de crecimiento, la firma *Zpryme Research and Consulting* acuñó el término «techno-Hispanics» (tecno-hispanos) para describir la realidad cada vez más grande de hispanos que usan tecnología.

El uso de tecnología en el ministerio católico hispano. El crecimiento rápido y decisivo en el uso de nuevas tecnologías mediáticas entre los hispanos tiene implicaciones profundas en cuanto a la manera como los católicos hispanos en los Estados Unidos viven su fe y, por consiguiente, la manera como los agentes pastorales les sirven en el ministerio. Para comenzar, ayudaría mucho entender cómo se usa actualmente la tecnología en el contexto del ministerio católico hispano. Desafortunadamente no se han hecho estudios que describan prácticas relacionadas con el uso de tecnología en el ministerio hispano. Por ello, a comienzos del año 2014 se condujo una encuesta electrónica para obtener información en la cual participaron dieciséis organizaciones ministeriales y teológicas, movimientos apostólicos y agentes pastorales hispanos no necesariamente asociados con los anteriores grupos[8].

En general, la encuesta reveló que los agentes pastorales y los académicos usan tecnología ampliamente. Cerca del 60% de quienes participaron se identificaron como personas que están acostumbradas y se sienten cómodas usando nuevas tecnologías. Cerca del 70% reportaron usar un teléfono inteligente en su ministerio/trabajo profesional, el 54% usa un teléfono inteligente varias veces al día, y el 62% envía mensajes de texto varias veces al día como parte de su ministerio/trabajo profesional.

Los medios de comunicación social juegan un papel importante en la vida de los agentes pastorales y teólogos hispanos. El 89% indicó que usa medios de comunicación social tanto para asuntos personales como profesionales. Los tres espacios de comunicación social que los agentes pastorales hispanos usan más

---

7 VOZ DE AMÉRICA, «Los Hispanos Usan Más Las Redes Sociales», *VOANoticias.com*, 26 de diciembre del 2012, disponible en http://www.voanoticias.com/content/eeuu-redes-sociales-facebook-latinos-hispanos-argentina-peru-/1572679.html (documento visitado el 22 de enero del 2014).

8 En este ensayo un «agente pastoral hispano» se define como cualquier persona sirviendo a los hispanos estadounidenses de habla inglesa o hispana.

son Facebook (71%), YouTube (51%) y Google (47%). El 40% de los participantes que usa medios de comunicación social lo hace primordialmente en inglés, el 38% en inglés y español, y el 22% sólo o primordialmente en español. La encuesta reveló la necesidad de formación y capacitación para usar los nuevos medios de comunicación social pues sólo el 40% ha recibido capacitación formal para usar computadores, el 24% ha sido capacitado para usar los nuevos medios de comunicación social, y sólo el 44% ha recibido orientaciones para usar tecnología y nuevos medios de comunicación social[9].

Las organizaciones nacionales y los nuevos medios de comunicación social. Se les preguntó a los miembros de las mesas directivas de las organizaciones ministeriales hispanas cómo usan los nuevos medios de comunicación social. Aunque las organizaciones sociales hacen uso de medios de comunicación social, dicho uso es limitado y no es consistente con las exigencias diarias y semanales de los hispanos que usan estos medios. Las dieciséis organizaciones reportan tener una página web. Sin embargo, sólo diez de ellas actualizan su página varias veces al año y sólo siete dicen tener herramientas de la generación web 2.0 tales como blogs e integración de medios de comunicación social.

Innovación en cuanto a los nuevos medios de comunicación social y tecnología en el ministerio hispano. A pesar de que el uso de los medios de comunicación social en el ministerio hispano no es el más adecuado, hay algunas instancias de creatividad en el uso de estos recursos. Por ejemplo, USHispanicMinistry.com es un portal electrónico que compila artículos, videos, recursos, organizaciones, programas de formación y oportunidades de trabajo en el ministerio hispano en los Estados Unidos. Teólogos y agentes pastorales contribuyen artículos y videos desde perspectivas únicas y diversas. El portal ofrece recursos en inglés y español e integra plataformas de medios de comunicación social. El *Instituto Fe y Vida* tiene una página en Facebook — *Biblia Católica para Jóvenes*— enfocada en recursos bíblicos para jóvenes hispanos y tiene más de medio millón de seguidores a nivel nacional e internacional.

Las universidades y las diócesis también usan las nuevas tecnologías con el propósito de ofrecer programas de formación. Muchas diócesis como San Ber-

---

9 Véase JIMÉNEZ, P., *Hispanic Ministry Technology and New Media*. Para más información detallada sobre los resultados, ver el resumen del reporte (en inglés), *Summary Report*, disponible en www.ushispanicministry.com/tr.

nardino, Stockton, y Fresno han usado sistemas de teleconferencias para ofrecer programas que cubren sus extensos territorios. Algunos programas se enfocan en certificación de catequistas que no pueden viajar a los centros de capacitación mientras que otros ofrecen educación continua en línea. Algunos de estos programas son en inglés ofreciendo títulos a nivel de postgrado mientras que otros son programas de certificación ofrecidos en español. A nivel universitario, la Universidad de Dayton (*La Comunidad Cibernética Para la Formación en la Fe*) y la Universidad de Notre Dame (*Camino*) ofrecen programas en línea en español que forman comunidades educativas virtuales. Estos programas tienen el potencial de trabajar con las diócesis estadounidenses usando el modelo de grupos definidos que toman clases al mismo tiempo, mientras que los estudiantes reciben orientación presencial en su parroquia o en su diócesis para familiarizarlos con la tecnología. Aunque estos programas en línea están diseñados más para formar y certificar agentes pastorales, hay una gran necesidad de programas, tanto en inglés como en español, que ofrezcan títulos universitarios en línea en el área del ministerio hispano.

2

Tecnología, medios de comunicación social y la realidad social católica hispana

~~~

Más que una manera de pasar el tiempo, comunicarse o crear redes de contactos, la tecnología y los medios de comunicación gozan de seis características que pueden ser compatibles con la experiencia religiosa y cultural de los católicos hispanos.

Una antropología comunitaria. Un estudio local conducido en la Diócesis de Fresno, CA encuestó a varios católicos hispanos sobre el uso y las motivaciones para usar los medios de comunicación social. El 92% de quienes fueron encuestados usan los medios de comunicación social regularmente (diaria o semanalmente) para relacionarse con amigos. El 81.7% los usa para conectarse con familiares y el 64.4% los usa regularmente para formar comunidad[10]. El 80% afirma que los medios de

---

10 Véase JIMÉNEZ, P., *Buenas Noches Facebook Familia: How Social Media is Redefining the Social Location of the Christian Community among Hispanics/Latinos in the U.S.*, tesis doctoral (D.Min.) no publicada, Barry University, 2014.

comunicación social forman comunidad[11]. El 92% de los encuestados en la encuesta nacional de organizaciones hispanas confirma estas observaciones[12].

Lo material y lo espiritual. En el contexto de la espiritualidad católica hispana, la mística con frecuencia se define como una manera de experimentar la realidad en la cual lo espiritual y lo material siempre se entremezclan[13]. Para muchos hispanos esta visión de «mística» también se hace vida en los nuevos medios de comunicación social en los cuales la tecnología, los salones de chat (*chatrooms*), los espacios mediáticos de comunicación social y los teléfonos inteligentes son mediadores de lo espiritual y lo material de una manera casi sacramental. Un ejemplo de ello es cuando las personas no pueden ir a Misa y se conectan a la liturgia por medio de la tecnología, experimentando gracia y presencia, a pesar de no estar físicamente presente en el evento. Aunque estas realidades son complejas y nos interrogan sobre lo que significa ser comunidad espiritual, no las podemos descontar.

El carácter público. Una de las características de la visión religiosa hispana del mundo es su dimensión pública. Hoy en día las fotografías de los altares del Día de los Muertos que se hacen en los hogares y la comunidad se publican en Facebook; el santo del día es compartido vía Tweeter; el viacrucis parroquial se disemina por medio de YouTube. Aparte de muchos otros eventos, la celebración de la Fiesta de Nuestra Señora de Guadalupe en la Arquidiócesis de Los Ángeles se transmite en vivo por medio del internet y se disemina por medio de blogs. Los hispanos siguen expresando y dando testimonio de su fe y prácticas populares, pero ahora lo hacen de manera muy pública en los «*tecno barrios*».

Vida y muerte. El catolicismo hispano exhibe una fascinación especial con la idea de la muerte y la convicción de que las relaciones personales con quienes han muerto continúan, como lo demuestra la celebración del *Día de los Muertos* y las novenas por los difuntos. Los nuevos medios de comunicación social ofrecen espacios nuevos que eclipsan la separación entre la vida y la muerte. Los

11 Ibid.
12 JIMÉNEZ, P., *Hispanic Ministry Technology and New Media.*
13 Véase GOIZUETA, R.S., «The Symbolic World of Mexican American Religion», en MATOVINA, T. y RIEBE-ESTRELLA, G. (eds.), *Horizons of the Sacred: Mexican Traditions in U.S. Catholicism*, Cornell University Press, Ithaca, NY 2002.

perfiles en Facebook y Tweeter con frecuencia permanecen después de que una persona ha muerto y muchos hispanos, por lo general católicos, siguen recordando a quienes están en la presencia de Dios publicando mensajes memoriales en sus perfiles.

Lo Cotidiano. Los católicos hispanos estadounidenses también marchan por este mundo buscando sentido en lo cotidiano, la experiencia y la lucha diaria. La teóloga Ada María Isasi-Díaz se refirió a lo cotidiano como un situarnos en nuestras experiencias[14]. Los nuevos medios de comunicación social permiten a los católicos hispanos la oportunidad de expresar lo cotidiano por medio de imágenes, frases y videos, al igual que darse a conocer y cambiar por medio de un encuentro con otras personas.

Liderazgo innovador. Finalmente, Alicia Marill y Fr. Jorge Presmanes han resaltado la importancia de la eclesiología que ha permeado el Plan Nacional Pastoral como una de comunión y participación[15]. Bajo este estilo de liderazgo, todos los bautizados comparten igualmente en la misión de Cristo por medio de su vocación bautismal. Uno de los aspectos fundamentales de los nuevos medios de comunicación social es su sentido democrático y su estructura de distribución del poder. Dentro de un contexto cristiano, la estructura y funciones de los medios de comunicación social abren espacios para ejercer creativamente nuestro llamado bautismal. Cualquier bautizado puede evangelizar compartiendo un recurso, una imagen, una oración o una devoción. Más importante aún es el hecho de que estas acciones ocurren fuera del contexto de las celebraciones litúrgicas oficiales y pueden ser expresiones de la gracia de Dios en nuestras vidas.

Es importante resaltar estas seis características de los nuevos medios de comunicación social puesto que son compatibles con la visión del mundo religioso hispano, el cual rechaza una comprensión dualista de la realidad[16]. Al considerar dicha realidad y la abundancia de la presencia hispana en los medios de comunicación social nos tenemos que preguntar: ¿cómo hemos de preparar a los agentes pastorales para que sean eficaces en su ministerio en el siglo XXI?

---

14 ISASI-DÍAZ, A.M., *La Lucha Continues: Mujerista Theology*, Orbis, Maryknoll, NY 2004, 95.
15 MARILL, A. y PRESMANES, J., «El ministerio hispano y la reflexión teológica», en OSPINO, H. (ed.), *El ministerio hispano en el siglo XXI: Presente y Futuro*, Convivium Press, Miami, FL 2010, 309.
16 GOIZUETA, R.S., «The Symbolic World of Mexican American Religion», 120-121.

3
La tecnología y los nuevos medios de comunicación social en la nueva realidad social

La tecnología actual y los nuevos medios de comunicación social han surgido como maneras viables para compartir y vivir el Evangelio, especialmente en el contexto hispano. Sin embargo, después de más de veinte años de la revolución digital, las iglesias católicas —con ministerio hispano y el resto— siguen rezagadas en comparación al mundo de los negocios, los grupos sociales y las organizaciones caritativas en cuanto a la interacción con sus públicos. Hay mucho para considerar a medida que la Iglesia avanza estrategias para usar medios de comunicación social en el ministerio. Las siguientes son cuatro preocupaciones que necesitamos tener en cuenta al momento de una conversación sobre el ministerio en un mundo digital:

La flexibilidad de respuesta como elemento fundamental. Encontrar el camino entre muchas opciones disponibles exige estar informados sobre las posibilidades para interactuar tecnológicamente con los fieles. El primer reto será seleccionar el medio (o medios) más adecuado. Desde el mismo momento en que aparecen los sistemas digitales, nos hemos encontrado con una verdadera explosión de maneras para comunicarnos. Mensajes de texto, correo electrónico, páginas web, blogs, medios digitales (film, video, e imágenes), redes para compartir archivos, sistemas de videoconferencia y videojuegos ofrecen una riqueza de maneras para informarnos y conectarnos con los demás. Por cada plataforma hay distintas aplicaciones (*apps*) que se pueden escoger. ¿Hemos de escoger Facebook, Google+, o LinkedIn? ¿YouTube, Vevo, o Vine? ¿Facetime, Skype, o Hangouts? Las posibilidades parecen interminables.

Navegar eficazmente este mar de opciones exigirá una disposición de adaptabilidad y apertura. La industria de la tecnología es volátil y crece gracias a la disrupción. Como resultado, aplicaciones y plataformas pueden hacerse populares o dejarlo de ser, ganar o perder millones de usuarios en cuestión de semanas. En este ambiente, los agentes pastorales tendrán éxito sólo cuando sean capaces de abandonar mecanismos de comunicación social anticuados y adaptarse a tecnologías que son más eficaces. Segundo, los agentes pastorales necesitarán estar abiertos y responder ágilmente a la particularidad de las personas a quienes sirven. Conocer la audiencia a la que se sirve es una de las condiciones fundamentales para los comunicadores, al igual que lo es para la metodología ver-juzgar-actuar al centro del ministerio hispano y la Doctrina Social de la Iglesia. En el siglo XXI, esto exige estar atentos a los grandes cambios demográficos. Hoy en día las preferencias de los usuarios son mucho más específicas[17]. Las personas esperan tecnologías que se ajusten a ellos en la particularidad específica de sus vidas. Cuando las tecnologías no hacen esto, las personas las ignoran. Como resultado, los agentes pastorales necesitan estar «en tiempo real» en donde los miembros de sus comunidades eclesiales están, no donde dichos agentes pastorales piensan que sus miembros están o deben estar.

Ciertamente dicha flexibilidad de respuesta exigirá que los líderes pastorales examinemos nuestros presupuestos ministeriales, aún aquellos que nada tienen que ver con tecnología. Por ejemplo, uno de los presupuestos más comunes en el ministerio hispano en los Estados Unidos es que aquellas personas que servimos sólo hablamos español, por consiguiente los programas deben ofrecerse en español. Sin embargo, un número cada vez mayor de grupos que se identifican como católicos hispanos, especialmente entre los jóvenes, prefieren el idioma inglés. Los agentes pastorales que usan medios de comunicación pero no reexaminan sus percepciones, confiando sólo en aquello que funcionó con generaciones anteriores, seguramente dejarán atrás a sus comunidades.

La flexibilidad de respuesta también exigirá, por supuesto, una evaluación crítica de lo que creemos con relación a la tecnología. Por ejemplo, cuando estalló el escándalo de abuso sexual, la Arquidiócesis de Filadelfia publicó nuevas orientaciones para quienes se comunican con menores de edad. Bajo el subtítulo «*E-Mail, Instant Messaging, and Text Messaging (sms —short message service)*» (correo electrónico, mensajería instantánea y comunicación usando mensajes de texto) las orientaciones dicen:

> Los maestros y el personal administrativo deben comunicarse con los estudiantes por medio de las cuentas de correo electrónico proveídas por la escuela y/o las páginas web patrocinadas por la escuela[18].

17 Véase MADRIGAL, A., «How Netflix Reverse Engineered Hollywood», *The Atlantic.com,* 2 de enero del 2014, http://www.theatlantic.com/technology/archive/2014/01/how-netflix-reverse-engineered-hollywood/282679 (documento visitado el 9 de enero del 2014).

18 ARQUIDIÓCESIS DE FILADELFIA, OFICINA PARA LA PROTECCIÓN DE NIÑOS Y JÓVENES, *Addendum to the Standards of Ministerial Behavior and Boundaries,* efectivo el 1 de julio del 2011, Filadelfia, PA, 2.

Dicha regla en principio tiene sentido: al comunicarse con los jóvenes, use siempre un medio tecnológico de difusión amplia y que se pueda monitorear, administrado por personal trabajando para la Iglesia. Las tecnologías que no se mencionan, mensajería instantánea y mensajes de texto, son más difíciles de monitorear.

Notemos, sin embargo, lo que en el fondo se asume con relación a la tecnología: las páginas web y el correo electrónico son medios eficaces para comunicarse con los jóvenes. Desafortunadamente dicha convicción sólo tiene algo de cierto. Según el Centro Pew para el Internet y la Vida en América (*Pew Center for Internet and American Life*), en el año 2013, el 78% de adolescentes tenían un teléfono celular, de los cuales casi la mitad (47%) eran teléfonos inteligentes[19]. Los adolescentes hispanos son el grupo más grande usando teléfonos inteligentes (43%) comparados con adolescentes de raza negra que no son hispanos (40%) y adolescentes de raza blanca que no son hispanos (35%). Sin embargo, estos jóvenes hispanos son los que menos acceso tienen a tecnología móvil para usar el internet (quizás debido al alto costo de los planes de datos), dejándolos sin capacidad de acceder a su correo electrónico y páginas web desde sus teléfonos. Los adolescentes hispanos, por el contrario, tienen un índice más alto de uso de sistemas de mensaje de texto comparados con otros grupos. Es notable resaltar que en el año 2012 el centro Pew reveló que los adolescentes hispanos en promedio envían 100 mensajes de texto al día, mientras que los adolescentes de raza blanca, no hispanos envían en promedio sólo 50[20]. Los adolescentes hispanos envían el doble de mensajes de texto a pesar de que tener un 16% menos de posibilidades de poseer un teléfono celular.

En un esfuerzo por proteger a los jóvenes, la arquidiócesis no practicó flexibilidad de respuesta eficientemente con relación a la tecnología, asumiendo que el correo electrónico y las páginas web servirían igualmente las necesidades de comunicación de todos los adolescentes. Usando un punto de partida incorrecto, se estableció un sistema que favorece las prácticas de uso de tecnología de un grupo particular de adolescentes, dejando a aquellos jóvenes que no tienen ac-

---

19 MADDEN, M., LENHART, A., DUGGAN, M., CORTESI, S. Y GASSER, U., «Teens and Technology 2013», *Pew Internet & American Life Project*, Pew Research Center, Washington, D.C. 2013, http://www.pewinternet.org/Reports/2013/Teens-and-Tech.aspx (documento visitado el 23 de mayo del 2013).

20 LENHART, A., «Teens, Smartphones & Texting», *Pew Internet & American Life Project*, Pew Research Center, Washington, D.C. 2012, http://pewinternet.org/Reports/2013/Teens-Social-Media-And-Privacy.aspx (documento visitado el 12 de mayo del 2013).

ceso fácil a correo electrónico y páginas web casi desinformados de las actividades parroquiales. Teniendo en cuenta las realidades tecnológicas en la realidad diaria, es altamente probable que aquellos jóvenes en este último grupo sean hispanos.

El factor de confianza ante un riesgo mayor al incrementar participación. Una segunda consideración que debe informar el uso de la tecnología en el ministerio es el carácter conversacional de la cultura tecnológica. Las páginas web actuales se caracterizan por la idea de que los usuarios pueden alterar el contenido de lo que se presenta. Los lectores comentan en los blogs, los programadores comparten sus códigos, los fotógrafos aficionados distribuyen electrónicamente imágenes que toman y cualquier persona puede subir videos al internet. Como resultado, nos encontramos con una cultura en línea que valora la interacción, el compartir y la contribución. Aunque es fácil criticar el ruido y la superficialidad que hay en el internet, son muchas las comunidades de discurso que existen allí en donde las personas intercambian ideas, se preocupan unas por otras y aprenden mutuamente. En estas comunidades se pueden observar instancias de una antropología comunitaria y un espíritu de *pastoral en conjunto* que es esencial para el liderazgo y el ministerio hispano.

En este contexto, los ministerios digitales necesitarán dar más voz a los usuarios para que contribuyan y participen. Los jóvenes tendrán la expectativa de crear videos sobre sus actividades y los usuarios de Facebook querrán hacer comentarios sobre los eventos en sus parroquias, y todo esto deberá ser supervisado pues el abrirse a la contribución de los usuarios siempre trae consigo algo de riesgo. Sin embargo, las estrategias ministeriales que excluyen esta clase de prácticas seguramente no durarán mucho. La tradición católica romana por lo general ha favorecido un enfoque magisterial con relación a los medios de comunicación que evita cualquier riesgo de ambigüedad y disentimiento. Por ejemplo, las diócesis emiten mensajes definitivos, claros y uniformes que expresan la posición de la Iglesia sin vacilación o variaciones locales. En un día de formación para los sacerdotes en la Arquidiócesis de Filadelfia, los sacerdotes reunidos expresaron con claridad sus reservas e incluso inconformidad con la idea de que los usuarios pudieran publicar en el internet críticas relacionadas con la enseñanza de la Iglesia o algún sacerdote en particular[21]. Para algunos de ellos ésta era razón suficiente para incluso rechazar por completo el uso del internet en el ministerio.

21 James F. Caccamo estuvo presente en este día de formación para los sacerdotes, Parroquia Saint Helena, Blue Bell, PA, el 29 de septiembre del 2010.

Pero los agentes pastorales han de considerar seriamente otro factor en esta ecuación: confianza. La confianza ha sobresalido como un factor crítico en el auge de la tecnología y los nuevos medios de comunicación social[22]. Uno de los elementos claves de establecer con éxito relaciones de confianza en línea es el tomar riesgos[23]. De hecho, crear una comunidad virtual es más que simplemente aparecer allí. Las comunidades virtuales exigen acciones recíprocas en las que todos los miembros toman riesgos, con ciertos niveles de incertidumbre y responsabilidad. Por naturaleza el diálogo auténtico siempre involucra algo de riesgo que hace que exista la comunidad. Así que mientras promover la participación conlleva algo de riesgo, las comunidades eclesiales que se cierran a esta práctica seguramente no engendrarán la confianza necesaria para un ministerio digital vigoroso. Es importante tener en cuenta que este proceso tiene que ocurrir involucrando todas las estructuras, pidiéndoles a los líderes eclesiales que inviertan en laicos competentes que estén bien capacitados con quienes puedan tener una línea abierta de comunicación y en quienes puedan confiar el uso responsable y eficaz de la tecnología para avanzar el bien de la comunidad eclesial. Porque el mundo de los medios de comunicación social cambia rápido, los agentes pastorales necesitan tener la libertad para hablar según sea necesario sin tener que pasar por círculos innecesarios de aprobación, lo cual seguramente creará la necesidad de corregir errores. Si el modelo pastoral que impera es aquel de manejo minucioso de líderes pastorales y los feligreses en lugar de uno basado en la confianza, el uso eficaz de la tecnología no será posible.

Recursos para un ministerio digital. Una tercera consideración que debe informar el uso de la tecnología en el ministerio es la evaluación equilibrada de los recursos necesarios para implementar iniciativas asociadas con un ministerio digital. Mientras que la Iglesia ofrece a sus sacerdotes educación y salario, muchos programas de ministerio hispano sobreviven gracias a la labor de un grupo muy pequeño de agentes pastorales con credenciales y un ejército de voluntarios, por lo general mujeres, o personal pobremente remunerado. El manejo de las páginas web y los medios de comunicación social con frecuencia es asignado a personal administrativo y a voluntarios con poco tiempo en sus agendas. Para reducir la carga, algunos buscan al número creciente de jóvenes católicos his-

---

22 Véase SOLOVE, D., *The Future of Reputation*, Yale University Press, New Haven, CT 2007.

23 FORD, H., «A Sociologist's Guide to Trust», *Phys.org*, 29 de marzo del 2012, http://phys.org/news/2012-03-sociologist.html (documento visitado el 10 de abril del 2012).

panos que están familiarizados con las herramientas digitales, los cuales pueden proveer una solución gratuita a nuestros desafíos relacionados con los medios de comunicación social pero también exigirán supervisión.

Desde una perspectiva razonable, estrategias sostenibles que involucren el uso de tecnología a largo plazo exigirán inversión en recursos adecuados en cuanto a personal, computadores y programas. Por ejemplo, los agentes pastorales necesitan ser capacitados en cuanto al uso de tecnología. Las necesidades que surgen con el uso de los nuevos medios de comunicación social deben ser parte integral de la formación ministerial. En este sentido el Vaticano ha invitado a que haya mayor capacitación en cuanto a las comunicaciones, aunque la respuesta hasta ahora ha sido modesta[24]. Hay que afirmar que la época en que los agentes pastorales pueden hacer un buen trabajo sin capacidades para usar medios digitales está llegando a su fin.

Segundo, si vamos a invitar a los jóvenes que están familiarizados con los nuevos medios de comunicación social a participar en el ministerio, se necesita una gran variedad de recursos para su formación. Los agentes pastorales hispanos deben conocer su tradición y entender la realidad humana profunda y compasivamente. También deben tener un nivel básico de conocimiento de los recursos tecnológicos y de los límites personales. El mundo digital valora muchas conductas que cuando son practicadas por los agentes pastorales desdicen de su labor. Compartir demasiado, imponer posiciones ideológicas, publicar fotografías comprometedoras, y usar el botón «me gusta» cuando se trata de organizaciones cuestionables por su valor irónico, entre otras acciones, puede estar bien para personas privadas pero no son apropiadas en el caso de agentes pastorales que representan a la Iglesia y están llamados a ser modelos de vida para otras personas.

Tercero, siendo consecuentes con el compromiso católico con la justicia, se deben adjudicar recursos para compensar a quienes avanzan ministerios digitales. Los católicos que son parte de la «Generación del milenio» y han sido formados en una cultura digital participativa están acostumbrados a pasar horas creando información mediática sin compensación. Teniendo en cuenta las limitaciones económicas, es tentador aceptar su servicio entusiasta como volun-

24 CONGREGACIÓN PARA LA EDUCACIÓN CATÓLICA, *Orientaciones sobre la formación de los futuros sacerdotes para el uso de los instrumentos de la comunicación social*, Vaticano, Roma 1986, http://www.vatican.va/roman_curia/pontifical_councils/pccs/documents/rc_pc_pccs_doc_190319 86_guide-for-future-priests_sp.html (documento visitado el 11 de mayo del 2014).

tarios, ignorando nuestra responsabilidad de pagar salarios justos. Además, los agentes pastorales deben tener las herramientas necesarias para hacer su trabajo, por ejemplo teléfonos inteligentes, computadores, y aplicaciones. En última instancia, somos testigos del surgir de nuevas formas de liderazgo dentro de la Iglesia que son consistentes con las sensibilidades eclesiológicas de la comunidad hispana. La creación de programas ministeriales sostenibles y eficaces que involucren el uso de los nuevos medios de comunicación social sólo será posible en donde se inviertan los recursos para apoyar a estos nuevos líderes.

Privacidad en cuanto a las opciones tecnológicas. Un último aspecto que necesita informar el uso de los nuevos medios de comunicación en el ministerio es el uso de la privacidad. Como buenos administradores de los recursos de la Iglesia, los agentes pastorales tienden a usar instrumentos de comunicación, sistemas de compartir información y herramientas para la creación de información mediática que están disponibles gratuitamente. Sin embargo, es fundamental conocer las implicaciones de nuestras decisiones para salvaguardar la privacidad de quienes servimos. En parte, esto apunta a una preocupación legal. Uno elemento de información que más se valora es la ubicación del usuario, la cual muchas aplicaciones graban, incluyendo aquellas que parecieran no tener componentes interesados en este tipo de información como en el caso de juegos, medios de comunicación social y portales para compartir videos. La información sobre la ubicación del usuario es especialmente un asunto sensible para la comunidad hispana, para quienes el contacto con extranjeros o personas indocumentados no es inusual. Queremos asegurarnos que el compromiso católico a la libertad de movilizarse no se infrinja por el uso de la tecnología.

Más allá de las preocupaciones legales, los agentes pastorales tienen que tener sensibilidad con relación a lo que se puede llamar necesidades de «privacidad existencial». Los agentes pastorales ya usan herramientas digitales en su trabajo para comunicarse y reflexionar. Pueden invitar a un grupo de católicos a usar una aplicación de fotografías para expresar algo muy personal o invitar a grupos para usar un video que les ayude a interpretar sus experiencias. En estos casos, la tecnología facilita el desarrollo humano integral al crear espacios personales, privados y sin censura para explorar y abrirse. Sin embargo, Hayden Ramsey ha propuesto el argumento de que la privacidad es una precondición necesaria «para participar eficazmente en cada realidad humana buena», incluyendo la vida espiritual[25]. Sin «la libertad para que la persona no sea intervenida y observada» y «cierta medida de intimidad », careceríamos de la «libertad para crecer y la seguridad para experimentar» lo necesario para un descubrimiento personal necesario[26]. Por consiguiente, la privacidad es clave en la acción pastoral.

Desde una perspectiva crítica podemos observar que mientras las herramientas digitales se pueden usar para crear espacios privados, la función de compartir información ampliamente que es parte integral de la mayoría de aplicaciones significa que siempre existe el peligro de que lo privado se haga público. En una cultura como la norteamericana, la cual valora la contribución y la creatividad del usuario, compartir —a veces en exceso— es una tentación constante. Desafortunadamente, las motivaciones para compartir información son muchas, aun excluyendo aquellas que involucran el mundo legal. Según un estudio en el año 2012, el 37% de las compañías estadounidenses usas los medios de comunicación social para investigar a posibles empleados[27]. Lo hacen por varias razones y el 34% de administradores encargados de contratar personal que miran a los medios de comunicación social deciden no proceder con muchos candidatos después de hacerlo. La razón más citada es que el 49% encontró material que de alguna manera consideran provocativo o inapropiado. Al compartir imprudentemente, muchas cosas reveladoras a las que invitamos a las personas a crear en privado pueden fácilmente convertirse en obstáculos.

Es importante afirmar el énfasis que la tradición católica hispana hace en expresar la identidad religiosa de la persona de manera pública y en acciones no litúrgicas. Sin embargo, dichas acciones tienen grandes implicaciones en una sociedad conectada. Los agentes pastorales tienen que tener estas realidades en cuenta para evitar comprometer la privacidad de las personas a quienes sirven. Ente las prácticas sencillas que los agentes pastorales pueden usar están el escoger servicios anónimos que cifren la información y educar a los miembros de las iglesias con relación a técnicas de privacidad. Una práctica más compleja es usar un servidor privado en la parroquia. En cualquier caso, desarrollar programas de ministerio hispano que utilicen tecnología exigirá que tomemos decisiones inteligentes para que las prácticas religiosas no le hagan daño al pueblo al que servimos.

---

25 RAMSAY, H., «Privacy, Privacies and Basic Needs», *Heythrop Journal* 60 (2010) 294.

26 Ibid., 295.

27 CARREERBUILDER, «Thirty-Seven Percent of Companies Use Social Networks to Research Potential Job Candidates, According To New Careerbuilder Survey», http://www.careerbuilder.com/share/aboutus/pressreleasesdetail.aspx?id=pr691&sd=4%2F18%2F2012&ed=4%2F18%2F2099 (documento visitado el 12 de mayo del 2014).

Conclusión

∽

En este ensayo hemos sugerido que la tecnología que nos permite informarnos y comunicarnos ofrece nuevas oportunidades para el ministerio que son consistentes con las convicciones básicas de la tradición católica hispana. Los hispanos en los Estados Unidos han adoptado el uso de la tecnología y los nuevos medios de comunicación social a un ritmo acelerado, sobrepasando a otros grupos demográficos en estas áreas. Sin embargo, los agentes pastorales todavía no usan las herramientas digitales de manera amplia. Los líderes pastorales en la comunidad católica hispana harán bien en establecer programas sólidos para interactuar con los católicos en sus nuevos mundos digitales. Hemos sugerido que como agentes pastorales y líderes adopten una actitud de flexibilidad de respuesta, faciliten procesos para afirmar las contribuciones de las personas a quienes sirven, se aseguren de que suficientes recursos se dediquen a estos esfuerzos, y se ponga atención al tema de la privacidad de las personas con quienes se comparte en los espacios de los nuevos medios de comunicación social. El observar estas dinámicas ayudará a establecer nuevas conexiones con las personas a quien sirven.

Lo que no hicimos, sin embargo, ha sido delinear lo que se pudieran considerar como «mejores prácticas» para usar la tecnología en el contexto del ministerio católico hispano. Los católicos pueden medir su progreso usando herramientas de medición prestadas del mundo de los negocios o de la comunidad evangélica protestante. Pero el hacer esto puede conducir a la Iglesia a adoptar prácticas que no son necesariamente compatibles con las convicciones que afirman el desarrollo integral de la persona y las iniciativas de justicia social propias de la educación y la acción pastoral católicas. Así que un paso clave en el desarrollo de programas que sean parte de un ministerio digital será reunir a los agentes pastorales y los expertos en tecnología para identificar las metas que se pueden lograr auténticamente con la tecnología. Este diálogo de colaboración habrá de responder a los nuevos interrogantes relacionados con la misión de la Iglesia, las necesidades de la gente y la manera como el ministerio digital puede ser el puente que sirve estas dos dimensiones. Estas realidades han de tratarse como prioridades.

Por último, es importante afirmar que el catolicismo no es una tradición que menosprecia la tecnología. Los Papas del siglo xx y del siglo xxi se han valido ampliamente de los medios de comunicación: el Papa Pío xii con la radio, San Juan Pablo ii con la televisión, y el Papa Francisco con Twitter e Instagram. Muchos agentes pastorales católicos están reconociendo que los instrumentos de comunicación social funcionan mejor cuando se usan para responder a las realidades morales y espirituales urgentes de la liberación de las comunidades humanas. Por consiguiente, las decisiones que se hagan con relación a la tecnología siempre han de tener en cuenta dichas realidades urgentes. No estamos sugiriendo que los medios de comunicación hispanos serán o deberán ser completamente digitales. El mundo de los medios de comunicación es complejo y la flexibilidad de respuesta exige que nuestras decisiones respeten dicha complejidad. En última instancia, el ministerio católico hispano se beneficiará significativamente de un gran conjunto de espacios de comunicación social en el proceso de servir las necesidades de la Iglesia. La tecnología y los nuevos medios de comunicación social jugarán un papel central en la tarea pastoral de la Iglesia el siglo xxi.

El ministerio hispano y el liderazgo

Hilda Mateo, *MGSpS*

¿Dónde ha de comenzar el esfuerzo de identificación del itinerario para fomentar un auténtico liderazgo latino?
—ALLAN FIGUEROA DECK, SJ[1]

Luciendo su distintivo sombrero de vaquero mexicano y botas, José, un hombre de mediana edad, de baja estatura, con ingenio, humor y convicción se presentó frente a cuarenta hombres y mujeres católicas en una zona rural de su diócesis en el suroeste de los Estados Unidos en una fría mañana de noviembre. Acomodó el podio, subió al segundo escalón que rodea la chimenea de piedra —jocosamente recordándole a la gente que necesitaba un poco de ayuda para verlos— y comenzó su reflexión teológica sobre el «Éxodo y la experiencia migratoria». Usando «palabras de la vida diaria» contextualizó las Escrituras judías dentro del marco general de la Doctrina Social de la Iglesia e hizo comparaciones entre la movilidad y las dificultades de los israelitas en la antigüedad y la de los inmigrantes hispanos contemporáneos en los Estados Unidos. A lo largo de su discurso, José, aparentemente confiando más en su experiencia que en las notas que llevaba, no dudó en hacer conexiones explícitas entre los opresores egipcios y la «migra»[2]. Invocando la fe y la confianza en el Dios del Éxodo, concluyó su discurso con una exhortación clara a sus hermanos católicos, la cual suscitó aclamaciones por parte de quienes le escuchaban y una ovación de pie: «Lo que hace falta hoy son nuevos Moiseses, nuevos líderes; y, ¿por qué no? también nuevas Moisesas, sí, hombres y mujeres que respondan al llamado de Dios de guiar a su pueblo inmigrante».

La reflexión de José fue la tercera charla como parte del currículo para participantes en el primer nivel de un programa de dos días copatrocinado por el Centro Cultural México Americano (MACC, por sus siglas en inglés)[3] y la Red Católica del Campesino Migrante (RCBM, por sus siglas en inglés). José había participado hacía tres años en los dos niveles del programa de formación y sabía bien que el objetivo de ese fin de semana era ayudar a «*fomentar* el potencial de *liderazgo* de los trabajadores campesinos migrantes católicos con el objetivo

---

1 FIGUEROA DECK, A., «Latino Leaders for Church and Society: Critical Issues», en CASARRELLA, P.J. y GÓMEZ RUÍZ, R. (eds.), *El Cuerpo de Cristo: The Hispanic Presence in the U.S. Catholic Church*, Academic Renewal, Lima, OH 2003, 184.

2 La palabra «migra» se usa generalmente entre los inmigrantes hispanos para referirse al Servicio de Inmigración y Control de Aduanas (ICE, por sus siglas en inglés), que se encarga de aplicar leyes federales que rigen el control de fronteras, aduanas, comercio e inmigración. Véase https://www.ice.gov/espanol.

3 En el año 2008 MACC se convirtió en una universidad: Mexican American Catholic College.

de que conocieran sus derechos y responsabilidades en la Iglesia y en la sociedad»[4].
Aunque la terminología para hablar de liderazgo se suponía en el contexto, el
uso recurrente de la palabra «líderes» y la inclusión consciente de las mujeres en
su discurso fue particularmente notable. Sin embargo, lo que cautivó al público
fue el testimonio enérgico de José: encarnaba las palabras y los conceptos, los
cuales compartía desde su propia experiencia.

Una vez terminada la charla, una mujer emocionada se me acercó. Quería
hablar conmigo sobre el liderazgo de José. Se trataba de una abogada experta en
derecho civil que había inmigrado recientemente a los Estados Unidos y había
conocido a José hacía unos pocos meses a través de sus respectivos trabajos en
la campaña *Justicia para los inmigrantes*[5]. Con algo de escepticismo, ella se pre-
guntaba cómo un hombre con tan poca educación formal había adquirido la
habilidad de movilizar a otros de manera tan eficaz. Su comentario me hizo reflexionar sobre las diversas interpretaciones que hay sobre la noción de liderazgo. Cada interpretación nos invita a preguntarnos no sólo *quién* puede ser un
líder competente, sino también *dónde* y *cómo* diferentes personas son llamadas
para ejercer roles de liderazgo. ¿Qué distingue a un «líder» de una persona que
«no es líder»? Si los líderes, según las definiciones clásicas, existen dentro de una
dinámica relacional que requiere «seguidores», entonces tenemos que preguntarnos: ¿quién lidera a quién, hacia dónde, con qué fines y en pos de qué resultados? ¿Se limita la terminología que usamos para hablar sobre liderazgo en la
Iglesia al papel de los obispos, sacerdotes, religiosas y religiosos, y los ministros
eclesiales laicos que sirven en posiciones «oficiales», ya sea remuneradamente o
como voluntarios dentro de las estructuras jerárquicas eclesiales? Aún más, ¿se
convierte una persona automáticamente en un líder al recibir la ordenación o
la consagración, o la autorización en el caso de los ministros laicos que han recibido una formación formal, usualmente estudios universitarios, y algún tipo de
credencial oficial? ¿Cuál es, entonces, la relación entre el fomento del liderazgo
y el discernimiento, la vocación y la misión? ¿Puede alguien como José ser reconocido estrictamente —y se considerado seriamente como una voz clave en la

---

4   Este fue el objetivo del programa en diciembre del año 2006 tal como se leía en el plan de estudios.
5   En junio del año 2004, el Comité para la Migración y la junta directiva de la Red Legal Católica
    de Inmigración (Catholic Legal Immigration Network, Inc.) de la Conferencia de Obispos Ca-
    tólicos de los Estados Unidos (USCCB, por sus siglas en inglés) decidieron hacer de la reforma
    migratoria integral una prioridad de la política pública de la iglesia al lanzar la campaña *Justi-
    cia para los Inmigrantes: Un viaje de esperanza*. Véase http://www.justiceforimmigrants.org/
    en-espanol.shtml

conversación— como «líder» según los estándares presentes que se presuponen para servir en el ministerio pastoral en la Iglesia Católica en los Estados Unidos? Si es así, ¿qué faculta a José para servir? La educación formal académica y la autorización oficial de la jerarquía no parecen haber jugado papel alguno en este caso. Sin embargo, decenas de miles de católicos latinos como José ejercen su liderazgo en sus comunidades de fe de maneras muy influyentes. Quiero sugerir que es su capacidad de reconocer y reclamar su propia identidad bautismal como discípulos misioneros de Jesucristo lo que los impulsa a asumir compromisos que con frecuencia se identifican con categorías como «liderazgo».

El papel del agente pastoral, sin embargo, refleja la manera práctica como la comunidad entiende la tarea pastoral. Si el ministerio es una actividad reducida a pasar día y noche en una oficina tomando decisiones ejecutivas, recaudando y administrando fondos, y tomando decisiones sobre empleados, por consiguiente el mejor modelo de liderazgo es el de un director ejecutivo (*Chief Executive Officer* o CEO, en inglés). Estos directores ejecutivos normalmente llegan a estas posiciones gracias a sus credenciales, sus conexiones en altos niveles y sus habilidades para tomar decisiones prácticas. ¿Cuántas personas hemos conocido en el mundo del ministerio que sean excelentes directores ejecutivos? Lo más probable es que muy pocos son como José, quizás con alguna excepción. Sin embargo, en esta reflexión sobre el liderazgo pastoral latino nos desafían las palabras del Papa Francisco:

> La pastoral en clave de misión pretende abandonar el cómodo criterio pastoral del «siempre se ha hecho así». Invito a todos a ser audaces y creativos en esta tarea de repensar los objetivos, las estructuras, el estilo y los métodos evangelizadores de las propias comunidades. Una postulación de los fines sin una adecuada búsqueda comunitaria de los medios para alcanzarlos está condenada a convertirse en mera fantasía[6].

Datos estadísticos recientes indican que hay una brecha cada vez más grande entre el número de agentes pastorales dedicados al ministerio hispano y la creciente población latina[7]. Según la Oficina del Censo de los Estados Unidos y el Centro de Investigación Pew: «La población hispana creció un 47.5% entre el

---

6 PAPA FRANCISCO, *Evangelii Gaudium*, n. 33.
7 Véase THE PEW FORUM ON RELIGION AND PUBLIC LIFE, *Changing Faiths: Latinos and the Transformation of American Religion*, Pew Hispanic Center, Washington, D.C. 2007; OSPINO, H., *El ministerio hispano en parroquias católicas: Reporte inicial de los resultados del Estudio Nacional de parroquias católicas con ministerio hispano*, Our Sunday Visitor, Huntington, IN 2015.

año 2000 y el año 2011»[8]. Este aumento es similar en términos de afiliación eclesial, para el cual las cifras indican que «cuarenta por ciento del crecimiento total de feligreses registrados en las parroquias estadounidenses entre el 2005 y el 2010 se debe a los hispanos/latinos»[9]. Al reconsiderar las metas y los métodos para un ministerio pastoral eficaz se nos exige identificar maneras creativas para inspirar una visión de liderazgo desde la perspectiva hispana que ofrezca posibilidades para que mujeres y hombres se preparen para ser «discípulos misioneros» latinamente[10].

Sin lugar a duda, el liderazgo es y ha sido, como nuestra memoria histórica atestigua, una preocupación central para los ministerios hispanos[11]. Una manera en que esto se ha demostrado es a través del uso común y frecuente del lenguaje de «liderazgo» entre los agentes pastorales y teólogos católicos hispanos en los Estados Unidos, especialmente en documentos oficiales. El *Plan Pastoral Nacional para el Ministerio Hispano* (1987) claramente presenta como prioridad el fomento de «liderazgo por medio de la educación integral que sea fermento del Reino de Dios en la sociedad»[12]. En *Encuentro y Misión* (2002), los obispos católicos estadounidenses declararon que habían «escuchado las voces de *líderes* hispanos —de los laicos y del clero», y se dirigieron con el documento a «todos los católicos, particularmente a los *líderes* pastorales involucrados en el ministerio con hispanos»[13]. Pero, ¿a qué se refieren exactamente estos documentos al usar la palabra «líder»? ¿Estamos usando el término al igual que se usa en con

---

8 DESILVER, D., «5 facts about Hispanics for Hispanic Heritage Month», http://www.pewresearch. org/fact-tank/2013/09/17/5-facts-about-hispanics/ (documento visitado el 28 de octubre del 2013).

9 GRAY, M., «Special Report: Multicultural Findings», *Emerging Models of Parish Leadership*, Center for Applied Research in the Apostolate, Washington, D.C. 2012, 11. Este reporte también pone de relieve que «nueve de cada diez líderes parroquiales se identifican racialmente como blancos, no hispanos».

10 La categoría «discípulos misioneros», estrechamente asociada con el pontificado del Papa Francisco, es también el enfoque distintivo de la v Conferencia General del Episcopado Latinoamericano y del Caribe en su documento final, conocido familiarmente como *Aparecida* (2007).

11 Para un análisis todavía relevante de la realidad y de los retos de los ministerios hispanos véase OSPINO, H. (ed.), *El ministerio hispano en el siglo XXI: Presente y Futuro,* Convivium Press, Miami, FL 2010. Llamo la atención en particular a la sección de consideraciones importantes en el capítulo de OSPINO, H. y MIRANDA, E.M., «El ministerio hispano y la formación para el liderazgo», 418-422.

12 CONFERENCIA NACIONAL DE OBISPOS CATÓLICOS (ahora CONFERENCIA DE OBISPOS CATÓLICOS DE LOS ESTADOS UNIDOS), *Plan Pastoral Nacional para el Ministerio Hispano*, USCC, Washington, D.C. 1987, n. 2-21. El documento se encuentra en UNITED STATES CONFERENCE OF CATHOLIC BISHOPS, *Ministerio Hispano: Tres Documentos Importantes*, USCCB, Washington, D.C. 1995.

13 CONFERENCIA DE OBISPOS CATÓLICOS DE LOS ESTADOS UNIDOS, *Encuentro y Misión: Un Marco Pastoral Renovado para el Ministerio Hispano*, USCCB, Washington, D.C. 2002, n. 1. Énfasis añadido.

textos que no son eclesiales, en particular el mundo de los negocios o la esfera política?

Escritos recientes revelan que el tema del fomento del liderazgo es un campo de estudio de rápido crecimiento en los Estados Unidos entre investigadores en las áreas de ciencias políticas, sociales y del comportamiento. De hecho, las últimas dos décadas han demostrado «un interés explosivo» en la proliferación y aplicación de «métodos eficaces de fomento del liderazgo»[14]. Etimológicamente, la palabra «liderazgo», tal como se usa en la cultura angloamericana, exalta «la iniciativa, la responsabilidad y las virtudes cívicas»[15]. Ciertamente, consciente de los méritos que los modelos de negocios ofrecen al ministerio en las áreas de organización, responsabilidad y eficacia, cabe preguntar si *todos* los católicos estadounidenses entienden lo mismo cuando se habla de «liderazgo» eclesial[16]. Por ejemplo, Colaboradores en la Viña del Señor (*Co-Workers in the Vineyard of the Lord*, originalmente escrito en inglés), un documento eclesial fundamental que expone detalladamente una visión para el ministerio eclesial laico en los Estados Unidos, habla del «liderazgo en un área particular del ministerio» como una de las cuatro características principales del ministro eclesial laico, sin embargo omite una definición del término «liderazgo»[17]. Al reflexionar sobre el desarrollo del ministerio eclesial laico en el país, H. Richard McCord, señala que «liderazgo es un término que no tiene un significado teológico o bíblico particular»[18]. Se hace imprescindible, entonces, explorar cómo la omisión de una de-

14 HERNEZ-BROOME, G. y HUGHES, R.H., «Leadership Development: Past, Present and Future», en *Human Resource Planning* 27, n. 1 (2004) 25-27.

15 FIGUEROA DECK, A., «Latino Leaders for Church and Society: Critical Issues», 186. Véase también MOLE, G., «Can Leadership Be Taught?», en STOREY, J. (ed.), *Leadership in Organization: Current Issues and Trends,* Routledge, New York 2011, 114-126. Mole destaca el uso positivista del término en el contexto de nuestra sociedad estadounidense e indica la necesidad de plantear desafíos a dicha interpretación.

16 Preocupaciones y cuestionamientos similares con relación al término «ministerio» fueron planteados por los participantes del simposio del año 2009 en el área de «Formación para el liderazgo». Se señaló que «las definiciones predominantes del ministerio eclesial en los Estados Unidos… con frecuencia reflejan perspectivas que muchas veces no tienen en cuenta las voces de los grupos que todavía son considerados como minorías», los autores se preguntan: «¿qué es lo que exactamente tenemos en mente cuando hablamos de ministerio eclesial?». Véase OSPINO, H. y MIRANDA, E.M., «El ministerio hispano y la formación para el Liderazgo», en OSPINO, H. (ed.), *el ministerio hispano en el siglo XXI*, 418; 398-400.

17 CONFERENCIA DE OBISPOS CATÓLICOS DE LOS ESTADOS UNIDOS, *Colaboradores en la viña del Señor: Un recurso para guiar el desarrollo del ministerio eclesial laico*, USCCB, Washington, D.C. 2005, 7-12.

18 MCCORD, H.R., «Lay Ecclesial Ministry: Pastoral Leadership in a New Era», en CAHOY, W.J. (ed.), *In the Name of the Church: Vocation and Authorization of Lay Ecclesial Ministry,* Liturgical Press, Collegeville, MN 2012, 5.

finición básica de liderazgo afecta la manera en que la evangelización, la catequesis y la formación ministerial de los hispanos son concebidos en el medio intercultural de la Iglesia en los Estados Unidos.

A principios de los años dos mil, Allan Figueroa Deck ya había señalado que en nuestras comunidades latinas los «fundamentos teológicos del ministerio y su relación con la noción secular de "liderazgo" han sido poco elaborados». Desafió en aquel entonces a los católicos hispanos a «elaborar una visión específicamente latina del liderazgo» adecuada para las nuevas generaciones[19]. Aludiendo a un estudio realizado entre los miembros del Consejo Nacional Católico para el Ministerio Hispano (NCCHM, por sus siglas en inglés) a mediados de la década de los años noventa, Figueroa Deck observa que cuando se preguntó a los participantes sobre las palabras que venían a su mente cuando pensaban en liderazgo, mencionaban «el servicio, la iniciativa, la responsabilidad y la solidaridad» conjuntamente con ideas negativas, autoritarias y abusivas sobre el liderazgo, tales como «caudillismo» y «caciquismo»[20]. En el año 2012 se llevó a cabo un estudio con el fin de «entender el papel que juega la cultura en la transformación y adaptación de modelos de liderazgo en la Iglesia». Dicho estudio corroboró las observaciones de Figueroa Deck. El proyecto fue parte de una iniciativa más amplia llamada Modelos emergentes de liderazgo pastoral (*Emerging Models of Pastoral Leadership* o EMPL, por sus siglas en inglés)[21]. El Padre Richard Vega en su crónica del proceso describe la dificultad de utilizar el léxico asociado con el término liderazgo entre las llamadas minorías étnicas:

> En cuanto a la formulación del diálogo se refiere, la [iniciativa] *Cultura y su impacto sobre el liderazgo*, el grupo asesor dedicó mucho tiempo analizando el fundamento cultural que permea el concepto de liderazgo entre las poblaciones de inmigrantes. Del diálogo afloró una preocupación clave sobre el liderazgo entre los grupos inmigrantes: el liderazgo puede suscitar sospechas porque evoca privilegio y jerarquía... El

---

19 FIGUEROA DECK, A., «Latino Leaders for Church and Society: Critical Issues», 186, 189. Relacionado con esta conversación, aunque en un contexto no eclesial, véase DAY, D.V., «Leadership Development: A Review in Context», en *Leadership Quarterly*, 11, n. 4 (April 2001) 581-613.

20 Véase FIGUEROA DECK, A., «Latino Leaders for Church and Society: Critical Issues», 189.

21 VEGA, R., «Report on the Culture and Its Impact on Leadership Initiative», *Emerging Models of Pastoral Leadership* (October 2012), 3, http://emergingmodels.org/wp-content/uploads/2013/05/Final-Report-on-Culture-and-Leadership.pdf (documento visitado el 8 de octubre del 2013). Para mayor información sobre la iniciativa *Emerging Models of Pastoral Leadership* visite www.emergingmodel.org

grupo asesor vio la necesidad de desarrollar un nuevo punto de partida para el diálogo sobre el tema del liderazgo, el cual habría de trascender el contexto cultural particular[22].

Una de las diez recomendaciones finales en el informe de Vega fue que «quienes participan en las diversas etapas del trabajo de formación con líderes laicos y ordenados deben tratar de incorporar la vocación bíblica y bautismal al liderazgo» en su vocabulario[23]. Para el grupo asesor, el «llamado al liderazgo desde una postura bautismal [implica] un cambio significativo en el paradigma a través del cual se interpreta el término *liderazgo*»[24]. El grupo sugirió un lenguaje que enfatizara la noción bíblica de *pastoreo,* la cual «permite que el Espíritu otorgue una variedad de habilidades basadas en distintos niveles de relaciones con diferentes roles dentro de una comunidad, en lugar de percibir el modelo jerárquico como la única alternativa para hablar de liderazgo»[25]. Del mismo modo, el informe final de la iniciativa Modelos Emergentes de Liderazgo Pastoral resalta que los participantes afirmaron la necesidad de enmarcar la «conversación sobre el liderazgo pastoral, no a la luz de prerrequisitos académicos», sino desde el «llamado bautismal común al ministerio»[26].

Al recordar aquel día frío de noviembre en el que José proclamó proféticamente el mensaje liberador del Evangelio, estoy convencida de que él modeló la clase de discipulado que cada persona bautizada involucrada en el ministerio hispano debe encarnar, ya sea laico, religioso consagrado, ordenado. Aún así, me pregunto, ¿sería José reconocido como un «líder» ministerial en su diócesis y en su parroquia? ¿Hubiera sido contratado para dirigir el ministerio en un contexto eclesial? No es descabellado sugerir que la actual escasez de agentes pastorales hispanos comprometidos puede ser sintomática de lo que el teólogo franciscano Kenan B. Osbourne ha identificado como una «insuficiente comprensión del ministerio común que pertenece a todos los cristianos por el Bautismo y la Confirmación»[27]. Es posible también que la mayoría de los latinos y latinas

22 Ibid., 5.
23 Ibid., 12.
24 Ibid., 5.
25 Ibid.
26 PARENT, N.A., «Final Report Executive Summary», *Emerging Models of Pastoral Leadership* (1 de junio del 2013), 7, http://emergingmodels.org/wp-content/uploads/2013/06/Final-Report_ Executive-Summary.pdf (documento visitado el 8 de octubre del 2013).
27 OSBOURNE, K.B., «Envisioning a Theology of Ordained and Lay Ministry», en WOOK, S.K. (ed.), *Ordering the Baptismal Priesthood: Theologies of Lay and Ordained Ministry,* Liturgical Press, Collegeville, MN 2003, 203.

no se identifiquen con el lenguaje de liderazgo y todo lo que presupone según la cultura predominante. Consciente de los temas, visiones, retos y preguntas planteadas por el Simposio nacional sobre el presente y futuro del ministerio católico hispano en los Estados Unidos que tuvo lugar en el año 2009, se mantiene la necesidad urgente de aceptar conscientemente el desafío que propuso Figueroa Deck de elaborar una «visión contemporánea del liderazgo que esté a la vez arraigada en la particularidad de las culturas y las tradiciones religiosas latinas y fundamentada también en la universalidad de la comunión católica»[28].

> La Iglesia tendrá que iniciar a sus hermanos —sacerdotes, religiosos y laicos— en este «arte del acompañamiento», para que todos aprendan siempre a quitarse las sandalias ante la tierra sagrada del otro (cf. Ex 3,5). Tenemos que darle a nuestro caminar el ritmo sanador de projimidad, con una mirada respetuosa y llena de compasión pero que al mismo tiempo sane, libere y aliente a madurar en la vida cristiana. Los discípulos misioneros acompañan a los discípulos misioneros[29].

En la edición de mayo del 2007 de la revista *Leadership*, Keith Grint escribe: «Las organizaciones que tienen muchos líderes, es decir, organizaciones que fomentan el liderazgo en todos los niveles, tanto líderes formales como infor-

---

28 Véase FIGUEROA DECK, A., «Latino Leaders for Church and Society: Critical Issues», 189. Vale la pena señalar, a fin de no restar importancia a la complejidad de la realidad, que cuando se habla de agentes pastorales hispanos estamos hablando de un grupo diverso en términos de nacionalidad, clase social, dominio de los idiomas inglés y español, niveles de educación formal e incluso niveles de educación religiosa. Por ejemplo, Allan Figueroa Deck invita a reconocer que hoy «nuestro liderazgo está compuesto por cuatro generaciones, cada una con su experiencia eclesial propia y particular, y con diferentes niveles de participación en los procesos eclesiales durante los últimos 60 años. Esas generaciones a veces se clasifican de esta manera: 1) Pre-Vaticano II, 2) Vaticano II, 3) Generación X, y 4) Generación del Milenio». Véase FIGUEROA DECK, A., «Reflections on the Hispanic Catholic Moment», ponencia presentada en *Raíces y Alas* 2010 (26 de septiembre del 2010). A su vez, Timothy Matovina sostiene que el conjunto básico de las percepciones y prioridades que dan forma a los «enfoques ministeriales» revela también cuán diversos son los agentes pastorales hispanos. Él clasifica estos enfoques en cuatro grupos: 1) católicos hispanos que han sido parte del ministerio hispano como un *movimiento* (líderes veteranos que ayudaron a aclarar una identidad única y forjaron una memoria histórica), 2) los nuevos inmigrantes (quienes tienden a equiparar el ministerio hispano con el idioma español), 3) los integracionistas, y 4) los agentes pastorales de estilo carismático (que ponen el énfasis primario en la evangelización directa y tienden a involucrarse en movimientos apostólicos). Véase MATOVINA, T., *Latino Catholicism: Transformation in America's Largest Church*, Princeton University Press, Princeton, NJ 2011, 145-155; MATOVINA, T., «El ministerio hispano y el catolicismo en los Estados Unidos», en OSPINO, H. (ed.), *El ministerio hispano en el siglo XXI*, 249-252.
29 PAPA FRANCISCO, *Evangelii Gaudium*, 169; 173.

males, son las que tienen más probabilidades de tener éxito a largo plazo»[30]. Para afirmar, como lo hace el documento *Colaboradores en la viña del Señor,* que «todos los bautizados son llamados a trabajar para la transformación del mundo», implica volver a una visión de la Iglesia en la que todos los «fieles son continuamente capacitados para estar abiertos a los demás»[31]. Con la esperanza de fomentar más instancias de reflexión teológica, concluyo invitando a concentrarnos con un espíritu renovado en una «eclesiología de la vocación» a la luz del Concilio Vaticano II, enraizada en el sacerdocio bautismal de todos los fieles y «situada tanto histórica como culturalmente» en la experiencia de la comunidad hispana[32].

El Nuevo Testamento sugiere que la Iglesia primitiva «no conoció distinción formal entre líderes de la Iglesia y el resto de la comunidad»[33]. Los discípulos cristianos son mujeres y hombres que responden conscientemente a la llamada de seguir a Jesucristo como comunidad de discípulos con el fin de llevar la Buena Nueva de la salvación de Dios: «Vayan y hagan que todos los pueblos sean mis discípulos, bautizándolos en el nombre del Padre y del Hijo y del Espíritu Santo, y enseñándoles a cumplir todo lo que yo les he mandado» (Mt 28,19-20a). Aunque algunos términos bíblicos de los tiempos de las primeras comunidades cristianas tales como apóstoles, gobernantes, anfitriones, *episkopoi y diakonoi* sugieren grados de responsabilidades formales a nivel ministerial, la manera como los entendemos hoy en día en nuestra Iglesia ha evolucionado en gran parte con el transcurso de los años. No olvidemos que desde una perspectiva paulina, «todos los creyentes… participan en la edificación de la vida de la comunidad y su misión en el mundo»[34].

El teólogo Richard Gaillardetz observa que, desde una perspectiva bíblica, la iniciación cristiana por medio del Bautismo conduce al creyente a una relación «ordenada» (es decir que sigue un orden particular del que se derivan implicaciones para la identidad y la acción) con la Trinidad y con la comunidad de los creyentes. Esta relación con Dios y la comunidad de los creyentes nos ordena a su vez hacia una tercera relación, o mejor un «movimiento hacia fuera,

---

30 GRINT, K., «Learning to Lead: Can Aristotle Help Us Find the Road to Wisdom?», en *Leadership* 3 (2007) 233.

31 USCCB, *Colaboradores en la Viña del Señor,* 8; HAHNENBERG, E.P., *Awakening Vocation: A Theology of the Christian Call,* Liturgical Press, Collegeville, MN 2010, 161.

32 HAHNENBERG, E.P., *Awakening Vocation,* 161; GAILLARDETZ, R.R., *Ecclesiology for a Global Church: A People Called and Sent,* Orbis, Maryknoll, NY 2008, 162.

33 GAILLARDETZ, R.R., *Ecclesiology for a Global Church,* 174.

34 Ibid., 29-32.

hacia el mundo en la misión». La esencia del Bautismo cristiano es «ser llamados *y* enviados». Es un compromiso con una nueva forma de existir como discípulos y una «nueva manera de entender la vocación humana», principalmente como vocación misionera[35]. Aunque esto es cierto e inspirador, Edward Hahnenberg observa que «la categoría de vocación [bautismal] ha sido ignorada» y subestimada entre los católicos[36], lo cual exige de los teólogos y ministros una reflexión más profunda. ¿Dónde nos ubicamos como teólogos y agentes pastorales hispanos en esta conversación? Mi experiencia de servicio a nivel de parroquia, decanato y estructura diocesana me dice que la mayoría de los hispanos se mantienen al margen del liderazgo público ya que, como la mayoría de los católicos, tienen dificultades para hacer realmente suya la vocación bautismal, reduciendo así el lenguaje de vocación y liderazgo a unos pocos estados de vida mientras limitan la llamada de Dios a expresiones institucionalizadas[37].

Para las familias católicas hispanas el bautizo de niños es «casi una experiencia universal»[38]. Bautizar un niño tiene connotaciones religiosas y culturales. Es posible que la mayoría de los católicos hispanos no tengan mucha claridad sobre las implicaciones vocacionales del Bautismo, y tal vez están más preocupados por el impacto del pecado original en el individuo que por la incorporación de la persona en la vida y misión de Jesucristo. No obstante, el carácter relacional que define la celebración hispana de los sacramentos, incluyendo los nuevos vínculos familiares que se establecen (por ejemplo, padrinos, madrinas, compadres), ofrecen posibilidades concretas para fomentar en nuestras comunidades procesos prácticos de iniciación a una vida cristiana consciente que cultiven los espacios para que las personas disciernan cómo vivir la vocación cristiana en la comunidad de fe.

La catequesis familiar como parte de la preparación sacramental es una de las áreas que se debe considerar seriamente en la conversación general sobre el fomento del liderazgo entre los católicos hispanos. Esta catequesis ocurre usualmente en la parroquia. Hosffman Ospino nos recuerda que «las parroquias importan»[39]; las parroquias «siguen siendo lugares privilegiados donde los católicos

---

35 Ibid., 186-7.
36 HAHNENBERG, E.P., *Awakening Vocation*, xi –xii.
37 Ibid., xiv, xvi.
38 EMPEREUR, J. y FERNÁNDEZ, E., *La Vida Sacra: Contemporary Hispanic Sacramental Theology*, Rowman & Littlefield, Lanham, MD 2006, 62.
39 Véase HOOVER, B.C. y OSPINO, H., «El ministerio hispano y la vida parroquial» en este volumen.

más activos aprenden, viven y celebran su fe»[40]. El hecho de que millones de niños latinos crezcan acompañados por cuatro adultos bautizados en promedio brinda una oportunidad de elaborar en nuestras comunidades parroquiales un marco de referencia desde las bases para conversar sobre el Bautismo y la vocación cristiana con el objetivo de fundamentar una teología del ministerio y de la acción pastoral en la llamada universal a la misión y al discipulado.

Una manera de proceder es explorar las posibilidades de una reflexión sobre el discipulado cristiano comprometido basada en lo que Roberto S. Goizueta ha llamado «teología de acompañamiento». Tal reflexión sobre el discipulado intencional tendría en cuenta la experiencia histórica, así como la sabiduría antropológica y teológica que emerge del mundo del catolicismo popular hispano en los Estados Unidos[41]. El acompañamiento para Goizueta no es sólo un asunto de acción ética. También incorpora una dimensión afectiva, una dimensión geográfico-espacial (por ejemplo, la ciudad, el hogar), una dimensión de interioridad (compromiso personal y apropiación) y una dimensión espiritual[42]. Caminar con los demás se convierte en una praxis liberadora que da testimonio de Reino de Dios. Tal como indica Goizueta, si la comunidad es el «lugar de nacimiento del yo», ¿cómo podemos encontrar maneras de educar formalmente a los católicos en todos los niveles en el arte o el ministerio del acompañamiento mutuo para promover personas como agentes-sujetos-en-relación con Dios y con los demás para la transformación de las estructuras de muerte *en* el mundo?[43] Antes de que los posibles «líderes» sean formados y enviados, necesitan primero ser reconocidos, acompañados y apoyados en su vocación bautismal.

Ciertamente quedan muchos desafíos que deben ser discutidos. En su reciente estudio sobre las parroquias católicas con ministerio hispano, Hosffman Ospino destaca que una de las áreas que requieren atención pastoral inmediata es el desarrollo de programas y recursos que sirvan a sectores poco tradiciona-

---

40 OSPINO, H., *El ministerio hispano en parroquias católicas: Reporte inicial de los resultados del Estudio Nacional de parroquias católicas con ministerio hispano,* Our Sunday Visitor, Huntington, IN 2015, 54.

41 GOIZUETA, R.S., *Caminemos con Jesús: hacia una teología del acompañamiento,* Convivium, Miami, 2009, 11. Mi deseo es centrar nuestra atención en la praxis liberadora de acompañamiento como un posible medio para referirse a la acción pastoral.

42 Ibid., 271.

43 Véase GOIZUETA, R.S., *Caminemos con Jesús,* 75-115; PAPA FRANCISCO, *Evangelii Gaudium,* n. 169; y MATEO, H., «*Hermenéutica Guadalupana:* Toward an Explicit Pedagogy for the Formation of Lay Associates of the *Guadalupan Missionaries of the Holy Spirit* in the United States Province», disertación doctoral (D.Min.) no publicada, Barry University 2010, 176-77.

les de la comunidad hispana en el contexto de la actividad pastoral[44]. Ospino observa que más de dos terceras partes de los agentes pastorales latinos en parroquias con ministerio hispano nacieron en el extranjero. Estos agentes pastorales prestan sus servicios a menudo siguiendo modelos de ministerio y liderazgo aprendidos en sus países de origen, los cuales tienen mucho que ofrecer y enriquecen la vida ministerial de nuestras comunidades de fe, pero con frecuencia entran en conflicto con modelos ministeriales y de liderazgo que predominan en los Estados Unidos. Esto corrobora los argumentos presentados en este ensayo. Ospino observa también que nueve de cada diez hispanos menores de 18 años han nacido en los Estados Unidos. Sin embargo, este grupo se involucra mucho menos en el ministerio. Irónicamente —o quizá escandalosamente— los jóvenes católicos hispanos se han convertido en un grupo *de facto* «no tradicional» en la Iglesia en los Estados Unidos. La gran mayoría de estos jóvenes católicos no se involucran en programas parroquiales de catequesis, iniciativas de pastoral juvenil, ni escuelas católicas[45]. La mayoría no van a la iglesia con regularidad. ¿Cómo van a discernir su vocación bautismal si están aislados del resto de la comunidad?

Otro desafío es la necesidad de estudiar y afirmar las expresiones de «liderazgo» en aquellas áreas menos estructuradas de la vida católica hispana (por ejemplo, los movimientos apostólicos, los grupos de oración, las hermandades), especialmente los casos en que tales prácticas de liderazgo son percibidas como abusivas y controladoras. Las dinámicas de «liderazgo» tal como se practican a nivel de las bases en nuestras comunidades, los diferentes movimientos y grupos merecen recibir más atención por parte de investigadores y programas intencionales de formación. Y tal vez uno de los desafíos más urgentes siga siendo la falta de reconocimiento y afirmación de las dimensiones públicas y oficiales del liderazgo de las mujeres en nuestras comunidades de fe —la mayoría de los agentes pastorales en el ministerio hispano al nivel de las bases en las parroquias y las diócesis son mujeres latinas.

La teóloga Carmen Nanko-Fernández nos recuerda que «La comunidad latina no es la diversidad de la Iglesia»[46]. «Nosotros *somos* la Iglesia»[47], y ¡*ahora!* es

---

44 OSPINO, H., *El ministerio hispano en parroquias católicas*, 91.
45 Véase OSPINO, H. Y MIRANDA, E.M., «El ministerio hispano y la formación para el Liderazgo», 180-184.
46 NANKO-FERNÁNDEZ, C., *Theologizing en Espanglish: Context, Community, and Ministry*, Orbis Books, Maryknoll, NY 2010, 73.
47 Ibid., 20.

el momento de delinear nuevos objetivos y «buscar juntos los medios para lograrlos»[48] que incluya las voces de los muchos Josés y Josefas en nuestras comunidades. A medida que la comunidad hispana crece, surge también la oportunidad de ofrecer a la Iglesia en los Estados Unidos una teología más integral de la vocación misionera de todos los fieles, una teología que cuestione el «modelo de profesionalismo ministerial norteamericano», el cual está influenciado profundamente por ideas seculares sobre el liderazgo[49]. Tal como insiste el Papa Francisco, sólo con la audacia de reconfigurar creativa y comunitariamente las costumbres, el lenguaje y las estructuras de la Iglesia, seremos capaces de formar una nueva generación de ministros y agentes pastorales hispanos para el ministerio hispano que sean conscientes de ser discípulos misioneros que acompañan a otros discípulos misioneros[50].

48 PAPA FRANCISCO, *Evangelii Gaudium*, 33.
49 GAILLARDETZ, R.R., *Ecclesiology for a Global Church*, 292.
50 CELAM, *Documento de Aparecida*, n. 276.

El ministerio hispano y el estudio de la Biblia

DAVID A. SÁNCHEZ

El fundamento del Catecismo es la Sagrada Escritura[1]

«Les fallamos. Les fallamos por completo». Esto fue lo que le dije a una religiosa una semana después de que abandonó apresuradamente de una de las sesiones del estudio bíblico que yo dirigía. El tema de esa noche era el tercer capítulo del Evangelio de Marcos y habíamos llegado a los versículos 31 al 34, los cuales hablan de los familiares de Jesús. Desafiaba a la clase a considerar las posibles implicaciones teológicas de la idea de que Jesús en verdad tuviera hermanos. Este tema, de hecho, era razón de conversaciones intensas en seminarios universitarios a nivel de postgrado y en muchas conversaciones apasionantes entre católicos y no católicos leyendo la Biblia. Fue en ese momento cuando la religiosa se levantó y abandonó la clase diciendo que nunca había escuchado algo tan irreverente durante su vida. Le fallé porque esa noche yo no entré en diálogo con una comunidad particular de feligreses viviendo en la actualidad, sino con una tradición de siglos interpretando las Escrituras. Al hablar del tema de los hermanos de Jesús, debí haber reconocido la larga tradición de interpretación bíblica católica que niega esta perspectiva y ofrecer mi lectura como una posibilidad que expertos bíblicos contemporáneos han debatido recientemente. Al mismo tiempo, ella falló al no demostrar el mínimo de tolerancia por una realidad más allá de su lectura limitada de la tradición. En el fondo su lectura exhibe un carácter fundamentalista. Nos fallamos mutuamente porque fuimos incapaces de modelar para la audiencia presente, la cual estaba sedienta de las Escrituras, lo que debió haber sido una conversación fiel e intelectual sobre la Biblia y la Tradición. Perdimos una oportunidad, pero aprendimos la lección.

Como latino y experto bíblico, reconozco lo difícil que es dialogar sobre asuntos relacionados con el conocimiento de la Sagrada Escritura en el contexto del ministerio pastoral. Por un buen tiempo he observado la brecha que existe entre el estudio académico y «científico» de la Biblia y el uso diario de las Escrituras en la vida pastoral de la Iglesia. Una separación radical entre estas dos áreas de la vida de la Iglesia puede restringir severamente su misión. En un reporte enviado al Papa Juan Pablo II en 1993, la Pontificia Comisión Bíblica advirtió sobre los efectos nocivos de una exégesis bíblica que empuja «a algunos exégetas a tomar posiciones contrarias a la fe de la Iglesia sobre cuestiones… importantes» y actitudes inadecuadas entre los files que ignoran el valor de los estudios bíblicos en favor de «acercamientos más simples» que conducen nada más y nada menos que a interpretaciones fundamentalistas del texto sagrado[2].

---

1 UNITED STATES CONFERENCE OF CATHOLIC BISHOPS, *Directorio Nacional para la Catequesis*, 24C.
2 Véase PONTIFICIA COMISIÓN BÍBLICA, *La interpretación de la Biblia en la Iglesia*, Roma, 1993.

Con esta realidad en mente, los agentes pastorales trabajando en el ministerio hispano debemos preguntarnos: ¿qué significa para los católicos leer la Biblia dentro de los contextos hispanos? ¿Qué contribuimos los católicos hispanos a la interpretación de las Escrituras a medida que las leemos con la Iglesia en nuestras comunidades particulares? ¿Cuáles son algunos de los mayores obstáculos que los agentes pastorales trabajando en el ministerio hispano y sus comunidades encuentran para situar las Escrituras al centro de sus vidas? Propongo que nos dispongamos a responder a estas preguntas comenzando con una definición inicial de lo que es el conocimiento bíblico, usando como guía al Magisterio de la Iglesia y ciertas contribuciones claves propuestas por expertos bíblicos hispanos. Describiré luego algunos desafíos relacionados con la lectura bíblica que han impedido fomentar un mejor conocimiento de la Biblia entre los latinos. Los agentes pastorales tienen que saber sobre estas limitaciones para así poder imaginar modelos eficaces de lectura de las Escrituras en sus ministerios. La contribución más importante de este ensayo es la propuesta de cuatro estrategias de lectura alternativa que buscan cerrar la brecha entre el acercamiento académico y el acercamiento pastoral a las Escrituras en el contexto del ministerio hispano. Concluyo con varias recomendaciones para la vida pastoral.

1

¿Qué significa tener conocimiento bíblico?

Ésta es una pregunta fascinante. He enseñado Sagrada Escritura por una década y media, y ésta es una pregunta que nunca deja de invitarme a hacer un alto en el camino y reflexionar. También es una pregunta que los católicos hispanos debemos tomar seriamente respondiendo al llamado del Concilio Vaticano II en su Constitución *Sacrosanctum Concilium* a abrir «los tesoros de la Biblia, de modo que… se lean al pueblo las partes más significativas de la Sagrada Escritura»[3]. Dentro de la tradición de la fe católica debemos poner atención suficiente a lo que puede llamarse una invitación *reformadora* por parte de la Iglesia —haciéndole eco, por ejemplo, a la invitación de Martín Lutero a que los laicos leyeran la Biblia— para afirmar aquello que es fundamental para una buena catequesis de la comunidad.

---

3 Concilio Vaticano II, *Sacrosanctum Concilium*, n. 51.

Desde la perspectiva de la tradición católica, la urgencia de fortalecer el conocimiento y el estudio de la Biblia nunca cesará, tal como lo afirma la Constitución del Vaticano II sobre la Divina Revelación, *Dei Verbum*:

> Este Santo Concilio… se propone exponer la doctrina genuina sobre la divina revelación y sobre su transmisión para que todo el mundo, oyendo, crea el anuncio de la salvación; creyendo, espere, y esperando, ame[4].

Por consiguiente, queda claro que desde la perspectiva de las enseñanzas de la Iglesia, la revelación divina está encarnada en parte en la Sagrada Escritura, la cual contiene el mensaje cristiano de salvación y el acceso de la Iglesia a ese mensaje en cuanto encarnado en la Palabra. Una lectura más cercana de *Dei Verbum* indica cómo la comunidad que interpreta debe acercarse a ese rico conocimiento de la Sagrada Escritura, lo cual es parte de lo que llamamos conocimiento bíblico:

> Pues para entender rectamente lo que el autor sagrado quiso afirmar en sus escritos, hay que atender cuidadosamente tanto a las formas nativas usadas de pensar, de hablar o de narrar vigentes en los tiempos del hagiógrafo, como a las que en aquella época solían usarse en el trato mutuo de los hombres[5].

Además, el reporte de la Pontificia Comisión Bíblica, «La interpretación de la Biblia en la Iglesia», especifica claramente que este conocimiento se fortalece, desde la perspectiva tanto de una lectura individual como comunitaria de las Escrituras, por medio de la práctica de *lectio divina*, una estrategia familiar para leer e interpretar la Biblia entre los católicos[6].

En cuanto al proceso de interpretación de las Escrituras, *Dei Verbum* nos indica que la Iglesia, sumergida en la riqueza de la Tradición, es el lugar por excelencia en donde esto ocurre: «Por esta Tradición conoce la Iglesia el Canon íntegro de los libros sagrados, y la misma Sagrada Escritura se va conociendo en ella»[7]. Para los católicos, el Magisterio es el árbitro que en última instancia determina la validez y utilidad de toda interpretación bíblica para los fieles: «Pero el oficio de interpretar auténticamente la palabra de Dios escrita o transmitida

4 Concilio Vaticano II, *Dei Verbum*, n.1.
5 *Dei Verbum*, n.12.
6 Véase por ejemplo PONTIFICIA COMISIÓN BÍBLICA, *La interpretación de la Biblia en la Iglesia*, n.181-86.
7 *Dei Verbum*, n.8.

ha sido confiado únicamente al Magisterio vivo de la Iglesia»[8]. Aun así, el oficio eclesial de enseñar, ejercido especialmente por aquellos cuyo ministerio involucra predicar la Palabra de Dios, ha de llevarse a cabo con *un oído en el pueblo*, tal como lo observó recientemente el Papa Francisco en su Exhortación Apostólica *Evangelii Gaudium*, prestando atención «al pueblo concreto con sus signos y símbolos, y respondiendo a las cuestiones que plantea». Estos son elementos esenciales en el proceso interpretativo[9]. Por consiguiente, el oficio vivo de la enseñanza de la Iglesia es llamado a un diálogo directo y activo con aquellos a quienes sirve, es decir los fieles, y los laicos están llamados a participar en el ministerio de la Palabra compartiendo sus experiencias de vida a la luz del Evangelio. El resultado es una interpretación de la Palabra completamente encarnada, la cual reconoce las realidades diarias de los fieles en diálogo con aquellos llamados a servirles.

Un enfoque católico de acercamiento a la Biblia exige lo siguiente:

1 Exégesis. Entrar en contacto con el texto en sí mismo y su mundo de una manera crítica, con la ayuda de los expertos bíblicos,

2 Interpretación histórica. Leer el texto en diálogo con la Tradición,

3 Interpretación contemporánea. Entender la realidad actual o la situación de la comunidad.

Éste es precisamente el tipo de acercamiento a la Biblia que debe estar presente en cualquier forma de acción pastoral asociada con el ministerio hispano. Como líderes académicos y pastorales, sabemos que el contexto y la identidad cultural determinan profundamente la relación del pueblo con Dios y con los demás. Por eso tenemos que preguntarnos: ¿podemos hablar de una(s) lectura(s) e interpretación(es) hispana(s) de la Biblia? Sí podemos y de hecho lo hacemos. Tales lecturas e interpretaciones contribuyen algo importante al enfoque católico que acabamos de describir.

Las palabras del teólogo protestante Justo González de hecho nos pueden ayudar a responder a esta pregunta:

En la comunidad hispana, le interpretación bíblica más apreciada no es la que nos ayuda a entender los pasajes difíciles en el texto sino más bien aquella que nos ayuda en nuestros propios pasajes en el camino de obediencia[10].

8 *Dei Verbum*, n. 10.
9 PAPA FRANCISCO, *Evangelii Gaudium*, n. 154.
10 GONZÁLEZ, J.L., *Mañana: Christian Theology from a Hispanic Perspective*, Abingdon Press, Nashville, TN 1990, 87.

Esta observación reconoce correctamente que la interpretación bíblica ocurre en distintos niveles. El primero, como nota González, ocurre al nivel de la interpretación del texto y el mundo del texto. Luego procede a resaltar el nivel de interpretación que es más relevante en el contexto del ministerio hispano: la aplicabilidad del texto bíblico a la vida de los hispanos en el aquí y el ahora mientras negociamos *nuestro propio* caminar en la realidad contemporánea. Desde esta perspectiva, nos encontramos una vez más con el esquema de interpretación bíblica de los varios niveles que identificamos anteriormente: el mundo ante el texto y el mundo del texto (exégesis bíblica); la vida del texto en la tradición cristiana/católica (historia de interpretación); y el entendimiento moderno y aplicabilidad (interpretación contemporánea). Éste es el tipo de lectura sofisticada de las Escrituras que idealmente los agentes pastorales deben fomentar en las comunidades hispanas en nuestro tiempo. Los agentes pastorales tienen que leer la Biblia con las comunidades hispanas realmente teniendo en cuenta el conjunto de situaciones de vida comunitaria y de vida pastoral, las enseñanzas de la Iglesia y la sabiduría que viene del estudio académico de la Biblia. La formación académica y fiel de los agentes pastorales en la tradición bíblica facilitará el encuentro de la comunidad con Dios en el aquí y el ahora. Al mismo tiempo, los expertos bíblicos latinos no se tienen que limitar sólo a estudiar el mundo frente al texto y el mundo del texto, sino que también han de estudiar la rica historia de interpretación del texto y las situaciones actuales desde las cuales interpretamos la Biblia como latinos y como católicos en nuestro caminar. Con todo esto se ha establecido un círculo hermenéutico: lo antiguo, lo histórico, y lo contemporáneo. Cada uno informa a los demás. Cada uno permanece incompleto sin el otro en el proceso de interpretación.

Cuando Justo González habla de «obediencia», creo que se ha de hablar más bien de *liberación*[11]. Este cambio de enfoque es especialmente importante para los católicos latinos cuando tenemos en cuenta los encuentros colonizadores que trajeron el catolicismo a las Américas y las muchas condiciones de marginalidad que actualmente definen las vidas de millones de católicos en los Esta-

---

11 Contrario a la idea de obediencia como un sometimiento pasivo, las Escrituras nos llaman a escuchar y a seguir el camino que Dios propone (por medio de Moisés, los profetas, Jesús, por ejemplo), el cual conduce a la liberación. En el Antiguo Testamento se usaba la palabra hebrea *shama*, la cual significaba «oír, escuchar, obedecer». En el Nuevo Testamento la palabra *hupakou* significaba «escuchar al alguien en una posición más alta, obedecer». Ciertamente la etimología de la palabra obediencia sugiere escuchar —*ob*, «hacia» y *oedire*, «oír o escuchar». Todas estas palabras tienen un carácter profundamente relacional y personal.

dos Unidos[12]. Por ello, el mensaje del Evangelio al centro de las Escrituras conduce a la liberación y a la emancipación de nuestros pueblos más que ser una simple llamada a la obediencia —un concepto bastante rico cuyo significado se distorsiona frecuentemente. El conocimiento de la Biblia presupone, entonces, preocupaciones de este mundo y más allá. Leer la Biblia sólo con la mirada a lo que ocurrirá más allá de nuestras existencias actuales es reducirle el valor único al texto sagrado de nuestras vidas históricas, aquí y ahora, haciéndolo casi irrelevante y reduciendo nuestra existencia humana a una vida (especialmente desde una perspectiva latina) de sumisión obediente y silenciosa ante las fuerzas que nos deshumanizan. Me gustaría hacerle eco a las observaciones del experto bíblico afroamericano Vincent Wimbush, quien por mucho tiempo ha resaltado la relevancia del elemento «*este mundo*» en el estudio de la Biblia como recurso tanto para la esperanza social y política, como la crítica y el desafío *en este mundo*[13].

El conocimiento de la Biblia exige familiarizarse con los textos y las historias que están en el conjunto de libros sagrados, los elementos de sabiduría que los católicos y otras comunidades cristianas han descubierto interpretando esos textos a través de los siglos, y el estudio crítico de aquellos pasajes que se consideran más difíciles. Pero el conocimiento bíblico no termina allí. Tal no puede ser el final. La meta última del conocimiento bíblico en el contexto del ministerio hispano es potenciar a latinos y latinas para que hagamos nuestros aquellos pasajes que le dan sentido al caminar de nuestras propias vidas, aquí en los Estados Unidos, ahora en el presente que compartimos.

2

Desafíos que limitan el conocimiento bíblico

Antes de considerar algunas estrategias alternativas de lectura bíblica que han sido implementadas históricamente en contextos pastorales latinos, es necesario hacer una serie de observaciones sobre ciertos desafíos que limitan el cono-

---

12 Recordemos que muchos latinos estadounidenses nunca cruzaron la frontera sino que la frontera se les impuso en 1848 cuando los Estados Unidos anexaron una gran parte de México a su territorio. En 1898 Puerto Rico se convirtió en una colonia de los Estados Unidos. Millones de personas de Latinoamérica y del Caribe llegaron a los Estados Unidos huyendo de condiciones de pobreza, violencia e incluso persecución, y actualmente confrontan nuevos desafíos en una sociedad que con frecuencia se rehúsa a reconocerles plenamente.

13 WIMBUSH, V.L., «Reading Darkness, Reading Scriptures», en WIMBUSH, V.L. (ed.), *African Americans and the Bible: Sacred Texts and Social Textures*, Continuum, New York 2001, 12.

cimiento bíblico. El primer desafío a un conocimiento bíblico sólido entre los latinos es la falta de recursos en nuestra comunidad que permitan un acercamiento más profundo y organizado a las Escrituras. Allan Figueroa Deck observa:

> A pesar del crecimiento robusto de la presencia hispana en los últimos 50 años, no nos acercamos al desarrollo de lo que yo llamaría una infraestructura adecuada para el ministerio hispano[14].

Esta falta de estructura afecta directamente la manera cómo los hispanos se acercan a las Escrituras. Dicha carencia se puede atribuir a causas múltiples. Seamos claros. Es mucho más que simple acceso a la Biblia. A lo que Figueroa Deck se refiere es una estructura organizacional permanente con suficientes recursos que responda a las preocupaciones de los católicos hispanos. A medida que los hispanos se convierten rápidamente en la mayoría de los católicos en muchas partes del país, es urgente que los líderes de la Iglesia hagan mucho más para preparar al clero y a otros agentes pastorales para que sirvan adecuadamente a esta población[15]. Esto implica preparar sacerdotes y agentes pastorales que conozcan la Biblia. La mayoría de latinos, mujeres y hombres, llamados al ministerio pastoral no tienen los medios económicos y los recursos (ej., títulos universitarios) para matricularse en escuelas especializadas de teología a nivel de postgrado o seminarios. Así que la mayoría de oportunidades de capacitación que tienen disponibles se concentran en los institutos pastorales, grupos parroquiales de estudio bíblico o formación a nivel individual. Esta falta de capacitación formal en estudios bíblicos corrobora la observación de Hosffman Ospino:

> [O]bservaciones empíricas por parte de profesionales y líderes eclesiales indican que muchos, quizás la mayoría de líderes y catequistas en estos grupos están insuficientemente preparados en cuanto al estudio de la Sagrada Escritura. Las consecuencias inmediatas de esta falta de preparación son lecturas e interpretaciones erróneas de la Biblia al igual que la tendencia a leer el texto sagrado de manera fundamentalista[16].

14 FIGUEROA DECK, A., *Hispanic Ministry: New Realities and Choices*, ponencia presentada durante el simposio sobre los católicos hispanos/latinos en los Estados Unidos, Center for Applied Research in the Apostolate, Georgetown University, Washington, D.C. 5-6 de octubre del 2008, 6.
15 Véase MATEO, H., «El ministerio hispano y el liderazgo», y HOOVER, B.C. Y OSPINO, H., «El ministerio hispano y la vida parroquial» en este volumen.
16 OSPINO, H., «La Biblia y la catequesis», en RUÍZ, J.P. Y PAREDES, M.J. (eds.), *La Palabra de Dios y los católicos latinos: La lecciones del camino a Emaús*, American Bible Society, New York 2011, 71-72.

Segundo, quienes hemos sido educados y tenemos títulos avanzados en estudios bíblicos somos muy pocos para poder responder a las necesidades de los grandes números de católicos hispanos que desean prepararse mejor en el estudio de las Escrituras para mejorar sus ministerios. Simplemente no hay suficientes expertos bíblicos latinos para llevar a cabo dicha preparación. Esto se complica ante el hecho de que la mayoría de expertos bíblicos latinos trabajan de lleno en universidades y seminarios con casi todo nuestro tiempo dedicado a las debidas responsabilidades dentro de estos espacios.

Otro reto al conocimiento bíblico desde una perspectiva latina es que en muchos ambientes católicos se asemeja el conocimiento bíblico a una lectura al estilo de los cristianos evangélicos, quienes enfatizan la memorización de textos, lo cual es común en muchas iglesias protestantes latinas, incluyendo movimientos fundamentalistas y grupos similares. Raúl Gómez-Ruíz ofrece la siguiente ilustración que seguramente les será familiar a los agentes pastorales trabajando en el ministerio hispano:

> [S]e me acercó un grupo de feligresas hispanas pidiendo que les instituyera un estudio de Biblia. Deseaban saber más sobre la Biblia por varias razones, una de las cuales era que se habían dado cuenta que se leía más ahora en la Eucaristía y segundo que los evangélicos les desafiaban declarando que los católicos ni usan ni conocen la Biblia[17].

La meta aquí, por supuesto, no es escarnecer la lectura fundamentalista o evangélica de las Escrituras. No debemos olvidar que el fundamentalismo bíblico hace posible que millones de cristianos se relacionen con la Palabra de Dios. Sin embargo, no es así como lo católicos leemos las Escrituras puesto que dicha lectura fundamentalista ignora el diálogo crítico con la Tradición. Desde una perspectiva protestante, dicha estrategia de lectura tiene sentido. Lo que podemos aprender de nuestros hermanos y hermanas protestantes con perspectivas fundamentalistas es el acercamiento amplio y en ocasiones «rabínico» de la Biblia. Cuando enseño en contextos fundamentalistas y evangélicos no dejo de sorprenderme constantemente, muchas veces con gusto, el gran conocimiento del contenido de la Biblia por parte de mis estudiantes. Como católicos romanos podemos aprender mucho de ese nivel de conocimiento bíblico textual, aunque en diálogo con el círculo hermenéutico articulado anteriormente.

---

17 GÓMEZ-RUÍZ, R., «Al partir el pan: la Biblia y la liturgia», en RUÍZ, J.P. Y PAREDES, M.J. (eds.), *La Palabra de Dios y los católicos latinos*, 37-38.

El último reto que quisiera resaltar está relacionado con el uso del Leccionario. Este reto tiene que ver con el hecho de que muchos agentes pastorales, tanto ordenados como laicos, ven el Leccionario como una estrategia completa de lectura bíblica. Gómez-Ruíz observa:

> [El] leccionario se convierte en otra «Biblia», una biblia litúrgica que escoge selectivamente cuáles textos serán utilizados/leídos/considerados con el fin de comunicar lo que la Iglesia cree tocante lo que es esencial en la revelación de la obra salvadora de Dios en la creación y para fomentar su aplicación a la vida cotidiana de los fieles[18].

Lo que escucho decir a Gómez-Ruíz en su observación es que no se trata de que el Leccionario sea un obstáculo a un acercamiento profundo a la Biblia, sino que quienes escuchamos los textos del Leccionario tenemos que hacer un estudio más profundo examinando la lectura que se nos propone oficialmente para cada día. Es responsabilidad del clero y de otros agentes pastorales en particular usar las lecturas propuestas por el Leccionario como una invitación a estudiar el pasaje en su contexto histórico, atentos a la historia de interpretación mientras consideramos la aplicación a la realidad actual.

3

Estrategias alternativas de lectura bíblica: lecturas desde una perspectiva latina

En décadas recientes han surgido varias estrategias de investigación bíblica que tienen en cuenta la realidad de la vida diaria de los lectores. Estas estrategias han desafiado a los expertos bíblicos latinos a considerar cómo nuestras propias realidades influyen en el proceso de interpretación de la Sagrada Escritura. Estas lecturas personales —o subjetividades— no son necesariamente una imposición en cuanto al proceso de interpretación bíblica[19]. De hecho, son factores vitales que enriquecen el ejercicio contemporáneo de interpretación bíblica. Hoy en día se acepta ampliamente la convicción de que aquellos enfoques de estudio bíblico considerados «objetivos» realmente distan mucho de serlo y, por consi-

---

18 Ibid., 38.
19 Los expertos bíblicos llaman a este modelo de lectura *eiségesis*: interpretar un texto primordialmente a la luz de las presuposiciones y las convicciones ideológicas de quien realiza el ejercicio de interpretación.

guiente, el tema de la verdad bíblica. El proceso interpretativo se lleva a cabo por seres humanos. Necesitamos reconocer que lo que en algún momento se percibió como investigación «objetiva» en el mundo de los estudios bíblicos, de hecho se trataba de «una clase específica de práctica cultural» de la visión noratlántica de los expertos bíblicos que han predominado históricamente[20]. Por consiguiente, la investigación bíblica «objetiva» que se ha practicado tradicionalmente por más de dos siglos es una manera culturalmente específica y política de leer la Biblia que pocas veces se nombra como tal. Dicha investigación tiene que ver muy poco con las realidades diarias de los católicos latinos. Porque las historias del pueblo de fe son importantes, al igual que su ubicación sociocultural, propongo las siguientes cuatro estrategias de lectura como modelo para nuestra consideración colectiva.

308   *Estrategia de lectura 1: Leer en comunidad: Clero, académicos y comunidades de fe.* Para confrontar las lecturas bíblicas que predominan y sus agendas subjetivas que con frecuencia no se reconocen como tales, Jean-Pierre Ruíz propone:

> [La] investigación bíblica latina insiste no únicamente que sea imposible de comprobar suposiciones y presunciones de entrada antes de envolverse en la interpretación bíblica, pero dichas presuposiciones presuntas (teológicas, socioculturales y demás) no son menos importantes para la interpretación bíblica que las destrezas gramaticales, lingüísticas e históricas que son el equipamiento estándar para la interpretación académica bíblica[21].

Esta observación básicamente consiste en una invitación al clero y a los agentes pastorales latinos a integrar seriamente sus contextos sociales y sus preocupaciones ministeriales en el momento de acercarse a la Biblia. Por consiguiente, el modelo tradicional de carácter unidireccional por medio del cual los expertos bíblicos educan al clero, a los agentes pastorales y a los laicos se transforma en un verdadero *diálogo* en el cual todos los involucrados en el proceso de estudio de las Escrituras entran en diálogo crítico con los expertos bíblicos dando a conocer la realidad de sus vidas en su caminar mientras que buscan liberación y

---

20 WIMBUSH, V.L., «Reading Darkness, Reading Scriptures», 10.
21 RUÍZ, J.P., «Comenzando con Moisés y todos los profetas: la investigación bíblica entre los latinos y la Palabra de Dios en la Iglesia», en RUÍZ, J.P. y PAREDES, M.J. (eds.), *La Palabra de Dios y los católicos latinos*, 109-110.

salvación (teología de conjunto). Ruíz resume esta estrategia de lectura colectiva de la siguiente manera: «El trabajo de la teología se lleva a cabo no en primera persona singular, sino en primera persona plural, ya que el primer destinatario de la reflexión teológica es la comunidad —la Iglesia»[22].

Estrategia de lectura 2: El lector de carne y hueso. El experto bíblico cubanoamericano Fernando Segovia ha promovido una segunda estrategia de interpretación bíblica. Al igual que Jean-Pierre Ruíz, él «cuestiona la idea de un lector *neutral y desinteresado* que presupone el historicismo crítico»[23]. Segovia promueve como alternativa que se considere el valor del lector de carne y hueso (*flesh-and blood reader*, en inglés) en el proceso de interpretación bíblica. Él reconoce que desde el comienzo el lector de carne y hueso está «siempre posicionado y tiene un interés particular, social o históricamente condicionado, y no puede presumir que vive fuera de esas condiciones»[24]. La estrategia de Segovia hace un puente entre el mundo de los estudios bíblicos y el de los estudios culturales: «un estudio crítico en conjunto de textos y lectores, perspectivas e ideologías»[25]. Esta estrategia para el estudio de las Escrituras es una invitación para que los agentes pastorales involucren abiertamente tanto sus identidades como sus realidades sociales y culturales en la interpretación de la Biblia —y capaciten a otras personas a hacer lo mismo.

Estrategia de lectura 3: Leer la Biblia «en español». Justo González, quien no habla desde una perspectiva católica pero ha tenido gran influencia entre los teólogos católicos hispanos en los Estados Unidos gracias a la profundidad de sus contribuciones, argumenta:

> Si es cierto que traemos una perspectiva particular a la historia y a la teología, entonces también traemos una perspectiva particular a la interpretación de las Escrituras. Una vez más, puede ser que esta perspectiva sea de gran uso no sólo para nosotros sino para el resto de la iglesia[26].

22 Ibid., 110.
23 SEGOVIA, F.F., «And They Began to Speak in Other Tongues: Competing Modes of Discourse in Contemporary Biblical Criticism», en SEGOVIA, F.F. y TOLBERT, M.A. (eds.), *Reading From this Place: Social Location and Biblical Interpretation in the United States,* vol. 1, Augsburg Fortress Press, Minneapolis, MN 1995, 28, énfasis añadido.
24 Ibid., 28-29.
25 Ibid., 29.
26 GONZÁLEZ, J.L., *Mañana,* 75.

González propone que una subjetividad latina de hecho puede ofrecer una ventaja en el momento de interpretar las Escrituras, una ventaja hermenéutica que desafía las estrategias de lectura que predominan. González hace un llamado a una lectura *no inocente* de la Biblia «en español»:

En resumen, la historia bíblica es una historia más allá de la inocencia… Puesto que ésta es la naturaleza de la historia hispana, ciertamente puede ser que desde esta perspectiva tengamos una ventaja hermenéutica sobre aquellas personas que todavía se encuentran en el nivel de una inocencia culpable y seguramente tienen que leer las Escrituras de la misma manera que leen su propia historia[27].

González continúa: «Es impresionante observar el paralelo entre las "historias bíblicas" que leemos en la escuela dominical y las "historias estadounidenses" que son presentadas diariamente como historia oficial en nuestras escuelas»[28]. Como alternativa a dichas lecturas «inocentes» —y con frecuencia cómplices— de la Biblia, González promueve una lectura que no es inocente, la cual tiene en cuenta los ejemplos positivos y negativos de las Escrituras. En lugar de simplemente resaltar las historias de triunfo y victoria o a los personajes más justos en la Biblia, González propone una lectura más profunda y honesta de las Escrituras. El experto bíblico nos desafía a hacerle frente a historias tales como la que narra la mentira de Abraham con relación a su esposa Sarah para salvar su propia vida, la indecisión de Moisés para aceptar su llamada, la compleja apostasía que se detalla en el Libro de los Jueces, el error grave de David de provocar la muerte de uno de sus generales para quedarse con su esposa, y las varias limitaciones de los discípulos de Jesús en el Testamento cristiano. ¿Cuáles son los resultados de entrar en diálogo con estas historias a medida que hacemos interpretación bíblica? ¿De qué manera la disrupción de una lectura inocente de las Escrituras desafía nuestra relación con la Biblia y los mundos inocentes (y triunfalistas) que nacen de dicha lectura? Más importante aún, ¿de qué manera esta lectura no inocente de las Escrituras hace posible una evaluación más crítica de nuestro caminar como expertos bíblicos, clero y agentes pastorales latinos con el pueblo que buscamos servir en nuestras parroquias?

27 Ibid., 77.
28 Ibid., 79.

Estrategia de lectura 4: A través del lente del catolicismo popular. La última estrategia de lectura que propongo es una a la que he dedicado la mayor parte de mi tiempo como académico: la lectura bíblica a través del lente del catolicismo popular latino. La categoría teológica «catolicismo popular», según el teólogo Orlando Espín, es vital para referirse a cualquier noción de espiritualidad latina, desde una perspectiva bíblica o no, puesto que la mayoría de los católicos latinos lo son «usualmente de una manera "popular"»[29]. Según Espín,

> Al hablar de «popular» no me refiero a «muy conocido», aunque el catolicismo popular es bien conocido. «Popular» más bien es el adjetivo correspondiente al sustantivo «pueblo». Por consiguiente, el catolicismo popular es «popular» porque le pertenece al pueblo. Aunque es evidente que no toda persona católica latina participa en esta tradición dentro del catolicismo, la mayoría de latinos lo hacen, y todas nuestras culturas claramente están enraizadas en ella[30].

No debería ser una sorpresa para nadie leer que la religiosidad popular tiene una larga historia en nuestras comunidades de fe. Es tan central para algunas de nuestras expresiones teológicas latinas que Espín la ha categorizado como un «verdadero [espacio teológico] *locus theologicus* y no simplemente o principalmente como un problema pastoral o catequético»[31]. Es la fe del pueblo, la *fe de nuestro pueblo*, y merece ser parte esencial de nuestra reflexión teológica. Según Hosffman Ospino, «[El] catolicismo popular es simultáneamente una manera de conocer y el lenguaje más disponible a la mayoría de latinos católicos, muchos de los cuales viven en las márgenes de nuestra sociedad, para expresar nuestra fe de una manera que es accesible y familiar»[32]. El catolicismo popular tiene un gran impacto y da vida a las comunidades en las que existe y a las que sirve.

En mi propia investigación sobre la tradición de murales con la imagen de Nuestra Señora de Guadalupe en el Este de Los Ángeles, he descubierto que algunas expresiones de catolicismo popular latino son fruto de un buen conocimiento bíblico y proponen interpretaciones que exhiben gran sabiduría[33]. Cuan-

29 ESPÍN, O.O., *The Faith of the People: Theological Reflections on Popular Catholicism*, Orbis Books, New York 1997, 3.
30 Ibid.
31 Ibid., 2.
32 OSPINO, H., «La Biblia y la catequesis», 67.
33 Véase SÁNCHEZ, D.A., *From Patmos to the Barrio: Subverting Imperial Myths*, Fortress Press, Minneapolis, MN 2008.

do comencé a coleccionar fotografías de murales con la imagen de Nuestra Señora de Guadalupe en el Este de Los Ángeles, pronto observé que las representaciones modernas, al igual que la imagen original, le hacen eco al capítulo 12 del libro de la Revelación: «Y apareció en el cielo un gran signo: una Mujer revestida del sol, con la luna bajo sus pies y una corona de doce estrellas en su cabeza» (Ap 12,1). Estas representaciones demuestran un conocimiento complejo del mundo antiguo y de las historias bíblicas que permiten apropiaciones modernas sofisticadas. Tal conocimiento revela también una impresionante apreciación bíblica por el texto como tal, la cual es parte íntima del catolicismo popular contemporáneo.

Los expertos bíblicos, teólogos y agentes pastorales podemos aprender mucho al poner atención a estas conexiones profundas entre las Escrituras y las expresiones de catolicismo popular. Por mucho tiempo nos hemos acercado a las expresiones de catolicismo popular como si fueran contrarias o mucho menos que la doctrina y las prácticas oficiales. Una mirada más de cerca revela que hay mucho más allí. Nos encontramos ante una tradición interpretativa a partir de la cual vale la pena realmente hacer una reflexión teológica seria y continua.

4
Epílogo

A medida que la Iglesia en los Estados Unidos se hace cada vez más hispana y se necesiten modelos creativos de ministerio y evangelización, la recepción pasiva de la Biblia simplemente no es una opción viable. Quienes están encargados de la actividad pastoral tienen la responsabilidad específica de escuchar las orientaciones de *Sacrosanctum Concilium* citadas anteriormente: hay que abrir «los tesoros de la Biblia, de modo que… se lean al pueblo las partes más significativas de la Sagrada Escritura». Las estrategias alternativas de lectura que se proponen en este ensayo, nacidas en medio del diálogo con expertos bíblicos y teólogos hispanos, todas enraizadas profundamente en la vida pastoral, afirman el papel de la experiencia diaria en el proceso de interpretación bíblica. El trabajo y las experiencias de compromiso pastoral de estos expertos, el mundo de la investigación y el análisis bíblico, y la rica tradición de la Iglesia constituyen el círculo hermenéutico que mueve la interpretación bíblica latina.

Todos los líderes pastorales involucrados en el ministerio hispano pueden mejorar el nivel de conocimiento bíblico. Esto ya está ocurriendo en gran parte cada semana por medio de la catequesis, la predicación, los grupos de oración y sesiones de estudio bíblico en miles de comunidades sirviendo a los católicos latinos en el país. Sus ministerios con frecuencia reciben el apoyo de esfuerzos como la *Biblia Católica para Jóvenes* (patrocinada por el Instituto Fe y Vida), la *Biblia Católica de la Familia* (patrocinada por el Center for Ministry Development y la editorial Verbo Divino), Renew International, el Estudio Bíblico de Little Rock, entre otros. Se necesita hacer mucho más para fomentar un amor más profundo por las Escrituras. Éste es el momento para que los agentes pastorales latinos asuman su debido papel en este círculo fiel y así todos seamos uno.

El ministerio hispano y la Iglesia en Latinoamérica y el Caribe

Allan Figueroa Deck, SJ *y* Teresa Maya Sotomayor, CCVI

La Iglesia Católica en los Estados Unidos se ha convertido en la comunidad ecle-sial más globalizada del mundo[1]. Ninguna otra comunidad eclesial en el planeta ha experimentado las realidades multiculturales e interculturales como lo han hecho las parroquias y las diócesis católicas en los Estados Unidos[2]. Los retos pa-ra la tarea pastoral son evidentes, sin embargo el potencial que dicha híper-diversidad tiene para el futuro de la Iglesia Católica es bastante prometedor. Nuevo vino se vierte en la vida de nuestra Iglesia. ¿Tenemos listos los odres nuevos? Esta diversidad es el «lugar teológico» apropiado para re-imaginar a la Iglesia en un mundo globalizado que cambia rápidamente. El ministerio con la población ca-tólica hispana ha sido por décadas el espacio por excelencia en el cual este pro-ceso de re-imaginación ha ido teniendo lugar de manera creativa y dinámica.

¡Las posibilidades de un sueño «panamericano» que imaginaron quienes participaron en luchas independentistas desde Nueva Inglaterra hasta Buenos Aires, o la realización de la profecía de Karl Rahner de una «Iglesia mundial»[3], o simplemente la idea de una iglesia continental que proclamó Juan Pablo II en *Ecclesia in America*, se están haciendo realidad en muchas parroquias en los Es-tados Unidos! La intersección de culturas y tradiciones que el ministerio hispano representa está creando un modelo eclesial nuevo que es único para el tercer mi-lenio y la tarea de la nueva evangelización. La tensión tradicional entre lo caris-mático y lo institucional se ha comenzado a reintegrar de maneras esperanza-doras en el ministerio hispano en donde el Sur global y el Occidente global se encuentran[4]. La Iglesia de «las Américas» se presenta así como un paradigma para el futuro: acompañando pastoralmente en la diversidad, creando un nuevo mes-tizaje que integra las contribuciones de la Iglesia en Latinoamérica con aquellas de la Iglesia en Norteamérica dando vida a algo nuevo.

La Iglesia en los Estados Unidos ha estado vinculada a la Iglesia en Latinoa-mérica por siglos, pero los vínculos cada vez son más fuertes y sistemáticos des-de comienzos de la década de los 1960s. En este ensayo exploramos la fusión de

1 Véase CENTER FOR APPLIED RESEARCH IN THE APOSTOLATE, *Cultural Diversity in the Catholic Church of the United States,* CARA, Washington, D.C. 2014, http://www.usccb.org/issues-and-action/cultural-diversity/upload/cultural-diversity-cara-report-phase-1.pdf (documento vi-sitado el 26 de Agosto del 2014).
2 Véase HOOVER, B.C. y OSPINO, H., «el ministerio hispano y la vida parroquial» en este volumen.
3 SAMMON, S.D., «The Birth of a World Church», en *America Magazine,* 15 de octubre del 2012, http://americamagazine.org/issue/100/birth-world-church (documento visitado el 23 de Agos-to del 2014).
4 ALLEN, J.L., *The Future Church: How Ten Trends Are Revolutionizing the Catholic Church,* Dou-bleday, New York 2009, 17-20.

culturas eclesiales y las contribuciones de la Iglesia latinoamericana al ministerio hispano actual, delineando cómo el ministerio hispano a su vez tiene algo que ofrecer a Latinoamérica. Nuestra meta es identificar varias fuentes para una visión pastoral que gana nuevo vigor bajo la guía reformadora del Papa Francisco, el primer Papa latinoamericano. El ministerio hispano se convierte así en el lugar de intercambio entre el Sur global y la cultura occidental ofreciéndole a toda la Iglesia nuevas expresiones y métodos.

1

¿Cuál Latinoamérica? Hacia un contexto

El ministerio hispano en los Estados Unidos tiene raíces profundas en la acción pastoral de la Iglesia en Latinoamérica desde el Concilio Vaticano II. Esa influencia comenzó con los intercambios que tuvieron lugar entre las conferencias de obispos católicos. Las recomendaciones de las conferencias generales del episcopado latinoamericano (CELAM) siempre se sintieron en los Estados Unidos. Los esfuerzos de colaboración ya habían comenzado antes, pero después de los años sesenta los obispos católicos del Norte y del Sur comenzaron a reunirse de manera más regular. Estas iniciativas fueron apoyadas por la Oficina para Latinoamérica de la Conferencia de Obispos Católicos de los Estados Unidos en Washington, D.C., establecida como mecanismo para diseminar en los Estados Unidos la extraordinaria visión eclesial que surgía de Medellín, Puebla y otras iniciativas pastoral del CELAM. Estos contactos llevaron al establecimiento de la Oficina Regional del Noreste para los católicos de habla hispana (*Northeast Regional Office for the Spanish-speaking*, en inglés). El sacerdote colombiano, Édgar Beltrán, quien había trabajado para el CELAM en Bogotá, fue contratado por la División para los católicos de habla hispana de la Conferencia Nacional de Obispos Católicos (*Division of the Spanish-Speaking of the National Conference of Catholic Bishops,* en inglés). El carismático Padre Beltrán viajó por todo el país y comunicó un mensaje extraordinario de conversión pastoral, el cual era explícito en las iniciativas pastorales de la Iglesia en Latinoamérica[5]. El corazón de una

5 Los agentes pastorales latinoamericanos han estado familiarizados con la idea de «conversión pastoral» por varias décadas. Recientemente el documento de Aparecida (2007) la retomó. Por ejemplo: «Ninguna comunidad debe excusarse de entrar decididamente, con todas sus fuerzas, en los procesos constantes de renovación misionera, y de abandonar las estructuras caducas que ya no favorezcan la transmisión de la fe» (n. 365); «De allí nace la necesidad, en fidelidad al Espíritu

generación completa de líderes pastorales hispanos ardía y un nuevo período de renovación eclesial en los Estados Unidos comenzó a surgir en el contexto de los ministerios hispanos.

La influencia latinoamericana también se sintió por medio de los encuentros convocados por los distintos institutos religiosos masculinos y femeninos. En 1971 se reunió la Asamblea Interamericana de Religiosas y Religiosos, y desde entonces ha habido conversaciones entre todas las conferencias de religiosas y religiosos en la región. Nuevas corrientes de pensamiento y acción llegaron desde Latinoamérica gracias al trabajo de miles de misioneros estadounidenses —sacerdotes, religiosos y laicos. Estos habían fundado misiones en todo el continente, respondiendo a la llamada de San Juan xxiii al apostolado misionero. Misioneros apasionados regresaron con experiencia de primera mano en cuanto a cómo la visión pastoral que surgía en Latinoamérica se hacía vida por medio de teorías y prácticas. Estos misioneros inmediatamente comenzaron a aplicar lo que habían visto y aprendido en su experiencia de misión a los contextos pastorales en todos los Estados Unidos. Así fueron plantadas las semillas de una orientación pastoral distintiva que sería promovida por la Oficina para Católicos de Habla Hispana (*Office of the Spanish-Speaking*, en inglés)[6] de la Conferencia de Obispos Católicos y más tarde sería eje central de lo que se llamó el proceso de Encuentro, el cual ha influenciado al ministerio hispano desde entonces.

Otra fuente importante de influencia de Latinoamérica en la Iglesia en los Estados Unidos son los inmigrantes mismos que se han integrado activamente a nuestras comunidades. La sola presencia numérica de estos inmigrantes ha transformado la realidad demográfica de la Iglesia en los Estados Unidos. Ésta no es una ola más en la historia de migraciones que los Estados Unidos asimila como rutina. El movimiento constante de personas, ideas y recursos en toda di-

---

Santo que la conduce, de una renovación eclesial, que implica reformas espirituales, pastorales y también institucionales» (n. 367); «La conversión pastoral requiere que las comunidades eclesiales sean comunidades de discípulos misioneros en torno a Jesucristo, Maestro y Pastor» (n. 368); «La conversión pastoral de nuestras comunidades exige que se pase de una pastoral de mera conservación a una pastoral decididamente misionera» (n. 370). Véase CELAM, *Documento de Aparecida*. El Papa Francisco también la ha hecho una categoría central de su pontificado: «La reforma de estructuras que exige la conversión pastoral sólo puede entenderse en este sentido: procurar que todas ellas se vuelvan más misioneras, que la pastoral ordinaria en todas sus instancias sea más expansiva y abierta, que coloque a los agentes pastorales en constante actitud de salida y favorezca así la respuesta positiva de todos aquellos a quienes Jesús convoca a su amistad», *Evangelii Gaudium*, n. 27.

6   Esta oficina más adelante se convirtió en el Secretariado de Asuntos Hispanos y actualmente es parte del Secretariado de Diversidad Cultural en la Iglesia.

rección en el continente crea un efecto dinámico en la región que ha exigido al mismo tiempo perspectivas pastorales dinámicas. El ministerio hispano ha ido aprendiendo por décadas a servir a hispanos tanto inmigrantes como de segunda y tercera generación al mismo tiempo, experimentando pérdidas en el proceso, y a convivir con la diversidad. Esta realidad exige que el ministerio hispano en los Estados Unidos se mantenga en conversación con los cambios que también ocurren en Latinoamérica desde el Concilio Vaticano II.

Latinoamérica ha experimentado cambios dramáticos a nivel político, social y económico durante los últimos cincuenta años. El progreso económico es evidente en algunos sectores, pero regiones enteras todavía sufren por causa de una pobreza deshumanizadora. Las violaciones graves a los derechos humanos todavía abundan y la plaga de la violencia asociada con el tráfico de drogas es una epidemia. El cambio social ha mantenido el rápido ritmo de transición de la población a las grandes ciudades. Hoy en día, a pesar de las diferencias regionales, la mayoría de la población latinoamericana vive en sectores urbanos. Las migraciones masivas se han convertido en una característica importante de la vida en Latinoamérica. Movimientos migratorios de áreas rurales a las ciudades, y luego entre ciudades y países ha incrementado exponencialmente al punto de que es una de las regiones con mayor población en medio de movimientos migratorios en el mundo[7]. Las familias cada vez más se encuentran divididas en varias ciudades y países. Esta diáspora latinoamericana constante tiene repercusiones tanto culturales como religiosas.

Las culturas y las ciudades latinoamericanas reflejan estos cambios. Las ciudades por lo general comparten características tales como falta de planeación urbana, crecimiento caótico y cinturones de pobreza que les rodean. Las culturas de los más jóvenes al igual que la secularización comienzan a forjar la identidad de la cultura urbana. La erosión paulatina de la religiosidad popular entre los latinoamericanos jóvenes es un fenómeno evidente en años recientes. La distancia cada vez mayor entre las tradiciones de los jóvenes y las de sus familias nos dejan con una población que busca la espiritualidad pero está más abierta a lo secular (lo que no es religioso) en el trascurso de una generación. El resultado final no es muy optimista cuando los porcentajes de afiliación eclesial cada vez

---

7   Véase HOOVER, B.C., *The Shared Parish: Latinos, Anglos, and the Future of U.S. Catholicism,* NYU Press, New York 2014,165. También, INTERNATIONAL ORGANIZATION FOR MIGRATION, *Facts and Figures,* http://www.iom.int/cms/en/sites/iom/home/about-migration/facts—figures-1.html (documento visitado el 19 de septiembre del 2014).

son más reducidos en todos los países latinoamericanos. El hecho es que Latinoamérica alardea de tener la población católica más grande del mundo, pero no está muy lejos de las iglesias en Europa y Norteamérica en cuanto a la disminución de la práctica de la fe[8].

El pluralismo religioso está incrementando gradualmente en Latinoamérica. El pentecostalismo ha crecido de manera exponencial en las Américas durante los últimos 50 años. Aunque reconociendo su limitación, las encuestas muestran tendencias que están transformando dramáticamente los perfiles religiosos de países como Guatemala, El Salvador, Uruguay o Nicaragua en done los católicos posiblemente ya no son la mayoría de la población[9]. La ciudades en todas partes son centros de diversidad religiosa. La tensión acompaña este pluralismo y el continente poco a poco deja de ser mayoritariamente católico. Las estructuras eclesiales en Latinoamérica parecen no reconocer todavía que los cristianos de otras confesiones ya no son necesariamente conversos que vienen del catolicismo. Ciertamente algunos de ellos son tercera y quinta generación de cristianos no católicos[10].

La erosión del catolicismo cultural y del paradigma constantiniano del Cristianismo ha creado las condiciones para un nuevo momento. La posición de la Iglesia institucional ha sido reaccionaria desde la perspectiva de una religión mayoritaria, con frecuencia protegida legalmente del proselitismo protestante. Dentro de este paradigma las parroquias funcionan como estaciones sacramentales más que otra cosa. Algunas costumbres y tradiciones heredadas de las concesiones asociadas con aquellos arreglos que datan de la época colonial (ej., *el Patronato Real*) persisten. En la gran mayoría de territorios latinoamericanos, los católicos encuentran una iglesia con la cual se sienten conectados. La idea de inscribirse o registrarse en una parroquia local o de tener un equipo administrativo parroquial para hacerle seguimiento a quienes se han registrado es casi impensable para la mayoría de parroquias en el continente. La parroquia todavía carece del tipo de organización administrativa que es común en los Estados Uni-

---

8 Véase CHESTNUT, A.R., citado por GOODWIN, L., «First Latin American Pope Could Counter Declining Catholicism», 13 de marzo del 2013, http://www.news.yahoo.com/blog/the-lookout/first-latin-american-pope (documento visitado el 17 de septiembre del 2014).

9 LATIN AMERICAN PUBLIC OPINION PROJECT, Vanderbilt University «Nota metodológica: midiendo religión en encuestas de Latinoamérica», http://www.vanderbilt.edu/lapop/insights/I0829es.pdf (documento visitado el 19 de septiembre del 2014).

10 MARTÍNEZ, J.F., *Los Protestantes: An Introduction to Latino Protestantism in the United States*, Praeger, Santa Barbara, CA 2011, 55.

dos. Es más, los arreglos económicos por medio de los cuales las parroquias regularmente apoyan a las diócesis en términos de impuestos parroquiales son más pocos y con menos impacto en las diócesis en Latinoamérica y el Caribe que en las diócesis en los Estados Unidos. Las parroquias en Latinoamérica no son muy estructuradas en comparación al modelo institucional estadounidense.

La participación organizada de los laicos es una característica importante en la cultura católica latinoamericana. Las parroquias con frecuencia son administradas por voluntarios laicos u organizaciones laicales que normalmente cubren los vacíos que dejan la falta de sacerdotes. Las razones históricas y sociológicas de este elemento de identidad de la Iglesia en la Latinoamérica tanto de habla hispana como portuguesa se remontan a los primeros días de la evangelización en el continente. El número escaso de ministros ordenados para acompañar pastoralmente las necesidades de las iglesias locales, la cultura dinámica de las confraternidades medievales que cruzaron el Atlántico, y la separación racial que fue prevalente como una estrategia para avanzar la evangelización condujeron a que se formaran grupos independientes que respondieran a las necesidades pastorales de las comunidades. La religiosidad popular es una de las consecuencias de esta organización independiente, no su causa. Las organizaciones laicales florecieron tanto en los contextos urbanos como rurales. Dependiendo de la región, un porcentaje extraordinario de católicos no participan en la vida sacramental de la Iglesia, pero se identifican como católicos[11]. En las regiones más remotas es normal ver a sacerdotes haciendo «recorridos» de visitas pastorales periódicas. En las ciudades más pequeñas y medianas puede haber más sacerdotes concentrados, sin embargo el número de Misas que ofrecen en unos pocos lugares los domingos y el gran tamaño de la población bajo su responsabilidad pastoral hacen que la gran mayoría de los católicos no los conozcan y los sientan distanciados.

La Iglesia en Latinoamérica tiene muchos desafíos en el área de formación en la fe o catequesis. Las nuevas generaciones de padres de familia católicos no siempre matriculan a sus hijos en los programas catequéticos locales y las escuelas católicas son menos del 7% de todas las escuelas en un país como México. Los obispos latinoamericanos identificaron en el documento de Aparecida la for-

---

11 La Iglesia Católica en México reporta que sólo entre el 6% y el 9% de los católicos van a Misa los domingos en un país en donde el 84% de la población se identifica como católica según el censo del año 2010. Véase, OFICINA DE PLANIFICACIÓN Y ESTADÍSTICA DE MÉXICO, «Disminuye la asistencia a Misa», Línea Directa, http://www.linearecta.com.mx/?p=1356. Sistema Informativo de la Arquidiócesis de México, http://www.siame.mx/ (documento visitado el 16 de diciembre del 2013).

mación como un desafío significativo e invitaron a todo el continente a un proceso de formación en la fe centrado en el encuentro personal con Jesucristo[12]. Las conferencias de obispos católicos han declarado una «emergencia educativa» en Latinoamérica porque el compromiso a ser discípulos y misioneros «requieren una clara y decidida opción por la formación de los miembros de nuestras comunidades»[13]. El Papa Francisco afirma este enfoque con vigor renovado, llamando a una reforma de los seminarios y las casas de formación de religiosos y religiosas al igual que de los programas catequéticos[14]. El desafío a los seminarios y los programas de formación de religiosas y religiosos en Latinoamérica seguramente surge como respuesta al uso prevalente de una pedagogía inadecuada: memorización, compilaciones y resúmenes de libros de texto, pero poco énfasis en el fomento del pensamiento crítico. En algunos países y ciudades, la falta de profesores con credenciales apropiadas usualmente conduce a prácticas de enseñanza que dejan mucho que decir. Sin embargo, los sacerdotes, las religiosas y los religiosos que acompañan a los inmigrantes en las comunidades eclesiales en los Estados Unidos con frecuencia tienen que recibir formación más rigurosa, pues estando aquí son confrontados con la gran diferencia de trabajar en una de las comunidades católicas más educadas del mundo entero y una comunidad eclesial en donde el nivel de profesionalización de quienes trabajan en la parroquia ha alcanzado niveles que quizás nadie imagina en sus países de origen. Como resultado, los agentes pastorales que migran a los Estados Unidos experimentan tensiones asociadas con los niveles más sofisticados de formación teológica entre los agentes pastorales euroamericanos e hispanos, especialmente las mujeres preparadas ampliamente para el trabajo pastoral, de quienes las parroquias dependen en gran parte.

Éstas son apenas algunas de las luces y sombras en medio de las cuales la Iglesia en Latinoamérica maduró después del Concilio Vaticano II. Haciendo vida las palabras del Papa Francisco, «las realidades son más importantes que las ideas», El Consejo Episcopal Latinoamericano (CELAM) ha estado discerniendo para entender cuál es el lugar apropiado de la Iglesia en una Latinoamérica moderna a la luz de estos retos urgentes[15]. Éste es el contexto en el cual la Iglesia en

---

12 CELAM, *Documento de Aparecida*, n. 246-247.
13 Ibid., 276, 328.
14 SPADARO, A., «¡Despierten al mundo! Diálogo con el Papa Francisco sobre la vida religiosa», en *La Civiltá Cattólica*, 1 (2014) 3-17, disponible en línea, http://www.laciviltacattolica.it/articoli_download/extra/Despierten_al_mundo.pdf.
15 PAPA FRANCISCO, *Evangelii Gaudium*, n. 231-233.

Latinoamérica ha florecido. Las respuestas pastorales a estas realidades están al centro de muchas iniciativas positivas que han tenido impacto en la Iglesia en los Estados Unidos.

2

Contribuciones latinoamericanas a la vida pastoral en los Estados Unidos

∽

Timothy Matovina ha identificado varias contribuciones del catolicismo hispano a la vida de la Iglesia en los Estados Unidos[16]. Estas contribuciones se explican en gran medida por la visión eclesial renovadora que, como observamos, comenzó en Latinoamérica después del Concilio Vaticano II. Esta reforma se llevó a cabo por medio del liderazgo del CELAM con el apoyo de la reflexión profunda de una nueva generación de pensadores latinoamericanos, entre los cuales se encuentran teólogos de la liberación como Gustavo Gutiérrez[17]. Algunas de las características centrales de este movimiento de renovación resonaron fuertemente en los Estados Unidos: 1) la visión de la misión de la Iglesia como un movimiento de evangelización en salida en lugar de concentrarse en asuntos internos o de adoptar una posición defensiva; 2) la opción por los pobres, la cual incluye un compromiso para trabajar por el cambio socioeconómico; 3) una teología de la Iglesia como el Pueblo de Dios peregrino en la historia y no como una «sociedad perfecta» estática; 4) énfasis en la Iglesia como comunidad y como jerarquía, y por consiguiente la parroquia como «comunidad de comunidades»[18].

Durante los últimos cincuenta años estos elementos han echado raíces en la vida pastoral de la Iglesia Católica en los Estados Unidos en conexión con la presencia hispana y se han manifestado al menos de cuatro maneras. Primero, con relación a la liturgia, la religiosidad popular Latinoamericana ha traído color, movimiento, pasión y belleza no sólo a las comunidades hispanas que crecen rápidamente en el país sino también a la experiencia católica estadounidense

324

---

16 MATOVINA, T., *Latino Catholicism: Transformation in America's Largest Church,* Princeton University Press, Princeton, NJ 2011, 98-131.

17 Con relación a lo que el Cardenal Muller piensa sobre la actitud del Papa Francisco ante la teología de la liberación, véase PONGRATZ-LIPPITT, C., «CDF Head: Pope Francis has close ties with Liberation Theology», *The Tablet* (2 de mayo del 2014).

18 CONFERENCIA NACIONAL DE OBISPOS CATÓLICOS (ahora CONFERENCIA DE OBISPOS CATÓLICOS DE LOS ESTADOS UNIDOS), *Plan Pastoral Nacional para el Ministerio Hispano,* USCC, Washington, D.C. 1987, n. 2-21. El documento se encuentra en UNITED STATES CONFERENCE OF CATHOLIC BISHOPS, *Ministerio Hispano: Tres Documentos Importantes,* USCCB, Washington, D.C. 1995.

en general. Las tendencias naturales de las culturas latinas a acentuar el rito, la narrativa y el símbolo han contribuido a renovar el carácter sacramental de la tradición católica, la cual es desafiada por la tendencia de nuestro mundo contemporáneo a silenciar símbolos, eliminar ritos y negar la experiencia del misterio y lo trascendente. De manera interesante, el catolicismo hispano no se dedica a promover la restauración de prácticas litúrgicas de otros siglos o de impulsar la antigua liturgia en latín. En lugar de ello fomenta la integración de los símbolos, ritos y narrativas vitales del pueblo en las expresiones litúrgicas oficiales.

Los latinos llevan prácticas de religiosidad popular a las parroquias, movimientos, escuelas y otras instituciones de la cuales son parte. Al integrar la piedad y la liturgia oficial, los latinos siguen el espíritu de la Constitución sobre Sagrada Liturgia, *Sacrosanctum Concilium*, del Concilio Vaticano II, promoviendo una participación plena y consciente en la liturgia. La fiesta de Nuestra Señora de Guadalupe es de hecho la fiesta mariana más popular en los Estados Unidos, pero el día de obligación es el que corresponde a la Inmaculada Concepción[19]. Es más, el espíritu devocional del catolicismo latino, con su rico repertorio musical, modera aquellas tendencias en nuestro día a un formalismo litúrgico que a veces predomina en contextos mono-culturales y de clase media. La presencia latina sirve como elemento moderador de tendencias a imponer normas doctrinales frías en la práctica litúrgica que buscan limitar la expresividad, la espontaneidad y la vida del culto. Además, el sentido de fiesta que caracteriza las culturas hispanas fortalece la naturaleza celebrativa que es esencial a los sacramentos[20].

La segunda contribución del catolicismo latino es en el área de renovación espiritual. ¿Qué sería del catolicismo en los Estados Unidos sin los cursillos, los encuentros matrimoniales, los grupos de la Renovación Carismática Católica, los retiros de búsqueda para adolescentes, o las comunidades cristianas de base? Todas estas expresiones de espiritualidad que han prosperado en los Estados Unidos durante los últimos cincuenta años vinieron de España y Latinoamérica o fueron implementadas por católicos latinos en los Estados Unidos. Al fondo de estas prácticas de renovación de vida cristiana se encuentra un aprecio espiritual por la afectividad humana y la vida interior. Así, muchos aspectos de la vida parroquial y espiritual se han beneficiado al adoptar las características de

---

19 PALMO, R., «A Morenita Mass and Procession», 2011, http://whispersintheloggio.blogspot.com/2011/12/big-week-begins-in-la-mass-and.html (documento visitado el 24 de febrero del 2014).
20 Véase BURGALETA, C., *La fe de los hispanos: diversidad religiosa de los pueblos latinoamericanos*, Liguori, Liguori, MO 2013.

ciertos movimientos que hacen que las riquezas de la fe sean más accesibles y más atractivas a los creyentes en la vida diaria.

La tercera contribución de los latinos a la vida de la Iglesia en los Estados Unidos es en el esfuerzo de relacionar la fe con la justicia. A mediados del siglo XX el catolicismo estadounidense pasó de ser una tradición asociada con la clase trabajadora y los grupos inmigrantes de origen europeo a una experiencia eclesial decididamente de clase media. La elección de John F. Kennedy como presidente sirvió como evento catalizador de este proceso. Mientras que la presencia de los latinos de hecho precede la de los euroamericanos en este país, fue en el siglo XX que comenzó una nueva migración latinoamericana hacia el Norte. Aunque esta migración ha traído desafíos, son muchas más las bendiciones las que le acompañan. De manera notable, la presencia latina ha ayudado a preservar y expandir la profunda tradición católica de abogar por los inmigrantes, los trabajadores y la dignidad humana en general en los Estados Unidos. Expresiones de organización comunitaria en el contexto de la Iglesia tales como PICO (por sus nombre en inglés, *Pacific Institute for Community Organizations*) e IAF (por su nombre en inglés, *Industrial Areas Foundation*), con frecuencia bajo el auspicio de líderes católicos y de naturaleza ecuménica, han crecido con fondos iniciales de la Campaña Católica para el Desarrollo Humano (CCHD, por sus siglas en inglés). Los latinos, los afroamericanos y otros grupos marginados que también experimentan el flagelo de la pobreza están presentes activamente en organizaciones que surgieron con el objetivo de confrontar asuntos serios de justicia social como el acceso a la educación, la atención médica y la seguridad. Hoy existe una nueva generación multicultural de laicos católicos preparados para la acción social bajo la inspiración de la Doctrina Social de la Iglesia, la opción por los pobres y la teología de la liberación.

Una cuarta contribución notable del catolicismo latino a la Iglesia Católica en los Estados Unidos es la aplicación de metodologías pastorales íntimamente asociados con los documentos que van desde Medellín hasta Aparecida en contextos pastorales a nivel parroquial, diocesano y nacional. Estas metodologías han sido adoptadas especialmente por los obispos católicos en los procesos de Encuentros celebrados entre el año 1972 y el año 2006. De especial importancia es el método del círculo pastoral para la planeación pastoral y las metodología que proceden inductivamente en lugar de deductivamente[21]. El acompaña-

326

21 WIJSEN, F., HENRIOT, P. Y MEJÍA, R. (eds.), *The Pastoral Circle Revisited*, Orbis Books, Maryknoll, NY 2005.

miento pastoral y la planeación primero deben evaluar la realidad y discernir usando las herramientas y procedimientos de las ciencias sociales antes de entretener consideraciones teológicas y doctrinales para tomar decisiones. La metodología de Encuentro insiste en una dinámica que busca entender la vida eclesial de tal manera que la misión evangelizadora exija atención constante a las realidades socioculturales junto con una planeación pastoral seria. Esto ha ocurrido en muchas diócesis y parroquias. La visión de tal Iglesia se encuentra en los documentos de los Encuentros publicados por la Conferencia Católica de Obispos de los Estados Unidos (usccb por sus siglas en inglés) durante los últimos sesenta años junto con diócesis, institutos pastorales, organizaciones ministeriales y movimientos en los Estados Unidos[22]. Varias diócesis han elaborado planes pastorales complejos siguiendo estas líneas.

3
Contribuciones de los Estados Unidos a Latinoamérica y al ministerio hispano

La relación entre las prácticas pastorales en Latinoamérica y los Estados Unidos ha sido de hecho recíproca y de interacción mutua. Esto lo vemos en el surgir de una nueva generación de agentes pastorales en el ministerio hispano que son inmigrantes pero que han llegado con una buena base de formación pastoral y teológica o, con los años, han sido formados gracias a su experiencia y estudios en universidades católicas en los Estados Unidos al igual que en institutos pastorales. El ministerio hispano ha prosperado en el ambiente estadounidense como resultado del énfasis que se ha puesto en la educación en este país y el impulso de la clase media a profesionalizarse, lo cual ha beneficiado a muchos agentes y programas pastorales hispanos. Institutos como el Centro Cultural México Americano o el Instituto Pastoral del Suroeste comenzaron lo que se convirtió en una relación permanente entre Latinoamérica y los Estados Unidos. Estos centros invitaron pastoralistas latinoamericanos a dar talleres y a entrar en diálogo con agentes pastorales hispanos sobre cómo traducir iniciativas latinoamericanas como las comunidades eclesiales de base o la planeación pastoral en contextos parroquiales y diocesanos estadounidenses.

---

22 Véase SECRETARIADO DE DIVERSIDAD CULTURAL EN LA IGLESIA, SUBCOMITÉ DE ASUNTOS HISPANOS, *A New Beginning: Hispanic Ministry-Past, Present, Future*, usccb, Washington, d.c. 2012.

Estas iniciativas ciertamente fueron inculturadas y adquirieron una identidad estadounidense. Por ejemplo, Renew International adoptó el modelo de comunidad eclesial de base y lo adaptó exitosamente al modelo de pequeño grupo parroquial para compartir la fe en los Estados Unidos. Movimientos eclesiales como la Renovación Carismática Católica o el Movimiento Familiar Cristiano, ambos con raíces latinoamericanas, encontraron un hogar en la estructura organizacional de la Iglesia en los Estados Unidos. El caso de la Renovación Carismática Católica es interesante en sí mismo. El movimiento de hecho comenzó en los Estados Unidos como es bien conocido, pero prosperó más en Latinoamérica. Al cabo del tiempo, los carismáticos hispanos en los Estados Unidos recibirían apoyo constante de los animadores latinoamericanos quienes acompañaban comunidades en varias partes del país. Las comunidades que se formaron, a pesar de algunas tensiones esporádicas con líderes oficiales a nivel local, por lo general tienen la habilidad de mantenerse en comunión con sus párrocos y conformarse con el esquema pastoral más estructurado de los Estados Unidos[23].

Estas interacciones son apenas una muestra del potencial que tiene del catolicismo hispano estadounidense de influir en la Iglesia en Latinoamérica. Durante las últimas cuatro décadas la cooperación interamericana ha incrementado por medio de organizaciones como *Catholic Relief Services*, *Jesuit Refugee Services*, y la Colecta para Latinoamérica de los Obispos Católicos, al igual que la participación de los obispos estadounidenses tanto en el Sínodo de las Américas en 1997 y en la Conferencia de Aparecida en el 2007, en la cual tuvieron voz y voto. La movilidad de sacerdotes, religiosas y religiosos, y laicos entre los Estados Unidos y Latinoamérica es más común que en cualquier otro momento de nuestra historia compartida. Ocurre en universidades católicas, seminarios y centros teológicos a medida que el porcentaje de sacerdotes, seminaristas, religiosas y religiosos y laicos latinos, nacidos en los Estados Unidos e inmigrantes, incrementa en el país. Al mismo tiempo un número significativo de latinoamericanos vienen a estudiar a los Estados Unidos y luego regresan a sus países de origen. Esto significa que muchos agentes pastorales latinoamericanos regularmente aprenden sobre la cultura y las prácticas pastorales estadounidenses por medio del idioma, los estudios de postgrado, experiencias de inmersión y programas de formación. Lo mismo ocurre con líderes pastorales estadounidenses.

23 Véase MATOVINA, T., *Latino Catholicism*, 118-19; También PEW FORUM ON RELIGION AND PUBLIC LIFE, *Changing Faiths: Latinos and the Transformation of American Religion*, Pew Hispanic Center, Washington, D.C. 2007, 23-30.

Actualmente somos testigos de la transformación de presbiterados completos en los Estados Unidos. Un número notable de sacerdotes sirviendo en las distintas diócesis son inmigrantes latinoamericanos y de muchas otras regiones del mundo. Las congregaciones religiosas estadounidenses están siendo transformadas por la inclusión de un número amplio de latinoamericanos[24]. Por ejemplo, los padres y los hermanos Trinitarios, fundados en los Estados Unidos, con su casa madre en Silver Spring, Maryland, han girado su atención a Latinoamérica en las últimas décadas. Con el tiempo seguramente serán una congregación primordialmente latinoamericana. Las congregaciones femeninas como la Compañía de María o las Hermanas de la Caridad de la Palabra Encarnada se están combinando con las provincias latinoamericanas para crear provincias internacionales. En lugares como la Arquidiócesis de Denver, programas creativos dentro del ministerio hispano como el que existe en el Centro San Juan Diego, combinan la visión pastoral latinoamericana con los desafíos de los latinos inmigrantes y de primera generación. El acceso a recursos electrónicos de excelente calidad y oportunidades de educación a distancia son ofrecidos por medio de las páginas web del CELAM y de los Obispos Católicos de los Estados Unidos. Así, en todo el hemisferio se han creado condiciones sin precedente para una verdadera relación de interacción mutua, un modelo de formación bilingüe y cros-cultural de agentes pastorales que trasciende fronteras.

Una de las áreas en las que se notan más la mutua influencia entre Latinoamérica y los Estados Unidos es en el área de ministerio con jóvenes y jóvenes adultos. Orientaciones recientes para la certificación de agentes pastorales han adoptado el concepto de Pastoral Juvenil Hispana para referirse al esfuerzo de acompañamiento espiritual y formación de jóvenes y jóvenes adultos, un esfuerzo con características y raíces profundas en la pastoral latinoamericana[25]. Este enfoque integra la metodología del círculo pastoral, el énfasis en un liderazgo activo por parte de los jóvenes y los jóvenes adultos, la formación de una conciencia social, la formación de pequeñas comunidades y muchas otras cualidades de

---

24 Mary Gautier y otros investigadores del Center for Applied Research in the Apostolate en Georgetown University están documentando la transformación cultural que ocurre actualmente en la Iglesia Católica en los Estados Unidos, incluyendo seminarios, universidades y presbiterados. Véase GAUTIER, M., *Catholic Ministry Formation Enrollment: Statistical Overview for 2013-2014*, CARA, Washington, D.C. 2014, http://cara.georgetown.edu/Overview201314.pdf (documento visitado el 28 de agosto del 2014).

25 Véase NATIONAL CATHOLIC NETWORK DE PASTORAL JUVENIL HISPANA - LA RED, *Conclusiones: Primer Encuentro Nacional de Pastoral Juvenil Hispana*, USCCB, Washington, D.C. 2008. También el Instituto Fe y Vida: www.feyvida.org

la visión pastoral latinoamericana contemporánea. Al mismo tiempo el Instituto Fe y Vida ha entrado en diálogo constante con los líderes de los ministerios con jóvenes y jóvenes adultos en los Estados Unidos y ha adoptado prácticas para buscar fondos y proveer capacitación profesional que son típicas de catolicismo estadounidense. Así, la Pastoral Juvenil Hispana se ha posicionado como una opción clara para el acompañamiento de los jóvenes y los jóvenes adultos católicos estadounidenses y gana reconocimiento como una alternativa a enfoques pastorales más euroamericanos al servicio de estas poblaciones[26].

4

Un Nuevo Papa: Los tiempos están cambiando

330   La multitud era impresionante en comparación a lo que se había visto en ocasiones anteriores. Millones de jóvenes se habían reunido en la playa de Copacabana para la liturgia final de la Jornada Mundial de la Juventud. ¡Los obispos bailaban! Sí, bailaban. El Papa argentino decía en español, «¡*Hagan lío*!». Agentes pastorales de toda clase seguramente se preguntaban sorprendidos si sus programas realmente respondían a este desafío[27]. Un capítulo nuevo se abre para la Iglesia bajo el liderazgo extraordinario del Papa Francisco. Él mueve a la Iglesia en el mundo entero de un estado de letargia y un período invernal caracterizado el trazo de líneas en la arena y obsesiones sobre ciertas enseñanzas, hacia un período de vivacidad, diálogo e inclusividad.

No es fácil para muchos agentes pastorales, desde obispos hasta catequistas parroquiales, entender las implicaciones de las reformas del Papa Francisco. Todavía hay mucha desorientación e incluso aflicción por el hecho de que aquella iglesia tridentina empecinada en una apologética anacrónica finalmente está quedando atrás. Él es un líder lleno de sorpresas y energía que vino, literalmente, «del fin del mundo» y tiene una manera de proceder que no encaja propiamente con las esquinas ideológicas de los católicos conservadores y progresistas. Sin

---

26   Véase CERVANTES, C.M., FIGUEROA DECK, A., y JOHNSON-MONDRAGÓN, K., «Pastoral Ministry and Vision: Latino/a Contributions to the Transformation of Practical Theology in the United States», en WOLFTEICH, C. (ed.), *Invitation to Practical Theology*, Paulist Press, Mahwah, NJ 2014.

27   Véase PAPA FRANCISCO, *Discurso durante el encuentro con los jóvenes argentinos en la catedral de San Sebastián, Viaje apostólico a Río de Janeiro con ocasión de la XXVIII Jornada Mundial de la Juventud*, 25 de julio del 2013, http://w2.vatican.va/content/francesco/es/speeches/2013/july/documents/papa-francesco_20130725_gmg-argentini-rio.html (documento visitado el 28 de agosto del 2014).

embargo, este análisis breve de las realidades pastorales actuales demuestra que el ministerio hispano constituye un punto de encuentro y un puente entre la visión fresca del Papa Francisco de una *Iglesia siempre en salida* y la visión y las prácticas de la Iglesia en los Estados Unidos. Los hispanos son mediadores de un proceso que exige crear y «poner vino nuevo en odres nuevos». Esto puede ocurrir aceptando devociones populares marianas, la fiesta de todos los difuntos renovada por las prácticas latinoamericanas del Día de los Muertos y la sensibilidad estética más expresiva de las representaciones hispanas de la muerte y de los que han fallecido. El esfuerzo constante de hacer de las parroquias comunidades de comunidades se fortalece por la presencia hispana que valora profundamente las comunidades pequeñas en las que se comparte la fe. Es más, la orientación robusta hacia la justicia social que es propia del catolicismo latinoamericano, su conexión con la Doctrina Social de la Iglesia y en la teología contextual, y la planeación pastoral modelada por el CELAM, representan una corriente con la que más y más agentes pastorales en los Estados Unidos se identifican.

En el contenido y las metodologías de los procesos de Encuentro durante las últimas cuatro décadas, la visión pastoral que vigorizó el pensamiento y la práctica pastoral de Jorge Mario Bergoglio y muchos otros agentes pastorales en Latinoamérica y el Caribe ha encontrado un hogar en los Estados Unidos. La eclesiología fundamental del Pueblo de Dios, la opción por los pobres, la justicia que brota de la fe, la metodología inductiva del círculo pastoral, el respeto profundo por la religión popular de los pueblos, y el espíritu misionero que inspiró los documentos básicos del ministerio hispano en los Estados Unidos, hoy se encuentran cristalizados en *Evangelii Gaudium,* el documento fundamental del ministerio petrino del Papa Francisco[28]. Tanto el ministerio hispano como las reformas del Papa Francisco para toda la Iglesia tienen sus raíces más profundas en las iniciativas creativas de la Iglesia en Latinoamérica después del Concilio Vaticano II.

He aquí que los Estados Unidos se han convertido en el espacio de gestación para una visión pastoral realmente interamericana, luchando por reconocimiento y con frecuencia víctima de una apatía condescendiente. El ministerio hispano en la era del Papa Francisco surge como una fuente de conocimiento, experiencias y visión para la Iglesia en los Estados Unidos, la cual sigue tratan-

---

28 Véase el *Plan Pastoral Nacional para el Ministerio Hispano (1987)* y *Encuentro y Misión (2002)* en SECRETARIADO DE DIVERSIDAD CULTURAL EN LA IGLESIA, SUBCOMITÉ DE ASUNTOS HISPANOS, *A New Beginning,* 123ff; 167-177.

do de comprender hacia donde le dirige este pontificado. La Iglesia en los Estados Unidos al mismo tiempo hace contribuciones importantes a este encuentro con su énfasis en la educación y la profesionalización. Las universidades católicas y los centros pastorales han estado a la vanguardia de esta tarea. Pero lo que estas instituciones ofrecen no es suficiente. Este encuentro ofrece una oportunidad única para cerrar la brecha. Las estrategias pastorales latinoamericanas que enfatizan el diálogo cultural, la inculturación y la liberación tienen que seguir en conversación con las iniciativas educativas y de formación en los Estados Unidos[29]. Algo nuevo y mejor surgirá de este encuentro. Por lo general, el énfasis latinoamericano en el discipulado misionero y la inclusión de todos los bautizados potencia al laicado más ampliamente que el modelo profesional —y posiblemente elitista— de ministerio eclesial laico que predomina en los Estados Unidos[30].

332   El ministerio hispano es el lugar privilegiado para encontrar maneras de relacionarse con todos los fieles en el discipulado, sin importar su nivel educativo, mientras crecen en conocimiento y habilidades[31]. Así el ministerio hispano ofrece modelos alternativos que encajan con un mundo globalizado mientras que afirma los beneficios de los logros educativos y técnicos de la cultura estadounidense. Finalmente, el ministerio hispano en los Estados Unidos, fruto de la experiencia pastoral latinoamericana y estadounidense, ofrece al mundo entero ejemplos y modelos de interacción pastoral que están fundamentados firmemente en la sabiduría de *Evangelii Gaudium*. Este ministerio es entonces un recurso creativo para avanzar el proceso de conversión pastoral que el Papa Francisco ha propuesto como meta para una Iglesia universal que siempre está en salida y busca mantenerse en estado permanente de misión.

29 IRARRÁZABAL, D., *Inculturación: Amanecer Eclesial en América Latina,* Ediciones Abya-Yala, Quito, Ecuador 2000, 169-75.

30 CELAM, *Documento de Aparecida,* n. 201-205.

31 Véase MATEO, H., «El ministerio hispano y el liderazgo» en este volumen.

Autores

James F. Caccamo, Ph.D., es profesor asociado de teología y director del departamento de teología y estudios religiosos en Saint Joseph University en Filadelfia, PA.

Antonia Darder, Ph.D., posee la cátedra presidencial Leavey y es directora del programa de liderazgo ético y moral en la Escuela de Educación de Loyola Marymount University, Los Ángeles, CA.

Lynette De Jesús-Sáenz, es directora de la oficina para la diversidad cultural y el instituto pastoral hispano de la Diócesis de Rochester, NY.

Allan Figueroa Deck, SJ, Ph.D., es investigador distinguido en teología pastoral y estudios latinos, y es catedrático en el departamento de estudios teológicos y el departamento de estudios chicanos/latinos en Loyola Marymount University, Los Ángeles, CA.

Brett Hoover, Ph.D., es profesor asistente de estudios teológicos en el departamento de estudios teológicos en Loyola Marymount University, Los Ángeles, CA; coeditor de este libro.

Donald Kerwin, Jr., es el director ejecutivo del Centro de Estudios Migratorios (*Center for Migration Studies*, CSM) en Nueva York.

Patricia Jiménez, D.Min., es fundadora de *ushispanicministry.com* y trabaja como investigadora independiente en California.

Ken Johnson-Mondragón, D.Min candidate, es director de investigación de temas latinos y producción de recursos para RCL Benziger.

Hilda Mateo, MGSpS, D.Min., es directora de investigación del carisma sacerdotal guadalupano, Provincia de Nuestra Señora de Guadalupe, Misioneras Guadalupanas del Espíritu Santo.

Teresa Maya Sotomayor, CCVI, Ph.D., actualmente sirve en el equipo de liderazgo de la Congregación de las Hermanas de la Caridad del Verbo Encarnado, San Antonio, TX.

Elsie M. Miranda, D.Min., es profesora asociada de teología práctica y directora de formación ministerial en Barry University, Miami, FL; coeditora de este libro.

Hosffman Ospino, Ph.D., es profesor asistente de ministerio hispano y educación religiosa; director de programas de postgrado en ministerio hispano en la Escuela de Teología y Ministerio de Boston College, Boston, MA; coeditor de este libro.

David Sánchez, Ph.D., es profesor asociado de estudios teológicos y director del programa de culturas americanas en Loyola Marymount University, Los Ángeles, CA.

*Rediscover the
Historical Praxis of Jesus
Through the Latest
Research*

Jesus. An Historical Approximation

José A. Pagola
ISBN: 978-1-934996-09-6
560 Pages
Series Kyrios

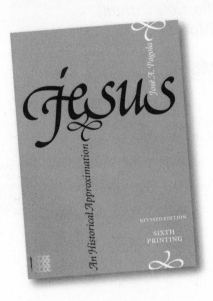

This is an extraordinary work of scholarship. Beautifully written, it is also an expression of the author's profound faith commitment… The author presents a compelling «approximation of that life»… A highly readable book that deserves a wide readership in the Church and the academy.

— Roberto Goizueta, Boston College, Former President of the Catholic Theological
Society of America

José Antonio Pagola was born in Spain in 1937. He completed his theological studies at the Pontifical Gregorian University and his studies in Sacred Scripture at the Pontifical Biblical Institute in Rome. He also studied Biblical sciences at the École Biblique in Jerusalem. He has dedicated his life to Biblical studies and Christology and has done research on the historical Jesus for more than 30 years, selling more than 60,000 copies of his recent theological bestseller *Jesús. Aproximación histórica*, now available in English by Convivium Press.

This controversial book is now available in English for the first time. In this bestseller, greeted with both enthusiasm and controversy in Europe, Pagola, criticized by some for depicting a too-human Jesus, offers a scholarly and thought-provoking biblical rereading of the life of Jesus. Pagola reconstructs the complete historical figure of Jesus with a scholarly exegetical and theological approach, in an easy to read language.

ERIC HOFFER
AWARD FINALIST

2014 Association
of Catholic Publishers
Excellence in
Publishing Awards
Winner
1ST Place
Theology

BUY IT AT: *www.conviviumpress.com*

*Is Life in Society
Possible without
Morality?*

Morality in Social Life

SERGIO BASTIANEL
ISBN: 978-1-934996-14-0
360 Pages
Series Episteme

*Morality in Social Life is a valuable work on the centrality of relationships, story, and virtue to morality
in the social sphere. Those who are quick to advocate for public policies based on theological principles will be
disappointed in this work, but they would do well to remember Bastianel's central thesis: …God
communicates himself in the man of Nazareth, in his gestures, words, his human way of living out relationships
on this earth, in his living and dying, in his remaining present through the gift of the Spirit.*

— National Catholic Reporter, Arlene Helderman Montevecchio,
   Director for Social Concerns, Gannon University

Sergio Bastianel SJ is currently professor of moral theology at the Pontifical Gregorian University in Rome and also serves as its academic vice-rector. He spent his early years teaching and lecturing at the Pontifical Theological Faculty of San Luigi in Naples, Italy, and in later years he served as dean of the theological faculty of the Pontifical Gregorian University.

Sergio Bastianel answers the question by addressing the responsibility of Christians to confront issues of justice within society in ways that promote the common good. The author, who views one's relationship with the «other» as foundational to the moral experience, places a priority on human relationships based on sharing and solidarity. He emphasizes the interconnections between personal morals and social justice and raises fundamental questions about such issues as political life and economics, about hunger and development, and about the true meaning of «charity», all of which are relevant issues in our contemporary societies.

BUY IT AT: *www.conviviumpress.com*

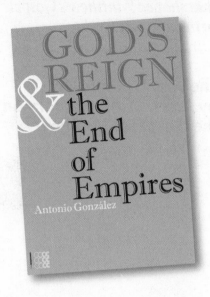

*Reclaiming
the Spirit and Praxis
of the Reign
of God*

God's Reign & the End of Empires

Antonio González
isbn: 978-1-934996-29-4
384 Pages
Series Kyrios

*González masters a vast variety of economic, political, sociological and theological issues with a high degree
of scholarly command, clarity, and elegance. He offers a meaningful way forward and the courage not to lose hope
—for those of us who have theoretically and academically struggled for quite some time with the structural,
cultural, psychological, and overt violence of imperial capitalism… and for those of us who simply feel in our
hearts that something is basically going wrong in our society, culture and world and are looking for
meaningful alternatives. **This is social theology at its best.**

— Ulrich Duchrow, Professor of Systematic Theology at the University of Heidelberg*

Antonio González, a leading Spanish theologian, was born in Oviedo (Asturias) in 1961. He has worked in El Salvador and in Guatemala at the Jesuit University, as well as in various centers of higher education in Europe. He shares with liberation theology the perspective of God's option for the poor and the centrality of praxis in the Christian message and life. He is a member of the Mennonite community and was the former General Secretary of the Fundación Xavier Zubiri in Madrid, Spain. González is a prolific author whose works include *Structures in Praxis* (1997), *Trinity and Liberation* (1993), and more recently, *Theology of the Evangelical Praxis.*

Post-resurrection communities continued to practice living in the reign of God. With the rise of Emperor Constantine, however, this vibrant counter-cultural movement of believers was institutionalized within the Roman Empire. Over time the institutional Church became the dominant power with all the trappings of empire. The author shows how regaining the practice of living in the reign of God can change the face of Christianity.

BUY IT AT: *www.conviviumpress.com*

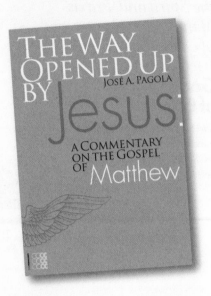

Exploring the context
that shaped Matthew's Gospel
in the context of today's
Christian communities

The Way Opened Up by Jesus. A Commentary on the Gospel of Matthew

José A. Pagola
ISBN: 978-1-934996-28-7
264 Pages
Series Kyrios

This new book is an insightful and careful walk through the gospel of Matthew that begins by making the argument (one that resonates with me) that «Christianity as most people live it today does not raise up "followers" of Jesus, but "adherents" to a religion». I am reminded of theologian Leonard Sweet's argument that Christianity should be a «movement», not an «institution», for an institution, he says, is mostly in the public's eye, whereas a movement is mostly in the public's hair…

— Bill Tammeus, Faith Matters

José Antonio Pagola was born in Spain in 1937. He completed his theological studies at the Pontifical Gregorian University and his studies in Sacred Scripture at the Pontifical Biblical Institute in Rome. He also studied Biblical sciences at the École Biblique in Jerusalem. He has dedicated his life to Biblical studies and Christology and has done research on the historical Jesus for more than 30 years, selling more than 60,000 copies of his recent theological bestseller *Jesús. Aproximación histórica*, now available in English by Convivium Press.

Matthew's perspective shows Jesus transforming the expectations of the People of Israel—He is the fulfillment of God's ancient promises to them; he is God's new presence with them after the destruction of the Temple; he is the Prophet of a new Law proclaimed from a new Mount Sinai; and he is the Messiah who calls together the new Israel, which Matthew calls the Church. He is also the Teacher of Life, whose surprising—and disconcerting— sermons and parables offer the new spiritual energy that today's churches need in order to be transformed from adherents into followers.

BUY IT AT: *www.conviviumpress.com*

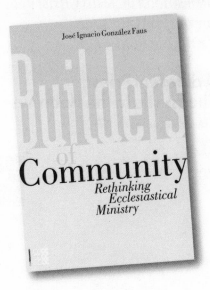

*Rethinking
the Crisis in Ordained
Ministry*

Builders of Community Rethinking Ecclesiastical Ministry

José I. González Faus
ISBN: 978-1-934996-25-6
176 Pages
Series Traditio

SCAN CODE
FOR MORE
INFORMATION
ABOUT THIS
BOOK

González Faus's analysis and vision of the future provide hope for the ministry for the twenty-first century. He offers a formidable challenge to those who characteristically view the ministry as consisting of «power, dignity, superiority and remoteness» and offers hope to those who view the ministry as consisting of «service, surrender, sameness and nearness».

— Anglican Theological Review, Scott M. Myslinski

José Ignacio González Faus was born in Valencia, Spain, in 1935. He has a PhD in Theology from Innsbruck and is currently Professor of Theology and Director of the Centro de Estudios (Cristianismo y Justicia) in Barcelona. He is dedicated to the promotion and defense of freedom and justice within the framework of an integral vision of the human person. His numerous published works include *La humanidad nueva: Ensayo de cristología* (1974), *Acceso a Jesús* (1979), *El proyecto hermano: Visión creyente del hombre* (1989), *Ningún obispo impuesto* (1992) and *Where the Spirit Breathes: Prophetic Dissent in the Church* (1989).

It is exceedingly possible that the Church might be reaching what has been called «the time of the laity», and yet it is also possible that we might pass through this time in a sterile way, not because of not having known of its arrival, or what it was about, but because of not having understood the specificity of the ordained ministry and that of other ministries within Christian communities.

BUY IT AT: *www.conviviumpress.com*

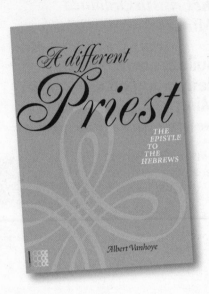

Understanding the unique
Priesthood of Jesus Christ
for the first Christian
communities

A different Priest.
The Epistle to the Hebrews

ALBERT VANHOYE
ISBN: 978-1-934996-20-1
456 Pages
Series Rhetorica Semitica

Vanhoye's main concern is to examine how the distinctive rhetorical and oratorical elements of Semitic rhetoric shaped the profound theology of Christian faith and how it was proclaimed through the distinctive literary genre of the sermon. His book is a unique contribution to biblical rhetoric and Christian theology, and it will be a fascinating resource —rare and invaluable— for preachers and scholars of preaching.

— Rev. Eunjoo M. Kim, Ph. D., Director of Ministry Program,
The Iliff School of Theology

Albert Vanhoye is one of the most recognized scholars on the Epistle to the Hebrews. He has taught it at the Pontifical Biblical Institute and published a great number of specialist articles and books on it, and now brings one of the most contemporary authoritative commentaries to a wider audience, contributing with the understanding of the unique Priesthood of Jesus Christ for the first Christian communities. He is honorary president of the International Society for the study of Biblical and Semitic Rhetoric. He was appointed Cardinal by Pope Benedict XVI in 2006.

In this work by Albert Vanhoye, a detailed analysis of the text known as the Epistle to the Hebrews enables us to conclude without a shadow of a doubt that this is the full text of a splendid Christian homily, which constantly conforms to the rules of Semitic rhetoric, including various genres of parallelism, synonymy, antithesis and complementarity, and obeying a concentrically symmetrical schema.

Opening Your Heart
to the Gift of God
through Major Existential
Questions

Transparencies of Eternity

RUBEM ALVES
ISBN: 978-1-934996-19-5
136 Pages
Series Sapientia

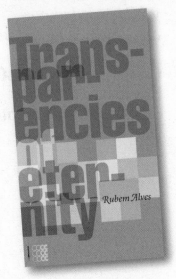

God is not a concept simply understood by many. **Transparencies of Eternity** *is scholarly prose and poetry from Ruben Alves, as his work studies the concept of God, faith, and the love that goes both ways, a study that presents much to ponder for readers and much to understand for those who want to more completely understand their world. Transparencies of Eternity is a strong addition to religious studies collections, highly recommended.*

— Midwest Book Review

A pedagogue, poet, philosopher, theologian and psychoanalyst, Rubem Alves is one of Brazil's most respected intellectuals. He is a prolific writer —with more than fifty titles in different languages— and one of the most brilliant craftsmen of the Portuguese language.

In this book are collected texts that masterfully comprise both a profound knowledge and the major existential questions of humankind. The texts flow with a simplicity of rare beauty, and the result could not be better: spirituality is presented through a new lens, attracting, instigating and enchanting readers who want to broaden their horizons. As a master of the word, Rubem Alves relates events and experiences in life where God, religiosity, love, beauty and the meaning of life are always present. The author draws transparent and multicolor stained glass windows, using as raw material the existence and the multiple faces of God.

WINNER 2012 MONTAIGNE MEDAL,
ERIC HOFFER AWARD TO THE
MOST THOUGHT-PROVOKING
TITLES EACH YEAR

BUY IT AT: *www.conviviumpress.com*

*Una nueva visión
de la persona de Jesús
y de la sociedad
desde la diversidad cultural*

Caminemos con Jesús: Hacía una teología del acompañamiento

ROBERTO S. GOIZUETA
ISBN: 978-1-934996-10-2
320 páginas
Serie Hispania

ESCAN
EL CÓDIG
PARA M,
INFORMACIĆ
SOBRE É!
LIBF

Roberto S. Goizueta es catedrático de Teología en el Boston College. Fue presidente de la Catholic Theological Society of America, y de la Academy of Catholic Hispanic Theologians of the United States. Se ha dedicado al estudio de la cristología y la antropología a partir del mundo de vida hispano/latino. Su libro, *Caminemos con Jesús. Toward a Hispanic/Latino Theology of Accompaniment,* se hizo merecedor del reconocimiento que otorga la Asociación de Prensa Católica en los Estados Unidos.

Hasta ahora no habíamos contado con ningún intento sistemático por definir una teología hispana. Roberto S. Goizueta, un teólogo laico cubano-americano, consciente de que «hispano» y «latino» pueden ser términos impuestos artificialmente a diferentes personas, encuentra un vínculo común en el idioma español y en una cultura compartida. Constitutiva de esta cultura es la experiencia del exilio, el ser un pueblo en los márgenes de una sociedad, que debe encontrar y hacer su camino como comunidad. Este libro reta tanto a las teologías europeo-norteamericanas tradicionales como a las modernas proposiciones epistemológicas occidentales, y nos propone una antropología y una cristología para el presente.

¿Cómo entiende el
cristianismo la vida eterna?
Un libro para repensar
el sentido de esta vida

Sorprendidos por la esperanza. Repensando el cielo, la resurrección y la vida eterna

N. T. WRIGHT
ISBN: 978-1-934996-15-7
408 páginas
Serie Traditio

Nacido en 1948, en Inglaterra, N.T. Wright es el actual obispo anglicano de Durham. Ha sido decano de Lichfield y profesor de Estudios del Nuevo Testamento en la Universidad de Oxford. También se ha desempeñado como investigador en el Worcester College, en Oxford, y como profesor de Lenguaje y Literatura del Nuevo Testamento en diferentes universidades de Inglaterra. Wright es doctor en Teología y Filosofía por la Universidad de Oxford y miembro de la Sociedad para el Estudio del Nuevo Testamento, la Sociedad de Literatura Bíblica, el Instituto para la Investigación Bíblica y la Asociación Anglicana de Académicos en el área de los Estudios Bíblicos.

¿Qué sucedería si mueres hoy? ¿Sabrías adónde irías y qué sería de tu vida a continuación? Según el eminente teólogo y profesor N.T. Wright, autor de innumerables libros, no se va al cielo, sino que hay que dirigir la mirada hacia la esperanza que nos coloca en el horizonte de la vida tal y como la vivimos hoy en nuestro presente. El autor nos habla de nuevos cielos y de una nueva tierra, revelando lo que le sucede a los difuntos hasta que alcanzan esa nueva condición de la vida. Lo que creemos de la vida después de la muerte afecta directamente lo que creemos sobre la vida antes de la muerte.

Explora la enorme experiencia de la libertad en la Biblia

Llamados a la libertad

Roland Meynet
isbn: 978-1-934996-03-4
304 páginas
Serie Rhetorica Semitica

Roland Meynet S.J. es actualmente profesor de Teología Bíblica en la Facultad de Teología de la Pontificia Universidad Gregoriana, en Roma, de la cual ha sido su director. Es miembro fundador y actual Secretario de la «Società Internazionale per lo studio della Retorica Biblica e Semitica», y es uno de los promotores más importantes y reconocidos del método retórico aplicado a los textos bíblicos y semíticos.

La libertad constituye, en esta obra, el eje que orienta y discierne la experiencia sociopolítica y religiosa del pueblo hebreo a lo largo de su historia. El autor nos presenta una lectura inesperada de la experiencia del éxodo, replantea el sentido de la ley según ha sido testimoniado en las dos narrativas del decálogo, y también nos introduce en la lectura de los himnos a la libertad, como fueron cantados y proclamados por Israel en los salmos en medio de sus más dramáticas experiencias humanas. Es un tópico relevante y pertinente para las sociedades y los sujetos modernos que proclaman la libertad.

adquiéralo en: *www.conviviumpress.com*

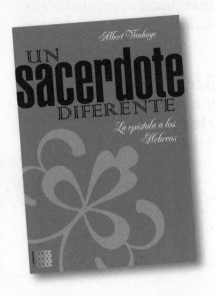

Comprendiendo el carácter único y definitivo del sacerdocio de Jesucristo para las primeras comunidades cristianas

Un sacerdote diferente. La epístola a los Hebreos

ALBERT VANHOYE
ISBN: 978-1-934996-21-8
456 páginas
Serie Rhetorica Semitica

ESCANEA
EL CÓDIGO
PARA MÁS
INFORMACIÓN
SOBRE ÉSTE
LIBRO

Albert Vanhoye, nacido en 1923 en Hazebrouck (Norte de Francia), entró en 1941 en la Compañía de Jesús. Obtuvo su licenciatura en Letras en la Sorbona, y las licenciaturas en Filosofía y Teología en los escolasticados de su Orden, así como el doctorado en Ciencias Bíblicas en el Pontificio Instituto de Roma. Luego fue nombrado profesor en el mismo Instituto, del que fue Rector y donde enseñó, de 1963 a 1998, Exégesis y Teología bíblica del Nuevo Testamento. También ha sido miembro de la Comisión Bíblica de 1984 a 2001, y su Secretario de 1990 a 2001. Ha publicado numerosos estudios de exégesis, de teología bíblica y de espiritualidad. Es Presidente honorario de la Sociedad Internacional para el estudio de la Retórica Bíblica y Semítica. En 2006 fue creado Cardenal por el Papa Benedicto XVI.

El eminente biblista Albert Vanhoye nos sorprende con su nueva publicación. En la primera parte del libro expone un sólo tema, «el nombre de Cristo», presentando una cristología fundamental. Las dos partes que siguen ofrecen una novedosa cristología sacerdotal, primero más general, y luego más específica. Las dos últimas partes, muestran el resultado de todo ello para la vida cristiana, vivida en la fe, la esperanza y la caridad. El autor nos ofrece su más reciente aporte a la interpretación de este texto del cristianismo originario y las consecuencias que tiene en la actualidad.

*Redescubre la novedad
de la vida cristiana desde sus
parámetros comunitarios
y sociales*

El cristianismo como comunidad y las comunidades cristianas

PEDRO TRIGO
ISBN: 978-1-934996-02-7
248 páginas
Serie Traditio

Pedro Trigo es uno de los teólogos jesuitas latinoamericanos más reconocidos de la actualidad. Es profesor de Teología en la Facultad de Teología de la Universidad Católica Andrés Bello de Caracas. También ha dedicado gran parte de su vida al estudio de la literatura hispana y a la historia de la evangelización en América Latina. De manera continua lleva su palabra autorizada a los escenarios académicos más prestigiosos de Europa y Latinoamérica en calidad de conferencista invitado sobre Teología de la Liberación.

Este libro presenta una perspectiva novedosa del cristianismo como comunidad, más allá de todo individualismo o colectivismo actual. Su autor, Pedro Trigo va abordando los diversos perfiles de vida que el cristianismo ofrece, dentro de sus parámetros comunitarios y sociales. Es un intento por presentar una visión actual del cristianismo y, en ella, del sujeto humano. Estamos ante una obra de madurez, escrita desde la más sentida experiencia de vida cristiana.

ADQUIÉRALO EN: *www.conviviumpress.com*

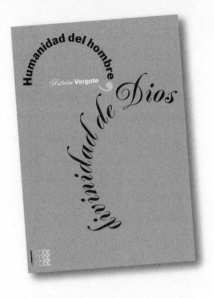

Repensando lo humano
y lo divino desde los aportes
actuales de la psicología
y la antropología

Humanidad del hombre, divinidad de Dios

ANTOINE VERGOTE
ISBN: 978-1-934996-13-3
328 páginas
Serie Kyrios

ESCANEA
EL CÓDIGO
PARA MÁS
INFORMACIÓN
SOBRE ÉSTE
LIBRO

Antoine Vergote nace en 1921, en Bélgica, y estudia psicoanálisis, filosofía y teología. Se ha dedicado a analizar el fenómeno religioso tal y como ha sido asumido por el sujeto moderno. Es profesor de Louvain, y fue discípulo de Jacques Lacan. Se ha interesado ante todo por el estudio de las relaciones entre el psicoanálisis, la antropología y la fe cristiana. Es el cofundador de la escuela psicoanalista belga donde ha buscado tratar de superar la concepción neurótica que se ha tenido de la religión, para encontrar, una experiencia de compasión y sentido capaz de desvelar verdad la historia humana.

Este libro de Antoine Vergote presenta un análisis antropológico, psicológico y religioso del sujeto contemporáneo. Aquí, se considera al hombre como un ser personal en relación, con un profundo anhelo de felicidad, capaz de amar y entregarse por otros pero, a la vez, consciente de un misterio divino que lo sobrepasa, cuya experiencia no puede definir. Un sujeto que se vive religiosamente en medio de los dramas y los traumas personales. Al final de la obra, el autor presenta una aproximación a la figura histórica de Jesús con los aportes de la psicología y la antropología modernas.

Hispanic Ministry in the 21st Century: Urgent Matters

El ministerio hispano en el siglo xxi: asuntos urgentes

This book was printed on thin opaque smooth white Bible paper, using the Minion and Type Embellishments One font families. This edition was printed in Panamericana Formas e Impresos, S.A., in Bogotá, Colombia, during the last weeks of the ninth month of year two thousand and sixteen.

Ad publicam lucem datus mense septembre in nativitate Sancte Marie

...continues to unfold with giant steps, U.S. Catholicism experiences major transformations at various levels thanks to the Hispanic presence. In many parts of the country, especially in the South and the West, to speak of Hispanic ministry is to speak of Catholicism in general. Without a doubt, the Church's evangelizing work in this country and the vitality of Catholic communities will be strengthened

...investment in Hispanic Catholics. In this book, theologians Hosffman Ospino, Elsie Miranda and Brett Hoover bring together pioneering voices reflecting on what many consider «urgent matters» in our day for Hispanic ministry and the overall U.S. Catholic experience. This collection of essays continues the important conversation that began in the previous work, *Hispanic Ministry in the 21st Century: Present and Future* (Convivium, 2010).

...agigantados, el catolicis-mo en los Estados Unidos experimenta una transformación acele-rada a distintos niveles gracias a la presencia hispana. En muchas partes del país, especial-mente el Sur y el Oeste, hablar del ministerio hispano es hablar de catolicismo en general. Sin lugar a duda, la labor evangelizadora de la Iglesia en el país y la vitalidad de las comu-nidades católicas serán

...cuando se invierta gene-rosamente en los cató-licos hispanos. En este libro los teólogos Hosffman Ospino, Elsie Miranda y Brett Hoover reúnen voces pioneras reflexionando sobre lo que muchos consideran «asuntos urgentes» en nuestro día tanto para el ministerio hispano como para el catolicismo en los Estados Unidos. La colección de ensayos continúa la conver-sación importante que comenzó en la obra anterior, *El ministerio hispano en el siglo xxi: Presente y Futuro* (Convivium, 2010).

ISBN: 978-1-934996-67-6